The Original Buffalo Bills

The Original Buffalo Bills

*A History of the
All-America Football
Conference Team, 1946–1949*

KENNETH R. CRIPPEN

McFarland & Company, Inc., Publishers
Jefferson, North Carolina, and London

LIBRARY OF CONGRESS CATALOGUING-IN-PUBLICATION DATA

Crippen, Kenneth R.
　The original Buffalo Bills : a history of the all-America
football conference team, 1946–1949 / Kenneth R. Crippen.
　　　p.　　cm.
　Includes bibliographical references and index.

　ISBN 978-0-7864-4619-3
　softcover : 50# alkaline paper

　1. Buffalo Bills (Football team) — History.　I. Title.
GV956.B83C75　2010
796.332'640974797 — dc22　　　　　　　　　　　　　2009036775

British Library cataloguing data are available

©2010 Kenneth R. Crippen. All rights reserved

*No part of this book may be reproduced or transmitted in any form
or by any means, electronic or mechanical, including photocopying
or recording, or by any information storage and retrieval system,
without permission in writing from the publisher.*

Front cover: Alex Wizbicki (82) returns a punt for the Bills against
the Los Angeles Dons on November 9th, 1947, at Civic Stadium in
Buffalo (Photograph from author's collection)

Manufactured in the United States of America

*McFarland & Company, Inc., Publishers
　Box 611, Jefferson, North Carolina 28640
　　　www.mcfarlandpub.com*

To Kristy,
for loving and supporting me ... and
to the players, coaches and administrators
who put Buffalo on the map
of the football world in the 1940s ...

Table of Contents

Acknowledgments	ix
Preface	1
Prologue	3
1. The AAFC Forms	9
2. The Bisons Take Shape	18
3. The Bisons Take the Field	27
4. Ratterman Arrives in Buffalo	44
5. The Third Season Begins	64
6. The Team Started to Gel	70
7. Clem Crowe Takes Over	85
8. The War Was Over	102
Epilogue	113
Appendix A: Schedules and Rosters	117
Appendix B: Detailed Game Summaries	127
Appendix C: All-Time Record versus Each Opponent	217
Appendix D: All-Time Roster	220
Chapter Notes	295
Bibliography	303
Index	313

Acknowledgments

No work of this sort can be completed without the help of others. First, I would like to thank my wife Kristy for her love and support. She was also instrumental in formatting and editing, as well as scheduling interviews. I will eternally be grateful for her love, assistance and encouragement throughout this process.

A special thank you goes to all of the players, family members of players and team administrators (in alphabetical order) who were willing to contribute to this project: Joseph Blount (son of Lamar Blount, 1946 Miami Seahawks, 1947 Buffalo Bills, 1947 Baltimore Colts), Jack Brennan (Public Relations Director, Cincinnati Bengals), George Buksar (1949 Chicago Hornets, 1950 Baltimore Colts, 1951–1952 Washington Redskins), James Cordovano (son of Sam Cordovano, Owner 1944–May 1946), Adrienne Dawson (daughter of Red Dawson, Coach 1946–1949), Jesse Freitas (1946–1947 San Francisco 49ers, 1948 Chicago Rockets, 1949 Buffalo Bills), Bill Gompers (1948 Buffalo Bills), Mike Gompers (son of Bill Gompers, 1948 Buffalo Bills), Susan Gray (daughter of Bill Stanton, 1949 Buffalo Bills), George Groves (1947 Buffalo Bills, 1948 Baltimore Colts), Hal Herring (1949 Buffalo Bills, 1950–1952 Cleveland Browns), Peter Kritzer (son of Cy Kritzer of the *Buffalo Evening News*), Chick Maggioli (1948 Buffalo Bills, 1949 Detroit Lions, 1950 Baltimore Colts), Zeke O'Connor (1948 Buffalo Bills, 1949 Cleveland Browns, 1951 New York Yanks), Gloria Poole (wife of Ollie Poole, 1947 New York Yankees, 1948 Baltimore Colts, 1949 Detroit Lions), Ollie Poole (1947 New York Yankees, 1948 Baltimore Colts, 1949 Detroit Lions), Ben Pucci (1946 Buffalo Bisons, 1947 Chicago Rockets, 1948 Cleveland Browns), Anne Ratterman (wife of George Ratterman, 1947–1949 Buffalo Bills, 1950–1951 New York Yanks, 1952–1956 Cleveland Browns), Matt Ratterman (son of George Ratterman, 1947–1949 Buffalo Bills, 1950–1951 New York Yanks, 1952–1956 Cleveland Browns), Don Schneider (1948 Buffalo Bills), Lilly Schneider (wife of Don Schneider, 1948 Buffalo Bills), Bill Stanton (1949 Buffalo Bills), Art Statuto (1948–1949 Buffalo Bills, 1950 Los Angeles Rams), Blair Stautzenberger (son of Odell Stautzenberger, 1949 Buffalo Bills), Roy Stuart (1942 Cleveland Rams, 1943 Detroit Lions, 1946 Buffalo Bisons), Jack Sutton (son of Joe Sutton, 1949 Buffalo Bills, 1950–1952 Philadelphia Eagles), Joe Sutton (1949 Buffalo Bills, 1950–1952 Philadelphia Eagles), George Terlep (1946–1948 Buffalo Bills, 1948 Cleveland

Browns), Lou Tomasetti (1939 Pittsburgh Pirates, 1940 Pittsburgh Steelers, 1941 Philadelphia Eagles, 1941 Detroit Lions, 1942 Philadelphia Eagles, 1946 Buffalo Bisons, 1947–1949 Buffalo Bills), Al Vandeweghe (1946 Buffalo Bisons), Betty Vogt (wife of Alois Vogt, 1946 Buffalo Bisons), Wilbur Volz (1949 Buffalo Bills), and Alex Wizbicki (1947–1949 Buffalo Bills, 1950 Green Bay Packers).

I am also grateful to the members of the Professional Football Researchers Association's All-America Football Conference (AAFC) Committee for taking the time to interview the players listed below. The transcripts of those interviews were invaluable in gaining perspectives from players from other AAFC teams: Ben Agajanian (interviewed by Andy Piascik), Bruce Alford, Sr. (interviewed by Jay Langhammer), Bill Boedeker (interviewed by Andy Piascik), Ray Ebli (interviewed by Andy Piascik), Dick Erdlitz (interviewed by Andy Piascik), Gene Fekete (interviewed by Andy Piascik), Verl Lillywhite (interviewed by Andy Piascik), Mo Scarry (interviewed by Andy Piascik), Otto Schnellbacher (interviewed by Andy Piascik), Dean Sensanbaugher (interviewed by Andy Piascik), Ken Stofer (interviewed by Mel Bashore) and George Terlep (interviewed by Andy Piascik).

Additionally, I would like to thank the following people for their help with research and advice: Mel Bashore (author, historian), Jill Birschbach (Senior Researcher-Getty Images), Ace Cacchiotti (NFL Films, retired; historian), Bob Carroll (Executive Director-Professional Football Researchers Association), Lori Chase (journalist, historian), Saleem Choudhry (Researcher-Pro Football Hall of Fame), Jerome Collins (author, historian), Joe Cronin (historian), Dennis Frank (University Historian-St. Bonaventure University), Bob Gill (author, historian), Joe Horrigan (Vice President of Communications/Exhibits-Pro Football Hall of Fame, author, historian), Sean Lahman (author, historian), Denny Lynch (Buffalo Bills Director of Archives, retired; historian), Tod Maher (author, historian), Joe Marren (author, historian), Sandy Marzullo (historian), David Neft (author, historian) Dennis O'Brien (St. Bonaventure University), Mark Palczewski (historian), Pete Palmer (author, historian), Bill Pepperell (historian), Andy Piascik (author, historian), Ken Pullis (author, historian), Pete Rosen (screenwriter), Steve Schott (lawyer), and Ron Wolf (NFL executive, retired).

Preface

This book explores the original Buffalo Bills franchise of the 1940s. The All-American Football Conference (AAFC) first took the field in 1946 and Buffalo was a charter member. Over the subsequent four years, Buffalo became a major factor in the Conference, including playing in the championship game in 1948. When the team disbanded, there was an outpouring of support from the community to get a team back in Buffalo. The lengths to which the city tried to convince the National Football League (NFL) to allow Buffalo into the league were nothing less than impressive, and the league noticed. However, the war with the AAFC left the NFL in tough financial shape and the NFL did not want to expand to fourteen teams.

There have been many books written about the current Buffalo Bills franchise, and many more are in the works. But none have spent appreciable time exploring this important part of professional football history in Buffalo. It is this author's humble opinion that the current Buffalo Bills franchise would not exist if it were not for the original Buffalo Bills of the 1940s. When Ralph Wilson was unable to get a team in Miami for the upstart American Football League, Buffalo was suggested as a possible alternative due to the success of the 1940s team and the fan support from the community. If it were not for that franchise, it is possible that Buffalo would not have been suggested to Wilson. Therefore, Wilson would have chosen another city for his club and Buffalo would have been out of the picture. The current Buffalo Bills are ingrained into the fabric of the community. The same can be said of the Buffalo Bills of the 1940s. In exclusive interviews for this book, members of the AAFC Bills mentioned time and again how they were welcomed into the community. It was as if they were members of the family for each and every fan.

This book is divided into two segments: the narrative and the reference materials. The narrative section goes into detail on the formation of the All-American Football Conference, the building of the team and how it evolved throughout its existence. It finishes with the dissolution of the AAFC and the dispersal of the players from the team. The reference materials give detailed game summaries and statistics for every game played. It also goes to great lengths to give information—including biographies and statistics—of every player that suited up for the club, regardless of whether they were in training camp or on the regular roster.

Preface

I have been studying professional football history for over twenty years and there is something truly special about the AAFC Buffalo Bills. While researching this book and talking with surviving members of the team, I have formed a bond with them. Many were very eager to be interviewed. Some hesitated to talk with me, wondering how they could possible contribute any valuable information towards this book, either because they were not a member of the franchise for a significant length of time or perhaps they didn't see much action on the field. I want them to know that every single piece of information they were able to share helped to shape this book into its final form and I am forever indebted to them. I am proud and honored to call them my friends. For the family members of players and coaches who have passed on, who have given so generously of their time, I am humbled. I can only hope that this book properly honors the players, coaches, owners and team personnel that made this franchise so special. It was their work that left a permanent mark on the history of professional football in Buffalo and it is my intention to make sure that they are never forgotten.

Prologue

Professional football in Western New York started in the early 1900s, with the Oakdale club being one of the first semi-professional clubs in the area. As the sport became more popular and players graduated from college, additional athletic clubs and local businesses formed aggregations. These teams tried to entice the best players to their squads to beat their area rivals. As they became stronger, they looked for competition outside of their local gridirons. Over time, regional rivalries became heated and smaller teams banded together to form larger all-star squads. Town pride was at stake with these all-star teams. Bragging rights for an entire year could be had with a single win, not to mention the money that could be made gambling on the contests. By the mid–1910s, All-Buffalo—otherwise known as the Buffalo All-Stars—started to become a force on Western New York gridirons. The Rochester Jeffersons also emerged and battled the Buffalo All-Stars for Western New York supremacy. Year after year, these two teams were the best that their respective cities could offer and the battles were intense.

With the arrival of Tommy Hughitt in 1917, Buffalo's team immediately became the best in Western New York. Hughitt—born Ernest Frederick Hughitt in British Columbia—moved to Michigan when he was young. While in high school, his football skills did not stand out. This changed once he started playing for the Michigan Wolverines, where he starred as their quarterback for three seasons. After graduation in 1915, Hughitt went on to coach the University of Maine football team, as well as play part-time ball for the Youngstown Patricians and the Detroit Heralds. Once in Buffalo, he became a leader on the field, taking Buffalo's strongest teams to championships in 1918 and 1919, as well as become the driving force on Buffalo's professional teams of the 1920s. After retiring from football, Hughitt became a well-respected official, working on games throughout the area including the Buffalo Bisons/Bills of the All-America Football Conference (AAFC).[1]

Buffalo had their first attempt at a formal football league in 1918. There were attempts at leagues before this time, but all were informal local circuits. The Buffalo Semi-Professional Football League was made up of four teams, although only three were from Buffalo. The Niagaras were by far the best team and were led by Tommy Hughitt and Warren D. Patterson. They went 5–0–0 for the season and outscored their opponents by an astonishing 109–7. The war factory Pierce-Arrows, the Hydraulics from the south side, and the Pittsburgh Colored Stars filled out the league; however, none could compete with the Niagaras.[2]

Hughitt again made waves on the Buffalo football scene when he led the Buffalo Prospects to glory in 1919. The team started the season with an upset loss to West Buffalo, but rebounded to finish their championship season with a record of 9-1-1, including a 19-0 victory in their rematch with West Buffalo. Several members of the Prospects found their way onto the roster of the Buffalo All-Americans—Buffalo's first NFL franchise.[3]

There are no official records indicating that the Buffalo All-Americans were actual members of the American Professional Football Association (APFA), the league that was renamed the National Football League (NFL) in 1922. A letter applying for membership was sent to the league, but no official response has been found. Couple this with the fact that official meeting minutes show that Buffalo was granted a franchise in 1921, all indications show that the team was not an official member of the 1920 league. In spite of this, their records are still included in the official league standings.

The 1920 Buffalo All-Americans were a strong team. Heading into their final contest of the season, the All-Americans needed to beat the 7-0-3 Akron Pros for the APFA championship. A tie or a loss would give Akron the inaugural league title and Buffalo was determined to prevent that from happening. Buffalo had a chance late in the fourth quarter, when Heinie Miller recovered Fritz Pollard's fumbled punt return. This put Buffalo on Akron's twelve-yard line and in position to strike for the first score of the game. Unfortunately, time expired before Buffalo could mount any sort of offensive attack and the game ended in a scoreless tie. The Akron Pros were the champions of the APFA and Buffalo claimed second place.[4] All Buffalo sports fans are painfully aware of this recurring theme throughout their history. "Wide Right" and "No Goal" are phrases that cause die-hard Buffalo sports fans to cringe.

Controversy arose during the 1921 season, as bitterness arose between the Buffalo All-Americans and the Philadelphia Quakers (previously the Union Athletic Association). In 1920, Buffalo manager Frank McNeil failed to pay promised bonuses to his players, thereby creating tension on the team. It was also discovered that several of his star players were playing for the Quakers on Saturday and returning to Buffalo to play on Sunday. Most professional games were played on Sunday, but Pennsylvania Blue Laws prevented teams from playing on that day. Therefore, all games played in the Keystone state were held on Saturday. That gave players an opportunity to earn additional money by playing for two teams over the weekend.

Buffalo scheduled a game with the Canton Bulldogs on November 20, 1921. Later, McNeil found out that the Quakers had a game scheduled with Canton for the previous day. Since his players also played for Philadelphia, McNeil felt that they would be too tired or injured to give Buffalo its best chance to beat Canton and informed the league of the situation. Once APFA

President Joe Carr found out about the conflict, he cancelled the Philadelphia-Canton game. This infuriated Leo Conway, manager of the Quakers. The gate receipts for that game were expected to be huge and McNeil ruined Conway's chances at the windfall. In the fallout of all of this, Lou Little, Heinie Miller, Johnny Scott, Joe Spagna and Lud Wray left the All-Americans and stayed with the Quakers. Needing to fill roster spots, Buffalo raided the roster of the recently defunct Detroit Tigers, grabbing guard Moose Gardner, center Charlie Guy, tackle Steamer Horning, back Walt Kuehl and tackle/end Tillie Voss. With little practice time, the All-Americans were only able to muster a 7–7 tie with Canton. Philadelphia quickly scheduled another game against an APFA opponent—the Rochester Jeffersons—to make up for the Canton game that was cancelled. In that game, Johnny Scott kicked a six-yard field goal after rushes by backs Robb and Smith failed to gain much ground deep inside Rochester territory. The Jeffersons were able to drive to the Philadelphia forty-yard line, where Rochester lined up for a kick. Jim Laird held the ball as Morrissey put it through the goal posts to even up the game. The score stood tied at 3–3 when the final whistle blew.[5]

The following week, the All-Americans met the Chicago Staleys (currently called the Chicago Bears) at Cubs Park in Chicago. The All-Americans won 7–6 and the Buffalo newspapers declared their local team league champions. Buffalo had a record of 8–0–2 and amassed an astounding seven shutouts. They faced the Dayton Triangles a few days later and generated their eighth shutout of the season and a 9–0–2 record. There was no question that Buffalo would be named league champion. That was until Buffalo manager Frank McNeil scheduled "exhibition" games against the Akron Pros and the Chicago Staleys. Buffalo beat Akron 14–0 and traveled to Chicago to play the following day. Battered from the Akron game, the Buffalo All-Americans lost 10–7 to the Staleys.

At that point, the All-Americans had a record of 10–1–2, while Chicago had a 9–1–1 season record. That meant that Buffalo was the champion, right? Chicago manager George Halas contended otherwise. The Buffalo win over the McKeesport Olympics was dropped from the standings, since McKeesport was not a member of the APFA. Now, Buffalo and Chicago had the same record (ties were not counted, so both teams were 9–1). Halas asserted that the second game between their two clubs should count more than the first since it was more difficult to win the second game. The league agreed and awarded the championship to Chicago.[6] Again, Buffalo came in second place. Halas went on to win five more league championships with the Chicago Bears and was inducted into the inaugural class of the Pro Football Hall of Fame in 1963.

Throughout the remainder of the 1920s, Buffalo professional football never reached the pinnacle of the 1920 and 1921 seasons. In 1929, after several name changes and facing financial difficulties, Buffalo fielded their last major-league professional team for over a decade.

Professional football in Buffalo reemerged in the form of the American

Football League (AFL) in 1940. The AFL was a minor league and was no real threat to the NFL. The Buffalo Indians, coached by Earl "Red" Seick, struggled their first season going 2–8–0. After losing four of his first five games that year, Seick was replaced by Ole Nesmith. He faired no better and only won one game the remainder of the season. Buffalo dropped out of the 1941 AFL season for financial reasons, but an unnamed Scranton businessman bought the franchise and renamed them the Buffalo Tigers. The team still struggled, going 2–6–0 and folded soon after the end of the season.[7] However, team president Fiore Cesare remained a fixture on the Buffalo football scene and later became a scout for the Buffalo Bisons of the All-America Football Conference (AAFC).

The Rival Leagues

The landscape has been littered with well-intentioned leagues who thought they could compete with the NFL. Grange's AFL of 1926 was the first major test for the relatively young NFL. After an intense and money-draining year, the AFL folded, while the battered and bruised NFL survived. Other minor American Football Leagues surfaced in the mid to late 1930s, as well as the 1940s, but none were of the same caliber as the NFL.

On December 7, 1941, the NFL was playing the last of their regular season games. It was also one of the darkest days in American history. On the morning of that fateful day, over 2,400 people were killed and more than 1,200 people were injured when the Japanese bombed Pearl Harbor. According to Mel Hein, Hall of Fame center for the New York Giants, "We knew something was going on because every few minutes during the game the PA announcer would call some military person to report to his post."[8] Two weeks later, the Chicago Bears beat the New York Giants 37–9 for the NFL Championship in front of a sparse crowd. The country had other things on its mind.

The following year, NFL rosters started to dwindle as players were drafted or enlisted in the military. A few stars remained, but there was a noticeable drop in the overall talent level. The league fell from ten teams to eight, with the Cleveland Rams suspending operations, and the Philadelphia Eagles and Pittsburgh Steelers merging to become the Steagles. The following year, the Steelers merged with the Chicago Cardinals before breaking off on their own in 1945.[9]

World War II almost ruined professional football as the bulk of the quality players were shipped overseas. A few leagues tried to form during this time, which included yet another incarnation of the AFL, the Trans-America League, the United States Football League (USFL) and the AAFC. Each of these leagues vied for the few remaining serviceable players and the battle between them was intense. In order to get a leg up on the USFL, the AFL tried to form an alliance with the NFL. The AFL asked NFL Commissioner Elmer Layden to protect the AFL players from scavenging until west coast teams could be established and become competitive. The AFL, however, made a crucial mistake when they allocated NFL players to the new west coast teams. Dean Hilmick and Bill Fisk of the Detroit Lions, as well as Vic Carroll of the New York Giants were in a pool of players set to work out for AFL teams. This ended their agreement before it could even be put on paper. Upon hearing this news, NFL publicity director George Strickler issued the following warning: "Any National league player who accepts a contract with any other league will be ineligible to play in our league for five years and none of our teams can play another team which has on its roster such a player." Strickler also added that there is room for another professional league, but none of the current crop of leagues was qualified.[10] Fearing reprisal, no NFL players suited up for the AFL. This relegated the AFL as a non-factor.

The Trans-America League was headed by former Manhattan College coach Chick Meehan. Meehan, as the AFL had attempted before, tried to work out a deal with the NFL to keep his league viable. He proposed that his Trans-America League merge with the NFL to form a 16-team league (eleven from the NFL and five from the Trans-America League). The proposal was to have the league operate like the American and National Leagues in baseball. Each "league" would compete individually, with the winners competing for the championship. The NFL was far superior to the Trans-America League, so the championships would be lopsided. Seeing no need to prop up a minor league, the NFL rejected this offer. Meehan's league was now in trouble and he rested its future on obtaining stadium rights in New York City.[11] Much to Meehan's chagrin, he never obtained those rights. According to Meehan, "Once Larry MacPhail, president of the baseball Yankees, told me he couldn't give me word on the stadium until 1946, I knew we were licked. So I notified my franchise owners that we were withdrawing."[12] They officially called it quits on June 5, 1945.[13] Two of the four leagues were now out of the picture, leaving just the USFL and AAFC to go against the goliath NFL.

While the USFL held its first organizational meeting on April 4, 1944, it was not until July before the league became official. In a meeting in Philadelphia, it was decided that the USFL would consist of ten teams broken up into two divisions. Two additional franchises were to be added in the future, but this never happened. In fact, the league dropped two of its clubs before the end of the year.

One of the franchises looking for admission into the USFL was Buffalo. A group headed by former Buffalo Tigers president Fiore Cesare could easily have made it into the USFL, as they were supported by league President *pro tem* Roland D. Payne, but financial backing was a problem. As a result, Buffalo withdrew their application before the end of the year. The final cities in the league were: Akron (headed by Charles Burns of the Akron Rubber Bowl), Baltimore (led by A.H. Ehlers, president of the Interstate Baseball League), Boston (ownership not announced), Chicago (under the direction of consulting engineer J.E. "Ned" Grimes, Honolulu (led by the team of businessman Ralph W. Olson, surgeon Dr. Samuel L. Lee and F.J. Brickner of the Navy), New York (headed by contractor W.S. Palmer), Philadelphia (owned by businessman J.J. Ahrin) and Washington (led by Lt. Harry L. Harris of the Coast Guard).[14] Due to the expense of travel during the war, Honolulu announced that they would play their games in Cincinnati.[15]

At the same time that these teams were announced, Harold "Red" Grange was brought on board. Up to this point, Pittsburgh businessman Roland D. Payne was in charge of the league, however, Payne was relatively unknown in sports circles. Adding the "Galloping Ghost" to their league gave the USFL instant credibility. His exploits on the Illinois gridiron were legendary and was arguably the greatest running back of his time. Grange was a football god.

The USFL did not want to create tension between their league and the NFL. In an attempt to avoid the mistake that doomed the AFL, they did not want to directly raid the NFL rosters. However, the college draft was another story. In discussing his new venture, Grange stated, "We will not attempt to sign any players under contract with the National league, but as far as players they claim under the draft, that's another story. The final choice should be up to the player, himself."[16]

Even though the USFL tried to avoid it, things started to become tense between the rival leagues and the NFL felt the heat. In an attempt to minimize the viability of these new leagues, NFL Commissioner Elmer Layden — in the NFL's publication to servicemen called *The Touchback* — went on the offensive, stating,

> Attempts to organize opposition to the National League were inevitable. But present efforts appear to be especially ill-timed. Despite the vaporizing of well-meaning neophytes, there is nothing to indicate that there is room for another major league. Fabulous offers are being made (by new leagues) to national leaguers and to National League prospects in an attempt to get them under contract. Far from the mainland in foxholes and out-of-the-way bases, these offers unquestionably appear exceedingly attractive. But they are only so much paper, merely a promoter's promise unless when the signee presents himself for collection there is a team for him to join and opponents for that team to play. To date, none of the proposed organizations has any idea when it can operate if ever.[17]

A few weeks after Layden's statement, Red Grange resigned as President of the USFL, putting the final nail in their coffin. Grange's reasoning for resigning was two-fold. First, the role as president required "a big promotional job and my insurance business prevents me from giving it the necessary time the office requires."[18] Additionally, he thought it was not the right time to go against the NFL. "Players are holding out for between $400 and $800 a game when they used to get $150,"[19] stated Grange. "Promoters will need to attract a helluva lot of people just to break even."[20] Grange did not want to be a part of another failed attempt to take on the NFL as he reminisced on his 1926 AFL days. The USFL folded at the same time as the Trans-America League.[21] This left just the AAFC as the sole rival to the NFL.

1

The AAFC Forms

"For over 40 years baseball has settled down to the acceptance of two major leagues, which have, made baseball what it is. The game was too great for just one league. It is my belief that pro football has a future that is too big for just one league. It is true that pro football has given us only four money makers from some 20 to 21 clubs. But if pro football in this vast expanse of football talent can't support two leagues, it may be there isn't room enough for even one league. It will only prove that pro football isn't a big league sport. I don't believe this."
— *Grantland Rice*[1]

To get insight into the formation of the AAFC, one must look to the beginning of 1944 when four groups of financial backers applied for franchises in the NFL. The first group—led by Bing Crosby—wanted a franchise in Los Angeles. This group consisted of Crosby, actor Don Ameche, Frank Mandel of Chicago (cousin of Fred Mandel, Jr. who was the owner of the Detroit Lions at the time), Graham Smith of the Marine Corps and A.G. Atwater of Chicago. Atwater was the brother-in-law of Philip K. Wrigley of baseball's Chicago Cubs. The second group was led by Anthony J. Morabito. Morabito, co-owner of Lumber Terminal Company, was looking for a franchise for San Francisco. The final two groups both looked for franchises in Buffalo. Charles Murray, a Buffalo sports promoter, was part of the first group and Sam Cordovano, president of Globe Construction Company, headed the second. Cordovano's group consisted of local businessmen, namely Frontier Oil Refining Corporation's President James F. Breuil, Treasurer William Bennett and Sales Manager Clayton Maxwell. All four groups deposited $25,000 checks, as well as their applications, to the league by January of 1944 and anxiously awaited the league's decision.[2]

Sam Cordovano was no stranger to football and to sports in general. A product of Canisius High School, Cordovano was an all-around athlete. He competed in football, baseball and basketball, as well as other sports. After an All-American football career at Georgetown—where he was a teammate of Cleveland Rams' owner Dan Reeves—Cordovano played nine games for the NFL's Newark Tornadoes in 1930 and built a reasonable name for himself as a professional wrestler. After his short playing career, Cordovano became an assistant coach under Lou Little at Columbia. He remained there for 14 years, including taking over the head spot while Little suffered from a variety of health ailments during the 1943 season. Cordovano said that he would resign his post as coach at Columbia if he were to get an NFL franchise.[3]

James F. Breuil had long been a supporter of Buffalo sports. Breuil had come to Buffalo in 1922 as an oil salesman and within seven years, established the Frontier Oil Refining Corporation. Less than ten years later, Breuil steadily expanded the company to employ over 300 workers.[4] The trio of Breuil, Bennett and Maxwell provided the financial backbone to the franchise-seeking group, while Cordovano was the face. Of the two Buffalo aggregations, the Cordovano-led contingent was the strongest. Murray's group failed to gain traction and the Buffalo focus went to Cordovano. With an estimated $250,000 in capital and wealthy businessmen associated with the group, there was no question that if Buffalo were to receive a franchise, it would go to Cordovano.[5] Since his group worked on getting a franchise for approximately a year and were far more established, Charles Murray's bid would become nothing more than a footnote in Buffalo football history.

Things looked good for Cordovano and his cohorts. If the NFL were to expand, Buffalo was considered to have the best chance at landing a franchise. Los Angeles and San Francisco were just too far away from the other clubs and travel expenses needed to be considered during those lean war years. Speculation was that Buffalo would join the reactivated Cleveland Rams, the Chicago Cardinals, Chicago Bears, Detroit Lions and the Green Bay Packers in the Western Division. This balanced the league at twelve teams, making it easier to form a schedule. The schedule, the franchise applications and the college draft would all be addressed at the league's spring meeting in April.[6]

Hopes were quickly dashed for the west coast teams. On January 14, 1944, the NFL owners tabled the applications for franchises from Los Angeles, San Francisco and Buffalo. They returned the $25,000 deposit to Los Angeles and San Francisco, but kept the Buffalo money stating that Buffalo might still be granted a franchise at the April meeting. All was not lost for Buffalo, even with that minor setback. The league did not say "Yes," but it definitely did not say "No." Cordovano, always the PR man, commented, "Buffalo would be a great football town. We can get almost 50,000 in our stadium and have a 2,000,000 population within a radius of 62 miles."[7]

Still, everything hinged on the whims of the owners and the ability of Buffalo to quickly put together a team. Even if Buffalo gathered enough players in time to start the 1944 season, the owners could still wait until after the war before admitting a new franchise. According to Cordovano, "If the Buffalo franchise is granted, we will follow the dictates of the other club owners on whether or not we can operate this year."[8] Cordovano also added, "We believe if Buffalo gets a franchise we can field a team this season. If our application is accepted we could use Municipal Stadium."[9]

Buffalo had only a few months to convince the league that they were serious and deserved a franchise. Cordovano stepped up the pressure and issued a statement that he would field a team "franchise or no franchise." This non-league squad would play exhibition matches with local community elevens. Cordovano added, "The city wants and will support a professional team and I'll give it to them, even if the only opposition they ever meet is composed of fellow squad members.... We have everything but the franchise.... We have the complete support of the mayor, board of supervisors and other city officials. We have a first rate football stadium that isn't used for any other sport. And, we already have football men scouting the country recruiting players."[10]

Jim Breuil, Bisons/Bills owner.

On April 21, 1944, Buffalo's chances at an NFL franchise for 1944 came to an end. The NFL owners voted to table all expansion applications until after the war. Buffalo, Los Angeles, San Francisco and a new group from Baltimore headed by Abe Watner, all had to wait.[11]

Seeing a golden opportunity, *Chicago Tribune* sports editor Arch Ward started the process of forming a rival league: the All-America Football Conference. He immediately went after the groups denied by the NFL, tapping Don Ameche's Los Angeles group, Anthony Morabito's San Francisco group and the Cordovano-Breuil contingent from Buffalo.[12] The makeup of the Los Angeles group changed somewhat from the original team that applied for an NFL franchise. Don Ameche took more of a public role in the organization, which was originally led by Bing Crosby. Ameche brought in Christy Walsh, who is arguably considered the first sports agent. In 1921, Walsh created a syndicate called the Cosmopolitan Book Corporation, where sports stars such as Babe Ruth and Lou Gehrig could generate additional revenue outside of the game.

In June of 1944, the AAFC held its first organizational meeting in St. Louis. Out of that meeting, charter franchises were awarded to Buffalo, Chicago, Cleveland, Los Angeles, New York and San Francisco. However, it would not be until September before the league was officially announced to the public. Hints of this league started appearing in August, as can be seen from an *Oakland Tribune* article from August 9, 1944:

> An Associated Press gossip yarn yesterday declared that Don Ameche, miffed because his application for a National Pro League franchise in Los Angeles had been tabled, has been secretly negotiating with interested parties with the idea of forming a new league. Others mentioned as being part of the Ameche plan are Christy Walsh of

New York, John Keeshin of Chicago, Tony Morabito of San Francisco and Sam Cordovano of Buffalo. Morabito applied for a National League franchise for San Francisco at the same time Ameche asked for one for Los Angeles—and received the brushoff just as did the actor man.[13]

With Cordovano now occupied with his duties as co-owner, general manager and interim head coach of the new Buffalo franchise, he needed to unload some of his other responsibilities. As previously mentioned, Cordovano stated that he would relinquish his coaching duties at Columbia if he were granted a franchise. True to his word, he did just that as Tad Wieman, former head coach at Princeton, took over for Cordovano as line coach at Columbia.[14]

There was another secret meeting in the beginning of September before the rival league was officially announced to the public. At that point, the newspapers were on top of the story and the announcement was more of a formality. Additional names started to come out. Ameche, Walsh, Morabito, Keeshin, Cordovano and Breuil were known at this point and L.T. "Buck" Shaw, Max Farrington, Ray Ryan and Vincent X. Flaherty were added to the list.[15] Things shaped up for the league, but they still only had six franchises. At the September meeting, owners of the charter franchises met to approve a seventh franchise, this one in Baltimore. Applications for an eighth club were accepted from Detroit, Boston and Philadelphia, but no franchise was granted. Coinciding with the meeting, the league's first four players were signed by the New York franchise: Tulsa back Glenn Dobbs; Minnesota and Michigan All-American back Bill Daley; Baylor end Jack Russell; and Texas A&M tackle Martin Ruby. The AAFC was now set and the names of the franchise owners slowly made it into the newspapers:

Baltimore: Gene Tunney (former heavyweight boxing champion)
Buffalo: James F. Breuil (president of Frontier Oil Refining Corporation), Sam Cordovano (President of Globe Construction Company), William Bennett (Treasurer of Frontier Oil Refining Corporation)
Chicago: John L. Keeshin (President of Keeshin Freight Lines)
Cleveland: Arthur McBride (Owner of a taxicab company)
Los Angeles: Don Ameche (actor) and Christy Walsh (former newspaper syndicate director)
New York: Eleanor Gehrig (widow of Lou Gehrig) and Ray J. Ryan (President of Ryan Oil Company)
San Francisco: Anthony J. Morabito and Allen E. Sorrell (co-owners of Lumber Terminal Company), Ernest J. Turre (General Manager of Del E. Webb Construction Company of Phoenix, AZ)[16]

With seven teams in the mix and a potential eighth franchise, they were ready to go public with their league. According to Ward, "The circuit is fully organized" and he characterized the owners of the seven clubs already granted franchises as "men of millionaire incomes."[17] As part of the announcement, Ward also announced two resolutions adopted by the owners, namely that the

AAFC forbid any franchise from trying to steal players from the NFL and that no player would be accepted into the league as long as they still had college eligibility remaining. He also stated that any AAFC franchise that is in a city that currently has an NFL franchise would make every effort to avoid conflicts in game dates and playing sites.[18]

The AAFC continued to organize and at a December organizational meeting, Lt. Commander James Crowley was named as permanent Commissioner, taking over for Arch Ward who had served as temporary leader. Crowley was the left halfback of Notre Dame's famed Four Horsemen backfield of the mid to late 1920s. Ironically, his backfield teammate was Elmer Layden, who was the Commissioner of the rival National Football League. Additionally at the organizational meeting, Christy Walsh (Los Angeles) was named Vice-President, Eleanor Gehrig (New York) was elected Secretary and Buffalo's Sam Cordovano became Treasurer. Each club put up a $10,000 franchise fee, except Baltimore, which was expected to do so at a later date. Ray Miller (Cleveland), Anthony Morabito (San Francisco) and John L. Keeshin (Chicago) were appointed to draw up a constitution and bylaws. Miller, a former Notre Dame star, was named legal counsel.

The league experienced its first conflict as New York owner Ray Ryan withdrew his franchise from the league. With the new vacancy, Baltimore owner Gene Tunney agreed to move his club to New York in order for the AAFC to keep a presence in the Big Apple. As if that were not enough, Tunney was forced to withdraw his franchise soon after when he was ordered to Pacific duty. This left a hole in the New York market and only six franchises. To make up for the lack of franchises, Harvey Hester's Miami group was awarded the seventh team.[19]

As 1945 progressed, the franchises started taking shape. Paul Brown, former Massillon High School, Ohio State and Great Lakes Naval Station football coach, was hired to coach the Cleveland squad. Northwestern and El Toro Flying Tigers coach Dick Hanley was signed to coach the Chicago club, while Duluth Eskimos and Chicago Cardinals star Ernie Nevers inked to be his assistant. Jack Meagher, coach at Alabama Poly, became the head man at Miami.

Still, the league was looking for an eighth franchise. At the April organizational meeting, a contingent from Kansas City made a proposal, but no decision was made. The lack of a decision was probably due to Tom Gallery's (representative of the NFL's Brooklyn Tigers) expressed interest in bringing his franchise into the league, as he no longer wanted to be a part of the NFL. This was a major coup for the AAFC, as it gave the AAFC instant credibility by adding an established franchise. By December of 1945, an official announcement was made. Dan Topping—owner of the Brooklyn Tigers—proclaimed that he was moving his team from the NFL to the AAFC. In return, it was agreed that the other seven AAFC owners would give Topping $75,000, plus an additional $25,000 to come out of the first year's gate receipts. This new team became the New York Yankees. In reality, Topping did not "transfer" his franchise to the AAFC. He needed to fold his Brooklyn Tigers franchise and start a new club in the AAFC. When he folded his franchise, all player contracts were given to Ted Collins' Boston Yanks team, who merged with the Tigers for the 1945 season. As it turned out, Topping was able to sign away most of the Tiger players from the Yanks and he essentially started the New York Yankees with the same players that he had the previous year with the Tigers.

To clean up the situation left by Ray Ryan and his New York franchise, Arch Ward talked with baseball's Branch Rickey about a new Brooklyn franchise to play at Ebbets Field. That new franchise was owned by William Cox, Gerald Smith and Dr. Mal Stevens of the Brooklyn Dodgers. Cox was banned from baseball for gambling and was the owner of the New York team in the defunct USFL and Gerald Smith was from Street and Smith publishers. The AAFC decided that all players signed by Ryan would be transferred to this new Brooklyn franchise. Rickey agreed to allow Brooklyn to play at Ebbets Field and the league was set.

Initially, the AAFC had no intentions of competing with the NFL. They felt that they could peacefully co-exist and went to work to hammer out an agreement between the two leagues. The NFL, however, did not see things the same way. In September of 1945, Cleveland coach Paul Brown and Chicago owner John Keeshin were appointed to confer with NFL Commissioner Elmer Layden regarding a working agreement between the two major leagues. They were unsuccessful in their efforts to meet with Layden and later attempts to discuss such agreements also failed. According to an article in the *Stars and Stripes Mediterranean,*

> The All-America League has petitioned the established National for recognition, but Layden was "not in" and inferred they should go get a reputation. That leaves the new league with no alternative but to offer higher inducements to college seniors who are controlled in a December draft by the National League. The National has threatened all players who jump to the rival league with disbarment for life.[20]

The NFL wanted nothing to do with the AAFC. Since they did not want to peacefully coexist, the AAFC started to play for keeps. In August of 1945, AAFC Commissioner Jim Crowley announced the signing of 150 players, including two NFL stalwarts: Bob Steuber of the Chicago Bears and Lou Rymkus of the Washington Redskins. Both became the newest members of the Cleveland franchise. According to Crowley, "We originally resolved not to tamper with National league players, but since the N.F.L. snubbed us we see no reason why we can't hire their players."[21] The theft continued as Miami signed Hampton Pool of the Chicago Bears and Jim Poole of the New York Giants.

Of course, the battles were not strictly between leagues, but also intraleague. In November of 1945, the league saw a battle between the college ranks, the NFL, and the Chicago and Buffalo franchises in the AAFC. Halfback Elroy

"Crazy Legs" Hirsch was claimed by Wisconsin, the Cleveland Rams of the NFL and the Chicago Rockets of the AAFC. Hirsh was on the Wisconsin team in 1942 before heading off to Michigan as a V-12 trainee in 1943. While in the Marine Corps, Hirsch played on the star-studded El Toro Flying Tigers team. Chicago claimed that they had signed Hirsch, but Badger coach Harry Struhldeher and Hirsch both denied that assertion. In 1945, Hirsch was drafted by the Cleveland Rams. To make things more complicated, Buffalo claimed that Hirsch made a "verbal commitment to play with Buffalo"[22] and filed a claim with commissioner Crowley.

Bills halfback Steve Juzwik. This photograph was taken while Juzwik was with the Fleet City Bluejackets.

According to Sam Cordovano, "I have no doubt that Crowley will recognize our claim."[23] Cordovano was wrong and Hirsch started the 1946 season with the Chicago Rockets. Hirsch played three years with Chicago before going to the Los Angeles Rams (formerly the Cleveland Rams) to end his Hall of Fame career.

Throughout 1945, Sam Cordovano was on a tear to add players to the newly named Buffalo Bison roster. By November, Cordovano claimed to have 35 players signed to contracts, including Paul Governali, All-American halfback out of Columbia.[24] Governali was one of the first players to sign with the Bisons.[25] Chicago Rockets coach Dick Hanley rated Governali as one of the country's best passers. Hanley had first-hand knowledge of the quarterback/tailback as Governali played for Hanley on the El Toro Flying Tigers team, completing 67 out of 125 attempts and nine touchdowns in seven games.[26]

By December, Cordovano had 37 players signed — 30 of them straight out of college and seven veterans of the pro gridiron. Details of when players were signed are sketchy. According to Cordovano, "I can't give you their names because some of the players still are in service, but I can tell you that our forward wall will average 235 pounds and our backfield 200 and they're all pretty good players." He added, "Our payroll will run well above the $100,000 mark."[27] If Cordovano were to announce the players still in the service, the

NFL would have time to try to "entice" them to drop the AAFC and join their league. Cordovano did not want that to happen and kept mum on his roster. Signing away NFL players, however, made for good press. To finish up 1945, Cordovano signed Nebraska star Harry Hopp of the Detroit Lions and Notre Dame's Steve Juzwik, who was on the Washington Redskins' reserve list of players in the armed forces. Both backs starred for the service champion Fleet City Blue Jackets.[28] Signing prominent college players was also good press. Along with Governali, Cordovano was quick to announce the signings of tackle Derrell Palmer of Texas Christian, tackle Al Klug of Marquette, tackle Frank Gnup of Manhattan and end John Kelleher — a Columbia teammate of Governali.[29] Gnup was an All-American Honorable Mention in 1939 and played professionally under an assumed name.

Cordovano left no stone unturned while he looked talent. Tapping into his professional wrestling background, Cordovano tried to get wrestling star Verne Gagne to play for the Bisons. He was not the only one interested in his services. According to Gagne biographer Bill Murdock,

> With the war ended, Verne's career was at a crossroads that not many 20-year-olds have to face.... Undecided between a return to the University of Minnesota, the college gridiron and the mat and pro football, Verne made his choice in an unusual way.... As Gagne recalls, 'Sam Cordovano, who was recruiting for the Buffalo Bills, entertained some of us one night in Los Angeles. Sam was trying to sign some of the Marines. I really couldn't make up my mind. Finally, I said to Sam, "I'll tell you what I'll do, I'll wrestle you. If I win, I go back to school, if you win, I'll sign." Cordovano was unbelievably strong. He had played football for Georgetown and later wrestled professionally. We wrestled in his room in the Biltmore Hotel. Well anyway, as you know, I went back to school.[30]

The Conference was under way. Throughout 1944 and 1945, there were six leagues competing on the professional gridiron circuit (PanAmerica, United States, National, American and Trans-America football leagues, and the All-America Football Conference). By 1946, all that remained were the National Football League (NFL) and the All-America Football Conference (AAFC).

It was at that point where the war really began. In the October 28, 1945, edition of the *Stars and Stripes*, the battle lines were drawn between the leagues and preparations were made for a slugfest.

> So the sport which has outright command of exactly one (1) stadium in the U.S., at Green Bay, Wisc., will now undergo a period similar to that through which the American and National baseball leagues struggled at the turn of the century — one of player-bidding, mud-slinging, snubbing, charges and counter charges.[31]

Comparisons were being made between the two leagues in order to determine who would come out on top. The most outstanding of the comparisons dealt with stadium rights. Most of the NFL teams played in baseball stadiums. The previous year, the baseball owners declared that football teams could not use the baseball stadiums until the baseball season was over. With the AAFC having only one team using a baseball stadium (the Brooklyn Dodgers using Ebbets Field), this gave a clear advantage to the upstart Conference, as they gained fan support before the NFL started their season. The only way the NFL could compete with this was to play on neutral fields, but this would not generate the necessary fan interest in their home towns. This also impacted revenue, as each team needed to pay 15 percent off the top for park rental. The Green Bay Packers were the only NFL team immune from these fees as they were the only team not playing in a baseball stadium. That was a factor in the battle, as there had only been four money-making teams in the NFL prior to the inter-circuit war.[32]

The struggle between the two leagues only got worse and neither league would be immune.

2
The Bisons Take Shape

The beginning of 1946 saw continued turmoil surrounding franchises in the AAFC. At a three-day organizational meeting to kick off the new year, Edwin Nielsen (New York oilman and Baltimore representative at the meeting) stated that there were delays in securing a lease to play at Baltimore Municipal Stadium. Nielsen also expressed doubts about his franchise's ability to get enough players to field a team in 1946. As a result, the owners agreed to the delay and stated that Baltimore could enter the league in 1947.[1]

In the end, this made things easier for the league, as now there was an even number of teams (eight), which were broken up into two divisions. The Eastern Division included Brooklyn, Buffalo, Miami and New York, while the Western Division was made up of Chicago, Cleveland, Los Angeles and San Francisco. The teams would play a fourteen game home-and-home season, with the winners of each division playing for the championship.

It was also decided at the organizational meeting that the clubs would contribute seven players to Dan Topping's New York team. Each club would allow New York their choice of a player from their roster, after scratching three of their best players from the list. This essentially gave Topping seven free players; a small price to pay for the coup described in the previous chapter.[2]

The most interesting development to come out of the organizational meeting in January was the institution of a draft for college players. The NFL had been holding college drafts since 1936, so the concept was not new. The AAFC, however, decided to take a different approach with their "secret" draft: They only drafted players with no college eligibility remaining and who showed a desire to play professional football. In past years, the NFL drafted college all-stars who really had no desire to play professionally or who still had a year or two left in the collegiate ranks. According to Dr. Mal Stevens, former Yale and American University coach who was with the Brooklyn franchise, "The National League puts college seniors on the block like pieces of property with 500 or more names listed for hire. That practice has irked college athletic directors and coaches.... There is no sense in publicizing a list of players who have no intentions of entering the professional field. The National League has conducted this draft system mainly to advance its own game by flaunting names of college stars before the public eye."[3]

2—The Bisons Take Shape

The AAFC decided to write to the National Collegiate Coaches Association asking for a list of college players known to be interested in continuing football as a professional. They only approached interested players after receiving the approval of their coaches. This definitely made an impact with college coaches, as can be seen in a letter from Cornell University to Buffalo scout Fiore Cesare. In it, Cornell head coach Ed McKeever stated, "I think your idea of not drafting anyone eligible for college ball will get more cooperation for your league, as I had a bitter taste last year of the Cleveland Rams taking our best player."[4] Additional letters from collegiate coaches mirrored similar sentiments, as the coaches were more than happy to assist with requests for information.[5] The draft was held December 20 and 21 of 1946 and is described in further detail later.

Heading into 1946, the NFL changed commissioners. Out was Elmer Layden and in came Bert Bell. Bell, in association with Lud Wray, bought an NFL franchise in 1933 and named it the Philadelphia Eagles.[6] Buffalo football aficionados remember Lud Wray as the tackle/center out of the University of Pennsylvania who played for the 1920 and 1921 Buffalo All-Americans of the American Professional Football Association (renamed the NFL in 1922). After playing for Buffalo, Wray went into coaching and in 1932, he was the coach of the Boston Braves (currently the Washington Redskins). He became the Eagles' first head coach, lasting three seasons. The Eagles struggled and were put up for auction in 1934. Bell paid $4,500 and obtained sole ownership of the team. Pittsburgh owner Art Rooney sold the Steelers to Alexis Thompson and Rooney joined Bell as co-owner of the Eagles at the end of 1940 season. Thompson wanted to move his team to Boston, but the NFL owners refused. Fearing that Pittsburgh would be without an NFL franchise, Bell and Rooney decided to move their franchise to Pittsburgh (to be the new Steelers) and Thompson moved his franchise to Philadelphia to become the new Eagles.[7] This placated Thompson as it allowed him to move his franchise closer to his hometown of Boston and allowed Rooney to keep a team in Pittsburgh. Bell gave up his interests in the Steelers when he was named commissioner.

In his first test as NFL Commissioner, Bell had to address a franchise relocation situation. On January 12, Dan Reeves announced that he was moving his Cleveland Rams franchise to Los Angeles. This was an interesting move, as the Cleveland Browns would have been fighting the Rams for supremacy of the city. By leaving, the NFL abandoned the town and allowed the AAFC sole possession. With the Rams being the NFL Champion in 1945, this seemed like an unwise move. Other NFL owners agreed and voted 6–4 against the relocation. Reeves was determined and worked out deals with the Los Angeles Memorial Coliseum and the Cotton Bowl in Dallas to play games. In the end, the owners relented and agreed to allow Reeves to move to Los Angeles, where he went head-to-head with the Los Angeles Dons of the AAFC.[8] Only time would tell as to whether this was a good move.

The AAFC had a firm foothold on the west coast, with franchises in San

Francisco and Los Angeles. The NFL was just getting started with Reeves' Rams, but had no other presence out west. The NFL felt that more still needed to be done in order to compete. In stepped the Pacific Coast Football League (PCFL), a minor league consisting namely of teams in California. Three owners of the league: J. Howard Sullivan (attorney from Los Angeles), Frank Ciraolo (owner of Dugan's Café in San Francisco) and Clyde Mowdy (printer from Oakland), signed a working agreement with the NFL and "immediately proclaimed themselves the instruments which will break the rival millionaire-supported All-America football conference."[9] In the agreement, four PCFL teams would work with four NFL teams to hurt the AAFC: the Los Angeles Bulldogs would work with the Los Angeles Rams, the San Francisco Clippers with the New York Giants, San Diego Bombers with the Green Bay Packers and the Hollywood Bears with the Washington Redskins. It was agreed that the PCFL would not play in the same city as the NFL on the same day. Additionally, when the NFL was not playing a game on the West Coast, the PCFL would schedule a game to rival the AAFC. This forced the AAFC to take on both the NFL and the PCFL at the gate, while the NFL just battled the AAFC. The PCFL also agreed not to employ any AAFC players on their roster. In return for their help, the PCFL was promised two future franchises in the NFL, presumably Los Angeles and San Francisco. According to J. Howard Sullivan of the Los Angeles Bulldogs, "This fall will be tough on us, but we don't have to worry too much. The NFL has guaranteed to make up the deficit which we will suffer. No, we aren't worried. But what we want to do is start taking in money by the wheelbarrow full instead of the bucket full."[10] According to an article in the *Syracuse Herald Journal*, "In the National-A.A. battle, it figures close to $30,000 in expenses to take a club to the west coast under the new transcontinental setup. Every buck at the gate is going to count terrifically and the PCFL through its schedule maneuvering is going to chisel away at the A.A. gate while leaving the N.F.L. a clear path."[11]

Why would the NFL help out the PCFL? The PCFL was just a minor league and had no impact on the NFL. None of the teams were at the same talent level as the NFL, so bringing in a PCFL team did not make sense. Since the NFL was not keen on expansion, it also did not make sense to promise a franchise or two to the PCFL. The PCFL had to have known this from the beginning. The only explanation that makes sense was that the PCFL rosters were being raided by both the NFL and AAFC, and the deal was probably made to stop the hemorrhaging and to keep the PCFL somewhat intact.

* * *

Throughout the first part of the year, Sam Cordovano continued his blistering pace of signing talent for the squad. John "Bat" Batorski, Rocco Pirro, Bill Daddio, William Dutton, Sam Porazinsky, Joe Pezelski and Vic Kulbitski

2—The Bisons Take Shape

were inked to contracts in a matter of a couple of months. Batorski, a 215-pound end out of Colgate, was serving at the 43rd field hospital in the Pacific for twenty-two months before he returned to sign with Buffalo.[12] Pirro was an All-District selection while at Catholic University and played on the National Champion Fleet City Blue Jacket team in 1945. He was drafted in the twelfth round of the 1940 NFL draft by the Pittsburgh Steelers and played for the Steel City team in the 1940 and 1941 seasons. Daddio and Dutton were both University of Pittsburgh stars before coming to the Bisons. Daddio was drafted in the fifth round of the 1939 NFL draft by the Chicago Cardinals and is best known for scoring in 17 consecutive games between 1941 and 1942, as well as being named all-pro second team in 1942. Porazinsky and Pezelski played at Villanova, where Pezelski was named All-American Honorable Mention for two years before they reunited on the El Toro Flying Marines squad.[13] The signing of Kulbitski, former Minnesota and Notre Dame star, brought the number of players under contract to 38.[14] The next players signed were from the NFL. Michael Kostiuk (tackle with the Detroit Lions), Stephen Benchwick (guard with the New York Giants) and Chuck Cherundolo (center with the Cleveland Rams and Pittsburgh Steelers) helped fill out the lines.[15] Kostiuk's professional experience included playing a year each with the minor-league Jersey City Giants and the NFL's Detroit Lions. He also played a game for the Cleveland Rams in 1941. Cherundolo, a 225-pound center, played seven years in the NFL and doubled as an assistant coach while on the Miami Naval Training Station eleven.[16]

With the signing of Jack Dugger, All-American from Ohio State, the roster stood at 42 players. Dugger resigned from his coaching job at Lancaster (Ohio) High School to join the team. The 6'4" 230-pound end was the captain of the 1943 Buckeye team in his junior year and was an All-American his senior year. While on the team, Ohio State won the Big Ten Championships in 1942 and 1944, a National Championship in 1942, and made the college all-star squad in 1943 and 1944. Dugger was an all-around athlete, being named second team All-American in basketball and won AAU shot put and discus titles three years in a row.[17] Three additional signings occurred in May: Ray Makofske, Dan Dalsando and Albert Shaw. Makofske was a halfback who converted to tackle while Cordovano was a line coach at Columbia. As a captain in the infantry, Makofske spent twenty-two months in the Pacific, earning two Bronze Stars and a Purple Heart. Dalsando was the captain of the 1941 Detroit Tech eleven before spending twenty-two months serving in the Army in Europe. Shaw spent the previous three seasons playing for the Naval Training Center squad in San Diego.[18] This brought the roster to 45 players:

PLAYERS SIGNED AS OF MAY 13, 1946

Name	College	Weight	Hometown (Pro Experience)
Jack Dugger	Ohio State	230	Canton, OH
Al Vandeweghe	William & Mary	210	Teaneck, NJ

The Original Buffalo Bills

Name	College	Weight	Hometown (Pro Experience)
John Batorski	Colgate	218	Lackawanna, NY
Bill Daddio	Pittsburgh	208	Pittsburgh, PA (Chicago Cardinals)
Nick Klutka	U. of Florida	215	New Breighton, PA
Jack Kelleher	Columbia	190	Flushing, NY
Tackles			
Al Klug	Marquette	225	Milwaukee, WI
Quentin Klenk	USC	230	Long Beach, CA (LA Bulldogs)
Ben Pucci		280	St. Louis, MO (Hollywood Rangers)
Mike Kostiuk	Detroit Tech	220	Hamt'mek, MI (Detroit Lions)
John Brandt	Marquette	260	Antigo, WI
Joe Amorosi	Canisius	230	Lackawanna, NY
Tony Sabella	Canisius	220	Niagara Falls, NY
Ray Zaso	Canisius	200	Niagara Falls, NY
Jim Larkin	Lock Haven	215	Oil City, PA
Ray Makofske	Columbia	215	Roosevelt, NY
Guards			
John Badaczewski	Western Reserve	220	Seanor, PA
Gene White	Indiana	205	South Bend, IN
Joe Cippiciani	Scranton	220	Scranton, PA
Bill Kennedy	Michigan State	225	Detroit, MI (Detroit Lions)
Chuck Menzemer	Canisius	210	Buffalo, NY (Cleveland Rams)
Steve Benchwick	Alabama, Tulsa	220	Campbell, OH (New York Giants)
Dan Dalsando	Detroit Tech.	205	Detroit, MI
Albert Shaw	USC	220	El Monte, CA
Centers			
Chuck Cherundolo	Penn State	235	Old Forge, PA (Pittsburgh Steelers)
Ray Whelan	Buffalo, Rochester	220	Indianola, MI (Redskins, S.D. Bombers)
Rocco Pirro	Catholic University	220	Solvay, NY (Pittsburgh Steelers)
Sam Brazinsky	Villanova	215	Kulpmont, PA
Pat Martinelli	Scranton	220	Dunmore, PA (Eagles, Wilmington Clippers)
Quarterbacks			
Paul Governali	Columbia	195	New York, NY
Frank Gnup	Manhattan	185	Warren, MA
Halfbacks			
Harry Hopp	Nebraska	215	Hastings, NE (Detroit Lions)
Ronnie Cahill	Holy Cross	185	Leominster, MA (Chicago Cardinals)
Dan DaSantis	Niagara University	180	Niagara Falls, NY (Philadelphia Eagles)
Christy Stetzar	Scranton	200	Scranton, PA
Earl Dolaway	Indiana	198	Ft. Allegany, PA
Lou Tomasetti	Bucknell	198	Old Forge, PA (Philadelphia Eagles)
Steve Juzwik	Notre Dame	184	Chicago, IL (Washington Redskins)
Joe Pezelski	Villanova	182	Kulpmont, PA
Ken Germann	Columbia	195	Garden City Park, NY
Bill Dutton	Pittsburgh	180	Weston, WV
Fullbacks			
Walter Fedora	George Washington	195	Decatur, IL (Brooklyn Dodgers)
Vic Kulbitski	Minn. Notre Dame	204	South St. Paul, MN
Jim Oldenburg	Canisius	225	North Tonawanda, NY
Leo Gregory	St. Bonaventure	190	Jackson Heights, NY[19]

Sam Cordovano was a busy man. Throughout the course of the year, Cordovano reportedly traveled over 100,000 miles, scouting for the Bisons and doing AAFC administrative work.[20] As all of this transpired, his construction company was expanding and picking up work outside of the Buffalo area. Cordovano had a choice to make: Stay with the Bisons or leave and tend to his business. On May 28, 1946, it was announced that Sam Cordovano would step down as head coach and general manager of the Buffalo Bisons. He also relinquished his position as treasurer of the AAFC. In the announcement, Cordovano stated that with "recent and rapid development of new and important interests outside of Buffalo.... It has become necessary for me to dispose of all my interests and sever all my connections with the Buffalo club of the All-America Football Conference."[21] Co-owner Jim Breuil, at least publicly, was shocked at the move and quickly worked to find a replacement coach.

Cordovano did not want to be the head coach and tried to get someone to fill that position, but it never happened. It is uncertain how much effort was really put into the task, as Cordovano seemed to spend most of his time signing talent. The only reported candidate was Buff Donelli.[22] Cordovano tried to tap into his Columbia connections to get Donelli, but Lou Little thought that Donelli should remain coaching collegiate teams and Donelli's candidacy ended quickly. Aldo T. "Buff" Donelli was an outstanding halfback and punter while at Duquesne in the 1920s. He became head coach at Duquesne in 1939 and went 29-4-2 during the four years of his tenure. While at Duquesne in 1941, Donelli also took on the role of head coach for the Pittsburgh Steelers, making him the only coach to simultaneously lead both a college and NFL team. His stint with the Steelers ended quickly. After going 0-5-0, NFL Commissioner Elmer Layden forced Donelli to choose between the Pittsburgh and Duquesne jobs. Donelli chose the latter and Walt Kiesling took over the head job with the Steelers. Donelli returned to the pro ranks when he took over the head coaching position with the Cleveland Rams in 1944, going 4-6-0 in his only season at the helm. After that season, Donelli went into the Navy. Obviously, Donelli had the experience to lead the Bisons, but Cordovano was stymied by his former boss. Donelli went on to coach Boston University to a 46-34-4 record over ten years, followed by eleven years leading the Columbia program. Of note during his Columbia stint, Donelli went 6-1 in the Ivy League, tying Harvard for the league championship in 1961. He retired from coaching in 1967.[23]

The Bisons were now without a general manager *and* a head coach. The AAFC was also without their treasurer with Cordovano's departure. Eleanor Gehrig took over the duel role of secretary and treasurer until the league was able to find a replacement. This came at an August organizational meeting when William D. Cox of the Brooklyn Dodgers took on the task. Gehrig moved up to become vice-president and Louis B. Carroll of the Los Angeles Dons and AAFC attorney was elected secretary. Edwin S. Kosky, assistant to the commissioner, was elected assistant secretary of the Conference. Former sportswriter Francis W. Dunn took over the general manager duties for the Bisons and, after a thirty-five minute interview, "Red" Dawson was signed to a three-year contract to coach the team. Dunn was a reporter-columnist for the *Buffalo Times* and the former Assistant Director of Public Relations for Bell Aircraft Corporation.

Lowell "Red" Dawson started playing football in 1925, his senior year in high school. He then went to the University of Wisconsin-River Falls and helped the team to three straight conference and state championships. The 165-pound Dawson continued his playing career by playing halfback for Tulane, including time in the 1932 Rose Bowl against USC. While at Tulane, Dawson was named All-Southern Conference twice and an Honorable Mention All-American once. After graduating and working as a coach in Robbinsdale, Minnesota, Dawson's former coach Bernie Bierman hired Red to be his assistant at the University of Minnesota. Dawson was the backfield coach for four years and in 1936, Tulane hired him as head coach, where he coached the first game to be played in Civic Stadium (Tulane vs. Colgate). After six years, his teams went a total of 36-18-4. In 1939, his Tulane team went undefeated and won a berth in the Sugar Bowl against Texas A&M, where Texas won 14-13. In 1942, Red went back to Minnesota to be an assistant to Dr. George Hauser.[24] According to Bills back Alex Wizbicki, "Dawson was a very methodical coach. He was well organized. When he came in with information for a particular game, we had a great deal of information. We were well prepared for the games under him."[25] The team felt as though they were in good hands with Dawson.

Red Dawson, head coach from 1946 through mid-1949.

While the Bisons were going through a coaching and general manager change, the Boston Yanks of the NFL announced the signing of Notre Dame quarterback Angelo Bertelli, who had previously agreed to a contract with the Los Angeles Dons. Bertelli was a Heisman Trophy winner and was a major signing for the Dons. After signing with the Yanks, Bertelli reportedly returned the bonus money he was paid by the Dons. Los Angeles, obviously, was furious and filed a lawsuit against Bertelli and the Yanks. This lawsuit was not just about a player, but about the competition between the NFL and AAFC. Failure to win this lawsuit could prove to be disastrous to the upstart league and it was imperative for Los Angeles to win. After the Dons filed suit, they obtained a restraining order, preventing Bertelli from playing for any team other than the Dons. Bertelli counter-sued for fraud and misrepresentation. It was shortly after the start of the season, but the legal battle was won by the Dons and Bertelli reported to Los Angeles to play for the team.[26] Superior Court Judge Felix Forte upheld the equity of AAFC player contracts when he ruled that Angelo Bertelli was prohibited from playing for any professional team other than the Los Angeles Dons.

A week after Boston signed Bertelli, they also outbid Buffalo for the services of quarterback Paul Governali. Buffalo was willing to take the battle to the courtroom, but later decided to relinquish Governali to the Yanks.[27] Governali was Boston's insurance policy, in case the courts gave Bertelli back to the Dons. With the courts ruling in favor of Los Angeles, this was a wise decision. The Governali signing was also another blow in the already bitter interleague war.

The first major signing for Red Dawson was Al Dekdebrun. Sam Cordovano tried to get the local native under contract when he was first declared ineligible for college ball earlier in the year, but the deal could not be done. Dekdebrun was declared ineligible because he played four minutes in a preseason game for Columbia against Fort Monmouth a few years prior.[28] As a result, he lost a year of eligibility after only playing two-and-a-half years for Cornell. Dekdebrun considered heading to Canada to play rugby after seeing Warren Stevens of Syracuse play a year of rugby before becoming head coach and athletic director at Toronto University.[29] Negotiations continued and Dawson was able to get Dekdebrun to sign a contract at the Ithaca Airport, as final exams prevented Dekdebrun from traveling to Buffalo.[30]

Next up was Elmer "Buck" Jones, who became the fifty-third player on the Bison roster. A local kid, Jones played guard for Riverside High School under Bob Rich. In 1939, he won All-Western New York honors to finish out his senior year. The 225-pound guard played with Wake Forest from 1940–1942; making All-Southern Conference in his final year. He joined the Marine Corps and went to Franklin-Marshall College in 1943 and by 1944, Jones was enrolled in the Georgia Pre-Flight School and made the Marine All-Star team in 1945.[31]

Originally, the Bisons were to hold their training camp at St. Bonaventure College. Due to scheduling difficulties, however, the training camp location was changed to Spring Bank Manor in Oconomowoc, Wisconsin. Located thirty miles west of Milwaukee and ninety miles from Chicago, the serene location was perfect for the team as seventy players could fit at the main lodge and the coaching staff would stay at an adjoining cottage. Red Dawson also decided to move up the start date of camp from July 29 to July 22. According to Dawson, "This will give us six weeks of work before our exhibition game against Miami in Baltimore, August 30, and seven weeks before opening the season against Brooklyn in Buffalo."[32] He continued his discussion of training camp, "We are planning on having between sixty and seventy players report to camp, although the number may exceed the latter figure. Every player already under contract has been notified to report ready for work July 22. We will have two practice sessions daily, morning and afternoon, throughout. As material looks now, we will use the 'T' Formation although there is a possibility that we may go to the single wing. We plan to adapt the offense to the backfield material and a final decision may not be made until the candidates have demonstrated their ability to run from the 'T.'"[33] The team moved to Lackawanna Stadium shortly before the beginning of the season. According to Bisons' tackle Ben Pucci, "No cuts were made until the last week."[34]

3

The Bisons Take the Field

The roster started to take shape and competition was fierce. At the end position, two All-Americans—Bill Daddio from Pittsburgh and Jack Dugger from Ohio State—fought with Al Vandeweghe from William & Mary and Colgate's "Bat" Batorski for first string. Referred to as the human tank, 330-pound Forrest "Chubby" Grigg battled with former Tulsa teammate C.B. Stanley and USC's Quentin Klenk for the tackle position. John Matisi from Duquesne was also in the mix. Moving on to left guard, Elmer "Buck" Jones (All-Southern Conference out of Wake Forest) fought with Rocco Pirro for the starting nod. Pirro, from Catholic University, had prior pro experience with the Pittsburgh Steelers, but was recovering from a twisted knee. Right guard saw Marquette's Al Klug and Oklahoma's Hal Lahar—both of whom played under Bison's line coach Tom Stidham at one time—duke it out. Pat Martinelli out of Scranton was the leading candidate out of seven for the center position. The backfield battle was between Harry "Hippity" Hopp (quarterback from Nebraska with prior pro experience with the Detroit Lions), Steve Juzwik (Notre Dame), Lou Tomasetti (Bucknell), Vic Kulbitski (Minnesota), Lou Zontini (Notre Dame), George Terlep (Notre Dame), Joe Pezelski (Villanova), Curt Sandig (St. Mary's), Allie Vogt (Marquette), Ken Davis (Cornell), Ken Stofer (Cornell) and Al Dekdebrun (Cornell).[1]

To further shake things up in the backfield battle, just before the 1946 season, Cleveland traded halfback Chet Mutryn to Buffalo. Assistant coach Clem Crowe had coached Mutryn at Xavier and was familiar with Mutryn's abilities. He wasn't the fastest back, but he had an innate ability to use his blockers to his advantage. According to Art Statuto, who was Mutryn's teammate in 1948 and 1949, Mutryn "would gain yardage when you didn't think there was any yardage available for him"[2] Bills' teammate Chick Maggioli recalled that "he seemed to move as if he wasn't moving. He could follow his blockers and he could peel off of a block so easy. For some reason, he would just slide in there and get yardage."[3] *Buffalo Evening News* columnist Cy Kritzer called Mutryn "the modern Red Grange,"[4] referring to the legendary Illinois back. According to George Buksar, teammate with Chet Mutryn while with the 1950 Baltimore Colts, "I have a letter from Paul Brown telling me that the biggest mistake he ever made was to trade Chet to Buffalo."[5] Buksar continued, "Chet was a tailback while he was with Xavier. When he got to the Browns, he was considered a quarterback. It was a flip of the coin as to whether they would keep [Cliff] Lewis or Chet. And the mistake he made was that he gave Chet to Buffalo."[6]

While it was only a preseason game, for the first time in five years, Buffalo fielded a professional football team. On a crystal clear August night in Baltimore, the Buffalo Bisons took on the Miami Seahawks. The highest priority for both squads was talent evaluation, as both teams fielded their entire roster for the game. The clubs needed to cut their rosters to the league-mandated 33 players before the beginning of the season a mere nine days later and it was not easy for either squad.[7]

Both teams stuck to their ground attack, which paid dividends for Miami first. Fifteen seconds into the second quarter, former Alabama star Jimmy Nelson crossed the line on a six-yard run. Buffalo quickly answered with a 50-yard run from Notre Dame back Steve Juzwik. Buffalo racked up two more scoring drives in the second period: the first from Cornell's Ken Stofer, who ripped off a 32-yard scamper, and former Pittsburgh Panther and Chicago Cardinal player Bill Daddio capped the quarter's scoring with a 23-yard field goal.[8]

Buffalo's Bob Thurbon increased the Buffalo lead to 23–7 on a 55-yard run, but it was all Miami for the rest of the game. Preston Johnson out of S.M.U. had given his team a much needed spark with his 20-yard scoring run. Miami was down 23–14 when Jim Tarrant connected on a 35-yard pass to Jimmy Nelson, who made a heroic catch to bring the Seahawks to within striking distance. It was too little, too late as the final buzzer sounded with Buffalo taking the 23–21 victory and momentum going into the season.[9]

With AAFC Commissioner Jim Crowley and Conference founder Arch Ward in attendance, the Buffalo Bisons started the 1946 season at home against the Brooklyn Dodgers. Even though Glenn Dobbs—arguably one of the greatest passers in collegiate history—was sidelined with a chipped bone in his throwing hand, the Dodgers fought a tough battle.[10] Dobbs was a tailback and punter while at Frederick High School in Oklahoma. He then went on to the University of Tulsa, where he led the team to a 10–1 record and a Sun Bowl victory. This earned Dobbs the distinction of being the first back from the Missouri Valley Conference to be named to the Associated Press' All-America team.[11]

Buffalo looked like they would score first after Steve Juzwik tore off a 68-yard run to bring the Bisons to within inches of the Brooklyn goal, but the Dodger defense stiffened and Buffalo settled for a field goal attempt. Lou Zontini lined up for the kick, but it came up short. Mickey Mayne recovered the errant kick in the end zone and ran it back a record-setting 104 yards for the score and a 7–0 lead. Shortly into the third quarter, Caleb "Tex" Warrington recovered a Harry Hopp fumble to put the Dodgers into scoring position. Mayne was again involved in the scoring, as he tossed a pass to end Saxon Judd for a 14–0 Dodger lead.[12]

Buffalo fought back with two scoring drives to even the contest. Driving 70-yards, Juzwik scored on a Statue of Liberty play from the five-yard line. On the next series, Ken Stofer recovered a Mayne fumble, setting up Curt Sandig for the nine-yard touchdown run.[13]

The score was now 14–14 and the Dodgers, namely Glenn Dobbs, knew that extraordinary measures were needed. Removing the bandages protecting his throwing hand, Dobbs entered the game and went to work. He tossed a 50-yard pass to Joe Davis to set up a 31-yard scoring pass to Judd. Minutes later Dolly King fumbled a Hopp pass, giving the ball back to the opponents. Fullback Dom Principe raced 15-yards to start the offensive drive and Dobbs added another 20 yards before lateraling to 6'7½" center Russell Morrow for the final score and a 27–14 victory for the visitors.[14]

In an exclusive interview, Buffalo tackle Ben Pucci recalled that most of the game was played with the second string quarterback Mickey Mayne. Pucci knocked Mayne out of the game to the accolades of his teammates, but on the sidelines they cut off the cast on Dobbs' right hand and he led the team to two touchdown drives, giving Brooklyn the win.[15] Pucci regretted knocking Mayne out of the game.

Even with the loss, Buffalo was optimistic about their future. Facing a 14–0 deficit going into the fourth quarter, the team never gave up. That was a good sign for Dawson's squad as the schedule continued to get more difficult.

Next up for Buffalo was the New York Yankees, although the Bisons were not given much of a chance to win. New York Coach Ray Flaherty had an impressive lineup made up of University of Texas halfback Spec Sanders, the Kinard brothers (Frank and George), as well as Duke back Ace Parker.

New York scored first by capitalizing on a Buffalo fumble by Harry Hopp. Frank "Bruiser" Kinard recovered Hopp's fumble on the Buffalo twelve-yard line, with Parker and Pug Manders sharing the duty; the latter taking it over the line for the 7–0 lead. Buffalo answered with a fumble recovery of their own when end Al Vandeweghe picked up a Dewey Proctor miscue on the Buffalo five-yard line and streaked down the left side of the field to tie the game. Buffalo added a field goal after an interception by Pat Martinelli to take a 10–7 lead going into the half.[16]

After the Buffalo score, it was all New York Yankees. The rushing attack of the Yankees was too much for the Bisons as New York racked up 198 yards on an AAFC record 57 carries. Sanders took the ball over the line twice to give the Yankees a 21–10 victory, dropping Buffalo to 0–2 for the season.[17]

The week before the Cleveland Browns game, the Bills signed end Herb Nelson and back John "Blondy" Black. The 6'4" and 218-pound Nelson requested to be released from the New York Giants in order to sign with the Bisons.[18] Black, who was drafted by the Brooklyn Dodgers while still at Mississippi State, decided to sign with the Bisons to start his professional career, but he did not see game action for a few weeks. Along with the signings, the Bills made a few roster moves. Harry Hopp had been ineffective in his first two outings as the Bisons' quarterback, so Red Dawson shifted Hopp from quarterback to fullback and George Terlep took over the passing duties. Steve Juzwik was temporarily out of the lineup due to a pulled leg muscle.[19]

Leading the Browns' offensive attack was quarterback Otto Graham. New York Yankees defensive back Otto Schnellbacher remembered Graham's intelligence and attention to detail, "One of the games that we played in Cleveland and we beat them, we were able to pick up a couple of habits that Graham had; one foot back when he was going that way and another foot back when he was going the other way. We picked it up in the game somewhere and we called timeout and we discussed it and said we thought that was what was going on. The new tackles hold up your hand if its right and he would play his right foot back and sure enough they would run to the right. All we did was watch his feet and, of course, we beat them to the punch all the time and held them and kind of kicked their stuff. Next time we played against them he moved his right foot back but went left.... I think that he looked at himself in the film week after week to see if he developed any habits that he needed to change."[20]

The Cleveland Browns quickly made a statement in the first meeting of the season between the two teams. Buffalo started with the ball, but an ineffective first drive gave it to Cleveland on their 48-yard line. After two minutes and twenty seconds of game time, former Notre Dame end John Yonakor grabbed an Otto Graham pass and sprinted 20 yards for a touchdown. Buffalo tried to battle back, but Tommy Colella intercepted a George Terlep pass to start another Cleveland drive. The Browns started with a Graham to Dante Lavelli pass for five yards and Marion Motley picked up another twelve yards with a push through the center of the line.[21]

Motley was one was the fastest backs in football. He was a big, bruising running back who could block as well as he could run. Motley earned respect for his play on both sides of the ball. According to teammate and Hall of Fame end Dante Lavelli, "Motley really built the passing attack for the Browns because of his blocking." Coach Paul Brown added, "I've always believed that Motley could have gone into the Hall of Fame solely as a linebacker if we had used him only at that position."[22] Otto Schnellbacher summed up his first meeting with Motley on the field: "Motley was the greatest I've ever seen. He ran over me my rookie year. We were playing a 5–3–3 and I was the safety. The hole opened and the linebackers were gone and here comes Motley. He cuts towards the sideline and I was going to push him out of bounds, but he didn't go out of bounds. He turned suddenly, put an elbow in my nose, broke my nose, knocked me out, stepped on me and goes on and scored. I woke up and the coach said, 'You know you'll get killed tackling like that!' I said, 'Tell me about it.'"[23]

Mac Speedie got his first reception on a 19-yard toss from Graham. Motley got the call on the next play, bolting for the corner of the end zone. Harry Hopp and Ken Stofer were waiting to stop the big back, but guard Ed Ulinski bowled over both to clear a path for Motley to tally the second score. The Browns scored again in the first quarter when back Gaylon Smith caught a lateral from Cliff Lewis and swept around right end for a twelve-yard run and another touchdown. Things settled down for the next few quarters as neither team scored. Buffalo regained their composure and held the ball for the majority of the time. The Browns had a couple of scoring opportunities in the fourth quarter, but it took a Buffalo miscue to get the Browns on the board again. Halfback Al Dekdebrun attempted a lateral, but fumbled. Cleveland tackle Chet Adams picked up the ball and darted 25-yards for the final score and a 28–0 victory over the home team.[24]

Bills tackle Quentin Klenk. This photograph was taken while Klenk was with the Fleet City Bluejackets.

While it is unfair to use the Cleveland Browns as a benchmark for Buffalo's progress (or lack thereof), the Bisons seemed to be regressing. Cleveland quarterback Otto Graham completed 50 percent of his passes for an average gain of over 30 yards per completion. The defense was weak and the offense was weaker. The Bisons embarked on a stretch where they played three contests in eight days. There was not a lot of time to fix the problems before that brutal stretch of games. They had hoped that the hapless Chicago Rockets—their first opponent in the series—was the answer to their woes.

The Bisons had yet to win a game at this point and changes needed to be made. In the week before the Bisons took on the Rockets, both center Pat Martinelli and tackle Quentin Klenk were waived. Harry Hopp suffered from a swollen right ankle and was replaced by Vic Kulbitski. The Rockets were also winless at this point of the season, but had more confidence. "At last the Rockets are ready to roll," stated Rockets coach Dick Hanley. "I'm sorry it has to be the Bisons, but my boys have finally hit their peak offensively."[25]

One of Chicago's leaders was back Bob Hoernschemeyer. According to former NFL executive Ron Wolf, Hoernschemeyer "was a jack of all trades player in the AAFC. He was a single wing tailback and he could throw and he could run. He was a better runner than a passer and I would classify him more as a power back than a nifty, shifty sort although, at times, he could make you miss."[26]

Desperate for a win, both teams fought to the bitter end in what some considered the wildest professional game ever played in Chicago. Buffalo scored first when Vic Kulbitski took the ball and streaked 47 yards for the opening touchdown. The Rockets quickly retaliated when Elroy "Crazylegs" Hirsh caught a Bob Hoernschemeyer pass on the Buffalo 45-yard line and broke free to tie the game on a 67-yard play. Chicago took the lead after a Lou Tomasetti fumble on Chicago's 43-yard line. On the first offensive play after the turnover, Hoernschemeyer tossed to back Billy Hillenbrand, who juked his way for a 51-yard scoring play. The Rockets were up 14–7 in the second quarter. Buffalo, namely Tomasetti, got revenge when Buffalo tackle John Matisi recovered a Steve Nemeth fumble. Quarterback George Terlep tossed a 29-yard scoring pass to Tomasetti, who was waiting in the end zone and the score was tied 14–14 going into the half.[27]

Chicago regained the lead early in the third quarter on a Hillenbrand 34-yard run. Buffalo answered with a 52-yard strike from Al Dekdebrun to Dolly King, which resulted in a 21–21 tie. Two Steve Juzwik touchdown receptions from Terlep put the Bisons ahead 35–21 in the fourth quarter, but Chicago started to mount a comeback with two consecutive scores. The first was a Hillenbrand 68-yard punt return, followed by an eight-yard pass from Hoernschemeyer to end Ralph Heywood out of USC.[28]

The game was tied 35–35 late in the fourth quarter. The teams had witnessed three total lead changes at that point and both could taste victory. Chicago had the ball for their final drive. Slowly pushing down the field, the Rockets got to within scoring position and the clock was winding down. With four seconds left, Steve Nemeth lined up for the potential game-winning field goal attempt. The ball was snapped, set and kicked. The 29,618 attendees at Soldier Field held their collective breaths until the ball sailed through the uprights for the Chicago victory. There was elation in the stands and on the Rocket bench, and yet another bitter defeat for the now 0–4 Bisons.

Going into the fourth quarter, Buffalo had a two-score lead. The problem with this was that the Bisons had a history of collapsing late in the game. In both the Brooklyn game and the New York game, Buffalo was able to stay even with their opponents. Here, they had a lead, but still could not retain it down the stretch. They had put together an impressive offensive showing, but it was their defense that let them down. Things were not rosy in Chicago, either. Even with the victory, the day after the Buffalo game Chicago coach Dick Hanley was replaced by a player-coach group consisting of Bob Dove, Wilbur Wilkin and Ned Mathews.

Despite being 0–4 for the season and having their heart ripped out on more than one occasion, the Bisons did not give up. In their game with the Los Angeles Dons, they continued to fight just as hard, if not harder, to get that elusive first win. Led by Jarrin' John Kimbrough, an All-American for two years while with Texas A&M, the Dons entered Buffalo with an undefeated record. Regardless, the Bisons were ready for a fight.

Buffalo scored first on a 25-yard run from Chet Mutryn, capitalizing on an Al Dekdebrun interception. Los Angeles answered with two consecutive scores. The first was a five-yard run by Buffalo's own Johnny Polanski. The second came when Bill Kerr, an end out of Notre Dame, blocked a Buffalo punt in the end zone. Los Angeles had a 14–7 lead as the fourth quarter started, but Buffalo continued to fight. George Terlep — hampered by an injured right ankle — led the team down the field, capping the drive with an eight-yard touchdown pass to Al Vandeweghe to tie the game. The Bisons stymied a Los Angeles offensive drive and pushed their way down field on another impressive offensive attack. The Bisons were now on the Los Angeles four-yard line. C.B. Stanley, the Bisons' workhorse tackle that day, continued to blast holes through the Dons defense. Battling an injured arm, Stanley gave it everything he had to open yet one more hole for Lou Tomasetti, who rewarded Stanley when he scored a touchdown to give Buffalo a 21–14 lead.[29]

With less than seven minutes remaining in the game, Los Angeles needed one more offensive drive. Rotating between Heisman Trophy winner Angelo Bertelli and Boston College's Charlie O'Rourke, the Dons moved downfield. O'Rourke proceeded to toss a 28-yard pass to Joe Aguirre for the tying score. The Bisons felt the game slipping away, just as it had the previous weeks. Time ran out with the score 21–21. The Dons moved to a 2–0–1 record, while Buffalo had a disappointing 0–4–1 record.[30] Buffalo had scored 59 points in two games, only to end up with a 0–1–1 record over that span.

The Bisons were close, but still needed more work. Blondy Black, All-American from Mississippi State, was now ready to enter the lineup. Tulane fullback Jim Thibaut, as well as Notre Dame and former Chicago Cardinals end Ray Ebli, were brought in to boost the team.[31] The additions of these two ends were to replace the loss of Al Vandeweghe. Vandeweghe, an end out of the College of William & Mary, decided to retire from professional football. Vandeweghe recalled, "They changed head coaches before the season started and I was not happy with the conditions that existed at that time."[32] Vandeweghe received an offer to coach ends at his alma mater and accepted the position.

The Bisons' next opponent was the New York Yankees. The Yankees capitalized on a second quarter Steve Juzwik fumble of a Spec Sanders punt. New York guard Charley Riffle recovered the fumble and the Yankees proceeded to drive downfield with back Bob Kennedy taking it over the line for the score. Buffalo rebounded on a Yankee miscue as Bisons' tackle Ben Pucci stripped halfback Bob Perina of the ball. Three plays later, George Terlep scored for the Bisons. Two quick scores by the Yankees put Buffalo into a 21–6 deficit. Buffalo scored late in the fourth quarter, but ran out of time and lost 21–13.[33]

The return game shined against New York. Setting Conference records for best average kick return (37.4 yards), most yards in punt returns (187) and best average punt return (23.4 yards), the Bisons showed improvement. The biggest problem was on the offensive side of the ball. Even with the better field position that resulted from excellent punt and kick returns, the Bisons still were not able to capitalize. The winless Miami Seahawks were next.

During the preseason, Buffalo was able to beat the Seahawks 23–21, but now it counted. New to the Bison roster since that contest were former Seahawk players Preston Johnston and end Marty Comer, as well as Northwestern guard Jim Lecture. The Seahawks added halfback Stan Stasica and former New York Giant end Dick Horne. Both teams had yet to win that season and it showed in the disappointing 5,040 attendance figure.[34]

Buffalo stayed true to form, as fumbles were costly. Within the first ten minutes of the first quarter, the Seahawks built a 14–7 lead. Buffalo tied it up in the third quarter, when Ken Stofer tossed a nine-yard pass to end Dolly King. Heading into the final minutes of the fourth quarter, Miami took advantage of an errant punt and started their drive from the Buffalo 39-yard line. Lamar Davis grabbed an 18-yard pass from Chuck Price and Jimmy Reynolds added twelve more yards on the ground. This set up a Dick Erdlitz field goal, which was good for the 17–14 victory and Miami's first win of the season.[35]

At this point in the season, Buffalo set a conference record in consecutive games without a victory with seven and were sitting in the conference cellar with a 0–6–1 record. Red Dawson continued to make changes to his roster, focusing on the backfield. Lou Tomasetti and Preston Johnston were new the starting halfbacks, while Jim Thibaut was the fullback and George Terlep — still hampered by an ankle injury — was the quarterback.[36]

Attendance continued to drop with Buffalo's inability to win games. For the October 19 matchup with the San Francisco 49ers, a meager crowd of 6,101 was at Civic Stadium.[37] San Francisco — led by back Frankie Albert — was a tough competitor. Known for his ability to run all facets of the game — running, throwing and kicking — Albert was a leader and at 5'9" and 170 pounds, the southpaw from Stanford was a mainstay in the 49er offense for several years. According to Bills end Ray Ebli, "He's pretty clever at getting you committing. Having you come in and pinch on plays. He'll go around you so fast he will make you sick."[38]

Still suffering from an ankle injury, George Terlep stayed on the sidelines as Al Dekdebrun took his place. Buffalo scored first when in the closing minutes of the first quarter, Lou Zontini booted a 47-yard field goal. San Francisco took the lead early in the second quarter when halfback Len Eshmont intercepted a Dekdebrun pass and returned it to the Buffalo 27-yard line. Runs by Eshmont, Norm Standlee and Albert brought the ball to the Bison two-yard line, where Eshmont finished the scoring drive to give San Francisco a 7–3 lead. The teams exchanged scores in the remaining 13 minutes of play in the half, leaving Buffalo down 14–10. Continued missed opportunities by Buffalo plagued the team throughout the second half, until late in the fourth

3—The Bisons Take the Field 35

quarter. Albert punted to Buffalo and in a rare move for the Bisons in that game, Buffalo returned it. A couple of passes by Dekdebrun to Dolly King took the ball to the 49er four-yard line, where Lou Tomasetti carried the ball an additional two yards and Dekdebrun connected with King for the score and a 17–14 lead. Time elapsed and Buffalo was able to get their first victory of the season.[39]

Buffalo struggled in their kick return game. Five times San Francisco was able to punt without a return, a Conference record that stood all four years of its existence. Several times, the record was tied, but none were accomplished on so few punts (six). Typically, it took many more punts to accomplish the same feat.

Tulsa tackle Forrest "Chubby" Grigg returned to the Buffalo lineup for the game against the Rockets. Inactive since September 23 for being overweight, Grigg had worked to take off the pounds. Tipping the scales at a svelte 330 pounds, Grigg had hoped to be down to a slimmer 300 pounds by game time.[40] That did not happen and he played closer to 330 pounds. Coach Red Dawson used to joke at practice, "All right men, run that last play again and then everyone take two laps around Grigg."[41]

It is amazing what a win can do for attendance as 15,758 onlookers witnessed the Bison's last home game of the season and their battle with the Rockets. The first quarter saw no scoring, but the Buffalo offense exploded in the second, tallying twenty-eight points. Chicago started the scoring with an 18-yard field goal by Steve Nemeth, but that lead lasted only two minutes as Buffalo ripped off five straight touchdowns without allowing Chicago to see the end zone. In the end, Buffalo's best performance of the season gave them a 49–17 victory over the Rockets and a 2–6–1 record.[42] Not only did the offense step it up, but the defense played well. Several scores and scoring drives were a direct result of interceptions and fumble recoveries. It was a record-setting day for Buffalo. Not only were their 49 points (a Conference record at the time), but Buffalo also racked up other impressive Conference records: Most Punt Return Yards (119 yards on five returns), Best Average Punt Return Yardage (23.8 yards), Lowest Average Yardage per Punt by Opponents (25.3 yards), Most Kick Return Yards (458 yards on seventeen returns) and Best Average Kick Return Yardage (26.9 yards).

The Bisons were done with their home schedule and proceeded to play five games on the road. The first was a cross-country trip to play the San Francisco 49ers, who were coming off their upset win over the Cleveland Browns. The Bisons arrived two days before the game and stayed at the Old Hearst Ranch near Pleasanton, California.[43] Buffalo was feeling confident. Even with San Francisco's win over the mighty Browns, Buffalo had beaten the 49ers two weeks prior and had an impressive victory over Chicago.

The game started as a defensive battle and Buffalo had the edge. Stanford All-American Frankie Albert was held in check for most of the first half and the only scoring San Francisco could muster was a Len Eshmont fumble return for a touchdown. This tied the game at 7–7. Earlier, back Steve Juzwik had caught a 23-yard pass from Al Dekdebrun for Buffalo's first tally. Heading into the fourth quarter, the game was still tied, but it was at this point where Buffalo's defense started to collapse. San Francisco ripped off three touchdowns to take a commanding 27–7 lead with four-and-a-half minutes remaining in the game. Buffalo scored a late touchdown, but it did not matter. Buffalo's small winning streak was over and they fell to a 2–7–1 record, which guaranteed a losing season.[44]

The defensive collapse continued to be a problem. Buffalo could hold their opponents for three quarters, but lost momentum in the fourth quarter and the offense was absent for the majority of the season. With only four first downs and eight fumbles against San Francisco, it was no wonder they were only able to score seven points.

The Dodgers were a different team from what the Bisons faced earlier in the season. Back Glenn Dobbs was healthy and started the game. Dr. Marvin Stevens resigned as head coach and was replaced by former NFL star Cliff Battles. The Brooklyn had won two straight games and slowly crept up in the standings and this was a critical matchup for Buffalo in order to keep up with the Dodgers in the divisional standings.

Dobbs had a good day passing, completing twelve of 25 passes for 258 yards, but he wanted his first pass back. A few minutes into the first quarter, Dobbs dropped back and tossed a bomb to the Buffalo ten-yard line. Instead of the pass going to his receiver, it was intercepted by Felto Prewitt and returned to the Brooklyn 48-yard line. This set up Buffalo's first touchdown, when Preston Johnston capped the drive with a five-yard scoring run. Throughout the rest of the game, Buffalo never gave up the lead. Lou Zontini kicked a field goal in the first quarter and Al Dekdebrun connected with Ray Ebli in the third quarter to seal the 17–14 victory.

Shortly after the Bisons lost to the hapless Seahawks earlier in the season, Miami changed coaches. Jack Meagher was out and Hamp Pool was in, but the change did not help as the Seahawks continued their losing ways. With their only win of the season coming against Buffalo, the Bisons wanted revenge. The Bisons were also fighting for second place in the division as Buffalo was only one game behind the four-win Brooklyn Dodgers, who had lost the previous day.

Turnovers again plagued the Bisons. While deep in Miami territory, Buffalo turned the ball over twice. Miami was not able to capitalize on the first turnover, but drove down the field for a score on the second. Buffalo tied the score with three minutes remaining in the first half. Felto Prewit intercepted a Marion Pugh pass to start the drive. Al Dekdebrun tossed a pass to end Dolly King, who in turn lateraled it to back Andy Dudish, who then picked up eight yards. Vic Kulbitski added 24 more yards and Dudish plodded ahead for three yards. Dekdebrun faked a pass for six yards and then tossed a ten-yard pass to King for the score. Miami scored twice in short succession to put the Sea-

3—*The Bisons Take the Field* 37

Game program from November 24, 1946: Buffalo Bisons vs. Cleveland Browns. The Bisons lost the game 42–17.

hawks ahead for good to capture the 21–14 victory.[45] Miami now had two wins for the season; both against Buffalo. The Bisons slipped to a 3–8–1 record and third place within the division. This minimized the importance of the upcoming game with Cleveland, at least from Buffalo's perspective. Cleveland still had something to play for in the matchup.

Cleveland was heading into the Buffalo rematch with the Western Division Championship on the line. All they had to do was beat the Bisons. It was not easy, however, as both teams fought hard. with several 15-yard roughing penalties assessed throughout the game. In the second quarter, Lou Zontini and Cleveland back Ray Terrell got into an altercation at midfield, resulting in both players being ejected from the game.[46]

Buffalo received the kickoff to start the game, however ineffective execution forced Buffalo to punt and Cleveland was ready to go. Starting on their own 36-yard line, Terrell swept around end for a five-yard gain. Edgar "Special Delivery" Jones got the call, but lost a yard in the process. Dante Lavelli took the ball 14 yards to put the Browns on the Buffalo 46-yard line. Otto Graham lateraled to Jones, who tossed an incomplete pass to Mac Speedie. Even though the pass was incomplete, Graham thought that the play would work and called it again. This time, Jones kept the ball and ran it in for the first score of the game. The Bisons countered when George Terlep recovered a Tommy Colella fumble to start another Bison drive. After only three plays, Vic Kulbitski broke through the line for the one-yard scoring run. Buffalo took the first lead of the game when Zontini kicked a 40-yard field goal late in the first quarter. Starting from their own 39-yard line, the Browns drove down the field on short passes until they reached the Buffalo 34-yard line. Graham tossed a beautiful pass to Jones, who was downed near the Bison goal. After Jones added a yard on a line plunge, Graham tossed a pass to Speedie to take a 14–10 lead going into the half.[47]

In the third quarter, Buffalo stood tall and continued to advance on the Cleveland defense. Racking up four first downs, the Bisons drove to the Browns' 31-yard line. Here Cleveland's defense stepped up and Colella intercepted a Terlep pass on the Browns' 24-yard line. Motley got the call and outran the Buffalo defense on a 76-yard scoring run. The lead was now 21–10 and Buffalo's defense started to fall apart. On the very next Cleveland drive, Graham tossed a pass to Lavelli, who in turn lateraled it to Jones. Jones sprinted down the field and, with the aid of a Lavelli block, scored to increase Cleveland's lead to 28–10. It was all Al Akins on the next drive. He intercepted a Terlep pass on the Browns' 40-yard line and returned it ten yards and on the next play, Akins bolted 50 yards for yet another Cleveland score. The Browns scored again when Colella returned a punt 58 yards to put the ball on Buffalo's eight-yard line. Wilson "Bud" Schwenk lofted a pass to John Harrington, but a penalty on the play put the ball on the Bison one-yard line. From there, Schwenk put the ball over for the final Cleveland score. Buffalo tried to mount a comeback, but it was too late. Buffalo was able to drive 80 yards downfield for a touchdown, but the damage had been done. Cleveland won 42–17 to clinch the Western Division title and with this victory, the Browns were able to take it easy against the Seahawks and Dodgers in the final two regular season games.[48] The Bisons, however, needed help. Once again, their defense collapsed late in the game. With a 9.45 yard-per-rush average for the game and a record five rushing touchdowns, Cleveland was able to expose the porous run defense.

3—The Bisons Take the Field 39

Not much could be said about the final game of the season, other than it was an embarrassment. The Bisons seemed lost as the Dons had their way with the lowly Buffalo squad. A 62–14 beating resulted in Los Angeles setting the single game record for the highest score. It also cemented Buffalo as the most scored-upon team in the Conference. To give perspective to the "game," Los Angeles had a stretch where they racked up 294 straight yards before Buffalo could gain an inch. The Dons had 625 total yards of offense (337 passing and 298 rushing), nine touchdowns and a pass completion percentage of 90 percent.[49]

This left Buffalo with a 3–10–1 record, which surprisingly tied them with the Brooklyn Dodgers for second in the division. They each shared in a pool of money set aside to reward teams based on their final season standings. Buffalo's share was $3,784.48.[50] Obviously, the Eastern Division was not very strong, outside of the 10–3–1 New York Yankees.

As far as Buffalo's impact in the first year of the league, the results were mixed. From a team perspective, the Bisons were the best in the conference in Yards per Rush at 4.08 yards per carry. They also led the Conference in Most Touchdowns on Fumble Returns (4) and Most Yards on Fumble Returns (229 yards), but also led the Conference in Most Touchdowns Scored Against (49) and Most Points After Touchdown Scored Against (49). The Bisons had a total of 117,954 fans in attendance at their home games, which placed them sixth in the Conference. The only teams with lower attendance figures were the Brooklyn Dodgers and Miami Seahawks.

Individual accomplishments were just as mixed. End Al Vandeweghe had the longest fumble return for a touchdown at 97 yards, which placed him second over the previous 24 years behind Chicago Bears legend George Halas, who had a 98-yard return against the Canton Bulldogs in 1922. Halfback Chet Mutryn ranked first in the Conference in fumble recoveries with two and end Dolly King was third in receptions with 30. Halfback Steve Juzwik was in the top five for two categories when he placed first in kickoff returns with 21 and fifth in interceptions with five. Rounding out the top ten finishers was fullback Lou Zontini, who placed eighth in the Conference in punts with eight and fullback Vic Kulbitski, who placed tenth in total yards gained (605 yards on 97 plays). Just outside of the top ten were quarterback George Terlep, ranking eleventh in total yards with 603 on 159 plays. Back Al Dekdebrun finished 16th in total yards with 462 on 91 plays.[51]

Jim Breuil still remained optimistic and was looking forward to the 1947 season. Breuil was quoted as saying, "Just give me a year and watch that Bison Thunder!"[52]

* * *

The All-America Football Conference had finished its first year with the Cleveland Browns defeating the New York Yankees 14–9 for the Conference

Championship, but the league office saw continued turnover as Harvey Hester and John Keeshin resigned from their posts on the Executive Committee. Jim Crowley resigned as Conference Commissioner in order to take charge of the Chicago Rockets, accepting the positions of executive vice-president, general manager and coach of the team. According to the *1947 All-America Football Conference Record Manual,*

> The confidence of one individual who has never been accused of stupidity was shown in the decision of James H. (Sleepy Jim) Crowley to leave the commissionership with nearly four years to run on his $25,000 a year contract, in order to become general manager and head coach of the Chicago Rockets. There are two well-established National League clubs in that city, and the Rockets did only fairly well in 1946. Crowley had enough faith in the AAFC and in the ability of that lusty city to support a third major league team to cast his future with the Rockets.[53]

The Miami Seahawks were in trouble as the AAFC filed charges against the Seahawks for violating the Conference's indebtedness clause. Throughout the 1946 season, clubs within the Conference made attempts to help Miami stay financially sound, but attendance was just not there. In the end, they were expelled from the AAFC for failure to meet their financial obligations.

With the Seahawks finished for good, Baltimore stepped up to the plate, namely Robert Ridgway Rodenberg. Rodenberg—the son of an Illinois congressman—was a reporter for the Washington *Herald* and *Capital Daily* and served in Burma during World War II. With the help of Charlie McCormick, J.C. Herbert Bryant, Maurice (Maury) L. Nee and William R. Rodenberg (brother of Robert), Robert purchased the Seahawks franchise for $50,000 and moved them to Baltimore. This angered Washington Redskins owner George Preston Marshall, but since he could not exercise territorial rights on a team from a different league, there was not much he could do.

Despite the failure of the Miami Seahawks, the NFL was on notice that the All-America Football Conference was not a minor league. There were 110 former NFL players on AAFC rosters. Of those, only three made the official All-Conference first team and only eight were on the combined first and second team lists. Buffalo halfback Steve Juzwik was the lone Bison named, making the second team. Frank 'Bruiser' Kinard, tackle for the New York Yankees, was the only All-NFL player to make the cut.

The Conference had talent and they proved it by the end of the first season. Not only could you look at the All-Conference teams, but the AAFC also set 64 major league records. Some of those records could be explained by the AAFC playing a 14-game schedule, versus the ten or eleven game schedules in which the original records were set. Others could not be explained away as easily. A Field Goal efficiency of 48.5 percent, a Point After Touchdown efficiency of 92.9 percent and an average punt return of 13.7 yards were more impressive with the increased number of games.[54]

Regardless of records and All-Conference teams, the AAFC still wanted to tweak their system. Throughout the 1946 season, games were played on practically any night. This loose scheduling of games made it more difficult for fans. As a result, the Conference decided to play strictly on Sunday afternoons and Friday nights, except for Thanksgiving Day, which saw two games. They also needed to deal with the Cleveland and New York situation, where both teams clinched the division title early in the season. These two teams were obviously far superior to the rest of the Conference, so the AAFC decided to implement a player distribution system. In this system, the stronger squads each gave up players in order to help the other teams. It was hoped that this could keep fan interest alive throughout the season as teams would be more evenly matched.[55]

Over the course of two days, the All-America Football Conference held their first college draft. Similar to the system used by the NFL, the AAFC teams drafted in reverse order of finish from the 1946 season. Since Miami was no longer in the league, their draft picks were sent to the new Baltimore franchise, who replaced them. One difference in the AAFC draft was the special selections, which occurred before the start of the draft. Each team was given two picks, but Los Angeles and San Francisco each traded one of their picks to the Buffalo Bills. The first fifteen rounds of the draft went as expected. In additional rounds after the draft, certain teams did not select. For example, in rounds 16 through 20, Cleveland and New York did not select. From rounds 21 through 25, Cleveland, New York, San Francisco and Los Angeles did not select. This was designed to achieve parity in the league. The weaker teams had more draft selections.[56]

1947 BUFFALO BISONS DRAFT RESULTS
(DECEMBER 20–21, 1946)

Rd / (Overall)	Player	Position	College
0	Bob Fenimore	B	Oklahoma State
0	Frank Aschenbrenner	RB	Marquette, North Carolina, Northwestern
0	Cal Richardson	E	Tulsa
0	John "Red" Cochran	QB-FB-HB	Wake Forest
1 (2)	Al Baldwin	E-DB	Arkansas
2 (10)	Bob T. Davis	T	Georgia Tech
3 (18)	Ray Kuffel	E	Marquette, Notre Dame
4 (26)	Joe Andrejko	B	Fordham
5 (34)	John Mastrangelo	T-G	Notre Dame
6 (42)	Bert Corley	C	Mississippi State
7 (50)	Ernie Knotts	G	Duke
8 (58)	Joe Watt	HB-DB	Syracuse
9 (66)	Paul Gibson	E-QB-DB-DE	North Carolina State
10 (74)	John Maskas	G-T	Virginia Tech
11 (82)	Baxter Jarrell	T	North Carolina
12 (90)	Chet Liptka	T	Boston College
13 (98)	Joe Sowinski	G	Indiana

42   The Original Buffalo Bills

Rd / (Overall)	Player	Position	College
14 (106)	Bill Chipley	E-DB	Clemson, Washington & Lee
15 (114)	Bronco Kosanovich	C	Penn State
16 (122)	Frank Kosikowski	DE	Marquette, Notre Dame
17 (128)	Wash Serini	DG-G-T	Kentucky
18 (134)	Vinnie Yablonski	FB-LB	Columbia, Fordham
19 (140)	Chuck Compton	T	Alabama
20 (146)	Bill Swiacki	E	Columbia, Holy Cross
21 (152)	Hamilton Nichols	G-LB	Rice
22 (156)	John Furey	T	Boston College
23 (160)	Don Schneider	HB	Pennsylvania
24 (164)	Chan Highsmith	C	North Carolina
25 (168)	Frank Wydo	T-DT	Cornell, Duquesne

As is the case with today's game, not all of the players drafted made the team. Several of the players drafted by the Bisons eventually went on to play for other AAFC or NFL teams:

The "Blonde Blizz" or Robert Dale (Bob) Fenimore was a 6'1", 195-pound back out of Oklahoma State. He was drafted in the first round of the 1947 NFL draft by the Chicago Bears and chose to play for the Bears for the 1947 season before retiring from professional football.

Francis Xavier (Frank) Aschenbrenner, born in Heibuehl, Germany, was drafted in the sixth round by the Pittsburgh Steelers in 1947. Shortly into the 1947 season, the Northwestern halfback's rights were traded by Buffalo to the Cleveland Browns in exchange for end Alton Coppage, guard George Groves and tackle John Kerns. Aschenbrenner still had a year of eligibility left and waited before starting his professional career. In the end, he did not play for Buffalo, Cleveland or Pittsburgh, but instead the 5'10", 188-pound back played for the Chicago Hornets in 1949.

John Thomas Cochran, Jr. was drafted by the temporarily merged Chicago/Pittsburgh Cardinals/Steelers team in the eighth round of the 1944 draft. The 6'0", 190-pound all-purpose back decided to play with the Chicago Cardinals from 1947 through 1949.

Robert Thomas (Bob) Davis, Jr. was drafted in the sixth round of the 1947 NFL draft. The 6'4", 235-pound tackle played neither for Buffalo nor the New York Giants, but instead played for the Boston Yanks in 1948.

John Battista Mastrangelo was a 6'1", 228-pound guard/tackle out of Note Dame. He was drafted by the Pittsburgh Steelers in the third round of the 1947 NFL draft and played for them in 1947 and 1948. In his final season with the Steelers, Mastrangelo made All-Pro. Mastrangelo moved on to the New York Yankees in 1949, before ending his career in 1950 with the New York Giants.

Joseph Chester (Joe) Watt, a 5'11", 184-pound halfback out of Syracuse, was drafted in the seventh round of the 1947 NFL draft by the Boston Yanks. He split time between the Yanks and the Detroit Lions during the 1947 season and stayed with the Lions for the 1948 season, before moving on to the New York Bulldogs to finish his professional career in 1949.

William Allen (Bill) Chipley, the 6'3", 199-pound end out of Clemson and Washington & Lee, was also drafted by the Boston Yanks in the eighth round of the 1947 NFL draft. He played for the Yanks in 1947 and 1948, before moving on to the New York Bulldogs in 1949.

William Washington (Wash) Serini was only drafted by the Buffalo Bisons. Still, he did not play for the team and instead went to the NFL. The 6'2", 236-pound tackle out of Kentucky played for the Chicago Bears from 1948 through 1951. He finished his career by playing for the Green Bay Packers in 1952.

Ventan Constantine (Vinnie) Yablonski, a 5'8", 195-pound fullback out of Columbia and Fordham was drafted by the Chicago Cardinals in the twelfth round of the 1946 NFL draft. Staying with the Cardinals, Yablonski played for Chicago from 1948 through 1951.

William Adam (Bill) Swiacki was a 16th round draft pick for the Boston Yanks in 1946. The 6'2", 195-pound end did not, however, play for the Yanks. Instead, he played for the New York Giants from 1948 through 1950, before moving on to the Detroit Lions for the 1951 and 1952 seasons.

Hamilton James Nichols, Jr. was a 5'11", 209-pound guard out of Rice. Drafted by the Chicago Cardinals in the fourth round of the 1946 NFL draft, Nichols only played three years for them (1947–49). He finished his NFL career with the Green Bay Packers in 1951.

Frank Wydo was drafted by the Pittsburgh Steelers in the fifth round of the 1947 NFL draft. The 6'4", 225-pound tackle stayed with the Steelers from 1947 through 1951, before moving on to play for the Philadelphia Eagles from 1952 through 1957.

The remaining draftees never played professional football in either the AAFC or NFL during the regular season: Cal Richardson, Joe Andrejko, Ernie Knotts, Baxter Jarrell, Chet Liptka, Joe Sowinski, Bronco Kosanovich, Chuck Ompton, John Furey and Chan Highsmith.

The first season was complete and the draft was held. Going into 1947, the Bisons still had a lot of work to do if they wanted to improve on their 3–10–1 record.

During the off-season, end Ray Ebli was released by Buffalo. According to Ebli, Buffalo refused to give him a raise and he asked for his release. Buffalo told him that they tried to send him somewhere, but nobody wanted him. The day Buffalo informed him of his release, he received a call from Jim Crowley of the Rockets. They immediately offered him a contract.[57]

4

Ratterman Arrives in Buffalo

The 1946 season was behind him and Red Dawson started to make the team his own. The 1946 squad was pretty much Sam Cordovano's team, as he signed the majority of its players. With Cordovano gone, Dawson could mold the team in his image. He started by making some changes to his coaching staff. Gone were end coach Bill Daddio and line coach Tom Stidham. To replace them, Dawson brought in backfield coach Chuck Jaskwhich and end coach Red Conkright. The previous season's backfield coach, Clem Crowe, was moved to line coach.

Charles "Chuck" Jaskwhich was a graduate of Notre Dame and played quarterback on Knute Rockne's last team in 1930. He played two seasons under Hunk Anderson before he graduated and became the head coach at Holy Cross Prep School in New Orleans. After a short stint at Holy Cross, Jaskwhich became the backfield coach at the University of Mississippi, then the backfield coach for Georgia Preflight during the war. In 1945, Jaskwhich joined Clem Crowe as his backfield coach at Iowa. Once Crowe left Iowa to come to the Bisons, Jaskwhich became the head coach. Jaskwhich was a scout for the 1946 Buffalo team, but was not officially on the staff until he became the backfield coach in 1947.[1]

William "Red" Conkright came over from the Cleveland Browns, where he was an end and center coach for the AAFC Champions. After he graduated from Oklahoma University, Conkright played with the Chicago Bears and Cleveland Rams from 1937 through 1944. He scouted ends for the Rams in 1945 before he left for Cleveland.[2]

Only 16 members of the 1946 squad made it to the 1947 roster. Halfback Steve Juzwik and fullback Vic Kulbitski, end/guard Dolly King and halfback Chet Mutryn were the core players brought back. The rest of the roster was decimated. Former Illinois standout halfback Julie Rykovich and ex-New York Yankees back Clarence "Pug" Manders were added, along with Notre Dame quarterback George Ratterman.

Ratterman backed up Heisman Trophy winner Johnny Lujack at Notre Dame. After graduation from Notre Dame, Lujack had a short but relatively successful career with the Chicago Bears. *Buffalo News* writer Tony Wurzer, in commenting on the diminutive size of both players, noted, "On the football field these two are the All-America Conference's greatest one-two scoring punch. In street clothes they look like high school youngsters."[3]

As a freshman, George broke his collarbone during an inter-squad scrimmage, which limited his playing time. In his sophomore season, Ratterman threw just four passes, with two of them being intercepted. It was not until his junior year before he saw substantial playing time and Ratterman helped his team to the national championship. George was suspended for a semester in his senior year at Notre Dame, which lasted through part of the football season. Upset at losing playing time at Notre Dame, when the Buffalo Bills offered him a two-year contract, he became a professional football player at nineteen years of age.

Notre Dame and Bills' teammate Art Statuto recalled, "George was one of the smarter quarterbacks to have played the game. He had tremendous insight as to what was going on. His play selection was particularly unreal. I harken back to the '46 season at Notre Dame. Coy McGee was the left halfback. Ratterman, from his own 30-yard line, pitched a lateral to Coy McGee, who ran it 70 yards for a touchdown. It was called back because of an offside penalty. On the very next play, Ratterman called the exact same play and Coy McGee ran 75 yards for a touchdown."[4]

There was also a front office change for Buffalo. In February of 1947, Francis (Frank) Dunn, business manager of the Bisons, resigned. According to owner Jim Breuil, Dunn left to pursue public relations opportunities.[5]

Things also started to take shape in the Conference offices. Once Jim Crowley's resignation was officially accepted, Los Angeles Dons' owner Benjamin Lindheimer—the Chairman of the Conference's new Executive Committee—was appointed acting Commissioner and Dan Topping of the New York Yankees was named the Acting President of the Conference. These positions were only temporary and by February of 1947, they were permanently filled. Admiral Jonas H. Ingram was named the Conference's new Commissioner and O.O. Kessing was appointed the Deputy Commissioner.

Ingram was a four-star Commander-in-Chief of the Atlantic Fleet during World War II. Born October 15, 1886 in Jeffersonville, Indiana, Ingram attended Jeffersonville High School and Culver Military Academy. After he graduated from the academy, he entered the Navy in 1903 and caught Navy's first touchdown pass in 1906. While in the Navy, Ingram won the Congressional Medal of Honor for his service at Vera Cruz in 1914, was awarded the Navy Cross and received three Distinguished Service Medals. He coached the Navy football team in 1915 and 1916 and served as the Athletic Director at Annapolis from 1926 to 1930. After his stint at Annapolis, Ingram was a college official in the 1930s. Ingram was offered a five-year contract with the AAFC, but declined the offer and accepted a one-year deal. According to Ingram, "I may not like the job or you may not like me after a year."[6] Immediately, he made his presence known to the owners; "You don't own me or any part of me."[7] Ingram ran the AAFC as he saw fit and let the owners know that they were not the ones calling the shots.

Oliver Owen 'Scrappy' Kessing was born December 6, 1890, in Greensburg, Indiana. He operated the first Navy Pre-Flight School at Chapel Hill, North Carolina, and was later the Commodore of the Navy, directing base operations in the Pacific. Kessing entered Annapolis in 1910 and immediately tried out for football, boxing, wrestling and baseball. He became the Navy's first graduate manager of athletics from 1926 to 1929 while he served under Athletic Director Jonas Ingram. While in the military, he was twice led out to be shot by the enemy during the battle against Mexico in 1916. He volunteered to be a balloon pilot in World War I and became commander of the base at Tulagi. He directed advanced operations for the next three and a half years. After the war ended, Kessing served in General MacArthur's staff in the occupation forces. His distinguished military career saw Kessing win three Legion of Merit Awards, the Bronze Star, the Navy Marine Corps medal, two Secretary of Navy commendations and the combat V. He retired from the on Navy April 1, 1947, after accepting the position of Deputy Commissioner of the AAFC.[8]

* * *

To generate more fan interest and to separate themselves from the minor-league baseball and hockey teams of the same name, the Buffalo Bisons changed their moniker. The team ran a contest for fans to come up with the new name. In fourth place was the Buffalo "Blue Devils." Coming in third was the Buffalo "Nickels," followed by Buffalo "Bullets" in second place. James F. Dyson, a merchant marine during World War II, submitted the winning entry of Buffalo "Bills." According to author Dick Stedler, "Dyson depicted the team members as a posse of Buffalo Bills, harking back to the days of William F. (Buffalo Bill) Cody, legendary Pony Express rider and Indian scout. Cody symbolized the American frontier, and the new team was sponsored by Frontier Oil. Hence, the name 'Bills' marked the start of a new frontier in Western New York sports."[9] For his efforts, Dyson received $500.

The Bills opened their 1947 training camp in Hamilton, Ontario, with fifty players on the roster:

Player	Pos	Height	Weight	College
Joe Andrejco	B	6'0"	190	Fordham
Graham Armstrong	T	6'4"	240	John Carroll
Blondy Black	HB	5'11"	195	Mississippi State
Lamar Blount	FB	6'1"	190	Mississippi State
Sam Brazinsky	C	6'1"	215	Villanova
Ray Carlson	FB	6'1"	185	Marquette
Marty Comer	E	6'0"	202	Tulane

Player	Pos	Height	Weight	College
Al Coppage	E	6'1"	195	Oklahoma
Elbert Corley	C	6'2"	210	Mississippi State
Bernie Craig	G-E	—	—	—
George Doherty	T	6'1"	218	Louisiana Tech
Gil Duggan	T	6'3"	235	Oklahoma
Verne Erdman	T	—	—	—
Dippy Evans	QB	5'11"	185	Notre Dame
Paul Gibson	E	6'2"	190	North Carolina State
Chubby Grigg	T	6'3"	330	Tulsa
George Groves	G	5'11"	195	Marquette
Joe Haynes	C	6'3"	225	Tulsa
Buckets Hirsch	G	5'10"	205	Northwestern
Len Janiak	FB	6'1"	200	Ohio University
Steve Juzwik	HB	5'8"	184	Notre Dame
Mike Kasap	T	6'2"	255	Illinois
John Kerns	T	6'3"	245	Ohio University
Dolly King	E	6'2"	195	Georgia
Kit Kittrell	HB	5'9"	190	Baylor
George Koch	HB	6'0"	200	Baylor
Joe Kodba	C	5'11"	190	Purdue
Chet Kozel	G	6'2"	207	Mississippi
Vic Kulbitski	FB	5'11"	205	Minnesota
Jim Larkin	G	6'1"	230	Lock Haven
Pug Manders	FB	6'0"	200	Drake
John Maskas	G	5'11"	212	Virginia Tech
Vince Mazza	E	6'1"	210	{None}
Jack Morton	E	6'0"	200	Purdue
Chet Mutryn	HB	5'9"	180	Xavier
Bob Paffrath	FB	5'8"	190	Minnesota
Dick Pfuhl	FB	6'3"	230	St. Louis
Rocco Pirro	T	6'0"	235	Catholic
Ray Piskor	T	6'0"	245	Niagara
Felto Prewitt	C	5'11"	210	Tulsa
Ben Pucci	T	6'4"	260	{None}
George Ratterman	QB	6'1"	175	Notre Dame
Albie Reisz	QB	5'10"	180	Southeastern Louisiana
Julie Rykovich	HB	6'2"	200	Illinois
Bud Schwenk	QB	6'2"	200	Washington (St. Louis)
Vince Scott	G	5'8"	215	Notre Dame
George Terlep	QB	5'10"	180	Notre Dame
Dick Thames	G	—	—	—
Alex Wizbicki	HB	5'11"	188	Holy Cross
Ray Yagiello	G	6'0"	220	Catawba[10]

During camp, tackle Ben Pucci dislocated his jaw. As a result, his weight dropped from 260 to 235 pounds and he lost most of his strength. In Red Dawson's continued work to mold the team in his own image, the two largest members of the team—Pucci and Forrest Grigg—were sold to the Chicago Rockets. According to Pucci, "[Red] Dawson did not like big tackles."[11] With camp under way, it was time to start playing preseason games. The first game was against the Eastern Division Champion New York Yankees.

The Yankees stayed in the form that put them in the Championship Game the previous year. The Bills, however, struggled as fumbles and a weak pass defense were their undoing. New York scored 17 points in the first period. Ratterman, Rykovich, Hirsch and Kodba did not play in the contest. Meanwhile, the Yankees had their stars in the lineup: Sanders, Sinkwich and newcomer Buddy Young.[12] Sinkwich, a Heisman Trophy winner out of Georgia, earned NFL MVP honors while with the Detroit Lions before he entered the AAFC. The 29–7 defeat was not the start the Bills wanted. Next up were the Baltimore Colts.

The Bills built up a 20–6 halftime lead before Baltimore battled back to tie it at 20–20. Buffalo added a field goal and a touchdown to seal the victory. Even though the score did not provide any indication, Buffalo dominated the game. Baltimore's line was weak and had difficulty stopping the Bills' attack.[13] Buffalo was finally showing improvement, albeit against a relatively weak team. This was exactly what Dawson wanted heading into the first regular season game against New York.

The Yankees were coming off their Championship Game appearance against the Cleveland Browns and were confident. While Cleveland won the game, New York could still hold their head high and felt that they could repeat as Eastern Division champions. Stars like back Spec Sanders and end Bruce Alford were still on the roster and guard Dick Barwegan showed promise.

Dick Barwegan was MVP of the undefeated 1943 Purdue team. According to Paul Stenn, a teammate of Barwegan's while with the Chicago Bears in the 1950s, Barwegan's "quickness made him an ideal pulling guard, and don't forget, he could play defense as good as the best, too."[14]

The Bills also felt as though they made strides toward a divisional championship run. The time for speculation had ended, and the rest remained to be settled on the field. New York's offense struck first in the regular season opener. Spec Sanders tossed to back Eddie Prokop to put the ball on the Buffalo twenty-three yard line. Prokop stayed on the ground for the next play as he ran through right guard to place the ball on the Bills' four-yard line. Prokop got the call again and sprinted through the line for the score. Buffalo's ineffective first drive gave the ball back to the Yankees in short order. Buffalo's defense, however, picked up the slack. Back Vic Kulbitski intercepted a Sanders pass on the New York 40-yard line and returned it to the 23-yard line. Halfback Chet Mutryn ran around right end to the eight-yard line on a lateral from George Ratterman. Rushes by Mutryn and halfback George Koch put the ball on the Yankee one-yard line where Ratterman sneaked in for the touchdown.[15]

That gave the Bills' offense life. On their next series, Ratterman tossed a 39-yard pass to end Dolly King, who jumped to get the ball on the Yankee three-yard line. He fell back across the goal line to give the Bills the lead in

4—Ratterman Arrives in Buffalo

the game and Ratterman his first touchdown pass as a professional. In his book, *Confessions of a Gypsy Quarterback: Inside the World of Pro Football,* Ratterman recalled the play. "I faked handing the ball off to a halfback, squinted downfield and hit our right end as he broke behind the safety man for 32[16] yards and a touchdown. Smart play? You bet it was. My play? Not on your life."[17] Ratterman continued,

> Like any number of successful six-point plays that win games and occasionally championships, that one first evolved high over the playing field in the press box where a gimlet-eyed Buffalo assistant coach sat anxiously scanning the field with binoculars in search of specific weaknesses on the part of the opposition. On the normal handoff into the line he saw the rival safety man move up a few steps. Using a tie-line telephone to the Buffalo bench, he told the head coach to send the play into our huddle that eventually worked well enough for me to hang up my first touchdown pass as a pro.[18]

Late in the second quarter, New York moved into scoring position. Sanders tossed a pass to end Van Davis for an eight-yard gain. The New York drive continued on a pass to Young who pushed the ball to the Buffalo 34-yard line, and a 17-yard pass to end Harry Burrus who cut the distance in half. Sanders faked a pass and then scooted down the sideline for the score. This tied the game at 14–14 to end the half.[19]

The excitement continued in the second half. Sanders ripped off a 15-yard run to start another offensive drive for the Yankees. A pass to Young in the left flat resulted in a 50-yard play for a touchdown. Ratterman took the reigns and tossed a 34-yard pass to end Al Coppage to put the ball on the New York 34-yard line, while halfbacks Chet Mutryn and Steve Juzwik combined to drive the ball to the Yankee 20-yard line. A defensive holding penalty gave Buffalo a first down on the nine-yard line. After Juzwik lost three yards, Ratterman flipped the ball to Coppage — who was tackled on the one-yard line — where back George Koch took it over for the score.[20]

New York's next series saw the Yankees run around left end for a 15-yard gain to put the ball on the Buffalo 15-yard line. Spec Sanders and back Frank Sinkwich combined for three yards on three plays, but New York failed to gain a first down. Harvey Johnson kicked a 20-yard field goal to give the Yankees a 24–21 lead. Buffalo had one more opportunity to score before the end of the game. Starting on their 22-yard line, backs Julie Rykovich and Lou Tomasetti combined for three first downs to bring the ball to the New York 31-yard line. Rykovich caught a Ratterman pitch on the 16-yard line and ran to the eight before being tackled. Two Ratterman incomplete passes forced a third down. Lou Tomasetti took the ball to the four-yard line and the Bills faced a fourth-and-goal. Here, Ratterman dropped back to pass. Mutryn sneaked out to the left side of the line and stationed himself in the back of the end zone. Ratterman, seeing this, flipped the ball to Mutryn. Both Lou Sossamon and Van Davis saw this and raced to cover Mutryn. It was too late, however, as Mutryn got the ball unmolested to give the Bills a 28–24 lead. New York put together one last desperation drive late in the fourth quarter. Five consecutive completions drove the ball to the Buffalo 26-yard line and two more plays took the ball to the Bills' ten-yard line, but time ran out on the defending divisional champions. Buffalo got the 28–24 upset victory to start the season 1–0.[21]

New York's pass defense was their downfall. Several times, Buffalo was able to put a sustained scoring drive together based on their passing and the last touchdown to Mutryn in the back of the end zone was simply a matter of blown coverage on the part of the Yankee defenders. Mutryn was left alone while Lou Sossaman and Van Davis scrambled to recover. Back Alex Wizbicki recalled the strength of their defense in the win, "We used a new defense and that helped us in the game. It was five and six man lines and variations on maneuvers by these defensive men, which created some confusion and resulted in us playing a good defense. The Yankees were kind of befuddled by it."[22] Of note in the game, it was the first time that two teams combined for a record low one punt return.

Coming off their upset win over the Yankees, the Bills faced a tougher opponent in the AAFC Champion Cleveland Browns at Municipal Stadium. On Cleveland's third possession, halfback Edgar 'Special Delivery' Jones ran 43 yards to the Buffalo 16-yard line. Halfback Don Greenwood added four yards and Jones took the ball outside and ran it to the Buffalo two-yard line. Jones finished the drive for the first points of the game, but Lou Groza's extra point attempt was blocked by Felto Prewitt.[23] "That's the first time I've had an extra point blocked, I guess. I don't know just what happened, and I won't know until I see pictures of the game," recalled Groza. "I just concentrate upon the spot and kicking the ball."[24] Don Greenwood was Groza's usual holder, but Greenwood had been kicked in the stomach earlier in the drive and was on the sidelines being attended to by medical personnel. Otto Graham held for the extra point. Later in the game, Greenwood returned to the lineup and Groza converted all extra point attempts.[25] Three more touchdowns gave the Browns a 27–0 lead at halftime.

The third quarter was a different story. The Buffalo running game took hold and dominated the Browns. Starting on Buffalo's 16-yard line, the Bills drove the length of the field strictly on the ground. The Bills defense held Cleveland and Buffalo was again on the move. Mixing the run with short-to-midrange passes, Buffalo drove from their 24-yard line for their second score. Cleveland made the appropriate adjustments to their defense and Buffalo was again stymied. A lone field goal was all that was scored in the fourth quarter, giving Cleveland the 30–14 win.[26]

Both coaches commented after the game. "We got a good head of steam and took a commanding lead in the first half and then let down and looked bad in the last two periods,"[27] recalled Cleveland coach Paul Brown. "I started the kids in the second half, and Buffalo almost tore them apart. That just goes to show the difference between an experienced player and one just breaking in."[28] Buffalo coach Red Dawson expressed similar sentiments. "They out hustled us in the first half, and the team which shows the most hustle, generally wins," stated Dawson. "We were slow getting started, but we did get going and we gave them a battle. I think that we were down a bit after our victory over New York, but Cleveland is a much improved club over last year. This is the team's second year together, and the added experience makes the squad much stronger. My club is comparatively green, but it will come along. Mutryn played a fine game though. He's a good back."[29]

The Bills running game was responsible for the only points scored by the offense. "Buffalo is an improved squad. They have a strong dangerous running game, and that Chet Mutryn is a very good back who knows how to run,"[30] commented Paul Brown. "That run which set up Buffalo's first touchdown was a beauty. The hole was there, but Mutryn knew what to do when he got in the open."[31]

Buffalo's pass protection prevented George Ratterman from being effective. "Their line rushed me all night long and I didn't have much of a chance to get the ball away accurately,"[32] recalled Ratterman. Cleveland quarterback Otto Graham echoed those comments: "He's a good passer, but he didn't have too much protection tonight. Our line rushed him most of the night."[33]

Buffalo's next opponent was the Rockets. Chicago's first scoring opportunity came off Ray Ramsey's 54-yard dash to the Buffalo seven-yard line early in the first quarter. At that point, Chicago's offense sputtered and they faced fourth down. Former Buffalo back Al Dekdebrun dropped back to pass and tossed the pigskin toward the end zone. The ball bounced off the crossbar for an automatic touchback and Buffalo started their first offensive series. They, too, showed an inability to mount any sort of offensive attack as the Bills started their drive by fumbling the ball on their 29-yard line. Another former Bill, big tackle Ben Pucci, recovered the fumble for the Rockets, but their drive again came to a halt as Angelo Bertelli's pass to end Max Morris was intercepted by back George Koch.[34]

Early in the second quarter, Chicago had another scoring opportunity. Racking up 50 yards on the drive, the Rockets moved the ball to the Buffalo 25-yard line. Angelo Bertelli attempted to pass, but Buffalo safety Alton Baldwin intercepted and returned it 71 yards to the Rocket two-yard line where he was knocked out of bounds by linebacker Bill Daley. Fullback Vic Kulbitski finished the drive and gave Buffalo a 7–0 lead.[35]

Bertelli only played two minutes of the third quarter when he limped off the field with an injured right knee. This was the same knee that he injured the previous season with the Los Angeles Dons. Third-string quarterback Sam Vacanti came in to relieve Bertelli and drove the Rockets to the Buffalo 25-yard line. Rocket end John Harrington roughed up Buffalo fullback Lou Tomasetti, pushing his team back 15 yards and out of scoring range. After a change of possession, the Bills drove and scored when Ratterman tossed a five-yard pass over the center.[36]

The following kickoff saw Tod Scallisi boot the ball to the Buffalo 48-

yard line. Sam Vacanti worked his magic, completing a 21-yard pass to end Jerry Mulready. Scallisi caught the next pass, putting the ball on the Buffalo 15-yard line. Scallisi then lateraled to halfback Bill Schroeder for Chicago's first score, which closed the deficit to 14–6.[37]

Buffalo's offense opened up and Ratterman tossed a 28-yard pass to end Alton Baldwin. Halfback Mutryn and fullback Vic Kulbitski pushed the ball to the Chicago 13-yard line, where Mutryn ran off right tackle for the score. A few minutes later, back George Terlep tossed a 26-yard pass to halfback Dippy Evans for a 28–6 Buffalo lead.[38]

Two minutes remained in the game and Chicago faced a daunting task. Down by 22 points, Sam Vacanti went to the air and heaved a 40-yard touchdown pass to halfback Ray Ramsey. On Buffalo's subsequent drive, halfback Alex Wizbicki fumbled on the Bills' 31-yard line where Ben Pucci recovered his second fumble of the game. Vacanti flipped a 25-yard pass to Ramsey and a six-yard touchdown pass to end Max Morris for a 28–20 score. Unfortunately for Chicago, the game ended before the Rockets could mount another drive and Chicago suffered their third straight defeat of the season.[39] The Bills stood at 2–1 after their third game.

Chicago lost the game in the first half. Former Los Angeles Don Angelo Bertelli and former Buffalo Bill Al Dekdebrun were ineffective through the air. Bertelli had just joined the team five days prior, so it was understandable that he needed time to acclimate to his new team. Dekdebrun was hampered by a broken finger on his passing hand. Regardless of these setbacks, the Rocket offensive line failed to stop the Buffalo rush. The Bills traveled to Chicago to take on this same Rocket team.

On the fifth play of the game, Chicago sent a message that they were going to play tough. End Max Morris broke through the line and pummeled George Ratterman for an 18-yard loss, which pushed the Bills back to the Chicago 46-yard line. On the next play, Chicago again sent the pressure, but Ratterman expected it and he tossed a short pass to Lou Tomasetti. Excellent blocking allowed the nimble halfback to take the ball 32 yards to the Chicago 14-yard line. Three running plays later, the Bills were down to the Chicago five-yard line. Ratterman dropped back to pass and hit end Alton Baldwin for the score. A minute later, Buffalo took a 10–0 lead on a Steve Juzwik field goal, set up by a Rocco Pirro recovery of an Elroy Hirsch fumble. The Bills put together another drive; this time for 65 yards. The drive was highlighted by a 49-yard pass to Baldwin. Fullback Vic Kulbitski finished with a two-yard run for the 17–0 second quarter lead.[40]

At that point in the game, the Rockets found their offense. A 77-yard pass from Sam Vacanti to Elroy Hirsch cut the lead to 17–7. The pass was the longest pass of the 1947 season to that point. That was followed by a 73-yard drive, capped by a Hirsch two-yard run around right end to bring the score to 17–14. Chicago was only down by three points, but suffered a setback when Hirsch aggravated his chronic back injury. This was the third time in four games that season that Hirsch did not complete a game. End Jerry Mulready went down with a bruised shoulder.[41]

At the start of the second half, Chicago attempted to tie the score with a field goal from the Buffalo 45-yard line. The kick was short and Buffalo's offense went back to work. A quick touchdown strike—a 58-yard pass to Mutryn—increased their lead to ten. Ratterman tossed another two touchdowns in the fourth quarter, but only one counted, as a 22-yard toss to Mutryn was called back on a clipping penalty. Ratterman got the score back when he threw an 18-yard toss to Dolly King. The Bills picked up a 31–14 victory, a 3–1 season record and was in first place in the Eastern Division. Chicago, however, still looked for their first win in four attempts.[42]

George Terlep, Bills quarterback/halfback from 1946 through the beginning of 1948.

Buffalo's offense stepped up in the game with 448 yards of total offense. Ratterman threw four touchdown passes, which tied a Conference record (Otto Graham set the record in 1946 against the Chicago Rockets). Ratterman also set a Conference record with his 294 yards passing, which eclipsed Graham's 284 yards versus the San Francisco 49ers. Buffalo came home to face the 49ers.

Buffalo's first offensive drive lasted 80 yards and ended with a 14-yard run by Rykovich. San Francisco answered in the second quarter with a Frankie Albert run. Ratterman added to the score when he connected with Baldwin on a 58-yard strike. Buffalo finished the scoring of the half with an 18-yard field goal by Juzwik. This put the Bills up 17–7 at the midway point of the game. The Bills continued their scoring streak in the second half with an 87-yard run for a touchdown.[43]

By the third quarter, the Bills were up 24–7; that is when things started to fall apart for the Buffalo defense. San Francisco scored two touchdowns in the third quarter and three touchdowns in the fourth quarter to run away with the game. The 49ers won 41–24 and dropped the Bills to a 3–2 record for the season, while the 49ers moved to 4–1.[44] Bills' back Alex Wizbicki recalled the loss: "We beat ourselves. We just didn't execute like we were supposed to. We had fumbled, I think, two or three times in the game, which they recovered. Two of them they turned into touchdowns. We became very, very sloppy. We should have never lost it, but we did. It was one of those games where we had everything. We had statistics. Good statistics, but as you know, the score counts."[45]

The seesaw battle between these two teams set multiple AAFC records: Most Plays Attempted (83), Most Total First Downs (22), and Most Kickoff Return Yards (331). Another notable accomplishment was that the 36,099 fans at the game set an attendance record for Buffalo. The previous record was 33,648, which was set two weeks prior when the Bills met the Rockets at Civic Stadium. The Bills then faced a cross-country trip to take on the Dons.

It took slightly over two minutes for Buffalo to put the first tally on the board. Starting on their 30-yard line, the Bills used five plays to get the score. Dolly King started the drive with an eleven-yard reception, and it ended with Alton Baldwin catching a 32-yard strike from Ratterman. The Dons answered with an eleven-play, 64-yard drive with Charlie O'Rourke running it in from the five-yard line. Buffalo regained the lead on a 73-yard drive highlighted by a pass from Ratterman to King. On the Dons' next drive, O'Rourke handed off to fullback John Kimbrough. The ball rolled up Kimbrough's back and on to the ground and Buffalo's Ed Hirsch picked up the ball and ran it to the Los Angeles seven-yard line. On the next play, Mutryn went around left end for the score, which gave Buffalo a 20–7 lead at halftime.[46]

Alton Baldwin, Bills end from 1947 through 1949.

Los Angeles started to come back and by the fourth quarter, the Dons cut Buffalo's lead to 27–21. Ratterman took two safeties in the fourth quarter to preserve the lead, which brought the score to 27–25, but used up about a minute of valuable game time. The contest ended without the Dons having the opportunity to score again and Buffalo took the win.[47] Buffalo was 4–2 for the season and in good shape within the division.

The Los Angeles media blamed the loss on poor officiating. Dick Hyland in the *Los Angeles Times* described his opinion of the officiating: "The officials, as the Dons, were not having a good day as they missed fouls, called borderline cases and got in the way of tacklers."[48] Regardless of whether the officiating played a part in the Dons' loss, Los Angeles quarterback Charlie O'Rourke had a bad day. On Ratterman's first touchdown pass, O'Rourke was responsi-

4—Ratterman Arrives in Buffalo 55

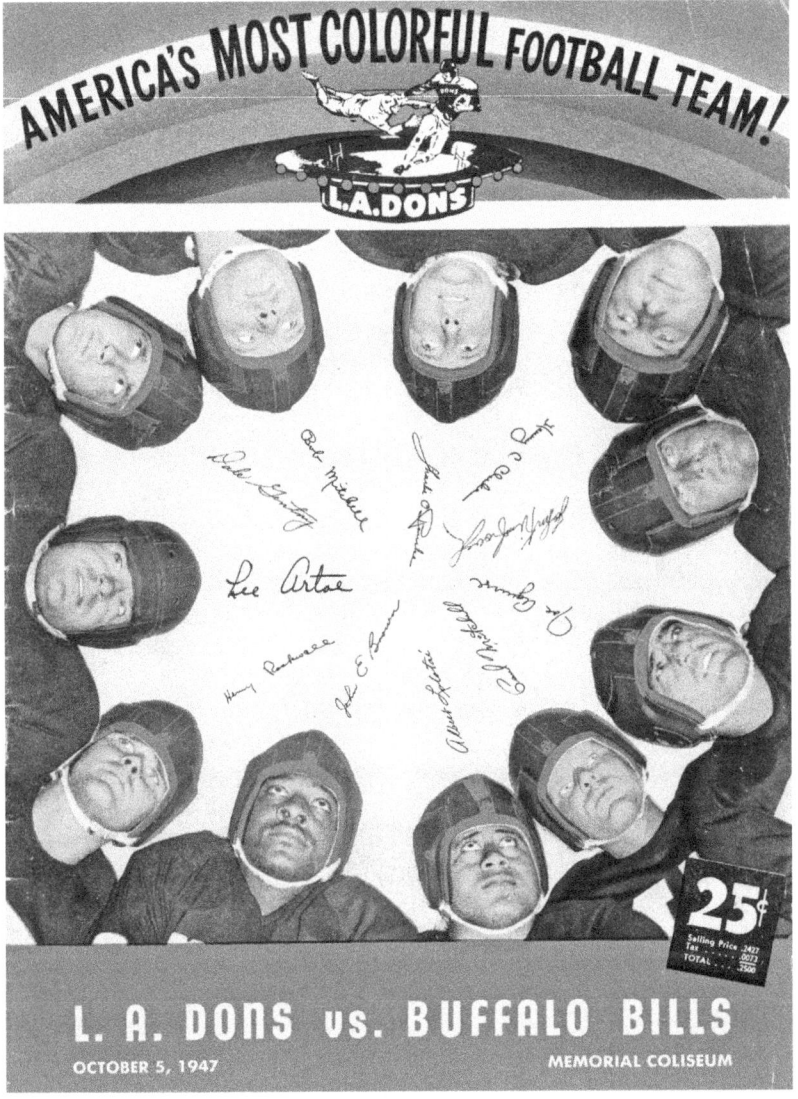

Game program from October 5, 1947: Buffalo Bills vs. Los Angeles Dons. The Bills won the game 27–25.

ble for covering Alton Baldwin. The result was a touchdown. Next, the Bills drove to the Buffalo 39-yard line. Ratterman dropped back to pass and tossed a 50-yard strike to end Dolly King. Who was O'Rourke responsible for covering on the play? King. The result was a touchdown. On a handoff to fullback John Kimbrough, O'Rourke fumbled the ball. The result was the Bills starting a one-play drive for a touchdown.[49]

On October 12, the Bills came home to take on divisional foe Baltimore. The Colts scored first when Augie Lio booted a 22-yard field goal late in the first quarter and they added two points when linebacker Mike Phillips dropped Ratterman in the end zone for a safety. On the next Colt drive, Baltimore moved the ball to the Buffalo six-yard line on the running of back Frank Sinkwich and a pass to end Lamar Davis. Bud Schwenk dropped back to pass, but decided to run the ball when he saw an opening in the Buffalo line. Schwenk crossed the line for the score and a 12–0 lead. The Bills finally showed some life in the second quarter as Mutryn finished a 66-yard drive with a two-yard scoring run. Baltimore tacked on three more points to give them a 15–7 halftime lead.[50]

Buffalo put together another long offensive drive in the third quarter. Ratterman guided the team down the field on three straight passes, the final pass being a 31-yard toss to Baldwin for the touchdown. Gone from the lineup, however, was Steve Juzwik, who dislocated his shoulder. Mutryn took over the kicking duties and closed the gap to a 15–14 Baltimore lead. The Bills' next offensive series started with a 32-yard reverse by Rykovich. Passes to King and Tomasetti drove the ball to the Baltimore eight-yard line. Mutryn finished the scoring drive, but missed the extra point. The Bills now had a 20–15 lead late in the fourth quarter.[51]

With seven seconds remaining in the game, Bud Schwenk dropped back and passed to end Lamar Davis. Davis caught the ball on the Buffalo 20-yard line and darted for the end zone. He appeared to have crossed the goal line, but field judge Eddie Tryon ruled that Davis stepped out of bounds just short of the goal. Approximately two seconds later, the final gun sounded to signal the end of the game. According to AAFC rules, the final gun cannot be fired while the play is in motion. The play must end before the gun can sound. This infuriated Baltimore coach Cecil Isbell, who joined the fans storming the field.[52]

Officially, Buffalo won the game 20–15. Baltimore contended that the Colts were victorious 21–20. Baltimore President Robert W. Rodenberg telegrammed Conference Commissioner Jonas H. Ingram, requesting that referee Ike Craig and field judge Eddie Tryon be called to the league offices to review the game film. According to a Baltimore spokesperson, "Davis caught the pass and said he was all the way over the goal line when his foot kicked the marker. He insisted he was in fair territory all the way."[53] He continued: "Johnny Vardian was right behind Davis, and he says Davis was at least a foot away from the out-of-bounds stripe. We're basing our protest purely on that angle."[54] Baltimore's appeal failed and Buffalo was declared the winner.

The Bills were in a first-place tie for the Eastern Division lead with the Yankees. The next two games for Buffalo were against division rival Brooklyn. If Buffalo won the games against the Dodgers, it would distance them from the hapless Brooklyn team and kept them in the hunt for the Eastern Division title.

In the first quarter, Buffalo drove down to within inches of the goal line, but was stopped by the Brooklyn defense. Runs by backs Bob Hoernschemeyer and Mickey Colmer moved Brooklyn down the field and six plays later, the Dodgers scored the first points of the game. The drive was finished when halfback Al Akins took the double-reverse from the 18-yard line and the Phil Martinovich kick made it 7–0. Buffalo answered on the subsequent kickoff when halfback Alex Wizbicki returned the ball 91 yards for the tying score.[55] Wizbicki recalled, "I remember most of all, the good blocking I got. A certain hole opened up and I took off after that."[56]

Heading into the second quarter, Buffalo put together an impressive offensive drive. Eight plays covered 80 yards, with halfback Chet Mutryn racking up the final 14 yards for the score and a 14–7 lead.[57]

Buffalo drove deep into Brooklyn territory in the third quarter, but came away empty. Neither team was able to sustain a drive the remainder of the quarter. Heading into the fourth quarter, Buffalo had a 14–7 lead, but Brooklyn had the ball. Lining up in their familiar double-wing, Hoernschemeyer swept wide around the right wing and streaked down the field 84 yards for the tying score. This 84-yard touchdown run set an AAFC record, eclipsing Bob Kennedy's 78-yard run against the Chicago Rockets.[58]

Buffalo's offense folded the remainder of the quarter as they were not able to get close to scoring. Brooklyn, however, kept the fans excited with their final drive. With three minutes to play, Brooklyn was facing fourth-and-one on their 25-yard line. The Dodgers went for it and converted the first down. With 45 seconds remaining, Brooklyn was again facing fourth down. This time, they needed seven yards in order to gain a first down. That fourth down was also converted. In a final desperation move, Hoernschemeyer heaved a pass to an open Monk Gafford for an apparent touchdown. Gafford, however, dropped the ball and the game ended in a 14–14 tie.[59]

The Dodger defense had trouble stopping the short passing game of the Bills. Conversely, Brooklyn's aerial attack was non-existent. Completing an anemic one pass out of seven attempts, the Dodgers relied solely on their ground game. Bob Hoernschemeyer racked up 179 yards on 19 attempts to carry the bulk of the 274-yard rushing load. This tie, coupled with the New York week off, prevented Buffalo from taking sole possession of the divisional lead.[60] Buffalo needed to win the rematch.

The Dodgers scored first when Mickey Colmer ran down the sideline for a 41-yard touchdown. The Bills came back when Ratterman lead a nine-play, 69-yard drive to tie the score. Halfback Julie Rykovich went over guard for the final five-yard run. Ratterman tossed a screen pass that lead to a 38-yard touchdown in the hands of fullback Vic Kulbitski. The Bills took a 14–7 lead into halftime.[61]

During the second quarter, guard Tex Warrington was called for unnecessary roughness. He argued with referee Bill Ohrenberger and Ohrenberger ejected Warrington from the game. After discussing Warrington's ejection with deputy commissioner O.O. Kessing — who was in attendance — Ohrenberger stated that Warrington "shoved him after the penalty had been called and slugged him after being ruled out of the game."[62] Kessing saw fit to suspend Warrington for the remainder of the season and levied a $500 fine.[63]

The offensive attack of the Bills continued early in the third quarter. Passes by Ratterman and runs by Rykovich and Tomasetti drove Buffalo to the Brooklyn two-yard line and Tomasetti took it over to increase the lead to 21–7. Not letting up, Buffalo ran an impressive play that got the fans to their feet. Ratteran dropped back and pitched the ball to end Dolly King on the Brooklyn 20-yard line. King, in turn, lateraled to Kulbitski who took the ball the remaining distance for the score.[64] Buffalo added another touchdown when Tomasetti intercepted a Hoernschemeyer pass on the Dodger 48-yard line and ran it in for the score and the 35–7 victory.[65]

The Dodgers were short-handed for the game as only 30 men dressed for the match-up, instead of the normal 33. With Warrington's ejection, Brooklyn was hampered further. The Bills next opponent was the Cleveland Browns.

The Browns took the opening kickoff with Tom Colella returning it 18 yards. Otto Graham tossed three straight times to move the ball 59 yards. They continued the drive to the Buffalo twelve-yard line, where Ed "Special Delivery" Jones took the handoff and smashed through the line for the score and a 7–0 lead.[66]

In the second quarter, the Browns started an offensive drive from their 31-yard line. Graham lobbed a screen pass to Marion Motley for an apparent touchdown, but it was called back to the Buffalo eleven-yard line on an offsides penalty. Dante Lavelli finished the scoring drive with a diving catch into the end zone. After a long, seventeen-play drive, Cleveland scored their second touchdown to take a 14–0 lead.[67]

Cleveland was pinned on their one-yard line about midway through the third quarter. The Bills had pushed the Browns into the shadow of their goal line, but the visitors' defense held for downs. With no room for error, Graham called a screen pass to Mac Speedie. The ball was put into play and Speedie blocked the incoming tackle. Breaking away from the block, Speedie ran along the goal line to receive the pass and Graham gently tossed the ball over the defensive rush to the waiting Speedie, who was protected by three of his teammates. Bursting down the field, the four players worked in tandem to push away any would-be tacklers. Around midfield, Chet Mutryn gained ground. Soon to be overtaken by the quick Mutryn, Speedie broke away from his protective front and sprinted the remaining distance for the score. It was a 99-yard pass reception which set a new AAFC record and tied an NFL record.[68]

Buffalo attempted a comeback, but Don Greenwood intercepted a pass on the Cleveland one-yard line. If he had failed to make the interception, the Browns would have had the ball on the Cleveland 37-yard line, but this mistake pinned the visitors deep in their own zone. Horace Gillom attempted to punt out of danger, but Mutryn put together a nice return to leave the Bills within scoring range. Five plays and 34 yards later, the Bills scored on an eleven-yard pass from Ratterman to Baldwin.[69]

Cleveland put another scoring drive together late in the fourth quarter and with a mere three minutes to play, the Browns drove 76-yards to finish with a 39-yard pass from Graham to John Yonakor for the 28–7 victory.[70]

Cleveland quarterback Otto Graham set a Conference record for Best Average Gain per Play at 14.6 (248 yards on 17 plays). Of note for Buffalo was another attendance record at Civic Stadium: 43,167. The Bills only had one more home game of the regular season and that was the following week against Los Angeles.

The field was ugly, as the snow-lined gridiron was thick with mud. As a result, the anticipated duel between Buffalo gunslinger Ratterman and his counterpart from Los Angeles Charlie O'Rourke was replaced by a slow, grinding running game.

After an ineffective first possession, Buffalo started their second drive on the Los Angeles 47-yard line. Ten plays later, the Bills drove to the Dons' 27-yard line. Facing third down, Ratterman dropped back and hurled a pass to Baldwin who was standing on the five-yard line. Baldwin caught the ball and sprinted to the corner of the end zone. That touchdown pass was be Ratterman's seventeenth of the season, which tied Otto Graham's Conference record.[71]

In the second quarter, the Dons' best offensive drive of the half took them to the Buffalo twenty-five yard line. Dons kicker Ben Agajanian attempted a field goal, but the snap from center was bobbled and recovered by the Bills. The half ended with Buffalo on top 6–0.[72]

Center Felto Prewitt intercepted O'Rourke on the second play of the half and returned it from the Dons 40-yard line to the 30-yard line. An illegal use of the hands penalty put the ball on the Los Angeles 26-yard line. Rykovich and Tomasetti drove the ball to the eleven-yard line and Mutryn ran through right guard for the score. The Bills went on offense again when two plays after kickoff, Rykovich intercepted O'Rourke's pass attempt to end Dale Gentry. Rykovich returned the ball to the Dons' nine-yard line. Fullback Vic Kulbitski pushed the ball two yards and Mutryn again went through right guard for the score. The Bills had the lead at 19–0 as they headed into the fourth quarter.[73]

Midway through the final period, the Dons took over on downs at the Buffalo 20-yard line. After an offsides penalty on Los Angeles, Gentry fumbled a pass from Glenn Dobbs and the ball was recovered by tackle John Kerns. Buffalo was not able to convert on the turnover and gave the ball back to the Dons. In the closing minutes of the game, end Vince Mazza intercepted O'Rourke's screen pass and returned it to the Los Angeles 16-yard line. Two plays later, George Terlep—substituting for a resting Ratterman—tossed a short pass to fullback Kulbitski for the score, a 25–0 victory and the first shutout in franchise history.[74]

1947 Buffalo Bills (left to right): Alex Wizbicki, Chet Mutryn, Stan Iwucz (assistant trainer), Steve Juzwik.

The win cemented Buffalo's second-place standing in the division with the Yankees a mere one game ahead. The Yankees faced that same Los Angeles team the following week, while Buffalo visited the Colts.

Buffalo scored first when Mutryn capped a 46-yard drive with a three-yard touchdown run. Midway through the second quarter, Ed Hirsch intercepted a Bud Schwenk pass on the Colt 45-yard line and returned it for a score. The Bills led 13-0 and Baltimore responded with a long eight-play, 80-yard drive that ended with a 17-yard pass from Schwenk to halfback Billy Hillenbrand to cut the lead to 13-7.[75]

In the third quarter, Ratterman tossed a 17-yard pass to end Marty Comer. After the catch, Comer turned up field and ran the remaining 41 yards for the score. On their next possession, the Bills increased their lead with a Rykovich two-yard run. Buffalo was on top 26-7 going into the fourth quarter.[76]

Baltimore put together another scoring drive early in the final period. Halfback Andy Dudish's one-yard run cut the lead to 26-14, but the Colts were running out of time and Buffalo had possession of the ball. On a long, sustained series, Rykovich and Mutryn drove the Bills 65 yards for the final score of the game and a 33-14 victory.[77]

All eyes were on the Yankees' game against the Browns. With Buffalo's victory, they needed the Yankees to lose, but the Yankees tied the mighty Cleve-

4—Ratterman Arrives in Buffalo 61

land team. That tie, coupled with Buffalo's victory over the Colts, moved the Bills to within one game of the divisional lead. The next game was crucial as Buffalo took on the Yankees. A New York win guaranteed the Yankees their second straight division title. A Buffalo win kept the Bills in the hunt going into the final week of the season and a chance to face the Browns for the AAFC crown.

New York's first drive consisted of nine plays that consumed 72 yards. Fullback Buddy Young was the workhorse who carried the ball five times for 46 yards and finished with a one-yard scoring run. New York center Lou Sossamon recovered a Ratterman fumble and rumbled into the end zone for a quick 14–0 lead as the first quarter came to an end. Buffalo bounced back late in the half when they put together a twelve-play, 82-yard drive. Rykovich's two-yard scoring plunge closed the gap to 14–6.[78]

In the second half, the Yankee offense exploded. An impressive five-play, 80-yard drive was highlighted by a 55-yard pass from Spec Sanders to end Van Davis. Runs by Young and Sanders pushed the ball to the Buffalo one-yard line, where Sanders went over for the score. Early in the fourth quarter, Ratterman tossed a 59-yard touchdown pass to Baldwin to bring the score to 21–13, but a 15-play, 75-yard drive sealed the victory for New York. The Yankees scored again late in the fourth quarter, but it was just icing on the cake as they took the 35–13 win.[79]

In the first half, Buffalo's defense held the New York running game in check. Sneaking their linebackers toward the defensive front, the Bills essentially created an eight-man line. In the second half, the Yankees exploited this by forcing the runs outside. This proved to be an effective tactic as the Yankee running game dramatically improved.

The Bills were officially eliminated from the race for the divisional title. For the second time, the New York Yankees (10-2-1) faced the Cleveland Browns (12-1-1) for the AAFC crown. The Bills traveled to San Francisco for the final game of the season.

Even though this was a meaningless game in the standings, the Bills and 49ers battled as though they were in a championship game. A steady rain hampered scoring early in the contest, as it was not until the second quarter before points were put on the board. A toss from Frankie Albert to left end Nick Suseoff put the 49ers on top 7–0. Buffalo started their drive on their 30-yard line. A 48-yard pass from Ratterman to end Paul Gibson ignited the offense and a seven-yard pass to end Alton Baldwin tied the score at 7–7.[80]

Late in the third quarter, Tomasetti recovered an errant lateral on the 49er twelve-yard line and a pass to end Paul Gibson put Buffalo ahead 14–7 in the fourth quarter. San Francisco retaliated with a 61-yard drive that ended with halfback Ned Mathews running around left end for the two-yard score to tie the game at 14–14.[81]

San Francisco took the lead on a Mathews interception of Ratterman as Mathews grabbed the ball on the Buffalo 35-yard line and returned it for a touchdown. With only a couple of minutes left in the game, San Francisco

4—Ratterman Arrives in Buffalo

1947 Buffalo Bills. Front Row (left to right): Steve Juzwik, Chet Mutryn, Stan Iwucz (Assistant Trainer), back row (let to right): Chuck Jaskwhich (Backfield Coach), John Kerns, Alex Wizbicki.

was up 21–14, but Buffalo put together an impressive drive. Three passes to Gibson pushed the Bills downfield and a toss to Dolly King in the end zone tied the score at 21–21, at which point the game ended.[82]

It was an exciting, but also disappointing season for the Bills. They had an opportunity to win their division, but just could not take that final step. However, their 8–4–2 showing was a marked improvement over the initial 3–10–1 campaign of 1946. This improvement in the team's performance also showed in the gate receipts. Attendance increased by 100,000 over the 1946 season and the Bills set a single-game city record of 41,167 against the Cleveland Browns. Individually, Chet Mutryn and George Ratterman were All-Conference selections; Mutryn being first-team halfback and Ratterman as second-team quarterback. The Bills were moving in the right direction heading into the 1948 season.

Opposite: 1947 Buffalo Bills. *Front row:* Albie Reisz, George Terlep, Graham Armstrong, Dolly King, Ray Kuffel, Elbert Corley, Vince Mazza, Jack Carpenter, Steve Juzwik, Vince Scott. *Second row:* Clem Crowe (Assistant Coach), Gil Duggan, Paul Gibson, Ed "Buckets" Hirsch, John Kerns, Lou Tomasetti, George Ratterman, Julie Rykovich, Alex Wizbicki, Chet Kozel, Vic Kulbitski, Felto Prewitt. *Third row:* Leland MacFarland (Treasurer), Chuck Jaskwhich (Assistant Coach), Tiny Dippery (Trainer), Pug Manders, Rocco Pirro, Alton Coppage, Marty Comer, Hal Lahar, George Groves, George Doherty, Chet Mutryn, Stan Iwucz (Assistant Trainer), Red Dawson (Head Coach), Jim Breuil (Owner). *Missing:* Alton Baldwin, Lamar Blount, John Black, William "Red" Conkwright (Assistant Coach), Fred Evans, Forrest Grigg, Joe Haynes, Mike Kasap, George Koch, Joe Kodba, Floyd Konetsky, John Maskas, John Morton, Ben Pucci, John Scafide (Assistant Coach).

5

The Third Season Begins

For the second year, the AAFC held their college draft and yet again the NFL refused to hold a common draft with the AAFC. A few subtle changes were made from the previous year. Most notable was that the draft increased to thirty rounds. The weaker teams still had additional picks, but they now occurred earlier in the draft. In the first round, all teams selected. In the second round, only Chicago and Baltimore had selections. At that point, things became a little more complicated. The third, seventh and ninth rounds saw every team select. Cleveland and New York did not have choices in the fourth and sixth rounds. Chicago, Baltimore and Brooklyn were the only teams to select in the fifth round. The eighth and tenth rounds had only Chicago, Baltimore, Brooklyn and Los Angeles selecting. After the tenth round, all teams were able to select.[1]

1948 BUFFALO BILLS DRAFT RESULTS (DECEMBER 16, 1947)

Rd /(Overall)	Player	Position	College
1 (6)	Clyde Scott	HB-DB	Arkansas, Navy
3 (16)	Bill Gompers	HB	Notre Dame
4 (24)	Bill O'Connor	E-DE	Notre Dame
6 (33)	Martin Wendell	G	Notre Dame
7 (39)	Bob Brugge	B	Ohio State
9 (51)	Lou King	B	Iowa
11 (63)	John Finney	B	Compton J.C.
12 (71)	Dick Johnson	G	Baylor
13 (79)	George Grimes	DB-WB	North Carolina, Virginia
14 (87)	Larry Joe	B	Penn State
15 (95)	Frank Ballard	G	Virginia Tech
16 (103)	Jim Walthall	B	West Virginia
17 (111)	Ray Coates	HB-DB	LSU
18 (119)	Dud Waybright	E	Notre Dame
19 (127)	Wade Walker	T	Oklahoma
20 (135)	Roger Stephens	B	Cincinnati
21 (143)	Howard Duncan	C	Ohio State
22 (151)	Ralph Sazio	T	William & Mary
23 (159)	George Bloomquist	E	North Carolina State
24 (167)	J.D. Cheek	T	Oklahoma State
25 (175)	Bob Rennebohm	E	Wisconsin

5—The Third Season Begins

Rd /(Overall)	Player	Position	College
26 (183)	Ted Andrus	G	Southwestern Louisiana
27 (191)	Ray Brown	B	Virginia
28 (199)	Lou Corriere	B	Buffalo
29 (207)	John Wosloski	C	Penn State
30 (215)	Talley Stevens	E	Utah State

As was seen the previous season, not all draft picks decided to play for the Bills, or even play professional football:

Clyde Luther (Smackover) Scott was a 6'0", 174-pound halfback out of Arkansas and the Navy. Even though Scott was the number one pick by Buffalo, he was also a first round selection by the Philadelphia Eagles. Scott chose to play for the Eagles and was on their squad from 1949–1951. In 1952, he split time between the Eagles and the Detroit Lions before retiring from professional football.

Martin Peter Wendell was another selection by the Bills who was also drafted by the Philadelphia Eagles (eighth round). Unlike Clyde Scott, the 5'10", 215-pound guard decided not to play for either Buffalo or Philadelphia, but signed on to play the 1949 season with the Chicago Hornets.

George Stanley Grimes was a defensive back out of Virginia. The 5'11", 190-pound Grimes was drafted by the Los Angeles Rams as well as Buffalo, but rebuffed both teams to play with the Detroit Lions in 1948. He retired from football after the 1948 season.

Buffalo's seventeenth-round selection was a 6'1", 195-pound halfback out of LSU named Raymond Jerald Coates. He was drafted by the New York Giants (eighth round) and played for them in the 1948 and 1949 seasons.

Philadelphia drafted (sixth round) another Buffalo pick, this time a 6'3", 225-pound center out of Ohio State named Howard Duncan. Turning down offers by both Philadelphia and Buffalo, Duncan opted to play for the Detroit Lions in 1948.

Ralph Joseph Sazio was taken by the Pittsburgh Steelers in the 28th round of the 1947 NFL draft. The 6'1", 250-pound tackle out of William & Mary chose to play with the Brooklyn Dodgers in 1948.

There are no records of Bob Brugge, Lou King, John Finney, Frank Ballard, Jim Walthall, Dud Waybright, Wade Walker, Roger Stephens, George Bloomquist, J.D. Cheek, Bob Rennebohm, Ted Andrus, Ray Brown, John Wosloski or Talley Stevens playing a professional football game in either the AAFC or NFL.

* * *

As the third season of the AAFC began, it became clear that something needed to be done to even the level of competition on the field. The Cleveland Browns dominated the league with the New York Yankees close behind. It was decided that the stronger teams would be forced to give players to the weaker teams.[2] Without this new rule in place, the AAFC faced its own extinction.

An item of contention was the ability of AAFC owners to accept financial losses as the Conference competed against the long-standing NFL. At the formative meetings in 1944, it was agreed that no owner would be allowed into the league if they could not accept losses for at least three seasons. As attendance continued to grow for AAFC games (total attendance in 1946 was 1.5 million and grew to 2.0 million in 1947), things shaped up nicely for the Conference to survive. More people attended the games, which obviously increased total revenues for each club. However, each team faced its own challenges heading into the 1948 season. A few clubs were sold to new owners and the AAFC was wondering if they could last the full three years.

The Baltimore Colts were a bad team and were sold to a civic group headed by Robert C. Embry. In spite of only winning two games in 1947, the fans still stepped up. Season ticket sales increased going into 1948 and an influx of money (a $200,000 stock sale), put the Colts in decent shape to make a run at the division crown. Of course, they still faced strong competition.

The Brooklyn Dodgers were taken over by Branch Rickey and the baseball Brooklyn Dodgers. Rickey planned on using his baseball scouting system to search for the best football talent for his team. With the successes that Rickey had on the baseball diamond (eight championships) and year-round scouting, it was expected that he would bring the same winning record to the football team. On paper, the Brooklyn Dodgers were a team on the rise.

The Chicago Rockets struggled from their inception and were in constant turmoil. As a result, ownership of the franchise was a revolving door. A civic group headed by R. Edward Garn was the latest to take the reins of the AAFC's cellar-dwellers and promised to right the ship. It was hoped that quarterback Angelo Bertelli, as well as backs Elroy Hirsch and Ray Ramsey, would be able to stay healthy for a full season, which they were unable to do in 1947. Rocket coach Ed McKeever (Notre Dame, Cornell and the University of San Francisco), needed his stars on the field if they had any hope of competing in 1948.

Merger talks with the NFL continued, but ended at an impasse. Both leagues knew that something needed to be done or they would go bankrupt. The latest merger proposal had the Cleveland Browns and the San Francisco 49ers enter the NFL, with all other teams disbanding. This was not acceptable to the AAFC and the offer was refused.

* * *

The 1947 Buffalo Bills improved over their disappointing 1946 start. Attendance nearly doubled (117,000 in 1946 vs. 217,699 in 1947) and heading into 1948, season ticket sales continued to rise. The Bills had all the marks of a successful season ahead of them.

The Bills had 23 players return from the 1947 squad: tackles Graham Armstrong, Jack Carpenter, Joe Haynes, John Kerns and Chet Kozel; guards

5—The Third Season Begins

Ed Hirsch, Hal Lahar, Rocco Pirro, Felto Prewitt and Vince Scott; center Bert Corley, ends Alton Baldwin, Marty Comer, Paul Gibson, Vince Mazza and Jack Morton; backs Vic Kulbitski, Chet Mutryn, Julie Rykovich, George Terlep, Lou Tomasetti and Alex Wizbicki; and quarterback George Ratterman. The most notable departures from the 1947 squad were end Dolly King and back George Koch.

The Bills opened training camp July 26 with 53 players on the roster. As the youngest team in the league — averaging just 24 years of age — Buffalo hoped that youthful speed would counteract the additional experience of the other squads. The Bills had three preseason games to test that theory.

On August 12, Buffalo took on the two-time defending Eastern Division champion New York Yankees. Spec Sanders was responsible for New York's first three touchdowns and had a large hand in the fourth. Two passes and a run by Sanders built up a 21–0 lead, while Bob Kennedy scored the fourth Yankee touchdown after Sanders broke off a 40-yard run. The Bills came back with two touchdowns by Kulbitski, but still trailed 28–14 in the fourth quarter. Rykovich added a touchdown to inch the Bills closer to the Yankees and in the closing minutes of the game, Jeff Durkota — who played on Penn State's undefeated Cotton Bowl team in 1947 — broke through the line and dashed 30 yards for the score. Bob Steuber kicked the point to tie the game at 28–28 when the final whistle blew.[3] The Bills held their own. Even though New York built up a commanding lead, Buffalo still fought back to gain a tie.

As Buffalo prepared to take on the Brooklyn Dodgers, Jim Breuil and Dodgers owner Branch Rickey met with the Buffalo Advertising Club. They discussed new ways to increase revenue and to make the AAFC more attractive to fans. Rickey proposed having two games per week for each team. Jim Breuil was on board with the idea. "Football is coming to a twice-a-week schedule anyway," stated Breuil. "We may as well pioneer it. We have pioneered a new major league. Why stop there?"[4] Rickey and Breuil stated that they would propose a 28-game schedule at the first winter meeting of the conference. Rickey added that it was "only fair to the thousands of fans who would like to see our teams and to the owners who are being whipsawed financially under the present setup."[5]

George Ratterman recalled in his autobiography *Confessions of a Gypsy Quarterback: Inside the Wacky World of Pro Football*, his experience with Branch Rickey's Brooklyn Dodgers in the preseason:

> With the emphasis not entirely on victory except in an ultimate regular-season sense, owners and coaches sometimes add a few harmless frills to the exhibitions strictly to pep up ticket sales among the hayseeds.... Among [Branch Rickey's] many innovations, the widely ballyhooed use of Pepper Martin, the balding old baseball slugger, as an extra point-kicker may have been the most enterprising. It was Rickey's assumption that if Martin the place-kicker could attract a few baseball fans who might not otherwise pay their way into a football game, well, their money was every bit as negotiable as anybody else's.[6]

5—The Third Season Begins 69

Paul Gibson caught the first two scoring passes from Ratterman, building a 14–0 Buffalo lead. The Dodgers fought back when a five-play, 40-yard drive resulted in a touchdown pass from Bob Hoernschemeyer to Lee Tevis. The Bills increased their lead when Ratterman connected with Mutryn for Ratterman's third touchdown pass of the game. Hoernschemeyer attempted to battle back with two more touchdown passes, but the Brooklyn kicking game failed to deliver. The final two extra point attempts by Pepper Martin missed the mark, leaving Buffalo's margin of victory at two points: 21–19.[7] Ratterman recalled, "We blocked Pepper's kick and the ball bounced back into his arms. He stood there, alarm registering on his face while several fierce 250-pounders bore down on him, wondering whether to bullyrag the officials or throw the ball to second base. As I recall now, he fell down in a protective heap instead."[8]

The final preseason game was against the Browns. The two-time AAFC Champion was a tough test for the Bills, but Buffalo needed to know where they stood against the best of the Conference. They were able to battle to a tie with New York, but Cleveland was undoubtedly the best. The Browns built up a 28–0 halftime lead before Buffalo started to fight back. Unfortunately for the Bills, time ran out before they could catch up. Using a strong aerial attack, Cleveland continued their winning ways by beating the Bills 35–21 in Akron, Ohio.[9]

Right: Lou Tomasetti, Bills halfback/fullback from 1946 to 1949.

Opposite page: 1948 Buffalo Bills. *Front row:* Stan Iwucz (Assistant Trainer), Ed "Buckets" Hirsch, George Ratterman, Lou Tomasetti, Ed King, Rocco Pirro, Hal Lahar, Rex Bumgardner, Carl Schuette, Felto Prewitt, Ed Balatti, Paul Gibson, Vince Scott. *Second row:* Chuck Jaskwhich (Assistant Coach), John Kissell, Al Akins, Gerry Whalen, Graham Armstrong, John Kerns, John Baldwin, Bill O'Connor, Al Baldwin, Jim Still, Art Statuto, John Wyhonic, Red Conkright (Assistant Coach). *Third row:* Red Dawson (Head Coach), Tiny Dippery (Trainer), Bob Callahan, Bill Gompers, Chick Maggioli, John Carpenter, Vince Mazza, George Kisiday, Alex Wizbicki, Don Schneider, Vic Kulbitski, Chet Mutryn, Clem Crowe (Assistant Coach). *Missing:* James Breuil (Owner), Marty Comer, Chet Kozel, Bob Leonetti, Julie Rykovich, Jim Smith, Bob Stefik, Bob Steuber, George Terlep.

6

The Team Started to Gel

The 1948 season started off slowly for the Bills. After playing three preseason games (going 1-1-1), the Bills opened their regular season with a game against the 49ers in San Francisco. With one touchdown in the first quarter and three more in the second, the 49ers put on an offensive display that was too much for Buffalo. The Bills scored once before the half and once after, but San Francisco never relinquished the lead. Buffalo's second score came shortly into the second half when fullback Norm Standlee fumbled deep in Bills territory. A Ratterman to Baldwin pass was good for 49 yards and end Bill O'Connor caught the touchdown pass to finish the drive. O'Connor recalled the play, "It was kind of a standard play-action pass run off a fake trap. It was crossing ends. I would delay and then cross in behind and came out pretty free. It was a nice pass, actually, from Ratterman that caused it. It was not a bad catch, either."[1] The final score was 35-14 and the Bills had their first loss of the season.[2]

With Steve Juzwik nursing a knee injury, he was relegated to just kicking duties against Buffalo's next opponent: the Chicago Rockets. Despite his absence from the offense, the Bills had an impressive showing against Chitown. Holding Chicago to a paltry 32 yards rushing, recovered five fumbles and intercepted four passes, the Buffalo defense took advantage and Buffalo scored two touchdowns in each of the first three quarters. In fact, the Rockets never stepped inside of Buffalo's 17-yard line until late in the fourth quarter. With Buffalo's quick and sustained scoring, Chicago resorted to a constant barrage of passing, setting a new Conference record with 49 pass attempts, which eclipsed the previous record of 46 set by the 1946 Brooklyn Dodgers. In the end, they could only score once and Buffalo took the easy 42-7 win to capture their first of the season.[3]

It did not take long for the Cleveland Browns to put the Buffalo Bills into a hole during their September 12th match up as within the first twelve minutes, the Browns were able to rack up two touchdowns. Cleveland's first scoring drive lasted eleven plays for a total of 54 yards. Three passes by Otto Graham highlighted the drive, with two of the passes going to Mac Speedie and the final went to Bob Cowan for the score. The second drive lasted 70 yards and was capped with Marion Motley bursting through the line for an 18-yard dash and the 14-0 lead. At this point, Edgar "Special Delivery" Jones

6—The Team Started to Gel

Game Program from August 29, 1948: Buffalo Bills vs. San Francisco 49ers. The Bills lost the game 35–14.

left the game after aggravating a rib injury sustained in the exhibition meeting between these two teams.[4]

The shell-shocked Bills were not out and started to move the ball. The Bills received the Cleveland kickoff and proceeded to drive 80 yards in ten plays. Rykovich's 25-yard run cut the Browns' lead in half. The Browns quickly countered with a nine-play, 82-yard drive to increase their lead back to 14. Not to be outdone, the Bills drove 77 yards to end the half at a 21–13 deficit.[5]

As the offense clicked in the first half for Cleveland, it was their defense that put on a show in the second half. The Bills were only able to drive the ball into Browns' territory once — it was only to the 43-yard line — in the last 30 minutes. The Cleveland offense still moved as easily as it did in the first half. After less than six minutes of play in the third quarter, Graham scurried across the goal line for the Browns' fourth touchdown and a 28–13 lead. They scored twice more in the fourth quarter to blast the Bills 42–12.[6]

The Bills' record was now 1–2 with a San Francisco rematch on tap. The Bills' first drive lasted 52 yards. Ratterman tossed to end Paul Gibson on the three-yard line and he ran the final distance for a score and a 7–0 lead. San Francisco retaliated by going 98 yards on nine plays, highlighted by a 38-yard pass from quarterback Frankie Albert to halfback Jim Cason. End Alyn Beals finished the drive with a 29-yard run for a tying score.[7] Beals, the 6'0", 188-pound end out of Santa Clara, was Albert's main weapon. In referring to Beals, Albert said, "Boy, did he have some great moves! He was a good faker. I can remember several times setting up to pass and watching the defensive back fall down after Alyn put a fake on him."[8]

Buffalo halfback Bob Steuber's 47-yard run increased Buffalo's lead to 14–7, but San Francisco halfback Jim Cason answered with a 59-yard run to tie the score. Buffalo halfback Chet Mutryn's miraculous catch in the end zone gave the Bills another lead and Joe Vetrano's 28-yard field goal ended the half with Buffalo on top 21–17.[9] Unlike the previous meeting, Buffalo was showing that they could stand tall against the powerhouse 49ers, but were they able to sustain that momentum?

The third quarter opened with Buffalo having the ball. Halfback Jim Cason intercepted a Ratterman pass and returned it 31 yards to the Buffalo 15-yard line. Halfback Johnny Strzykalski took advantage of the turnover and ran it in from the one-yard line. This gave San Francisco their first lead of the game. They extended their lead on a long scoring drive capped with Strzykalski tossing a lateral to Verl Lillywhite on the four-yard line, who ran it in. But Buffalo did not give up. On a drive highlighted with three passes by Ratterman, Baldwin caught a 14-yard toss for the score. A Lillywhite interception led to San Francisco's final score, as Albert ran around right end for the 20-yard touchdown.[10] This 38–28 victory gave the undefeated 49ers their fifth straight win, while Buffalo fell to 1–3 for the season.

Next up for the Bills was the winless Brooklyn Dodgers. Buffalo scored first on a Bob Steuber 24-yard field goal in the opening quarter. They extended their lead in the second quarter when halfback Lou Tomasetti took it across the line to make the score 10–0. The Dodgers answered on a four-play, 54-yard drive ending with fullback Hardy Brown running it in from the two-yard line. A Ratterman 43-yard pass to Mutryn made it 17–7 at halftime.[11]

Tackle Bulldog Williams recovered a Bob Steuber fumble on Buffalo's 25-yard line to start another scoring drive for Brooklyn, which ended when Hoernschemeyer threw a seven-yard pass to fullback Hardy Brown for the touchdown. Buffalo answered with an 80-yard drive ending with a nine-yard pass to halfback Chet Mutryn. Not giving up, Hoernschemeyer tossed passes of 20 and 27 yards—the latter for a touchdown—to close the gap to a 24–21 Buffalo lead. Buffalo put away the game with a quick drive that started with a 35-yard Rex Bumgardner punt return. Rykovich ripped off a 35-yard run through the middle of the line and finished the drive with a one-yard score with 16 seconds left on the clock.[12]

That was a desperately needed win for Buffalo. They were 2–3 for the season and were behind the 3–2 Baltimore Colts in the divisional standings. Both the offense and defense stepped up. The defense held the Dodgers to only nine yards rushing, compared to Buffalo's 222 yards. Halfback Chet Mutryn increased his consecutive game scoring streak to five, but hobbled off the field with an injury late in the game. His injury, however, was not serious enough to keep him out of the next game against the Yankees.

The Bills were up 13–0 at the half and New York stared at their fifth straight defeat of the season. But 30 minutes of football still needed to be played and the Yankees turned on the offense. In the second half, New York consistently put together long drives deep into Buffalo territory. The first score for the visitors came on a 68-yard drive highlighted by a 41-yard pass from Spec Sanders to end Bruce Alford. Their second scoring drive started at the Buffalo 47-yard line. Sanders faded right and tossed a pass to wingback Lowell Wagner, who fought off Alex Wizbicki and Vic Kulbitski for the ball and the touchdown. Harvey Johnson kicked the winning point to give the Yankees the 14–13 victory. Buffalo's offense did not get inside the New York 45-yard line the entire second half.[13]

With the win, New York moved into a tie for second place in the division with Buffalo. Even with Baltimore's loss to the 49ers, at 3–3, they still maintained a lead in the standings over the 2–4 Bills and Yankees.

Struggling to stay alive in the playoff hunt, the Bills faced the undefeated Cleveland Browns on October 17. Cleveland was searching for their seventh straight victory and 15th straight game without a loss. Ratterman was benched in an attempt to shake up the Buffalo squad and was replaced by Jim Still. Still, a tall and lanky quarterback, was signed in the off-season to be Ratterman's replacement in case of injury. George Terlep, Ratterman's original replacement, was traded to Cleveland and faced his previous team for the first time.

The Browns started the scoring with a Cliff Lewis return of a Jim Still punt, which put Cleveland in good starting field position. Fullback Marion Motley ran for ten yards before Otto Graham hooked up with halfback Edgar Jones for a 44-yard strike and a 7–0 lead. Bills center Art Statuto recalled, "I got stuck in on defense and I use that word advisedly. [Jones] looped around left end and headed down the sidelines. About 15 yards from the line of scrimmage, all I could see was his hand up in the air, shouting 'Hey, Otto!' The next thing I saw was the ball floating over my fingertips, into his hands and watching his feet lead me to the end zone, where he scored a touchdown. I think that was my last defensive play for Buffalo."[14] Buffalo took advantage of a Cleveland fumble to even up the score. With Cleveland having possession on their 39-yard line, Motley broke through the defense, but lost control of the ball. Mutryn picked it up and sprinted to the Cleveland three-yard line before being stopped. Four plays later, Jim Still tossed an easy fade to the corner of the end zone where end Alton Baldwin and defensive back Tommy James fought for possession. James tried to knock the ball down, but missed, which gave Baldwin the opportunity to grab it and the score was tied at 7–7. The Browns racked up another ten points before the end of the first quarter, taking the score to 17–7.[15]

Ratterman was put back in the lineup, but he was only able to drive the team for one more score. This happened in the fourth quarter, when the Bills were facing an 85-yard drive. Ratterman hit Mutryn on a 44-yard toss and the drive finished with Tomasetti catching a nine-yard dart from Ratterman for the touchdown. It did little as the Bills were down 24–14 at that point. Cleveland sealed the victory with another touchdown. Backs Cliff Lewis, Ara Parseghian, Dean Sensanbaugher and Ollie Cline combined to take the Browns to the Buffalo 30-yard line, where Mac Speedie caught a pass from Lewis for the score and a 31–14 win.[16]

Fortunately for Buffalo, New York lost their game with the 49ers, so the defeat did not drop the Bills in the standings. Both teams were 2–5 and tied for second place in the division, but Baltimore beat Los Angeles and moved to 4–3 for the season. This increased their lead for the divisional title. Buffalo had an opportunity to make some headway in the division and their next opponent was the 4–3 Los Angeles Dons. Both the Colts and the Yankees had more difficult opponents, as Baltimore faced the San Francisco 49ers and the Yankees faced the undefeated Cleveland Browns. Still, the Dons were not a team to be taken lightly.

With Ratterman back in as starter for the Bills, Buffalo hoped the offense would receive the kick start it needed. The Dons put together an impressive 64-yard drive for the first score of the game as passes to fullback Jeff Durkota and end Joe Aguirre quickly moved the ball into scoring territory. A strike from Glenn Dobbs to Aguirre put the first points on the board.[17]

Ratterman had a pass intercepted by linebacker John Brown on Buffalo's 25-yard line, which set up another drive for Los Angeles. Glenn Dobbs connected with Joe Aguirre for their second score and that was not the start the Bills had hoped for in that game.[18]

After a few ineffective series by both squads, halfback Rex Bumgardner stood deep in Buffalo territory to receive a Glenn Dobbs punt. The 47-yard punt was received by Bumgardner on the Buffalo nine-yard line who advanced slightly, faked a lateral to Mutryn and ran 91 yards for the score. This sparked the Bills' offense as Buffalo quickly tied the score on a 66-yard drive, capped with a Bob Steuber run. The score was tied 14–14 at the end of the first half.[19]

6—The Team Started to Gel 75

The Bills took the lead on a seven-play, 81-yard scoring drive and they followed it with another score before the end of the third quarter. Ratterman tossed a 19-yard pass to the grouping of Alton Baldwin, Jeff Durkota and Bill Reinhard. Reinhard and Durkota knocked each other away and Baldwin came down with it for the touchdown. Both teams scored again in the fourth quarter, but Glenn Dobbs re-injured his ribs and left the game, so the Dons did not have the same offensive firepower in the second half. Buffalo took advantage and returned home with a much needed 35–21 win.[20]

With losses by both Baltimore and New York, the Bills moved into sole possession of second place in the division and inched closer to the division leading Colts. Buffalo was now 3–5 for the season and played the 4–4 Baltimore Colts for a share of the divisional lead.

New to the Colts that year was quarterback Y.A. Tittle. According to former NFL executive Ron Wolf, "Tittle was an exceptional passer for his time and he was tough as nails. He had absolutely no protection with the old Colts and he found a way to get the football off.... He could set up quickly and he could get out of trouble.... Probably best in the AAFC, which is saying something when you think of Graham, Ratterman and Albert.... He was more mobile, for example, than Peyton Manning early on in his career."[21]

Buffalo started off on the wrong foot early into the game with the Colts. After 28 seconds, they were down 7–0 to the visitors as a screen pass from Tittle to halfback Billy Hillenbrand resulted in a 64-yard touchdown. The Bills fought back, however, and drove 89 yards to score on a Bob Steuber three-yard run. The Bills took the lead on a Bill Gompers 43-yard gallop in the second quarter.

Buffalo drove again, but defensive back Aubrey Fowler intercepted a pass from Ratterman on the Bills' 23-yard line. The Colts took advantage of this miscue when quarterback Charlie O'Rourke snuck in from the one-yard line. At the end of the half, the score was tied 14–14. Tittle had injured his knee and did not return to the game.[22]

Early in the third quarter, Baltimore took the lead on a 30-yard field goal from Rex Grossman. Buffalo regained the lead on a 70-yard drive with sixty-nine of those yards coming on passes from Ratterman to end Bill O'Connor. Mutryn finished the drive with a one-yard plunge and the Bills had a 21–17 going into the fourth quarter.[23]

At this point the Buffalo offense exploded. A pitch from Ratterman to Mutryn resulted in a 49-yard play. Mutryn, hit by center Mule Corley, ran 35 yards to finish the play and get the score. End Bill O'Connor finished an 89-yard drive with a 35-yard scoring reception and the Bills won 35–21.[24]

With this win, the Bills tied the Colts for the divisional lead at a record of 4–5. The offense was clicking for both teams as they combined for 893 total yards. This eclipsed the previous Conference record of 880 yards, set by the Bills and 49ers on August 20, 1948. The 3–6 New York Yankees also kept pace with their 42–7 win over the 1–9 Chicago Rockets.

Zeke O'Connor (#55) catching a touchdown pass against the Baltimore Colts on October 31, 1948. Jake Leicht (#81) is defending.

Next up for the Bills was a rematch with the 2–7 Dodgers. The Bills won 31–21 in their previous meeting and the Dodgers were coming off a 17–0 loss to the Los Angeles Dons. The Bills needed to win in order to at least stay even with the Colts and ahead of the Yankees. The Colts traveled to Cleveland to play the Browns, while the Yankees hosted the Los Angeles Dons. Both had difficult contests and Buffalo needed to take advantage of the situation with their weaker opponent.

Mutryn put the Bills on the board first when at 8:25 of the first quarter, he ran 68 yards for a touchdown. After an ineffective series by Brooklyn, Rex Bumgardner received the Mickey Colmer punt on the Brooklyn 43-yard line. Mutryn ran off right tackle for 18 yards and Tomasetti ran the same off-tackle play to add another 15 yards to the drive and a score. Buffalo was up 13–0 early in the second quarter, but Brooklyn worked to chip away at Buffalo's lead. Tailback Bob Chappuis passed to end Dan Edwards to start the next drive. Chappuis ran through the middle of the line for a 39-yard gain, which placed the ball on the Bills' 15-yard line. Passes to Dan Edwards and to end Saxon Judd drove the Dodgers down to the Buffalo three-yard line, and rushes by Mickey Colmer and Chappuis set up the final run by Colmer for the score. Buffalo answered with a nine-play drive finished by Mutryn to regain the advantage. The Bills were up 19–7.[25]

After a missed Steuber field goal attempt, Brooklyn took over on the Dodger 20-yard line. End Max Morris, end Saxon Judd and back Harry Burrus all had short pass receptions to move the ball away from the Brooklyn goal.

This is where their drive took a step backward, as Chuck Schuette intercepted a pass on Brooklyn's 40-yard line. Schuette streaked down the field, but fumbled short of the goal while attempting to lateral to end Vince Mazza. Mazza fell on it in the end zone to increase Buffalo's lead.[26]

Brooklyn attempted to battle back, but Chappuis fumbled the ball on the Buffalo 35-yard line. Buffalo in turn fumbled the ball back to the Dodgers, when end Hank Foldberg recovered the pigskin on the Buffalo 43-yard line. On the next play, Chappuis passed the ball to Judd, who was standing on the five-yard line. Judd caught the ball and ran it in for the score with a mere 1:20 left on the game clock. Brooklyn was not done, however, as wingback Ray Ramsey returned a Jim Still kick 70 yards for another touchdown. This cut Buffalo's lead to 26–21. Fullback Lee Tevis attempted an onside kick, but failed. The Bills controlled the clock and the game ended.[27]

Buffalo's offensive output sent a message to the other teams in the division. With 410 yards of rushing by the Bills—while holding their opponents to a paltry 54 yards rushing—Buffalo officially became a contender for the division title. Mutryn racked up 185 of the rushing yards, while Tomasetti added 141 yards on the ground. The Colts lost 28–7 to the Browns, so Buffalo was in sole possession of first place. The Yankees won 38–6 over the Dons, however, so both New York and Baltimore were in a tie for second place in the division and only one game away from the lead.

The team came together. Buffalo center Art Statuto remembered, "I don't know whether the opponents we played in the beginning were better prepared than we were, but it just took some time for us to gel and to be able to get things to move the way we wanted it to move. I think it was the normal progression of the team gelling."[28]

It was a cold, gray November day when the 5–5 Los Angeles Dons visited Civic Stadium to take on the Bills. Both quarterbacks—Ratterman and Glenn Dobbs—were seen blowing on their fingers to keep them warm.[29]

The Bills struck first as Ratterman tossed a pass to Baldwin, who was standing on the Dons' one-yard line. Glenn Dobbs went up to intercept the ball, but missed. Baldwin came down with it and scored, but the extra kick was no good. Two field goals by Ben Agajanian tied the score at 6–6 going into the half.[30]

The Dons opened the second half with an eight-play, 72-yard drive. Passes to fullback Walt Clay, end Burr Baldwin and wingback Herman Wedemeyer pushed the Dons downfield. Dobbs then broke through left tackle, cut back and ran 26 yards with guard Ray Frankowski's bone-shattering block against a Bills defensive back clearing the way. Wedemeyer got the call, but fumbled on the Buffalo 31-yard line. Four plays later, Ratterman tossed from the Buffalo 49-yard line to a waiting Mutryn on the Dons' 30-yard line. Back Mike Graham misread Ratterman's pass and was not able to catch up with Mutryn and the score was tied 13–13.[31]

The Dons put together an impressive seven-play, 60-yard drive to take the lead. The series started with a 29-yard reception by end Joe Aguirre and fullback Walt Clay pushed the Dons further downfield with his 19-yard reception. Dobbs went around right end for the six-yard scoring run, which put the Bills down 20–13 heading into the fourth quarter.

But the Bills still had some fight left in them. An eight-play, 80-yard drive was capped with an amazing touchdown reception by end Alton Baldwin. Ratterman dropped back to pass and lofted a 28-yard toss to Baldwin, who made a miraculous catch as he was falling into the end zone. That tied the score at 20–20.[32]

The Dons put together another drive, but Ben Agajanian's missed field goal on the Dons' 46-yard line gave the ball back to Buffalo on their eleven-yard line. Ratterman started the next offensive drive with a pass, but back Walt Heap intercepted that pass on the Buffalo 25-yard line, putting a quick end to the drive. Heap returned the interception to the Buffalo ten-yard line and the Bills were in trouble. Glenn Dobbs dropped back to pass and tossed it to Joe Aguirre, who faked twice to temporarily halt the Buffalo defenders and ran it in for the score.[33]

With thirty seconds left in the game and down 27–20, Buffalo had one more chance to salvage the game. Ratterman dropped back to pass and guard Al Lolotai broke through the line to race after the quarterback. Ratterman did not have a chance and was sacked for a seven-yard loss. The final play was a handoff to Tomasetti, who took the ball to the Buffalo 27-yard line as time expired and the Bills dropped to a 5–6 season record.[34]

This loss, combined with wins by both New York and Baltimore, put the Bills in a three-way tie for the division lead. There were three games left in the season, which included games against New York and Baltimore. But first, the Bills faced the lowly 1–11 Chicago Rockets on Thanksgiving Day. The Bills needed to take advantage of this opportunity, as Baltimore and New York both lost to stiffer competition earlier in the week. The Colts faced the 6–5 Los Angeles Dons and lost 17–14, while the Yankees faced the undefeated Cleveland Browns and lost 34–21. A win would put the Bills back into sole possession of first place in the division.

The Rockets started their first drive from the Chicago 14-yard line. Eighty-six yards later, former Bills halfback Julie Rykovich crossed the line to put the Rockets on top 7–0 (Rykovich played the first six games of the season with Buffalo before being sent to the Rockets). Not to be outdone, Ratterman connected with halfback Rex Bumgardner for a 64-yard strike, before Bumgardner was tackled by guard Joe Ruetz on the Chicago thirteen-yard line. Three plays later, Tomasetti broke through the line for a five-yard touchdown run, but with Jack Baldwin missing the kick, the Bills were down 7–6. Starting at their 38-yard line, quarterback Jesse Freitas connected with end Dolly King for a nine-yard gain. The drive finished with a 53-yard touchdown pass from Freitas to halfback Chuck Fenenbock. After a quick series ending in a Ratterman interception, Buffalo bounced back with a three-play, 47-yard

6—The Team Started to Gel 79

drive, capped by a Ratterman-to-Alton Baldwin pass from the Rocket's 33-yard line.[35]

Chicago still led 14–13 at this point. Buffalo started their next series on their one-yard line. Tomasetti fumbled and the ball was recovered on the Buffalo five-yard line by defensive end Bob Jensen. Two plays later, Chicago increased their lead to 21–13 on a five-yard run by fullback Bill Kellagher. It was now Buffalo's turn. Starting on the Bills 38-yard line, Buffalo drove to the Chicago five-yard line, aided by a Mutryn 43-yard run. With ten seconds to play in the half, Tomasetti crossed the line to make the score 21–19.[36]

Buffalo added to the score in the third quarter, starting their drive after recovering a Julie Rykovich fumble. Seven plays later, Tomasetti had his third touchdown of the game, giving Buffalo a 26–21 lead. A Freitas-to-Dolly King connection gave Chicago a 28–26 lead, which set up a wild fourth quarter.[37]

With five minutes left in the game, Mutryn received a Chicago kick on his ten-yard line. He lateraled to Bumgardner, who broke three tackles to run the ball 90 yards for a score and Buffalo went up 33–28. Freitas passed to Chuck Fenenbock, who took the ball to the Buffalo 40-yard line. Hit by Kulbitski, Fenenbock fumbled the ball and Kulbitski returned it 64 yards for the score and a 39–28 lead. Freitas connected with end Dolly King to close the gap to 39–35, but time ran out before the Rockets regained possession. The Bills pulled out the much-needed win.[38]

The Bills were 6–6 for the season and owned a one game lead over both New York and Baltimore. The Colts faced the 2–10 Brooklyn Dodgers, while the Bills met the Yankees. The first time the Bills played the Yankees that year, Ray Flaherty was the coach, but Red Strader was now in charge of the cross-state rivals. Norman "Red" Strader played fullback for Slip Madigan's St. Mary's teams in the early 1920s, earning the school's first All-American honor. After college, he experimented with professional baseball for a year before signing on with the Chicago Cardinals football team. After playing one season, Strader left to pursue a coaching position at Regis College before moving on to be an assistant coach at St. Mary's. He coached under Slip Madigan until Madigan's health problems forced him to retire at which point Strader took over the head coaching duties. Strader was hired to be the Yankees backfield coach in 1946. After their loss to the Colts in the fourth game of the 1948 season, head coach Ray Flaherty was gone and replaced by Strader. Over the next eight games, the team went 4–4 and was in the playoff hunt, but first they needed to get past the division-leading Buffalo Bills.

The Bills lost 14–13 in their last meeting with the Yankees in October. That was hardly the case in the rematch, as Buffalo took a commanding 21–0 lead in the second quarter. It was not until late in the half before New York would score as a 38-yard drive—finished by a six-yard pass from Spec Sanders to end Jack Russell—put the first points on the board for the home team.[39] Jimmy Powers of the New York *Daily News*, commenting on the game: "We have never seen a team as devastating as the Buffalo Bills in their first half against the Yankees."⁴⁰ Buffalo scored twice more before the end of the game to take the 35–14 victory.

The Buffalo line opened up huge holes for the Bills runners, taking advantage of the inexperienced Yankee defense. New York had a total of 70 yards rushing and 211 total yards, which did not help their cause. Buffalo, on the other hand, had 395 total yards, led by an outstanding performance by Mutryn. The diminutive back had nine rushes for 67 yards, four receptions for 65 yards and returned two punts for 99 yards and a touchdown.⁴¹

With the loss, the New York Yankees were officially eliminated from the division title race. It was now down to Buffalo and Baltimore.

Baltimore beat the Brooklyn Dodgers 38–20, which guaranteed the Bills at least a tie for the division lead. The Yankees had won the division the previous two years, but fell short in their quest for three straight division titles when they lost to the Bills. Buffalo (7–6) had a one game lead over the Baltimore Colts (6–7) heading into the final game of the season, which coincidentally, was against the Colts. A win and Buffalo clinched the division title. A loss and the Bills had to play a tie-breaking game against the Colts to determine who would play the Cleveland Browns in the AAFC Championship Game. The Browns won the Western Division after beating the San Francisco 49ers by a score of 31–28 in week 14 of the season.

It took four minutes and 37 seconds for the Buffalo Bills to get the first score against the Colts. A nine-play, 55-yard drive ended when Mutryn broke through the middle of the line for a one-yard plunge. Bob Stefik missed the kick and Buffalo had a 6–0 lead. The Baltimore defense stiffened and attacked Ratterman. As a result, the Buffalo offense sputtered. Not so for Baltimore, as quarterback Y.A. Tittle turned on the offense and the Colts started to move the ball. Beginning at their 41-yard line, the Colts drove deep into Buffalo territory. Halfback Billy Hillenbrand ran around the left flank and caught a Tittle pitch on the ten-yard line, turned up field and scored to give the Colts a 7–6 lead. On Baltimore's second drive, Hillenbrand returned a Buffalo punt 30 yards to start the drive on the Buffalo 40-yard line. Two Tittle-to-Davis passes put the ball on the Bills' eleven-yard line. Halfback Bob Pfohl added nine and fullback Bus Mertes took the ball to within inches of the goal, where Tittle ran it in to increase the lead to 14–6. Buffalo added a safety when Vince Mazza came off the end and crushed Tittle in the end zone, jarring the ball loose. This was the final scoring of the half.⁴²

Baltimore struck quickly in the third quarter when Tittle faked a handoff and tossed to end Lamar Davis, who outraced Mutryn for the 80-yard score. Tittle also engineered another scoring drive, which ended in his second sneak for a touchdown. Baltimore now had an insurmountable 28–8 lead in the fourth quarter. Ratterman put together another scoring drive late in the game, but with only a few minutes remaining, Buffalo could not recover from the Baltimore onslaught. The game ended when Davis intercepted a Ratterman pass and returned it to the Buffalo one-yard line. Halfback Jake Leicht

6—The Team Started to Gel 81

took it over on the next play to give the Colts a 35–15 victory.[43] Buffalo center Art Statuto recalled, "It was more of a letdown than anything else. Playing away from home. Away from our friendly fans. I think it was a normal letdown, that we realized that everything was coming to a close and we pretty well had everything under control. Unfortunately, we were wrong."[44]

It was the Colts' first win in four attempts over their divisional rival. It also gave Baltimore a share in the divisional lead, forcing a sudden death playoff game for the Eastern Division title. One week later, the Bills returned to Baltimore in the critical rematch. The season was on the line for both teams.

The first drive of the game saw Baltimore score on a Rex Grossman 16-yard field goal. Buffalo answered with a drive that started around midfield, early in the second quarter. It ended with a five-yard touchdown pass from Ratterman to end Bill O'Connor and Buffalo took a 7–3 halftime lead.[45]

Baltimore quickly scored two touchdowns to put the Bills in a hole. A 70-yard drive was capped with an eight-yard run by fullback Bus Mertes. He scored again a few minutes later on an 87-yard run from scrimmage and Baltimore had a 17–7 lead going into the fourth quarter. Buffalo had little time to find their offense and Ratterman took charge. Facing fourth-and-three on his 27-yard line, Ratterman waved off punter Jim Still and put the season on the line. Mutryn got the call and went off tackle for a six-yard gain and a first down. Ratterman then tossed a 66-yard scoring pass to halfback Bill Gompers to keep Buffalo alive. They were still down 17–14, but Buffalo had new life.[46] Gompers recalled that moment: "That was my only claim to fame. George Ratterman called a play. A pass play. I was there to block and I saw a hole on the side of the field, wide open. There was only one guy there with the linebackers. I came back into the huddle and thought to myself, 'You're a rookie. What the hell are you doing here?' I called to George, 'I apologize for talking, but please call the same play with me on the right side of it.' He did and it went for 65 yards, or something like that. We got back into the game and ended up beating them. It was the only time I ever talked in the huddle."[47]

At that point, things became a little strange. With about five minutes remaining in the game and in the midst of a Buffalo offensive drive, a Ratterman pass to Mutryn was dropped by the halfback at midfield. Baltimore guard Dub Garrett fell on the ball, where he apparently recovered a fumble for Baltimore. Head Linesman Fay Vincent—father of former Major League Baseball Commissioner Fay Vincent—ruled that the pass was incomplete, because Mutryn did not have possession and control of the ball. Baltimore obviously disagreed and argued that he had control and lost possession. The ball was given back to Buffalo and they continued the drive. After about a minute of play, Ratterman tossed the ball to Baldwin for a 25-yard touchdown and a 21–17 lead. The ruling by the head linesman gave the momentum to Buffalo and Baltimore struggled. Baltimore was desperate. With under three minutes to play, Tittle opened up an aerial assault in an attempt to move the Colts downfield. That ended quickly as fullback Ed Hirsch intercepted a Tittle pass on the Colt 18-yard line and returned it for the final score of the game. The Bills won 28–17 and faced the Cleveland Browns for the 1948 AAFC Championship.[48]

Bills back Alex Wizbicki recalled that it was the defense that made the difference from the previous week. "We put in special defenses. Special defensive maneuvers that were put in because of certain things they were doing. They revealed certain weaknesses, so we had a special defense set up for that particular game."[49] He commented further on the defensive schemes, "We used a defense where we had five man up fronts, three behind them. A 5–3–3. The linemen would go one way and the linebackers would go the other way in rushing into the line. So that, in itself, created confusion on the part of Baltimore."[50]

In spite of the defensive strategy changes, Baltimore still racked up an impressive 394 yards of total offense in the game, compared to Buffalo's 297 yards. Since Buffalo only had five offensive plays in the third quarter, it stood to reason that Baltimore had an easy victory. However, the pivotal point in the game was the referee call to give the ball back to Buffalo after an apparent fumble. Did Mutryn fumble or was it the correct call? Because of what happened on the field, the Baltimore fans were irate. Since Baltimore had a 17–14 lead and possession of the ball, the fans felt that their team could run out the clock or score again to put the game out of reach. In their opinion, bad officiating cost their team the game and the fans stormed the officiating crew. According to one report, "Numerous Colts fans, angered over penalties that had nullified some long gains, stormed the field and attacked the officiating crew. The officials were pummeled and sideline judge Thomas Whelan suffered a black eye before police could disperse the crowd."[51] Police and players from both teams held off the crowd to protect the officials. When asked about his memories of the incident, Bills' end Zeke O'Connor recalled, "Oh, yes. I do remember it. My family had come up from New York. The crowd got so unruly that I never got a chance to say 'Hello' to my dad or brother, who came, because they rushed us in and out to a bus so that we wouldn't be involved in any of the mêlée."[52]

The Cleveland Browns were still on their winning streak when they met up with the Bills in the AAFC Championship Game. At that point, the Browns were looking for their 15th victory of the season, 18th over two seasons and the 24th game without a defeat; an impressive feat by anyone's standards. With a win over Buffalo, the Browns would become the first team in professional football history to go undefeated throughout the regular season and playoffs and also become the first team to win three consecutive league championships. A lot was on the line for the Browns and by no means did they take the Bills lightly. Even though Buffalo failed to make their previous meetings competitive, Paul Brown did not allow anything less than perfection with his team, regardless of who they played.

Almost twenty-three thousand people weathered the 35-degree temperatures and snow-lined field to see these two teams meet. It took until the latter part of the first quarter, but Cleveland got on the board first. Defensive back Tommy James intercepted a Ratterman pass and returned it to the Buffalo 20-yard line. A few plays later, fullback Marion Motley drove the ball in from the three-yard line. Cleveland scored again in the second quarter, when defensive end George Young picked up a Rex Bumgardner fumble on the Buffalo 18-yard line and ran it in for the touchdown. The Bills were now down 14–0, but were still in the game. Halfback Don Schneider took the kickoff and returned it to the Buffalo 37-yard line. The Bills pushed downfield, driving to Cleveland's seven-yard line. Here, Buffalo had a first down and four opportunities to score. Continued efforts on the part of the Bills proved fruitless as the Browns repelled all Buffalo attacks. Ratterman dropped back to pass and was sacked by defensive end John Yonakor for a twelve-yard loss, ending the drive. The half came to a close with Buffalo down by two touchdowns.[53]

Ratterman left the game in the third quarter when he injured his shoulder and was replaced by Jim Still. When it looked like the Bills were stopped, Cleveland was charged with roughing the kicker and Buffalo continued their drive. When they got to the Cleveland ten-yard line, Still dropped back to pass and tossed a dart into the end zone. End Alton Baldwin made a miraculous finger-tip catch to secure the ball and the touchdown. At that point, the Bills were down 28–7 and hoped that this spark was enough to generate more offense. Unfortunately for Buffalo, Cleveland increased the pressure and scored two more times in the fourth quarter to build a 42–7 lead. Linebacker Lou Saban intercepted a Jim Still pass and returned it 39 yards for a score and the victory. This was the first time that Saban scored in his professional career.[54]

Fullback Marion Motley was the workhorse of the day, grinding out 133 yards on fourteen carries with three touchdowns to his credit. Bills' center Art Statuto recalled, "We were concentrating on Lavelli, Speedie and the two halfbacks and we forgot the guy by the name of Motley. He seemed to run wild the second half. If it wasn't for the stadium being enclosed, he'd still be running."[55] Statuto continued, "That's just the Browns. With Paul Brown and his coaching staff, they were able to pick out the flaws in our defense and our offense, and just picked us apart. With their guards in and out of every offensive play, they were aware of what was going on. Instead of the signals that they have today, it was done automatically from the sideline. We just weren't ready for that. We couldn't adjust our defense to their offense."[56]

As one can tell from the score, Buffalo's offense had a rough day. Their three fumbles were eclipsed by five interceptions. Ratterman threw three of the interceptions, with Jim Still tossing the final two. The roughing penalty in the third quarter was one of only two scoring opportunities for Buffalo. They were able to drive to the Cleveland seven-yard line in the second quarter, but they came away with no points.[57]

The Cleveland Browns captured their third straight title with the 49–7 victory. More importantly, they became the first team to finish the regular season undefeated and win a championship game. The previous two attempts were by the Chicago Bears. In 1934, the Bears went 13–0 in the regular season, but lost 30–13 to the New York Giants in the championship game. The Bears again went undefeated in 1942, racking up a regular season record of 11–0. Again, they lost in the championship game. That time, it was a 14–6 defeat to the Washington Redskins. At the time of the publishing of this book, only the 1972 Miami Dolphins have accomplished the same feat as the Browns.

* * *

As 1948 came to a close, merger talks between the All-America Football Conference and the National Football League became more serious. In a 14-hour secret meeting between owners, no agreement was produced; however, it became more apparent that a merger would eventually take place. The major sticking point at that meeting was raised by Washington Redskins owner George Preston Marshall. He opposed any merger that included the Baltimore Colts, as they infringed on his 75-mile territorial rights. He wanted Baltimore to pay $250,000 in order to agree to the merger. Any merger required unanimous consent of all of the owners, so resolution of this issue was paramount.[58]

On December 20, AAFC officials[59] met with NFL officials to discuss mutual concerns and attempted to end the war between the leagues. Again, no permanent solution was reached, but that marked the first time that the NFL publicly recognized the AAFC. Since April 20, 1945, the AAFC worked to obtain mutual agreements with the NFL to ensure the stability and solvency of major league football. After all of that time, the NFL finally relented, knowing that it was necessary for the survival of their league. Salaries took off and teams of both leagues needed to find a solution.

7
Clem Crowe Takes Over

With the 1948 season finished and Cleveland taking home yet another title, the franchises looked toward the annual draft. The 1949 draft was slightly different from the previous AAFC drafts in that a secret two-round draft was held before the 1948 season. The purpose of holding this draft was to allow AAFC clubs to get a jump on their NFL counterparts.

1949 BUFFALO BILLS DRAFT RESULTS (SECRET) (JULY 8, 1948)

Rd / (Overall)	Player	Position	College
1 (1)	Abe Gibron	G	Purdue, Valparaiso
2 (7)	Frank Tripucka	QB	Notre Dame

Of this secret draft, only Abe Gibron played for the Bills. The 5'11", 250-pound Abe Gibron lettered two years while at Purdue. He was unusually large and fast for a guard and his agility made him an asset to the Buffalo line. It should also be noted that Gibron was selected by the New York Giants in the 1949 NFL draft (sixth round).

Francis Joseph Tripucka was a 6'2", 192-pound quarterback out of Notre Dame. He was also drafted by the Philadelphia Eagles in 1949 (first round), but elected to play for the Detroit Lions that year. From 1950 through 1951, Tripucka played for the Chicago Cardinals and in 1952 he split time between the Cardinals and the Dallas Texans. He finished his career by playing for the Denver Broncos from 1960 through 1963. Tripucka was named All-Pro in 1962.

The regular AAFC draft was held in December of 1948. Since Buffalo and Baltimore tied at the end of the season, the playoff game between them was used to determine the draft order. This made the order Baltimore (7–8), Los Angeles (7–7) and then Buffalo (8–7). The rest of the draft order was clear, but as in other drafts, each round was different. All teams had a selection in the first round. Chicago, New York and Baltimore selected in the second round, while Brooklyn selected in the third round. Each team had selections from the fourth round through the 16th round. All teams, except Cleveland and San Francisco, had picks in rounds 17 through 21. Chicago, Brooklyn and New York selected in rounds 22 through 24. Every team selected in the 25th round and all teams, except for Chicago, Brooklyn and New York selected in rounds 26 through 29.

1949 BUFFALO BILLS DRAFT RESULTS (DECEMBER 21, 1948)

Rd / (Overall)	Player	Position	College
1 (6)	Bill Kay	T	Iowa
3 (15)	Hugh Keeney*	B	Rice
3 (19)	Vito Kissell	LB-FB	Holy Cross
4 (27)	Wilbur Volz	HB-DB	Missouri
5 (35)	Frank Gaul	T	Notre Dame
6 (43)	Frank Guess	B	Texas
7 (51)	Harold Ensminger	QB	Missouri
8 (59)	Vic Vasicek	LB-G-DG	Texas, USC
9 (67)	Alex Verdova	B	Ohio State
10 (75)	Al Russas	T-DE	Tennessee
11 (83)	Ernie Settembre	T	Miami
12 (91)	Milt Kormonicki	C	Villanova
13 (99)	Butch Songin	QB	Boston College
14 (107)	Leon Cooper	T	Hardin-Simmons
15 (115)	Clayton Tonnemaker	LB-C	Minnesota
16 (123)	Rob Goode	B	Texas A&M
17 (131)	Art Donovan	DT-T	Boston College, Notre Dame
18 (137)	Jim Goodman	T	Maryland
19 (143)	Merlin London	E	Oklahoma State
20 (149)	Marty Breen	C	Canisius
21 (155)	John Simon	G	Penn State
25 (170)	Bernie Hanula	T	Wake Forest
26 (175)	Bobby Deuber	B	Pennsylvania
27 (180)	Floyd Lewis	G	SMU
28 (185)	Tom Cochran	B	Auburn
29 (190)	Joe Leonard	T	Virginia

* From the Chicago Hornets

As had been seen the previous two seasons, not all draft picks decided to play for the Bills or even play professional football:

Francis Edward (Frank) Gaul was a 6'0", 200-pound tackle from Notre Dame who was drafted by the New York Bulldogs in the 20th round of the 1949 NFL draft and played one year for the Bulldogs. He declined to play for Buffalo.

Tennessee tackle/defensive end Alfred Victor Russas was drafted by the Detroit Lions (13th round), as well as the Bills. The 6'2", 210-pound Russas played for the Lions in 1949 before retiring from professional football.

Edward Frank (Butch) Songin was drafted by the Cleveland Browns in 1950 (19th round), but did not play major-league professional football until 1960. Joining the upstart American Football League, the 6'2", 190-pound Boston College quarterback played for the Boston Patriots from 1960 through 1961. He then joined the New York Titans for the 1962 season before retiring from football.

Frank Clayton Tonnemaker was drafted by the Green Bay Packers in 1950 (first round). The 6'2", 237-pound linebacker/center played with the Packers in 1950, 1953 and 1954; earning All-Pro honors each year. The Minnesota native was also elected to the Pro Bowl in 1953.

The 6'4", 222-pound Robert Leslie (Rob) Goode was drafted by the Washington Redskins in 1949 (first round). The Texas A&M back played with the Redskins from 1949 through 1954. In 1955, he split time between the Redskins and the Philadelphia Eagles. Goode earned two Pro Bowl berths (1951, 1954).

Arguably one of the best defensive tackles to play the game, Arthur James (Art) Donovan never had a chance to play for Buffalo as his professional career started after the Bills disbanded. The 6'2", 263-pound Donovan was drafted by the New York Giants in 1947 (22nd round), as well as Buffalo in 1948, but started his career with the Baltimore Colts in 1950. He went to the New York Yanks after Baltimore folded and followed the Yanks to Dallas in 1952. With the Texans folding after the 1952 season, Art was again without a home. The new version of the Baltimore Colts was formed and Donovan stayed for the next nine years. He finished his Hall of Fame career (Class of 1968) in 1963, making the Pro Bowl five times and gaining All-Pro honors six times.

Leon Thomas (Tom) Cochran was a 6'0", 209-pound fullback out of Auburn. The Bills were the only team that drafted him, but he decided to play for the Washington Redskins in 1949. He retired from football after only one year.

There are no records of Bill Kay, Hugh Keeney, Harold Ensminger, Alex Verdova, Ernie Settembre, Leon Cooker, Jim Goodman, Merlin London, Marty Breen, John Simon, Bobby Deuber, Floyd Lewis or Joe Leonard playing in a professional football game in either the AAFC or NFL.

* * *

The AAFC needed to make a change in order to stay viable, so rosters were cut from 35 to 32 players and the regular season schedule was reduced from 14 games to 12 games. Also, the Brooklyn Dodgers and the New York Yankees merged to form the Brooklyn-New York Dodgers-Yankees. With the Conference down to seven teams, the divisional format was eliminated. As a result, a new playoff system was adopted. In the first round, the first and fourth-place teams competed, while the second and third-place teams battled it out. The winners of each of those games faced each other for the championship.

The Chicago Rockets were in turmoil from the beginning. In what seemed like a yearly occurrence, the team was sold. The Chicago Rockets were purchased for $300,000 by James C. Thompson, owner of the Chicago Opera building. With this change, the Rockets were renamed the Hornets and were stocked with players from the former Brooklyn club. Six players from the orig-

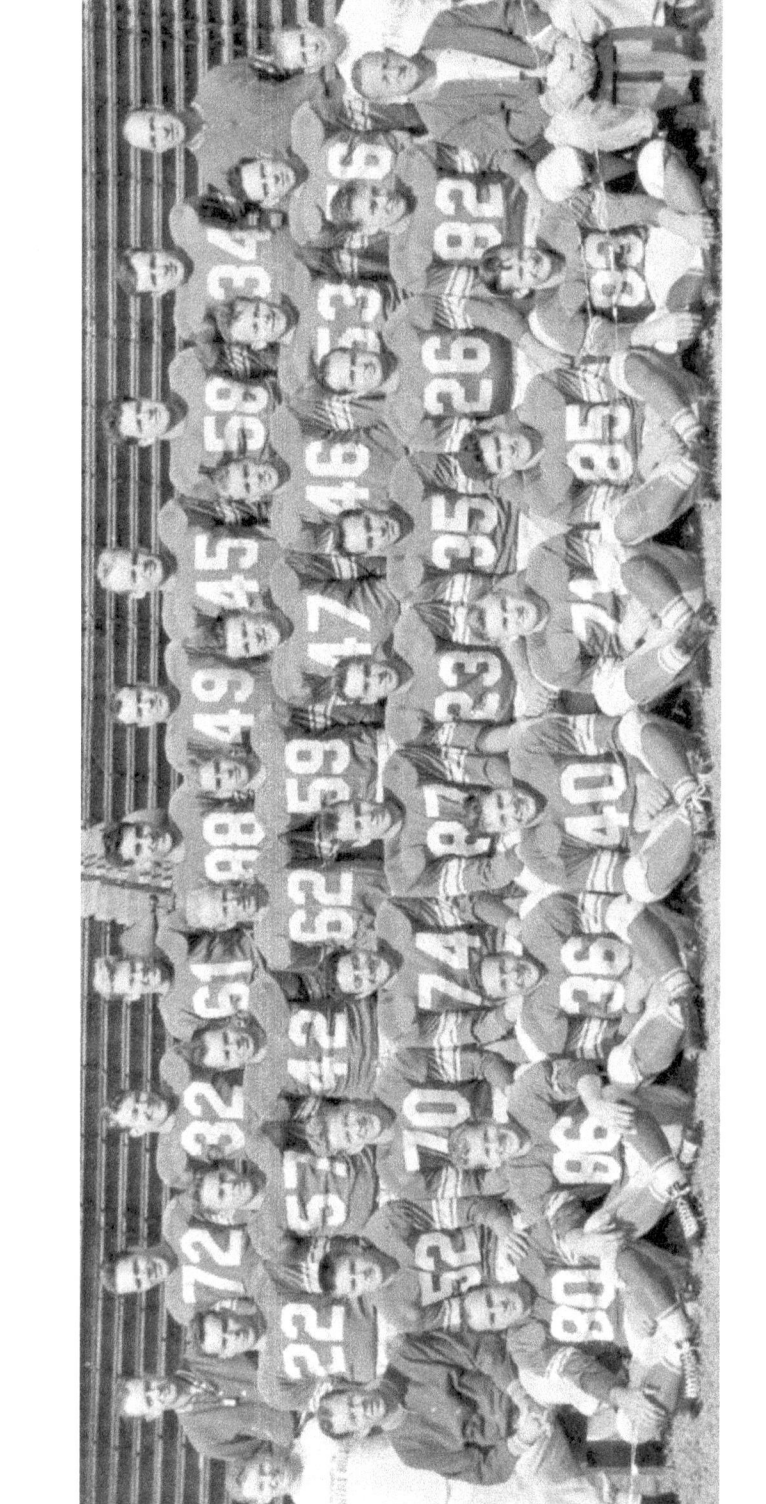

inal Brooklyn team went to the new Brooklyn–New York squad, while the remaining players were sent to Chicago. It was hoped that the influx of talent would help the struggling franchise.

In Conference news, Admiral Ingram resigned as commissioner and was replaced by Deputy Commissioner O.O. Kessing. According to Kessing, "I am not a rubber stamp. The rules will be strictly enforced. I firmly believe in the future of the Conference, and shall continue the policies of Admiral Ingram in protecting the best interests of the owners, the players, and the fans, and in guaranteeing the integrity of the game."[1] Dan Topping was elected vice-president of the Conference.

The major off-season move — or non-move — for Buffalo was Bills' owner Jim Breuil not renewing George Ratterman's contract. As a result, Ratterman returned to Notre Dame and signed a contract to play with the NFL's New York Bulldogs in 1950. With Ratterman not starting the season with Buffalo, the Bills needed to find another signal caller, so they picked up Jesse Freitas from Chicago. Freitas started his pro career with the San Francisco 49ers, but left after the 1947 season to play for the Rockets. With Frankie Albert on the 49ers roster, Freitas was expendable. Freitas recalled the situation that lead to his arrival in Buffalo, "Each year the Chicago team would go broke and new owners would come on. The year I was with them, they hired a new coach [Ray] Flaherty, who was a single-wing coach. Of course, I played single-wing in college, but they wanted a new look. I guess they weren't interested, so they traded me to Buffalo for a draft choice."[2] Freitas and Jim Still battled it out for the starting quarterback job.

Another off-season move for Buffalo was the acquisition of Tommy Colella. A Buffalo native and Canisius star, the "Albion Antelope" won three championships with the Cleveland Browns. Colella was one of those rare players who played for his hometown team in high school, college and professionally. He excelled in all facets of the game, especially on defense, and was a welcome addition to the Buffalo Bills squad.

In their first preseason game, the Bills crushed the Jersey City Giants 79–0 at Civic Stadium. The Giants were members of the American Football League and were a farm team for the New York Giants. By halftime, Buffalo was up 47–0 and did not let up. Jersey City was only able to generate two first downs and twelve yards of total offense. Joe Sutton, halfback from Temple, scored four touchdowns in the contest.[3] "I was contacted by Hank Reese, a scout for

Opposite page: 1949 Buffalo Bills. *Front row:* Larry Joe, Joe Sutton, Ed "Buckets" Hirsch, Abe Gibron, Vito Kissell, Alex Wizbicki, Chet Mutryn. *Second row:* Joel Hunt, Paul Gibson, Ollie Cline, Lou Tomasetti, Wilbur Volz, Chuck Schuette, Rocco Pirro, Hal Herring, Rex Bumgardner, Clem Crowe (Coach). *Third row:* Bobby Brown, Art Statuto, Al Baldwin, Chet Adams, Jim Still, Jim Lukens, John Kissell, Jack Kerns, Bill Stanton, Bob Oristaglio, Tony DiToma. *Fourth row:* Red Dawson (Coach), Bill Schroll, Odell Stautzenberger, George Ratterman, Tommy Colella, John Maskas, Jack Carpenter, Vince Mazza, Vic Vasicek, Hank Reese.

Buffalo, and asked if I would like to try out for the Bills," recalled Sutton. "I had a fairly good training camp, but I think I was on the cut list for Monday morning. We played the Jersey City Giants that weekend and that made the difference."[4] Sutton made the squad.

The Bills faced the Baltimore Colts in the next preseason contest. Before the game with Baltimore, the Bills cut former Wake Forest lineman Bernie Hanula and Rice Institute end Nick Lanza, while guard Bucky O'Connor and back Eddie Conwell were nursing injuries and did not make the trip to Wilmington for the game.[5]

The Bills scored first, going 99 yards on seven plays as Jim Still tossed a pass to Alton Baldwin to finish the drive. Baltimore answered with a Y.A. Tittle pass to Lu Gambino. The Colts racked up another three scores before Buffalo crossed the line again. It was too late, however, and Buffalo lost 28–12.[6] The Bills were 1–1 in the preseason as they faced the San Francisco 49ers.

Buffalo struggled against the 49ers. The Bills had only one pass completion and it came six plays from the end of the game. The Buffalo line held, but Jim Still made bad throws and bad decisions. However, the ground game was another story. West Virginia back Rex Bumgardner carried the ball nine times for an astounding 15.1 yards per carry average. Even with the passing difficulties, Buffalo was still able to go into the half with a 10–7 lead. It was all San Francisco in the second half, however. Touchdowns by Eddie Car and Len Eshmont sealed the 21–10 victory for the 49ers and the Bills needed to evaluate their quarterback situation. Jim Still was not getting the job done. Coach Red Dawson kept the locker room doors closed to the media after the game. Obviously disappointed in Still's performance, the team missed George Ratterman.[7]

For the second time in the 1949 exhibition season, the Bills played an American Football League team. This time, the Bethlehem Bulldogs were the victims. As with the game against the Jersey City Giants, the contest was not even close. Buffalo built a 42–0 halftime lead before taking it easy on the weaker team. Bethlehem left Civic Stadium with a 48–0 defeat and Buffalo headed into the regular season with a 2–2 preseason record.[8] What was misleading about the record was that both wins were against minor-league teams. When the Bills faced AAFC talent, they lost.

Buffalo was the Eastern Division champion of 1948. The Chicago Hornets (formerly the Chicago Rockets) went 1–13 the previous season. On paper, this should have been an easy game for the Bills. However, Chicago proved to be a tougher opponent than anticipated. The influx of talent from the defunct Brooklyn Dodgers during the off-season made a difference and Chicago was a new team.

In the first quarter, Chicago started an offensive drive after Chet Adams missed a field goal attempt. Quarterback Bob Hoernschemeyer tossed a pass to end Don Edwards, who streaked to the Buffalo 45-yard line before attempting to lateral to a teammate. The lateral was off target and the Bills recovered the pigskin. Six plays later, end Alton Baldwin caught a Jim Still pass for a score and the Bills were up 7–0.[9]

Chicago partially blocked a Still punt midway through the second quarter and the Hornets recovered the ball on the Buffalo 37-yard line. On the next play, Hoernschemeyer flipped the ball to back Ray Ramsey in the flat. Set up by excellent blocks, Ramsey outran Buffalo defenders to tie the score at 7–7. The Hornets scored again as former Pittsburgh Steeler back Johnny Clement passed to back Paul Patterson for a 35-yard touchdown strike and Chicago went into halftime with a 14–7 lead.[10]

Turnovers plagued both teams in the fourth quarter. A fumble by Ray Ramsey and an interception of a Jesse Freitas pass gave each team the opportunity to capitalize on mistakes, but neither could make headway. A blocked Chicago punt set up Buffalo for their best drive of the half. Five plays pushed the Bills 25 yards and into scoring position. Mutryn broke through the line for a 13-yard scoring run to tie the game 14–14. In the closing minutes of the contest, Freitas tossed another interception to give Chicago the ball on the Buffalo 18-yard line. The Bills' defense held strong — only giving up three yards — but the Hornets easily kicked a field goal. Buffalo did have a field goal attempt late in the game, but it was blocked. Chicago picked up the upset 17–14 victory and the Bills were 0–1 for the regular season.[11]

The Chicago defense stepped up and was strong the entire game. Their aerial assault provided two touchdowns, while Buffalo's passing attack was poor at best. Freitas' two interceptions were a low point, with one of them being extremely costly. The Bills missed Ratterman. Buffalo's defense, however recovered four fumbles. Again, the offense let the team down as they were only able to capitalize on one of the recoveries.

After the game, Freitas was released by coach Red Dawson. Freitas recalled the situation, "Still started the game, but he wasn't doing much. So I came in and I don't remember if we were ahead or was tied. It's been a long time ago.... I threw an interception and they ended up kicking a field goal to win the game."[12]

The Bills needed Ratterman in the lineup, so owner Jim Breuil went to South Bend to get him under contract. After receiving permission from the New York Bulldogs, Breuil signed Ratterman to a one-year contract and the Bills once again had their field general.[13]

The Cleveland Browns had been a thorn in the side of the Bills since the beginning. Buffalo just could not find a way to win against the powerhouse Browns in their seven previous meetings.

Cleveland got on the board first with a 68-yard drive that ended with a twelve-yard strike from Otto Graham to Edgar 'Special Delivery' Jones. After that drive, the Browns started to fall apart. Graham's passing was less than stellar and the team could not hold on to the ball. Horace Gillom — subbing for Dante Lavelli — was the first to fall victim. In the second quarter, the Browns were in punt formation when the ball was passed to Gillom. He dropped the pass, but was able to recover and tried running around left end. He failed to make a first down and the Bills took over on the Cleveland 32-yard line. Ollie Cline was a man possessed and took the ball over from the seven-yard line for the first Bills score to tie the game at 7–7. It was now halftime and the Bills were holding their own.[14]

Bill Boedeker fumbled the opening kickoff of the second half, but was able to recover. He fumbled on the next play, as well, and Chet Adams recovered. Adams rumbled into the end zone, but fumbled and Joe Sutton fell on the ball for the Bills. They started their drive from the Cleveland four-yard line. After three plays, Ratterman took the ball over from the one-yard line and the Bills were on top 14–7. The Bills put two more scores on the board in the third quarter to take a 28–7 lead. The Browns were reeling and the Bills capitalized on Cleveland's mistakes. At that point, Otto Graham changed tactics and went for short completions instead of the long ball. It turned the tide and the Browns saw success, driving for two quick touchdowns to make the score 28–21 in favor of the Bills. The Browns made fewer mistakes and this hurt the Bills as their offensive attack was not powerful enough to stay even with the Browns. They needed help in the form of turnovers, which is how the Bills were able to put up 28 points on the visitors.[15]

Could the Bills hold off the defending champions? At that point, the Browns were down by seven points with two minutes to play and the ball on the Buffalo 38-yard line. Graham had played miserably the first three quarters, but he was on fire in the final period. He took the snap and dropped back to pass as Gillom went deep into Buffalo territory. Amid triple coverage, Graham tossed a laser to Gillom, who grabbed it on the Bills two-yard line. There was a minute-and-a-half left in the game and Cleveland had four remaining tries for a score. Graham dropped back to pass and tossed an errant throw toward Mac Speedie. Speedie, on his knees in the goal, snared the ball inches above the turf for the score. With Lou Groza out with a pulled muscle, Lou Saban was responsible for the tying kick, which was good and the game ended in a 28–28 tie. For the first time in twenty-one games, the Cleveland Browns failed to win. They still, however, had an unbeaten streak at 25 games. After the contest, Jim Breuil was quoted as saying, "No, no, no! It can't be! We were 21 points ahead!"[16] For the eighth time in eight tries, the Bills failed to beat the Cleveland Browns. This was a devastating tie and not the way the Bills wanted to start the 1949 season. According to Bills center Art Statuto, "We hadn't beat Cleveland in two seasons. I think the closest we came was we had a 28–28 tie that shouldn't have been a tie. We were ahead 28–7. Graham, Speedie and Lavelli decided they weren't going to take that. We tried to get up in the game, but Cleveland at the time, as they proved in the NFL, they were a team to be reckoned with. They had the personnel. They had the coaching ability to do what they did accomplish."[17] The Bills were now 0–1–1 for the season.

Feeling confident — albeit disappointed — with their tie against the

7—Clem Crowe Takes Over

Game Program from September 25, 1949: San Francisco 49ers vs. Buffalo Bills. The Bills won the game 28–17.

Browns, the Bills faced the Brooklyn-New York Dodgers-Yankees.[18] Hitting his first three passes, Ratterman engineered a 68-yard drive to put the first points on the board for Buffalo. Within a few minutes, the Bills scored again when end Alton Baldwin snared a 23-yard strike from Ratterman. In less than seven minutes, Buffalo had amassed a 14–0 lead over New York.[19]

The Yankees' offense did not give up and their defense came up big. Center Frank Perantoni knocked a Ratterman pass to a waiting Martin Ruby on the Buffalo four-yard line. Ruby then stumbled into the end zone to cut the deficit to 14–7. In the fourth quarter, New York put together an impressive offensive drive, which started when quarterback Don Panciera tossed a 35-yard pass to halfback Tom Landry (future Hall of Fame coach for the Dallas Cowboys). Halfback Buddy Young and fullback Lowell Tew combined to drive the ball to the Buffalo 39-yard line where a pass to Young set up the final run by Tew for the tying score. Memories of the Cleveland Browns game the previous week started to fill the heads of the Buffalo players, as their commanding lead evaporated.[20]

The Bills had a final chance to regain the lead after an errant field goal attempt by the Yankees. Going for it on fourth-and-three in New York territory, the Bills converted. They attempted to convert another fourth down around midfield, but failed and the Yankees took over on downs. New York drove down to the Buffalo six-yard line on runs by fullback Lou Kusserow and Young. Harvey Johnson made good on his field goal attempt and New York had a 17–14 victory.[21]

The Bills again built a lead against their opponent only to let it slip through their fingers. The Buffalo defense stopped several Yankee charges deep into Bills territory, but the offense could not put together consistent drives. With a record of 0–2–1, the Bills were falling behind the division leaders and faced the undefeated San Francisco 49ers.

San Francisco scored first on a 23-yard field goal by Joe Vetrano. Taking the next drive 80 yards, Ratterman heaved a 39-yard pass to halfback Rex Bumgardner to take a 7–3 lead. Ratterman connected with end Alton Baldwin twice on the subsequent drive to build a 14–3 halftime lead.[22]

The Bills offense continued to dominate as Buffalo plodded 69 yards for their third straight touchdown and a commanding 21–3 lead. San Francisco, however, refused to collapse. Fullback Joe Perry caught a Frankie Albert pass in the flat, turned up field and scored. This reduced Buffalo's lead to 21–10. Bills halfback Chet Mutryn fumbled and San Francisco was back in action as defensive back Eddie Carr recovered the ball and darted into the end zone. San Francisco now trailed by only four points. In the fourth quarter, Buffalo's offense was back and drove 78-yards for a 28–17 victory. The Bills had their first victory of the season and it could not come at a better time.[23] The Bills outgained the 49ers 445 yards to 230 yards. In the previous games, the defense was Buffalo's downfall, but in this game, both sides of the ball held their own to produce the victory.

After the game, San Francisco quarterback Frankie Albert was involved in an incident with a fan who attended the game. The fan called out to "The Great Frankie Albert,"[24] which instigated the confrontation. Albert allegedly punched the fan in the cheek before 49er tackle Bob Mike broke up the scuffle. Cooler heads prevailed and Buffalo general manager Jim Wells convinced the fan to drop legal action against Albert.[25]

7—Clem Crowe Takes Over

The Bills opened October with a game against the Baltimore Colts. The Colts were winless in their first five games and the Bills had momentum after their victory over the 49ers. Trailing 21–14 going into the fourth quarter, the Bills drove 66 yards to tie the score. Baltimore answered with a 77-yard pass from Y.A. Tittle to end John North. North caught Tittle's pass on the Bills' 45-yard line, turned up field and outran defensive back Joe Sutton for the score. Not giving up, Ratterman tossed a 34-yard pass to end Alton Baldwin to again tie the score. With 24 seconds remaining in the game, Tittle flung a 52-yard strike to halfback Billy Stone for a touchdown and the 35–28 victory. Baltimore picked up their first victory of the season and Buffalo fell to 1-3-1. On the plus side for the Bills, they registered 23 first downs in the game, which tied a record set by the Cleveland Browns.[26] However, Buffalo again had a defensive letdown.

For the first time in 30 games, the Cleveland Browns lost. Falling 56–28 to the San Francisco 49ers, Cleveland registered their first defeat since October 12, 1947. Practically two years had elapsed since the Browns lost to the Los Angeles Dons 13–10.

The 1-3-1 Buffalo Bills faced the same Los Angeles Dons on October 9. Both teams had the ability to put points on the board, but failed to be victorious for one reason or another (Los Angeles was 1-4 for the season). What the more than sixteen thousand fans on hand did not expect was an offensive battle between Ratterman and his Los Angeles counterpart Glenn Dobbs that was one for the ages. Ratterman hit first less than two minutes into the game, when he engineered a drive that was capped by an Ollie Cline run for a touchdown. Both teams scored in the first quarter to give Buffalo a 14–7 advantage going into the second quarter.[27]

It was a wild second quarter and Glenn Dobbs stole the show. Within three minutes, the ex–Tulsa star engineered 66 and 65-yard scoring drives to take a 21–14 lead. Four of Dobbs' passes combined for 110 yards and two touchdowns. Not to be outdone, Ratterman came back to construct two scoring drives of his own to retake the lead 28–21. Before the half, Dobbs tossed a 32-yard strike to end Dick Wilkins to tie the score. In total, there were five touchdowns scored, which generated three lead changes in the second quarter alone.[28]

The Dons regained the lead in the third quarter and never looked back. Buffalo attempted several drives to tie the game, but were broken when halfback Joe Sutton fumbled on their 30-yard line and Wilkins recovered to score. The Dons won 42–28.[29]

To give an idea of the offensive display put on by both Dobbs and his Don teammates, Los Angeles needed a mere 20 plays to go from a 14–7 deficit to a 35–28 lead. With scoring drives of 66 yards, 65 yards, 80 yards and 38 yards, the Dons averaged over twelve yards per play. The Bills were snake-bit.

After the game, it was announced that Bills' owner Jim Breuil requested and accepted head Coach Red Dawson's resignation. According to Dawson, "We just could not agree."[30] Assistant Clem Crowe was promoted to head coach for the remainder of the season. Dawson compiled a 20–26–4 record in three-plus seasons with Buffalo, including a 1–4–1 record in 1949.

Clem Crowe, Bills assistant coach from 1946 through 1949 and head coach in 1949.

Players were stunned at the move, but not all were unhappy. According to halfback Joe Sutton, "Red Dawson was hard to play for as he didn't communicate very well with the players and you never knew where you stood with him."[31] Commenting on Clem Crowe, Sutton added, "Clem Crowe was the exact opposite, but he could never seem to get the team started."[32] Halfback Chet Mutryn added, "Red Dawson was a bit of a curmudgeon, and didn't know how to communicate with the players."[33] However, not all players had a negative opinion of Dawson. Asked whether Dawson should have been fired, Bills' back Alex Wizbicki replied, "No. It was a conflict between management and Red Dawson. To be honest with you, a lot of us were shocked at the firing of Red Dawson. We knew how we did with Red. What type of coach he was. His replacement wasn't what we called an improved replacement. They told us the front office disagreed on some policies. They held the upper hand and he was released, much to our surprise.... We, as a team, thought we lost a very capable coach."[34]

Bills' center Art Statuto recalled the first night after Dawson's firing: "It was a complete surprise to us. That happened when we were in Los Angeles. We were at the Green Hotel in Pasadena. This is another night that you don't really forget. We found out that Red had been let go and the Browns had come down from San Francisco. Paul Brown had put them all in a train and came down to Pasadena. Down to the Green Hotel. Frankie Albert had taken apart the Browns that afternoon. He beat them 56–28. He scored touchdowns against every defensive position, both backfield and line and of course Brown was fit to be tied. That night, we were falling over what we would do losing a coach and they were just losing, period. Lou Saban, around ten o'clock, said, 'Let's get back to the hotel. Brown is going to be mad and you don't know what is going to happen.' He was talking to all of us."[35]

The Bills were the only team to beat the 5–1 San Francisco 49ers, which also happened to be Buffalo's sole victory of the season. The 49ers had a statement to make in order to prove that they belong as an elite team in the Conference. To do that, they needed to beat the lesser teams. On the other hand, the Bills needed to prove that they were not as bad as their record indicated.

7—Clem Crowe Takes Over 97

Something had to give. Unfortunately for the Bills, the 49ers were better prepared. Other than Joe Sutton's touchdown in the first quarter, the Bills' offense failed to gain traction. In the second quarter, the Bills did not advance beyond their own 29-yard line. San Francisco's offense, however, never stopped. Racking up scores in every quarter and putting a staggering 37 points on the board in the first half, the 49ers made their statement.[36] The 51–7 defeat dropped the Bills to 1–5–1 and they were in serious trouble. Clem Crowe needed to stop the bleeding and get his team in order.

Putting aside their drubbing from the previous week at the hands of San Francisco, the 1–5–1 Bills came home for a rematch with the 2–5 Los Angeles Dons. Buffalo lost 42–28 to the Dons two weeks prior and needed to right the ship. Focusing on their ground game, Buffalo took their opening drive for a touchdown and a 7–0 lead. Buffalo scored another touchdown and added a field goal to take a 17–0 halftime lead.[37]

The Bills' defense held firm the first 30 minutes, allowing the Dons only 35 yards in total offense, but it was the Los Angeles defense that kept them in the game. In the third quarter, back Paul Crowe recovered Vito Kissell's fumble and ran it 56 yards for a score. Holding the Bills' offense in check, Los Angeles regained possession and drove for another score as Buffalo's lead diminished to a mere three points. The Dons had a final drive late in the game, but time expired before they could score. The Bills gained a much needed victory (2–5–1 for the season) and their first under new head coach Clem Crowe.[38]

Rumors of a merger between the AAFC and NFL persisted. According to a *Chicago Sun-Times* report, a merger "is on the verge of being declared."[39] The report stated that, "An arrangement has been worked out by interested members of both leagues which will find only three members of the AAC surviving the merger—Cleveland, San Francisco and the New York Yankees."[40] The report went on to say that two sets of teams would merge: the Los Angeles Dons would merge with the Los Angeles Rams, and the New York Bulldogs would merge with the New York Giants. This would form a twelve-team league with Buffalo, the Chicago Hornets and the Baltimore Colts disappearing. Los Angeles Rams owner Dan Reeves contradicted the report. "So far as I know, there is not a bit of truth in the Chicago report of a merger between the two football leagues,"[41] said Reeves. He continued, "No overtures have been made in recent months, and I am inclined to believe that none will be made in the near future."[42]

The Yankees looked to win their sixth straight game and to secure a playoff berth, but they needed to beat the Bills. Striking quickly in the first quarter, New York put up a 14–0 lead over Buffalo. It appeared that New York attained that much needed victory, but with only two and a half minutes elapsed, plenty of time remained for Buffalo. Late in the first quarter, George Ratterman tossed a 16-yard touchdown pass to end Alton Baldwin and Buffalo still showed life as they were only down 14–7.[43]

The second and third quarters were uneventful as neither team gener-

The 1949 Buffalo Bills Backfield: Rex Bumgardner (#82), George Ratterman (#61), Ollie Cline (#70) and Chet Mutryn (#83).

ated much offense. Things picked up in the fourth quarter, as Buffalo tied the score on a 45-yard pass from Ratterman to halfback Rex Bumgardner. Chet Adams added a twelve-yard field goal to put the Bills on top for good and they sealed a 17–14 victory.[44]

The Bills' defense kept the team alive and New York's passing game struggled. However, the Yankee's ground game was solid. Generating 226 yards rushing was helpful, but the Yankees failed to deliver when it counted. Buffalo relied on their aerial attack, albeit with their own difficulties. Ratterman connected on several long throws, but struggled in the short passing game.[45]

The Bills' victory over the Yankees had definite playoff implications. Buffalo moved from sixth place to fifth place and the loss dropped New York to second place behind the Cleveland Browns. The top four teams were to make the playoffs, so Buffalo needed wins over Cleveland, Chicago and Baltimore, as well as help from other teams if they were to make the cut. The next game was crucial as Buffalo faced the powerful Cleveland Browns.

The Browns scored first, capitalizing on a Buffalo interception. Ratterman dropped back to pass on first down and tossed the ball to Ollie Cline. Unfortunately for Buffalo, it landed in the arms of Cleveland's Tony Adamle, who returned it to the Bills' 24-yard line. Otto Graham lobbed a 13-yard pass to Horace Gillom and then focused on the running game. Dub Jones gained seven yards on the ground, followed by a Marion Motley plunge for four yards. Graham finished the drive with a run from the one-yard line. The Browns now had a 7–0 lead and only two-and-a-half minutes of playing time had elapsed. That did not look good for Buffalo.[46]

The Bills put together another good drive, but it was halted on an interception. It was not until a Cleveland miscue before the Bills generated a decent offensive series. Tommy Colella punted to Cliff Lewis. He called for a fair catch, but lost control of the rain-soaked pigskin and Odell Stautzenberger fell on it at the Cleveland 44-yard line to give Buffalo possession. Steadily, Buffalo pushed downfield and capped their nine-play drive with a four-yard run by Chet Mutryn. The game was tied 7–7.[47]

Cleveland and Buffalo battled for the remainder of the contest, with little to show for their efforts. Cleveland was able to drive down to the Buffalo four-yard line, but failed to put any points on the board. Buffalo tried a couple of field goal attempts, but failed to convert any of them. Late in the fourth quarter, Cleveland again drove deep into Buffalo territory, but Ollie Cline fumbled and Derrell Palmer recovered the ball on the Buffalo 32-yard line. The Browns then ran off five minutes of game clock, executed twelve plays and gained two first downs, but saw their team lose a total of six yards on the drive. Then, they started to move in the forward direction and drove to the Buffalo 13-yard line. Again, the Browns moved backwards and faced a fourth down situation from the Buffalo 45-yard line. Lou Groza stepped up to kick a field goal, but the kick went short and wide of the uprights. The game ended in a 7–7 tie. Buffalo was the first team to go through a regular season and not lose to the Browns.[48]

Weather was definitely a factor in the outcome of the game. Rain steadily fell throughout the contest, with the precipitation getting harder in the second half, which contributed to the lack of scoring. Statistically, the teams were matched. Buffalo gained 240 yards to Cleveland's 290 yards. Cleveland also had a slight edge in first downs 15–14. The 3–5–2 Bills closed in on fourth place within the Conference, while Cleveland still held on to first place. The next few weeks were critical.

The Buffalo Bills faced the 4–6 Chicago Hornets on November 20. The Hornets—perennial cellar-dwellers while named the Rockets—were in position for a playoff berth. A win over the Bills put them on solid standing for a post-season spot, but still needed help. Even with a victory over the Hornets, Buffalo still needed the 4–7 Los Angeles Dons (who beat the Baltimore Colts 21–10 later that day) to lose in their final game against the Yankees.

The field was ugly, as there had been snow and rain for a couple of days leading up to the game and the field was not covered. Thick, heavy mud was the result. Consequently, both offenses struggled. Halfback Bob Livingstone faced his former team for the first time. The former Notre Dame back played for the Rockets in 1948 and part of 1949, but he was cut about a month prior to the game and picked up by the Bills. His presence was felt in the second quarter, when he received a Chicago punt on the Buffalo 22-yard line. Livingstone broke through Hornet tacklers and darted into the end zone to give Buffalo a 7–0 lead.[49]

In the closing minutes of the second quarter, defensive back Paul Patterson intercepted a Ratterman pass and returned it to the Bills' eight-yard line. Chicago pushed their way to the one-yard line, when Johnny Clement dove over the pile. Witnesses claimed that Clement crossed the goal line, but referees disagreed and the Hornets came away empty-handed. The Bills added a Chet Adams field goal in the fourth quarter to seal the 10–0 victory.[50]

As mentioned previously, field conditions determined the outcome of the game as the thick mud prevented either team from gaining ground. In the process, several dubious records were established: Fewest Passes Attempted (Buffalo, 4), Fewest Passes Completed (Buffalo, 1), Fewest Pass Attempts per Game (6) and the Lowest Total Yards (75).[51]

With this win and Los Angeles' loss to Baltimore, the Bills moved into a tie with the Dons for fourth place and the final playoff spot. While Chicago was not officially eliminated, they were in a tough predicament. They needed both Buffalo and Los Angeles to lose, while also defeating the Cleveland Browns to secure the final berth. Everything rested on the final week of the season.

The Bills received a present on Thanksgiving Day, a full three days before their meeting with Baltimore: The Los Angeles Dons lost 17–16 to the Yankees and Chicago lost 14–6 to the Browns. A win or a tie against the Colts put the Bills in the playoffs. Already guaranteed postseason games were Cleveland, San Francisco and New York. The Yankees traveled to San Francisco for the first playoff round, while Cleveland awaited the results of the Bills game to determine if they hosted Los Angeles or Buffalo.

Even with a 1–10 record, the Colts were still a dangerous team for Buffalo. In the fifth game of the season, Baltimore beat the Bills 35–28 in a shootout. They had the offensive power to beat the Bills again, but which Baltimore team would show up?

Buffalo scored first on a 29-yard pass from Ratterman to halfback Rex Bumgardner. Chet Adams added a field goal to make it 10–0 in favor of Buffalo. End John North grabbed a Y.A. Tittle touchdown pass to close the gap to 10–7, but it was all Buffalo after that. Racking up four straight touchdowns, Buffalo built a dominating 38–7 lead. Tittle tossed a scoring pass to halfback Billy Stone, but Baltimore was beaten. For the second consecutive year, Buffalo defeated the Colts for a playoff berth.[52]

The Bills were set to take on Cleveland. They knew that the game would not be easy, but Buffalo had confidence. Bills' back Alex Wizbicki recalled, "We felt we could hold our own. We felt very confident that we could beat them. When they played us, they knew that they played a good football team and were in for a good game."[53] In the two prior meetings in the regular season, Buffalo battled the Browns to ties. In the first meeting, the Bills built a commanding lead only to squander it away. In the second contest, Buffalo battled back to earn a 7–7 tie. A difficult struggle awaited them in Cleveland.

Edgar Jones and Dante Lavelli returned from injuries to play in the game. The Browns started the scoring when Cleveland drove 75 yards for the touchdown. Lavelli, on his first play of the game, faked out the Bills defender and sprinted 51 yards for the score and the 7–0 lead. They extended their lead on a Lou Groza field goal to make the score 10–0. However, Buffalo countered with a scoring strike of their own. Ratterman threw into double coverage to hit Al Baldwin on a 39-yard reception. This put Buffalo on the Cleveland four-yard line, where Ratterman tossed a screen pass to Lou Tomasetti for the touchdown. The Bills scored again, late in the second quarter, when Ratterman connected with Mutryn for an eight-yard touchdown. The Bills had a 14–10 halftime lead and were in good shape going into the second half.[54]

The battle continued in the third quarter. Cleveland drove into Buffalo territory, but was unable to get past the Buffalo 30-yard line and lost the ball on downs. The Bills took over, but were incapable of make much headway on their first two plays. On third down, Ratterman dropped back to pass and flipped the ball to Mutryn. It hit him in the back and was intercepted by Lou Saban, who returned the ball to the Buffalo two-yard line. Edgar 'Special Delivery' Jones took the ball over on the next play and Cleveland recaptured the lead at 17–14. And if that was not enough excitement for the 17,270 fans in attendance, the Bills regained the lead on a 38-yard pass from Ratterman to Mutryn. With 1:35 left in the third quarter, the Bills had a 21–17 lead over the defending champions. Cleveland came back and score 45 seconds later when Dub Jones caught a 49-yard pass from Otto Graham, breaking a couple of tackles on the way to a 24–21 lead.[55]

The Bills drove to attempt a game-tying field goal, but Chet Adams came up short with his try. Cleveland tried to seal the game with another scoring drive. Deep into Buffalo territory, Graham tossed an apparent scoring pass to Mac Speedie, but the play was called back as Speedie was accused of pushing off of the defender. The game clock was ticking and Buffalo had one last opportunity to grab victory.[56]

Going into the final five minutes of the game, the Browns were up by a mere three points. Buffalo had the ball and was driving. Beginning at their own 20, Buffalo moved 26 yards on three plays: a Ratterman pass to Rex Bumgardner for ten yards, a Bumgardner ten-yard run and a Tomasetti plunge for six yards. Ratterman dropped back to pass and tossed to his receiver, however, Warren Lahr caught the ball instead and darted 52 yards for a touchdown and a 31–21 victory. The Bills failed — for the ninth time in the regular and postseason — to defeat the Cleveland Browns and their season was over. The Browns took on the San Francisco 49ers for the 1949 AAFC Championship. The Bills had played their last game.[57]

8

The War Was Over

On December 9, 1949, the All-America Football Conference and the National Football League announced a merger. It was not so much a merger as dissolution of the AAFC with three of its teams being admitted into the NFL. After five-and-a-half years of bitter rivalry and contention, the war was over. New York Bulldogs owner Ted Collins was reported to have lost over one million dollars in the fight, and the Green Bay Packers and Pittsburgh Steelers were on the verge of bankruptcy from the conflict.[1] The NFL needed this agreement to stay alive and the AAFC owners could not financially continue the skirmish.

The "merging" of the leagues took effect in 1950 and the new effort was called the National-American Football League (NAFL). The Cleveland Browns, San Francisco 49ers and Baltimore Colts were the only AAFC franchises to continue play in 1950. According to author and historian Mark L. Ford,

> As part of the merger agreement, New York Bulldogs owner Ted Collins had purchased the rights to all but six of the 32 players on the AAC's New York Yankees, gaining the right to play the 1950 season at Yankee Stadium. The Giants would have their choice of six players and keep playing at the Polo Grounds. Collins and Giants' owner Tim Mara couldn't reach an agreement on players, so Bell ordered both men to appear before him at 4:00 to determine which six players would be allotted to Mara. Unhappy with Bell's solution, Collins declined to appear.... Though the Colts, Browns and 49ers were the only 3 AAC clubs officially included in the merger agreement, the AAFC Yankees replaced the NFL Bulldogs for all practical purposes, surviving the merger nearly intact and becoming the New York Yanks.[2]

The remaining AAFC franchises were disbanded and players were allocated through a dispersal draft. The addition of the Colts was an interesting story. Washington Redskins owner George Preston Marshall consistently refused to include Baltimore in any merger talks, citing his exclusive territorial rights to the region. It was not until Baltimore paid him $50,000 before he saw the error of his ways and realized that a Baltimore franchise created a natural rivalry with his Washington team. As part of Marshall's agreement to allow Baltimore into the NAFL, Baltimore needed to show a profit after their first year.[3]

A month before the league merger was announced, Bills owner Jim Breuil dropped a bombshell on his fellow owners. Breuil stated that he would no longer run the Buffalo Bills. According to Breuil, "It just got to be too much for one man to handle."[4] Breuil claimed that he had lost over $700,000 over the four years he owned the team ($250,000 in 1946, $180,000 in 1947, $150,000 in 1948 and $125,000 in 1949). He added, "I had no choice in the matter. I was in a corner financially and had to stop.... The financial burden, as well as the drain on my time and energy was just too much."[5] Breuil noted that he did not announce this earlier because he thought that there was not enough time to put together another ownership group. As one of his final acts as owner of the Buffalo Bills, Breuil sold guard Abe Gibron, back Rex Bumgardner and tackle John Kissell to the Cleveland Browns in exchange for a 25 percent share in the Browns.[6]

Buffalo did not go quietly into the sunset. The Bills were not included in the merger between the leagues, however, the city of Buffalo did not take "No" for an answer. A few days after the merger announcement, Buffalo football fans formed the Buffalo Bills Football Club, Inc., with hopes of raising enough money to make the NAFL reconsider adding the Bills to the league. Albert T. O'Neill, president of the Buffalo Niagara Electric Company, was tapped to head this organization. O'Neill accepted the position on the condition that another spokesperson represented Buffalo at the NAFL owners meeting on January 19, 1950. He also made it clear that he would resign if Buffalo received a franchise. O'Neill stated,

> I believe that the reaction of the citizens of Buffalo and Western New York to the demand for a professional football franchise in this city merits continued wholehearted civic support. In view of that fact, I am willing to accept the presidency of the Buffalo Bills Football Club, Inc. without compensation, only until such time as a franchise is awarded by the National-American Football League and a sound working organization for a competent, progressive management is established. I do feel then when these two ends are accomplished, in justice to myself and to the office I hold at the Electric company, I must then resign, having complete confidence that the Board of Directors of the football club will then choose an adequate successor.[7]

John C. Stiglmeier, former business manager of the Buffalo Baseball Club and prominent local sports figure, was pre-eminent among those mentioned at the meeting as possible spokesman for the Bills at the NAFL gathering.[8]

More than 20,000 people of all walks of life showed up at Memorial Auditorium for an initial fundraising drive to "Keep the Bills in Buffalo." This was a mere few days after the formation of the Buffalo Bills Football Club. Sports booster clubs from Lancaster, Hamburg and Depew made their way to the event and one Tonawanda businessman donated 50 cars as free transportation to the fundraiser. That night, $74,770 was raised by selling five dollar shares in the company, with another $125,000 underwritten to bring the fundraising total to $199,770. In addition, $10,000 was donated by the Buffalo *Courier-Express* and, not to be outdone, the Buffalo *Evening News* handed over a check in the same amount. Fans in Hamilton, Ontario raised an additional $5,000 to keep the team alive. Arthur H. Rich, secretary-treasurer of the corporation, was shocked at the turnout. "Never saw anything like it. There just can't be another town like Buffalo. I don't see how this kind of spirit ... and cash ... can be turned down. Do you?"[9] Season ticket pledges were also sold. The goal was to sell 10,000 tickets, which was double the 1949 number. It took less than a week to reach the goal. An additional $15,073 in ticket pledges were received by January of 1950, shortly before Buffalo made their case to the NAFL for admittance.[10]

People of all walks of life contributed to the effort. It was a true community atmosphere, as people were concerned about getting a team and not notoriety. An anonymous fan commented, "My name? Aw, forget it. It's for the Bills. We want them here. They belong here." Kids broke into their piggy banks. Laborers stopped what they were doing to take time to support the cause.[11]

Even with the impressive fundraising going on, Buffalo still needed to convince the league that they should be admitted and they faced an uphill battle. NAFL Commissioner Bert Bell was adamant: "It is my opinion that the new league will operate with 13 teams."[12] After hearing of Buffalo's efforts to keep their team, Bell retreated slightly: "Developments within the last 24 hours at least entitle Buffalo to a hearing."[13] The community made a statement and the NAFL listened.

Bell met with representatives of the Buffalo Bills Football Club Executive Committee: Paul E. Fitzpatrick, Albert T. O'Neill, David B. West, Dr. James J. Ailinger and Jim Wells. Bell was "highly impressed" with the fundraising drive. "While I don't say Buffalo will get a franchise, I certainly can't say that the city will not. Buffalo, obviously, has a better chance now than it did a week or so ago."[14] Bell knew of "no one in the new National-American League setup who is against Buffalo's entry."[15] Bell continued, "All phases of the matter were discussed and it all (Buffalo's chances) now depends upon the presentation when Buffalo makes its formal application for a franchise."[16] Bell stated that he coached the committee on what owners wanted to know.

> Of paramount interest is a strong sale of season tickets. This cannot be stressed too strongly. This one factor is the most important facing Buffalo in its request for admission into the league. A sound season ticket sale, plus sound capital will be a great help. Although there are many stockholders in such a drive as Buffalo is conducting, there can be only one spokesman. The city must have one individual with power to act alone. The new league will function like the old National League. That means only one representative from each city.[17]

Heading into the January league meeting in Philadelphia, Buffalo had raised $252,170 in stock sales and capital investments, and over 15,000 season ticket pledges.[18] They also received the support of at least four NAFL owners: Art Rooney of Pittsburgh, Tim Mara of the New York Giants, George Preston Marshall of the Washington Redskins and Chicago Bears' owner George Halas. According to Rooney, "Frankly, I don't see how they can keep Buffalo out."[19] Everything was in the hands of the owners and the commissioner. According to Commissioner Bell, "We'll take up both Houston and Buffalo at the January 19 meeting here, but they'll have to meet two situations to make the league. First, they'll have to receive a unanimous vote of the 13 original franchises. Secondly, they'll have to fit into a schedule."[20]

Now, several questions arose throughout the fundraising campaign regarding a Buffalo franchise. The first was whether Buffalo actually had a team. As a result of an alleged merger with Cleveland, Buffalo really did not have a franchise. Bell did not recognize a merger between Buffalo and Cleveland: "I have heard of no such merger. It would be ridiculous for us to grant a franchise to Buffalo if the city didn't have a football team. The question of being able to field a good, strong team is one of utmost importance in a situation like this. If Buffalo gets a franchise, I'm certain it will also retain its team."[1] The next question dealt with climate, as Buffalo still had to overcome the city's reputation for snow. To negate that, the Buffalo contingent presented data showing that the weather in Buffalo during football season was actually more favorable than New York City, where the NFL already had two teams. In addition, the group presented plans for renovations to Civic Stadium in hopes of generating more ticket revenue.

The only thing that remained was the schedule. According to Bell, he had drawn up a 14-team schedule to be presented at the owners' meeting. Prior to the gathering, Bell wavered slightly and informed the Buffalo group that he had worked up the schedule—which included Buffalo—but needed a little more time to fine tune it before he presented it to the owners. At the meeting, Bell never presented the proposed schedule. When it was Buffalo's turn, George Preston Marshall made the motion to add them to the league and Baltimore's Abe Watner seconded the motion. Then, the meeting went behind closed doors. The first six owners voted in favor of Buffalo's admission, but Los Angeles Rams owner Dan Reeves cast the first negative vote, which ended Buffalo's chances of admission. Referencing the lack of a schedule, Reeves stated, "I felt it was silly to vote in a new city without first having a good idea where my team would play and when."[22] That takes us back to Bell's failure to present his 14-team schedule. According to Bell, "I told the owners that I would make a schedule, somehow, if they voted to increase the league to 14 teams."[23] This was obviously not enough, as judged by Reeves' comments. The final vote was 9–4 in favor of admitting Buffalo, but a unanimous vote was needed. According to Louis Effrat of the *New York Times*, "Dan Reeves of Los Angeles, Tony Morabito of San Francisco, and George Halas and Ray Bennigsen, both of Chicago, dissented. Their objections were not aimed against Buffalo, but at a 14-team league."[24] Buffalo did not get a franchise. A few weeks later, Albert O'Neill announced that he refunded the $180,690 generated by 9,700 stockholders.[25]

According to Pittsburgh Steelers owner Art Rooney, "It was a sad mistake not to include Buffalo."[26] Bills back Joe Sutton recalled, "I definitely think the fans in Buffalo deserved to have gotten a team in the NFL at the time. They did everything possible to show that they would support the team."²⁷ These sentiments were echoed by Bills back Chet Mutryn: "Buffalo fans were not only very supportive, but they treated Bills players like members of their family."²⁸ In reminiscing about his father, Blair Stautzenberger — son of Bills guard Odell Stautzenberger — stated, "My dad was always very disappointed that the Bills didn't join the NFL in 1950 like the other three teams. He thought that the team deserved to join the NFL and more importantly thought that the Buffalo fans would have supported the team, as attendance and city support was very good. My parents loved the people who lived in Western New York and had many, many friends while living there. My dad was very proud of playing for the 1949 Bills team."²⁹

Odell Stautzenberger, Bills guard in 1949.

This left the NAFL with a 13-team league, which was divided up into two divisions of six teams each. The 13th team floated between the divisions. Originally, the Cleveland Browns were designated as this floating team, but coach Paul Brown threatened to withdraw if that were the case. As a result, Baltimore was given that dubious title.³⁰ After a few months, the league took steps to minimize the AAFC by removing the "American" part of their new name, which reverted the name back to the National Football League (NFL).

The Buffalo Bills, Chicago Rockets and Los Angeles Rams were officially disbanded and the players from those teams were put into a dispersal draft. The draft order was determined by the order of finish of the 1949 season. Therefore, the draft order was: Baltimore, New York Yanks, Green Bay, Detroit, Washington, New York Giants, Pittsburgh, Chicago Cardinals (tied with Pittsburgh), Chicago Bears, San Francisco 49ers (tied with Chicago Bears), Los Angeles, Cleveland and Philadelphia. Since Baltimore and Green Bay were the weakest teams, they were given five extra draft picks each.

8—The War Was Over 107

DISPERSAL DRAFT

Round 1

No.	Player	Position	College	Drafted By	From (Reserve List Rights)
1	Chet Mutryn	HB	Xavier	Baltimore Colts	Buffalo Bills
2	George Taliaferro	HB	Indiana	New York Yanks	Los Angeles Dons
3	Billy Grimes	HB	Oklahoma A&M	Green Bay Packers	Los Angeles Dons
4	Bob Hoernschemeyer	HB	Indiana	Detroit Lions	Chicago Hornets
5	Jim Spavital	FB	Oklahoma A&M	Washington Redskins	Los Angeles Dons
6	John Rapacz	C-T	Oklahoma	New York Giants	Chicago Hornets
7	Robert Tinsley	T	Baylor	Pittsburgh Steelers	Los Angeles Dons
8	Robert Reinhard	T	Univ. of California	Chicago Cardinals	Los Angeles Dons
9	Harper Davis	HB	Mississippi State	Chicago Bears	Los Angeles Dons
10	Knox Ramsey	G	William & Mary	San Francisco 49ers	Los Angeles Dons
11	Art Statuto	C	Notre Dame	Los Angeles Rams	Buffalo Bills
12	Hal Herring	C	Auburn	Cleveland Browns	Buffalo Bills
13	Lindell Pearson	HB	Oklahoma	Philadelphia Eagles	N/A

Round 2

No.	Player	Position	College	Drafted By	From
14	Robert Livingstone	HB	Notre Dame	Baltimore Colts	Buffalo Bills
15	Nate Johnson	T	Illinois	New York Yanks	Chicago Hornets
16	Alton Baldwin	E	Arkansas	Green Bay Packers	Buffalo Bills
17	Lou Creekmur	T	William & Mary	Detroit Lions	(College in 1949)
18	Charles Drazenovich	FB	Penn State	Washington Redskins	(College in 1949)
19	Ollie Cline	FB	Ohio State	New York Giants	Buffalo Bills
20	Thomas Ray Richeson	G	Alabama	Pittsburgh Steelers	Chicago Hornets
21	Martin Wendell	G	Notre Dame	Chicago Cardinals	Chicago Hornets
22	Fred Negus	C	Wisconsin	Chicago Bears	Chicago Hornets
23	Edgar Henke	T	USC	San Francisco 49ers	Los Angeles Dons
24	Victor Vasicek	G	USC	Los Angeles Rams	Buffalo Bills
25	Leonard Ford	E	Michigan	Cleveland Browns	Los Angeles Dons
26	Jerry Krall	FB	Ohio State	Philadelphia Eagles	Los Angeles Dons

Round 3

No.	Player	Position	College	Drafted By	From
27	Albin H. Collins	HB	LSU	Baltimore Colts	Chicago Hornets
28	Dan Edwards	E	Georgia	New York Yanks	Chicago Hornets
29	Homer Paine	T	Oklahoma	Green Bay Packers	Chicago Hornets
30	Bob Jensen	E	Iowa State	Detroit Lions	Chicago Hornets
31	Roland Dale	T	Mississippi	Washington Redskins	(College in 1949)
32	Vince Mazza	E	(None)	New York Giants	Buffalo Bills
33	Tom McWilliams	HB	Mississippi State	Pittsburgh Steelers	Los Angeles Dons
34	Ray Ramsey	HB	Bradley	Chicago Cardinals	Chicago Hornets
35	James Clark	T	Mississippi	Chicago Bears	(College in 1949)
36	Odell Stautzenberger	G	Texas A&M	San Francisco 49ers	Buffalo Bills
37	Richard Wilkins	E	Oregon	Los Angeles Rams	Los Angeles Dons
38	Charles Schroll	HB	LSU	Cleveland Browns	Buffalo Bills
39	George Pastre	T	UCLA	Philadelphia Eagles	Los Angeles Dons

Extra Picks

No.	Player	Position	College	Drafted By	From
40	Arthur Donovan	G	Boston	Baltimore Colts	Buffalo Bills
41	James Lukens	E	Washington	Green Bay Packers	Buffalo Bills
42	Ed King	G	Boston College	Baltimore Colts	Buffalo Bills
43	Abner Wimberly	E	LSU	Green Bay Packers	Los Angeles Dons

Round 4

No.	Player	Position	College	Drafted By	From
44	George Buksar	FB	Purdue	Baltimore Colts	Chicago Hornets
45	John Clowes	T	William & Mary	New York Yanks	Chicago Hornets

The Original Buffalo Bills

No.	Player	Position	College	Drafted By	From (Reserve List Rights)
46	Wilbur E. Volz	HB	Missouri	Green Bay Packers	Buffalo Bills
47	William Kay	T	Iowa	Detroit Lions	Buffalo Bills
48	Lloyd Eisenberg	T	Duke	Washington Redskins	Los Angeles Dons
49	Alfred Schmid	E	Villanova	New York Giants	(Villanova in 1949)
50	Daniel Dworsky	C	Michigan	Pittsburgh Steelers	Los Angeles Dons
51	Ted Hazelwood	T	North Carolina	Chicago Cardinals	Chicago Hornets
52	Glenn Dobbs, Jr.	QB-HB	Tulsa	Chicago Bears	Los Angeles Dons
53	Earl Howell	HB	Mississippi	San Francisco 49ers	Los Angeles Dons
54	Wade Walker	T	Oklahoma	Los Angeles Rams	Buffalo Bills
55	Alex Wizbicki	HB	Holy Cross	Cleveland Browns	Buffalo Bills
56	Paul Gibson	E	North Carolina St.	Philadelphia Eagles	Buffalo Bills

Round 5

No.	Player	Position	College	Drafted By	From (Reserve List Rights)
57	Robert P. Oristaglio	E	Pennsylvania	Baltimore Colts	Buffalo Bills
58	Bob Kennedy	FB	Washington State	New York Yanks	New York Yankees
59	John E. Kerns	T	Ohio	Green Bay Packers	Buffalo Bills
60	Richard Rifenberg	E	Michigan	Detroit Lions	New York Yankees
61	Hardy Brown	FB	Tulsa	Washington Redskins	Chicago Hornets
62	Joe Sullivan	QB	Dartmouth	New York Giants	N/A
63	Herbert St. John	G	Georgia	Pittsburgh Steelers	Chicago Hornets
64	Jim Still	QB	Georgia Tech.	Chicago Cardinals	Buffalo Bills
65	Al Beasley	G	St. Mary's	Chicago Bears	New York Yankees
66	John Brown	C	North Carolina	San Francisco 49ers	Los Angeles Dons
67	Ernest Williamson	T	North Carolina	Los Angeles Rams	Los Angeles Dons
68	Walter Clay	FB	Colorado	Cleveland Browns	Los Angeles Dons
69	Joseph Sutton	HB	Temple	Philadelphia Eagles	Buffalo Bills

Extra Picks

No.	Player	Position	College	Drafted By	From (Reserve List Rights)
70	Robert Deuber	HB	Pennsylvania	Baltimore Colts	(College in 1949)
71	Ted Cook	E	Alabama	Green Bay Packers	Green Bay Packers

Round 6

No.	Player	Position	College	Drafted By	From (Reserve List Rights)
72	Michael Perrotti	T	Cincinnati	Baltimore Colts	Los Angeles Dons
73	Chester Adams	T	Ohio	New York Yanks	Buffalo Bills
74	Jason A. Bailey	T	West Virginia St.	Green Bay Packers	Chicago Hornets
75	Joyce Pipkin	E	Arkansas	Detroit Lions	Los Angeles Dons
76	Ed Hirsch	LB	Northwestern	Washington Redskins	Buffalo Bills
77	Richard Woodard	C	Iowa	New York Giants	Los Angeles Dons
78	George Grimes	HB	Virginia	Pittsburgh Steelers	Buffalo Bills
79	Jim Turner	T	Univ. of California	Chicago Cardinals	Chicago Hornets
80	John Cunningham	E	Univ. of California	Chicago Bears	N/A
81	George Murphy	QB	USC	San Francisco 49ers	Los Angeles Dons
82	Bill Renna	C	Santa Clara	Los Angeles Rams	Los Angeles Dons
83	George Strohmeyer	C	Notre Dame	Cleveland Browns	Chicago Hornets
84	Hosea Rodgers	FB	North Carolina	Philadelphia Eagles	Los Angeles Dons

Round 7

No.	Player	Position	College	Drafted By	From (Reserve List Rights)
85	Bill Gompers	HB	Notre Dame	Baltimore Colts	Buffalo Bills
86	Paul Crowe	HB	St. Mary's	New York Yanks	Los Angeles Dons
87	Denver Crawford	T	Tennessee	Green Bay Packers	New York Yankees
88	George Benigni	E	Georgetown	Detroit Lions	Chicago Hornets
89	Ed Smith	B	Texas Mines	Washington Redskins	N/A
90	Henry Foldberg	E	Army	New York Giants	Chicago Hornets
91	Ben Verick	FB	Wisconsin	Pittsburgh Steelers	N/A
92	Alex Sarkisian	C	Northwestern	Chicago Cardinals	N/A

8—The War Was Over

No.	Player	Position	College	Drafted By	From (Reserve List Rights)
93	John Donaldson	HB	Georgia	Chicago Bears	Los Angeles Dons
94	John Maskas	T	Virginia Poly. Inst.	San Francisco 49ers	Buffalo Bills
95	Jack Swaner	HB	Univ. of California	Los Angeles Rams	Chicago Hornets
96	Lynn Chewning	FB	Hampden-Sydney	Cleveland Browns	New York Yankees
97	Don Panciera	QB	San Fran. Univ.	Philadelphia Eagles	New York Yankees

Extra Picks

98	William Stanton	E	North Carolina St.	Baltimore Colts	Buffalo Bills
99	Charles W. Schuette	C	Marquette	Green Bay Packers	Buffalo Bills

Round 8

100	Vito Kissell	FB	Holy Cross	Baltimore Colts	Buffalo Bills
101	John "Mickey" Colmer	FB	Miramonte Jr. Coll.	New York Yanks	New York Yankees
102	Zigmont Czarobski	T	Notre Dame	Green Bay Packers	Chicago Hornets
103	Gerald Morrical	T	Indiana	Detroit Lions	New York Yankees
104	Leon McLaughlin	C	UCLA	Washington Redskins	Los Angeles Dons
105	Robert Heck	E	Purdue	New York Giants	Chicago Hornets
106	James Pearcy	G	Marshall	Pittsburgh Steelers	Chicago Hornets
107	Phil O'Reilly	T	Purdue	Chicago Cardinals	N/A
108	George Maddock	T	Northwestern	Chicago Bears	Chicago Hornets
109	Paul Cleary	E	USC	San Francisco 49ers	Chicago Hornets
110	Richard Scott	C	Navy	Los Angeles Rams	Brooklyn Dodgers
111	Paul Patterson	HB	Illinois	Cleveland Browns	Chicago Hornets
112	Caleb Warrington	C	William & Mary	Philadelphia Eagles	Brooklyn Dodgers

Round 9

113	Robert Hatch	QB-HB	Boston University	Baltimore Colts	N/A
114	Orban Sanders	HB	Texas	New York Yanks	New York Yankees
115	Victor Schleich	T	Nebraska	Green Bay Packers	Chicago Rockets
116	Warren Huey	E	Michigan State	Detroit Lions	Chicago Hornets
117	Murray Alexander	E	Mississippi State	Washington Redskins	Brooklyn Dodgers
118	Henry Kalver	T	Oklahoma City	New York Giants	N/A
119	Robert Forbes	HB	Florida	Pittsburgh Steelers	N/A
120	Ralph Sazio	T	William & Mary	Chicago Cardinals	Buffalo Bills
121	Robert Leonetti	G	Wake Forest	Chicago Bears	Buffalo Bills
122	Ernest Tolman	E	USC	San Francisco 49ers	New York Yankees
123	Edward Kelley	T	Texas	Los Angeles Rams	Los Angeles Dons
124	William Reinhard	HB	Univ. of California	Cleveland Browns	Los Angeles Dons
125	Carmen Falcone	QB	Pennsylvania	Philadelphia Eagles	N/A

Extra Picks

126	Louis Tomasetti	FB	Bucknell	Baltimore Colts	Buffalo Bills
127	Paul Duke	C	Georgia Tech.	Green Bay Packers	New York Yankees

Round 10

128	Lou Agase	T	Illinois	Baltimore Colts	Chicago Hornets
129	Tom Colella	HB	Canisius	New York Yanks	Buffalo Bills
130	R.M. Patterson	T	McMurray, Texas	Green Bay Packers	Chicago Hornets
131	Ray Coates	HB	LSU	Detroit Lions	New York Giants
132	Dewey Nelson	HB	Utah	Washington Redskins	New York Bulldogs
133	Dwight Eddleman	HB	Illinois	New York Giants	N/A
134	Robert Meinert	LB	Oklahoma A&M	Pittsburgh Steelers	Los Angeles Dons
135	Vaughn Mancha	C	Alabama	Chicago Cardinals	Boston Yanks
136	George Bernhardt	G	Illinois	Chicago Bears	Chicago Hornets
137	Dick Lorenz	E	Oregon State	San Francisco 49ers	Los Angeles Dons

No.	Player	Position	College	Drafted By	From (Reserve List Rights)
138	Dale Armstrong	E	Dartmouth	Los Angeles Rams	Brooklyn Dodgers
139	Lewis Holder	E	Texas	Cleveland Browns	Los Angeles Dons
140	Gil Johnson	QB-HB	SMU	Philadelphia Eagles	New York Yankees

There are arguments among historians as to whether the AAFC was on par with the NFL in terms of talent. According to George Ratterman, "There was not a lot of difference between the AAFC and the NFL. Cleveland showed how good it was in 1950 when it won the NFL Championship."[31]

Any doubt as to the strength of the top teams in the AAFC was quickly put to rest, as the Cleveland Browns sent a message early and often: "We are the best." Winning not once, but twice against the two-time defending NFL champion Philadelphia Eagles in the 1950 season bore this out.

The NFL was scared of the AAFC. They knew that the talent was strong, namely because they tried to sign the very same players. Sometimes, they were successful. Sometimes, they were not. The strength of the talent can be assessed by the number of All-Pros and Hall of Famers that came out of the AAFC. Over the same time period, the NFL and AAFC produced relatively the same amount of All-Pros and Hall of Famers.

The NFL refused to settle their disputes with the AAFC on the gridiron. Why? Because they knew that there was a realistic chance that the NFL would lose. Then, their argument that the AAFC was an inferior league was moot.

The downfall of the AAFC was in the way that the Conference was run. According to Paul Brown, the AAFC "had no direction from the top then, and it didn't help that the players and financial resources were always being used to help poorly run teams."[32] Brown was referring to the AAFC forcing the better teams to simply give players to the weaker teams without compensation. Combine that with relatively weak bottom franchises and the AAFC just could not continue. Of course, the NFL also had weak franchises, but the owners were involved with the league for a much longer time and therefore were in a better position to absorb losses.

The Impact of the Buffalo Bills

While Buffalo did not make it into the NFL, their impact on the AAFC cannot be ignored. When the 1949 season ended, Buffalo was getting stronger. Having a complete year with Clem Crowe at the helm could have produced a contender for the Conference Championship. According to George Ratterman, "In 1949 the Bills tied the Browns twice and played a good play-off game against Cleveland, so I think that the Bills would have fared quite well against NFL teams."[33] Statistically, the Buffalo Bills were at the top or near the top of a lot of major categories in the four years of the AAFC. They obviously had the talent. It was just a matter of Clem Crowe getting the final pieces to the puzzle.

- George Ratterman was fourth in total offense with 6,194 yards. The three players preceding him all played for four years in the league versus Ratterman's three. Cleveland's Otto Graham was first with 10,085 yards; San Francisco's Frankie Albert was second with 6,948 and Brooklyn Dodgers/Los Angeles Dons' Glenn Dobbs was third with 5,876 yards.
- Chet Mutryn was third in the league in rushing with 2,676 yards. Cleveland's Marion Motley was first with 3,024 yards and New York Yankees star Spec Sanders was second with 2,900 yards.
- George Ratterman was third in passing, going 438 for 831 and 6,194 yards. Cleveland's Otto Graham was first, going 592 for 1,061 and 10,085 yards. San Francisco's Frankie Albert was second with 515 completions out of 963 attempts for 6,948 yards.
- Chet Mutryn was first in kickoff return yardage with 54 returns for 1,494 yards. He was seventh in the league in punt returns with 35 for 492 yards. This placed Mutryn in first place in total returns with 89 for 1,986.
- Al Baldwin was tied for fourth in the league in receiving with 2,103 yards. Cleveland's Mac Speedie was first with 3,554 yards, Al Beals of San Francisco was second with 2,510 yards and Dante Lavelli of Cleveland came in third with 2,580 yards. Miami's Lamar Davis was tied with Baldwin at 2,103 yards. Fay "Dolly" King was in sixth place with 1,583 yards. King split his time between Buffalo and Chicago.
- Chet Mutryn was fifth in the league in total scoring with 229 points. San Francisco's Al Beals was first with 278 points, followed by Cleveland's Lou Groza (259), San Francisco's Joe Vetrano (247) and New York's Spec Sanders (240).

* * *

A few issues arose as to why Buffalo did not get a franchise in 1950. First, there was no schedule put forth by NFL Commissioner Bert Bell. Leading up to the January 1950 owners meeting, Bell told the Buffalo contingent that he had a schedule created. As time grew closer to the meeting, Bell wavered from this statement and said that he would create a schedule if they were admitted to the league. No schedule was produced at the meeting and the first "No" vote came specifically because there was no schedule on the table. Why did Bell do that? He obviously knew that having a schedule was paramount to Buffalo's case, yet he refused to present his preliminary schedule.

Second, going into the January 1950 meeting, Buffalo had no real ownership group in place. Even though the city showed its support with stock sales, capital investments and season ticket pledges, there was no owner. As Bell mentioned, there needed to be one person with the power to act alone. Buffalo was missing that piece. Would Buffalo have come up with a single owner to take charge of the team? Probably. While a group owned the team, there were enough prominent people in the community that one would step up to take the reins.

Third, the NFL did not want to expand beyond a 13-team league. With the financial losses accrued from their battle with the AAFC and the elevated player salaries from the conflict, the NFL wanted to take a step back and shore up their foundation. Taking talent from the Buffalo franchise strengthened the remaining NFL franchises. With the "bribe" given to George Preston Marshall to allow Baltimore into the NFL, it was pretty clear that Baltimore had the upper hand in negotiations. This was in spite of the fact that Baltimore was a weaker team, both financially and on the field. If the NFL truly wanted the best teams, they would have admitted Buffalo over Baltimore.

Finally, the NFL always thought that Buffalo was never able to support a franchise in the long term. This was mainly due to previous professional football teams failing to maintain financial stability. The Buffalo teams of the 1920s were strong the first two years of their existence, but steadily floundered as the decade wore on. Both of the American Football League teams of the 1940s—the 1940 Buffalo Indians and the 1941 Buffalo Tigers—failed to generate adequate support. While the Buffalo Bills from the AAFC showed solid fan support, owner Jim Breuil claimed to have lost money every year. The view that Buffalo cannot compete financially in the NFL continues today, even from current Buffalo Bills owner Ralph Wilson.

Regardless of the aforementioned issues, Buffalo has always struggled for major-league professional football respectability. In the 1920s NFL, they came in second place twice. In the AAFC, they came in second once. They won two American Football League Championships, but they are dismissed because it was considered an "inferior" league. The four Super Bowl appearances are regularly downplayed because Buffalo "could not win the big one." Regardless of what others say about professional football in Buffalo, the teams and the fans never give up. They fight to the end.

Epilogue

Thirteen players from the Buffalo Bills retired from professional football after the 1949 season ended: Jack Carpenter, Tom Colella, Jesse Freitas, Paul Gibson, Larry Joe, Jim Lukens, John Maskas, Rocco Pirro, Bill Stanton, Odell Stautzenberger, Jim Still, Lou Tomasetti and Wilbur Volz. Volz wanted to continue his football career and was drafted by the Green Bay Packers in the dispersal draft. However, he was called into the service and spent a year serving in the Korean War. When he returned stateside, he tried out for the Packers, but failed to make the cut. Other notable players from the 1949 squad that continued their professional careers are as follows:

- After leaving Buffalo, Chet Adams played twelve games for the New York Yankees in 1950.
- Alton Baldwin played twelve games for the Green Bay Packers in 1950.
- After being sold to the Cleveland Browns, Rex Bumgardner stayed with the Browns through the 1952 season.
- Ollie Cline played the 1950, 1951 and 1953 seasons with the Detroit Lions.
- Abe Gibron played the 1950–55 seasons with the Cleveland Browns. Partway through the 1956 season, Gibron went from the Browns to the Philadelphia Eagles, where he played the remainder of the 1956 and all of the 1957 seasons. He finished his professional career by playing two seasons for the Chicago Bears.
- Hal Herring was drafted by the Cleveland Browns in the dispersal draft. He played three years for the Browns before retiring.
- Ed Hirsch played in the Canadian Football League for the 1952 Hamilton Tiger-Cats.
- John Kerns also played in the Canadian Football League.
- Ed King played twelve games for the Baltimore Colts before retiring from professional football.
- John Kissell played the 1950–1952 and the 1954–1956 seasons with the Cleveland Browns.
- Vito Kissell played eleven games for the 1950 Baltimore Colts.
- Bob Livingstone played eleven games for the Baltimore Colts in 1950.
- Vince Mazza played from 1950–1954 for the Hamilton Tiger-Cats of the Canadian Football League.

- Chet Mutryn played twelve games for the 1950 Baltimore Colts.
- Bob Oristaglio played for three different teams after leaving Buffalo: In 1950, he played twelve games for the Baltimore Colts. In 1951, he played twelve games for the Cleveland Browns. He finished his professional career by playing four games with the 1952 Philadelphia Eagles.
- George Ratterman continued his professional career with the New York Yanks. After playing one year for the Yanks, Ratterman played for the Montreal Allouettes of the Canadian Football League in 1951. He finished the 1951 season with the Yanks, before he moved on to the Cleveland Browns, where he played from the 1952 through the 1956 seasons. His career came to an end in the fourth game of the 1956 season. "On a third down situation against the Redskins early in 1956," explained Ratterman. "I ran the sneak play Coach Paul Brown sent in from the sidelines. I ran it for profit, too, for Cleveland if not for Ratterman, moving the ball for a first down before the roof of my left knee fell in. My left foot pinned to the ground by a monstrous Redskin lineman, another player slammed into the knee and buckled it backwards from front to rear, which instruction sheets that accompany knees constantly warn the owner to guard against."[1]
- Bill Schroll was drafted by the Cleveland Browns in the dispersal draft. He did not play for the Browns, but instead played for the Detroit Lions in 1950. He finished his career by playing twelve games for the Green Bay Packers in 1951.
- Carl Schuette finished his playing career with the Green Bay Packers, playing 24 games over the 1950–1951 seasons.
- Art Statuto played twelve games for the Los Angeles Rams in 1950 to finish his professional career.
- Joe Sutton finished his playing career after three seasons with the Philadelphia Eagles.
- Vic Vasicek finished his playing career after twelve games with the 1950 Los Angeles Rams.
- Alex Wizbicki was drafted by the Cleveland Browns in the dispersal draft, but decided to play for the Green Bay Packers. He finished his career after eleven games with the 1950 Packers squad.

As far as the upper echelon of the Bills organization, owner Jim Breuil remained with the Browns for a few years before disappearing from the football scene. He moved to Oklahoma for semi-retirement. He then relocated to Florida, where he worked with his son to form Breuil Boat Company. Breuil passed away in 1978.

After the AAFC folded, Clem Crowe immediately signed on to become Baltimore's new head coach. After a 1–11 season, the Colts folded and Crowe went to coach the Ottawa Rough Riders to a Grey Cup victory. He stayed with Ottawa until 1955, at which point Crowe took over the reins of the British Columbia Lions for the next three years before retiring from football. He passed away in 1983.

County of Erie
Office of County Executive

PROCLAMATION

WHEREAS, CHET MUTRYN, the son of a Polish immigrant who settled in Cleveland, became a football star at Xavier University and was named Ohio's Outstanding Collegiate Football Player in 1944;

WHEREAS, CHET MUTRYN was drafted by the Cleveland Browns in 1946 of the newly formed All American Football Conference - Chet was a late cut and was picked up by the Buffalo franchise; and

WHEREAS, CHET MUTRYN soon made his way into Buffalo's starting lineup. Not only did he carry the load at running back, but he played defense, was a spectacular kick and punt returner, caught and threw passes, and often kicked and punted; and

WHEREAS, CHET MUTRYN averaged 5.4 yards a carry and ended his pro career with 3,031 yards rushing; and

WHEREAS, CHET MUTRYN gained All-Pro honors three times as a running back; and

WHEREAS, In 1987 CHET MUTRYN was rated the top running back of the pre-50's era. The rating was made by Dr. David Shapiro, a noted statistician, who ranked 'The Cleveland Butcher Boy' ahead of such greats as Bronko Nagurski and Steve Van Buren;

NOW, THEREFORE, I, DENNIS T. GORSKI, Erie County Executive, do hereby proclaim July 17th, Nineteen Hundred and Ninety as

"CHET MUTRYN DAY"

in this Great County of Erie, of the State of New York - The Empire State, in recognition of CHET MUTRYN'S outstanding personal achievements and his important role in establishing professional football in Western New York. I urge the Buffalo Bills to recognize CHET MUTRYN for his accomplishments by adding his name to the 'Wall of Fame' at Rich Stadium.

IN WITNESS WHEREOF, I have caused to be affixed the Seal of the County of Erie, this 17th day of July, 1990.

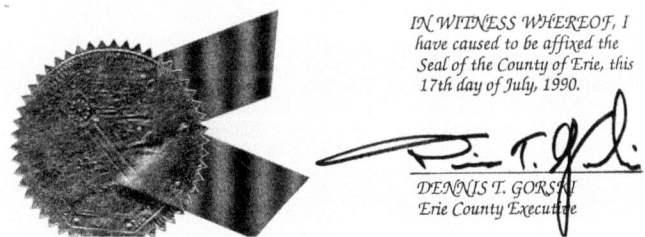

DENNIS T. GORSKI
Erie County Executive

Proclamation declaring July 17, 1990, Chet Mutryn Day

Red Dawson was an assistant under Biggie Munn at Michigan State before taking the head coaching duties at the University of Pittsburgh from 1951 through 1954. Dawson passed away in 1983.

Original Buffalo Bills owner Sam Cordovano left before training camp started in the 1946 season. After running the Globe Construction Company, Cordovano co-founded the Cordovano Company, a precision tool company in Buffalo. He retired to South Carolina and remained there until his death in 1995.[2]

There were varying degrees of success for the three remaining AAFC franchises. The Baltimore Colts went 1–11 in the 1950 season. At the February 1951 NFL owners meeting, Colts owner Abraham Watner sold the franchise back to the league with all players being dispersed through a draft. After the 1951 season, the New York Yanks became the Dallas Texans, but only stayed active for one season before folding. The team was reorganized and became the new Baltimore Colts and is currently the Indianapolis Colts.

The Cleveland Browns appeared in the first six NFL championship games after being admitted into the NFL. They won three of those games, forming arguably one of the greatest dynasties in professional football history. They appeared in ten straight championship games and won seven championships in two leagues. The Browns also won the championship in 1964. Owner Art Modell moved the team to Baltimore in the mid 1990s and formed the Baltimore Ravens. Cleveland received another franchise in 1999.

The San Francisco 49ers created one of pro football history's most memorable dynasties. Over their history, they won five Super Bowl championships, five conference titles and 17 divisional championships. In discussions of the greatest dynasties of all-time, San Francisco is always mentioned.

Buffalo had to wait another decade before major-league professional football returned. When Lamar Hunt formed the American Football League (AFL) in 1959, Detroit Lions minority owner Ralph Wilson purchased a franchise. Wilson tried to work with Miami to place his franchise there; however, the city was not interested. As Wilson was looking for a new location, Lamar Hunt mentioned Buffalo—as well as a few other cities—as a potential destination. Citing their success in the AAFC and the community support that franchise received, Buffalo was an attractive location. On October 28, 1959, Ralph C. Wilson, Jr. officially made Buffalo the seventh franchise to be admitted into the AFL. Wilson chose the name "Buffalo Bills" to honor the AAFC franchise.

Appendix A
Schedules and Rosters

Note: GP/GS Statistics are based solely on regular season games and do not include preseason and playoff games.

1946 Buffalo Bisons

Schedule

Record: 3-10-1
Points For: 249 (17.8/Game)
Points Against: 370 (26.4/Game)
Points For/Against Ratio: 0.67

Preseason

August 30, 1946   Buffalo Bisons 23 vs. Miami Seahawks 21 (@ Baltimore, MD)

Regular Season

September 8, 1946	Brooklyn Dodgers 27 @ Buffalo Bisons 14
September 14, 1946	Buffalo Bisons 10 @ New York Yankees 21
September 22, 1946	Cleveland Browns 28 @ Buffalo Bisons 0
September 25, 1946	Buffalo Bisons 35 @ Chicago Rockets 38
September 29, 1946	Los Angeles Dons 21 @ Buffalo Bisons 21
October 4, 1946	New York Yankees 21 @ Buffalo Bisons 13
October 11, 1946	Miami Seahawks 17 @ Buffalo Bisons 14
October 19, 1946	San Francisco 49ers 14 @ Buffalo Bisons 17
October 27, 1946	Chicago Rockets 17 @ Buffalo Bisons 49
November 2, 1946	Buffalo Bisons 14 @ San Francisco 49ers 27
November 10, 1946	Buffalo Bisons 17 @ Brooklyn Dodgers 14
November 18, 1946	Buffalo Bisons 14 @ Miami Seahawks 21
November 24, 1946	Buffalo Bisons 17 @ Cleveland Browns 42
December 1, 1946	Buffalo Bisons 14 @ Los Angeles Dons 62

Standings

	W	L	T	PF	PA
Eastern Division					
New York Yankees	10	3	1	270	192
Brooklyn Dodgers	3	10	1	226	339
Buffalo Bisons	**3**	**10**	**1**	**249**	**370**
Miami Seahawks	3	11	0	167	378
Western Division					
Cleveland Browns	12	1	1	423	137
San Francisco 49ers	9	5	0	307	189
Los Angeles Dons	7	5	2	305	290
Chicago Rockets	5	6	3	263	315

Roster

Owner: Jim Breuil; Head Coach: Lowell "Red" Dawson; End Coach: Bill Daddio; Backfield Coach: Clem Crowe; Line Coach: Tom Stidham; Line Coach: John Scafide

Name	Position	GP/GS
John Batorski	E	7/2
Blondy Black[a]	B	3/0
Sam Brazinsky	C	4/0
Marty Comer	E	7/2
Bill Daddio	E	3/1
Kenny Davis	-	*
Al Dekdebrun	B	13/7
George Doherty[a]	T	11/8
Andrew Dudish	B	12/2
Jack Dugger	E-T	6/0
Ray Ebli	E	9/8
Walter Fedora	B	*
John Fekete	B	2/0
Thaddeus Grabinski	C	1/0
Forrest Grigg	T	6/0
Harry Hopp[c]	B	9/2
Dick Horne[c]	E	1/0
Pres Johnston[b]	B	8/5
Elmer Jones	G	11/1
Steve Juzwik	B	12/9
Dolly King	E	12/0
Quentin Klenk[d]	T	2/2
Al Klug	T-G	11/5
Nick Klutka	E-B	10/4
Mike Kostiuk	T	2/0
Jack Kramer	T	10/2
Vic Kulbitski	B	13/7
Hal Lahar	G	12/3

Name	Position	GP/GS
Jim Larkin	G	1/0
Jim Lecture	G	2/0
Pat Martinelli	C	3/0
John Matisi	T	10/0
Chet Mutryn	B	13/8
Herb Nelson	E	12/8
John Perko	G	14/11
Rocco Pirro	T-G	13/12
Felto Prewitt	C	14/9
Ben Pucci	T	11/1
Curtis Sandig	B	9/1
Ralph Schilling	E	2/0
C.B. Stanley	T	12/11
Ken Stofer	B	13/1
Roy Stuart	G-B	9/0
George Terlep	B	13/5
Jim Thibaut	B	5/0
Bob Thurbon	B	2/0
Lou Tomasetti	B	13/2
Al Vandeweghe	E	5/3
Alois Vogt	B	1/0
Gene White	G	1/0
Al Wukits[c]	C	8/5
Lou Zontini	B	13/7

*On roster, but did not play.
[a]From New York
[b]From Miami
[c]To Miami
[d]To Chicago

1947 BUFFALO BILLS

Schedule

Record: 8-4-2
Points For: 320 (22.9/Game)
Points Against: 288 (20.6/Game)
Points For/Against Ratio: 1.11

Preseason

August 18, 1947   Buffalo Bills 7 @ New York Yankees 29 (@ Newark, NJ)
August 22, 1947   Buffalo Bills 29 vs. Baltimore Colts 20 (@ Hershey, PA)

Regular Season

August 31, 1947   New York Yankees 24 @ Buffalo Bills 28
September 5, 1947   Buffalo Bills 14 @ Cleveland Browns 30
September 14, 1947   Chicago Rockets 20 @ Buffalo Bills 28

Appendix A

September 19, 1947	Buffalo Bills 31 @ Chicago Rockets 14
September 28, 1947	San Francisco 49ers 41 @ Buffalo Bills 24
October 5, 1947	Buffalo Bills 27 @ Los Angeles Dons 25
October 12, 1947	Baltimore Colts 15 @ Buffalo Bills 20
October 17, 1947	Buffalo Bills 14 @ Brooklyn Dodgers 14
October 26, 1947	Brooklyn Dodgers 7 @ Buffalo Bills 35
November 2, 1947	Cleveland Browns 28 @ Buffalo Bills 7
November 9, 1947	Los Angeles Dons 0 @ Buffalo Bills 25
November 23, 1947	Buffalo Bills 33 @ Baltimore Colts 14
November 30, 1947	Buffalo Bills 13 @ New York Yankees 35
December 7, 1947	Buffalo Bills 21 @ San Francisco 49ers 21

Standings

	W	L	T	PF	PA
Eastern Division					
New York Yankees	11	2	1	378	239
Buffalo Bills	8	4	2	320	288
Brooklyn Dodgers	3	10	1	181	340
Baltimore Colts	2	10	1	167	377
Western Division					
Cleveland Browns	12	1	1	410	185
San Francisco 49ers	8	4	2	327	264
Los Angeles Dons	7	7	0	328	256
Chicago Rockets	1	13	0	263	425

Roster

Owner: Jim Breuil; Head Coach: Lowell "Red" Dawson; Line Coach: Clem Crowe; Backfield Coach: Chuck Jaskwhich; End Coach: William "Red" Conkright; Assistant Line Coach: John Scafide

Name	Position	GP/GS
Joseph Andrejco	B	*
Graham Armstrong	T	14/7
Alton Baldwin	E-B	13/5
Blondy Black[c]	B	0/0
Lamar Blount[a]	B	6/0
Sam Brazinsky	C	*
Ray Carlson	B	*
Jack Carpenter	T	13/4
Marty Comer	E	14/2
Al Coppage	E	14/11
Bert Corley	E-C	14/4
Bernard Craig	G-E	*
George Doherty	T	10/8

Schedules and Rosters

Name	Position	GP/GS
Gil Duggan	T	11/2
Verne Erdman	T	*
Frederick Evans[b]	B	4/0
Paul Gibson	E	13/8
Forrest Grigg	T	*
George Groves	G	8/0
Joe Haynes	G-C	10/0
Ed Hirsch	G-B	12/5
Len Janiak	B	*
Steve Juzwik	B	9/2
Mike Kasap[a]	T	0/0
John Kerns	T	13/2
Dolly King	E	14/2
Kit Kittrell	B	*
George Koch	B	13/3
Joe Kodba[a]	C	0/0
Floyd Konetsky[a]	E	0/0
Chet Kozel	T	11/5
Ray Kuffel	E	7/2
Vic Kulbitski	B	12/7
Hal Lahar	G	14/14
Jim Larkin	G	*
Pug Manders	B	3/0
John Maskas	G	9/0
Vince Mazza	E	13/0
Jack Morton	E	2/0
Chet Mutryn	B	14/11
Bob Paffrath	B	*
Dick Pfuhl	B	0/0
Rocco Pirro	G	14/14
Ray Piskor	T	*
Felto Prewitt	C	13/10
Ben Pucci[b]	T	0/0
George Ratterman	B	13/5
Albie Reisz	B	13/0
Julie Rykovich	B	13/11
Bud Schwenk[a]	B	0/0
Vince Scott	G	12/0
George Terlep	B	11/0
Dick Thames	G	*
Lou Tomasetti	B	14/8
Alex Wizbicki	B	14/2
Ray Yagiello	G	*

*On training camp roster, but did not make regular season roster.
[a]To Baltimore.
[b]To Chicago.
[c]Also played with Baltimore.

1948 BUFFALO BILLS

Schedule

Record: 7–7–0
Points For: 360 (25.7/Game)
Points Against: 358 (25.6/Game)
Points For/Against Ratio: 1.01

Preseason

August 12, 1948	Buffalo Bills 28 vs. New York Yankees 28 (@ Newark, NJ)
August 17, 1948	Brooklyn Dodgers 19 @ Buffalo Bills 21
August 22, 1948	Buffalo Bills 21 vs. Cleveland Browns 35 (@ Akron, OH)

Regular Season

August 29, 1948	Buffalo Bills 14 @ San Francisco 49ers 35
September 6, 1948	Chicago Rockets 7 @ Buffalo Bills 42
September 12, 1948	Cleveland Browns 42 @ Buffalo Bills 13
September 26, 1948	San Francisco 49ers 38 @ Buffalo Bills 28
October 3, 1948	Brooklyn Dodgers 21 @ Buffalo Bills 31
October 10, 1948	New York Yankees 14 @ Buffalo Bills 13
October 17, 1948	Buffalo Bills 14 @ Cleveland Browns 31
October 24, 1948	Buffalo Bills 35 @ Los Angeles Dons 21
October 31, 1948	Baltimore Colts 17 @ Buffalo Bills 35
November 7, 1948	Buffalo Bills 26 @ Brooklyn Dodgers 21
November 14, 1948	Los Angeles Dons 27 @ Buffalo Bills 20
November 25, 1948	Buffalo Bills 39 @ Chicago Rockets 35
November 28, 1948	Buffalo Bills 35 @ New York Yankees 14
December 5, 1948	Buffalo Bills 15 @ Baltimore Colts 35

Eastern Division Title

December 12, 1948	Buffalo Bills 28 @ Baltimore Colts 17

AAFC Championship

December 19, 1948	Buffalo Bills 7 @ Cleveland Browns 49

Standings

	W	L	T	PF	PA
Eastern Division					
Buffalo Bills	7	7	0	360	358
Baltimore Colts	7	7	0	333	327
New York Yankees	6	8	0	265	301
Brooklyn Dodgers	2	12	0	253	387

Schedules and Rosters

	W	L	T	PF	PA
Western Division					
Cleveland Browns	14	0	0	389	190
San Francisco 49ers	12	2	0	495	248
Los Angeles Dons	7	7	0	258	305
Chicago Rockets	1	13	0	202	439

Roster

Owner: Jim Breuil; Asssitant to Owner: Jim Wells; Coach: Lowell "Red" Dawson; Assistant Coaches: Clem Crowe, William "Red" Conkright, Charles Jaskwhich, John Scafide

Name	Position	GP/GS
Jim Aina	G	**
Al Akins[a]	B	4/0
Graham Armstrong	T	14/12
Ed Balatti[b]	E	7/0
Alton Baldwin	E	13/12
Jack Baldwin	C	3/0
Rex Bumgardner	B	13/4
Bob Callahan	C	7/0
Jack Carpenter	T	13/7
Bernie Check	E	**
Marty Comer	E	6/3
Bert Corley	C	**
Lou Corriere	B	*
John DiGangi	T	*
Jeff Durkota	B	*
Dominic Fusci	G	**
Paul Gibson	E	7/5
Don Giles	B	*
Bill Gompers	B	14/2
Joe Haynes	T	**
Thomas Heintz	T	**
William Heywood	B	*
Ed Hirsch	G-C	12/2
Robert Hodges	T	*
Richard Johnson	G	**
John Kerns	T	14/7
Ed King	T-G	13/0
George Kisiday	E-G	14/3
John Kissell	T	14/2
Frank Kosikowski	E	1/0
Chet Kozel[b]	T	1/0
Vic Kulbitski	B	13/4
Hal Lahar	G	13/11
Bob Leonetti[d]	G	2/0
Chick Maggioli	B	7/0

Name	Position	GP/GS
Vince Mazza	E	14/2
Jack Morton	E	1/0
Chet Mutryn	B	14/12
Zeke O'Connor	E	14/3
Joe Pasqua	T	**
Rocco Pirro	G	13/11
Frank Pizza	T	**
Felto Prewitt	G-C	6/6
George Ratterman	B	14/11
Ralph Ruthstrom	B	*
Julie Rykovich[c]	B	6/2
Don Schneider	B	9/1
Charles Schuette	B	13/2
Vince Scott	G	14/3
Marshall Shurnas	E	*
J. Bob Smith[d]	B	3/1
Art Statuto	C	13/6
Bob Stefik	E	1/0
Bob Steuber	B	9/7
Jim Still	B	12/1
Edward Swan	E	**
George Terlep[e]	B	3/0
Lou Tomasetti	B	14/7
Gerald Whalen	T-G	5/0
Alex Wizbicki	B	8/2
John Wyhonic	G	12/3
Steve Yelich	G	**

*On roster, but did not play.
**On training camp roster, but did not make regular season roster.
[a]From Brooklyn.
[b]Also played with New York and San Francisco.
[c]To Chicago.
[d]To Brooklyn.
[e]To Cleveland.

1949 BUFFALO BILLS

Schedule

Record: 5–5–2
Points For: 236 (19.7/Game)
Points Against: 256 (21.3/Game)
Points For/Against Ratio: 0.92

Preseason

August 5, 1949	Jersey City Giants 0 @ Buffalo Bills 79
August 10, 1949	Buffalo Bills 12 vs. Baltimore Colts 28 (@ Wilmington, DE)
August 14, 1949	Buffalo Bills 10 @ San Francisco 49ers 21
August 19, 1949	Bethlehem Bulldogs 0 @ Buffalo Bills 48

Schedules and Rosters 125

Regular Season

August 26, 1949	Buffalo Bills 14 @ Chicago Hornets 17
September 5, 1949	Cleveland Browns 28 @ Buffalo Bills 28
September 11, 1949	New York Yankees 17 @ Buffalo Bills 14
September 25, 1949	San Francisco 49ers 17 @ Buffalo Bills 28
October 2, 1949	Baltimore Colts 35 @ Buffalo Bills 28
October 9, 1949	Buffalo Bills 28 @ Los Angeles Dons 42
October 16, 1949	Buffalo Bills 7 @ San Francisco 49ers 51
October 23, 1949	Los Angeles Dons 14 @ Buffalo Bills 17
November 6, 1949	Buffalo Bills 17 @ New York Yankees 14
November 13, 1949	Buffalo Bills 7 @ Cleveland Browns 7
November 20, 1949	Chicago Hornets 0 @ Buffalo Bills 10
November 27, 1949	Buffalo Bills 38 @ Baltimore Colts 14

Playoff

December 4, 1949	Buffalo Bills 21 @ Cleveland Browns 31

Standings

	W	L	T	PF	PA
Cleveland Browns	9	1	2	339	171
San Francisco 49ers	9	3	0	416	227
Brooklyn Dodgers/NY Yankees	8	4	0	196	206
Buffalo Bills	5	5	2	236	256
Chicago Hornets	4	8	0	179	268
Los Angeles Dons	4	8	0	253	322
Baltimore Colts	1	11	0	172	341

Roster

Owner: Jim Breuil; Assistant to Owner: Jim Wells; Head Coach: Lowell "Red" Dawson; Line Coach: Clem Crowe; Backfield Coach: Joel Hunk; Assistant Coach: John Scafide; Assistant Coach: Hank Reese; After Red Dawson's firing: Head Coach: Clem Crowe; Assistant Coach: John Wyhonic; Backfield Coach: Joel Hunt

Name	Position	GP/GS
Chet Adams	T	12/0
Al Akins	B	*
Alton Baldwin	E	12/12
Rex Bumgardner	B	11/8
Jack Carpenter[b]	T	7/7
Ollie Cline	B	11/11
Tom Colella	B	12/0
Edward Conwell	B	*
Tony DiToma	B	*

Appendix A

Name	Position	GP/GS
Jesse Freitas	B	1/0
Bob Furse	B	*
Abe Gibron	T-G	10/9
Paul Gibson	E-T-G	11/2
Frank Guess	B	*
Bernard Hanula	T	*
Hal Herring	C	11/0
Ed Hirsch	G-C	10/0
Larry Joe	B	2/0
John Kerns	T	12/12
Ed King	G	4/0
Joseph Kirkland	T	*
George Kisiday	E	*
John Kissell	T	12/0
Vito Kissell	B	11/0
Milton Kormonicki	C	*
Nicholas Lanza, Jr.	E	*
Bob Livingstone[b]	B	5/0
Bob Logel	E	*
Jim Lukens	E	11/10
John Maskas	T	11/0
Vince Mazza	E	12/0
William McLellan	T	*
Chet Mutryn	B	11/11
Bucky O'Connor	G	*
Bob Oristaglio	E	12/0
Rocco Pirro	G	11/11
George Ratterman	B	11/11
William Schroll	B	11/0
Charles Schuette	C	12/0
Vince Scott	G	*
Bill Stanton	E	10/0
Art Statuto	C	12/12
Odell Stautzenberger	T-G	11/6
Jim Still	B	10/1
Joe Sutton	B	11/1
Lou Tomasetti	B	12/4
Vic Vasicek	G	12/3
Wilbur Volz	B	9/0
Alex Wizbicki	B	11/1
John Wyhonic	G	4/0

*On preseason roster, but not regular season.
[a] To San Francisco.
[b] From Chicago.

Appendix B
Detailed Game Summaries

Note: All game statistics were taken from the official All-America Football Conference score sheets. Where the score sheets were not available, statistics were recorded from newspaper accounts and compared to the official All-America Football Conference record books. Not all statistics may be complete for each game.

1946 BUFFALO BISONS

Preseason

August 30, 1946, Buffalo Bisons vs. Miami Seahawks
Location: Municipal Stadium (Baltimore, MD)
Attendance: 16,642

	1	2	3	4	F
Miami Seahawks	0	7	0	14	21
Buffalo Bisons	0	17	0	6	23

Scoring Summary

MIA	Nelson 6-Yard Run (Erdlitz Kick)
BUF	Juzwik 51-Yard Run (Daddio Kick)
BUF	Stofer 32-Yard Run (Daddio Kick)
BUF	Daddio 23-Yard Field Goal
BUF	Thurbon 54-Yard Run (Daddio Kick Failed)
MIA	Johnston 20-Yard Run (Erdlitz Kick)
MIA	Nelson 48-Yard Pass from Tarrant (Erdlitz Kick)

	Miami	Buffalo
First Downs	9	7
Total Yards	225	282
Yards Rushing	166	273
Passes Attempted	13	4
Passes Completed	3	1
Yards Passing	59	9
Interceptions	0	1
Punts/Average	8/37	6/35
Penalties/Yards	3/25	2/10

	Miami	Buffalo
LE	Ulrich	Klutka
LT	Olenski	Stanley
LG	Taylor	Perko
C	Whitlow	Wukits
RG	Jungmichel	Jones
RT	Ellenson	Klenk
RE	Scott	Vandeweghe
QB	Price	Hopp
LHB	Gafford	Tomasetti
RHB	Erdlitz	Juzwik
FB	Jones	Kulbitski

Substitutes

Miami
Ends: Plasecky, Comer, Sizemore, Kowalski, Blount, Ulrich, Scott
Tackles: Berezney, Reece, Olenski
Guards: Castronis, Bertagnolli, Cemore, McDonald
Centers: Tavener, Williams, Cato
Backs: Pugh, W. McDonald, Tarrant, Nelson, Mitchell, Butler, Crain, Fox, Craig, Reynolds, Kozlowski, Eakin, Johnston

Buffalo
Ends: Daddio, King
Tackles: Grigg, Kostiuk, Matisi, Pucci
Guards: Lahar, Pirro, Larkin
Centers: Grabinski, Prewitt, Martinelli
Backs: Dekdebrun, Terlep, Vogt, Pezelski, Sandig, Stofer, Thurbon, Dudish, Stuart, Zontini

Regular Season

September 8, 1946, Brooklyn Dodgers vs. Buffalo Bisons
Location: Civic Stadium (Buffalo, NY)
Attendance: 25,489

	1	2	3	4	F
Brooklyn Dodgers	0	7	7	13	27
Buffalo Bisons	0	0	0	14	14

Scoring Summary

BKN Mayne Field Goal Attempt Returned 100-Yards (Davis Kick)
BKN Judd 28-Yard Pass from Mayne (McCarthy Kick)
BUF Juzwik 5-Yard Run (Daddio Kick)
BUF Sandig 10-Yard Run (Daddio Kick)
BKN Judd 31-Yard Pass from Dobbs (McCarthy Kick)
BKN Morrow 58-Yard Run on Lateral from Dobbs (Kick Failed)

Detailed Game Summaries

Position	Brooklyn	Buffalo
LE	McCarthy	Klutka
LT	Ruby	Stanley
LG	Freeman	Lahar
C	Warrington	Wukits
RG	Bernhardt	Klug
RT	Hrabetin	Klenk
RE	Davis	Vandeweghe
QB	Shetley	Hopp
LHB	Connolly	Sandig
RHB	Colmer	Juzwik
FB	Principe	Zontini

Substitutes

Brooklyn
Ends: McCain, Adams, Perdue, Judd
Tackles: Perpich
Guards: Obeck
Centers: Morrow, Gibson
Backs: Mayne, Paffrath, Tackett, Dobbs, Timmons

Buffalo
Ends: Dugger, Batorski, Daddio, King
Tackles: Grigg, Matisi, Pucci, Kramer
Guards: Jones, Perko
Centers: Martinelli, Prewitt
Backs: Terlep, Stuart, Kulbitski, Stofer, Thurbon, Tomasetti, Mutryn

Individual Statistics

Brooklyn
Rushing: Mayne: 9-38, Dobbs: 4-37, Principe: 7-36, Connolly: 6-16, Paffrath: 4-11, Shetley: 2-4, Purdin: 2-(-3)
Receiving: David: 2-61, Judd: 2-59 2 TD, Colmer: 1-17
Passing: Dobbs: 2-3-80 1 TD, Connolly: 2-8-29 1 INT, Mayne: 1-1-28 1 TD
Punting: Dobbs: 6-274, Mayne: 1-40
Punt Returns: Colmer: 1-9, Connolly: 1-6, Mayne: 1-0
Kickoff Returns: Connolly: 1-27

Buffalo
Rushing: Juzwik: 11-88 1 TD, Sandig: 6-17 1 TD, Hopp: 13-10, Kulbitski: 1-2, Thurbon: 2-2, Terlep: 3-1, Stofer: 2-(-2)
Receiving: King: 3-61, Juzwik: 1-42, Vandeweghe: 3-35, Batorski: 1-16, Dugger: 1-15, Thurbon: 1-(-3)
Passing: Hopp: 10-18-166, Terlep: 1-0-0
Punting: Hopp: 3-94, Sandig: 2-82
Punt Returns: Juzwik: 2-24, Sandig: 1-14
Kickoff Returns: Juzwik: 3-66, Stofer: 1-45, Sandig: 2-43
Interception Returns: Jones: 1-7

September 14, 1946, Buffalo Bisons vs. New York Yankees
Location: Yankee Stadium (New York, NY)
Attendance: 40,606

	1	2	3	4	F
Buffalo Bisons	7	3	0	0	10
New York Yankees	7	0	0	14	21

Scoring Summary

NYY	Manders 2-Yard Run (Johnson Kick)
BUF	Vandeweghe 97-Yard Fumble Return (Daddio Kick)
BUF	Zontini 23-Yard Field Goal
NYY	Sanders 9-Yard Run (Johnson Kick)
NYY	Sanders 2-Yard Run (Johnson Kick)

	New York	Buffalo
First Downs	14	5
Total Yards	286	102
Yards Rushing	228	64
Passes Attempted	10	12
Passes Completed	4	2
Yards Passing	58	38
Interceptions	1	1
Punts/Average	5/39.4	9/29.4
Penalties/Yards	4/26	0/0

Position	Buffalo	New York
LE	Klutka	Masterson
LT	Stanley	F. Kinard
LG	Lahar	G. Kinard
C	Wukits	Robertson
RG	Pirro	Riffle
RT	Klenk	N. Johnson
RE	Vandeweghe	Alford
QB	Hopp	Morrow
LHB	Mutryn	Parker
RHB	Juzwik	Sweiger
FB	Zontini	Manders

Substitutes

New York
Ends: Schwartz, Burrus, Conger, Stanton
Tackles: Bentz, McCollum, Piskor
Guards: Karmazin, Doherty, Yackanich
Centers: Sossamon, Baldwin
Backs: Hare, Sanders, Perina, Wagner, Proctor, Kennedy, Prokop, H. Johnson

Buffalo
Ends: Batorski, Daddio, King
Tackles: Grigg, Matisi, Pucci, Kostiuk
Guards: Klug, Perko, Jones, Larkin, White

Centers: Prewitt, Martinelli, Grabinski
Backs: Terlep, Dekdebrun, Sandig, Thurbon, Stofer, Tomasetti, Fekete, Dudish, Kulbitski, Vogt

Individual Statistics

New York
Rushing: Sanders: 16–105 2 TD, Manders: 14–67 1 TD, Proctor: 9–33, Perina: 3–7, Sweiger: 1–6, Kennedy: 1–0, Wagner: 3–(–5), Parker: 10–(–15)
Receiving: Schwartz: 1–24, Burrus: 1–18, Masterson: 1–13, Proctor: 1–3
Passing: Sanders: 3–8–45 1 INT, Parker: 1–2–13
Punting: Parker: 2–77, Sanders: 2–77, Perina: 1–43
Punt Returns: Parker: 3–34, Chratham: 1–26, Prokop: 1–7, Sanders: 1–4
Kickoff Returns: Sweiger: 1–23, Sanders: 1–14, Chratham: 1–7
Interception Returns: Perina: 1–23

Buffalo
Rushing: Juzwik: 6–35, Terlep: 7–23, Mutryn: 3–7, Stofer: 3–3, Kulbitski: 1–0, Thurbon: 1–0, Hopp: 3–(–2), Zontini: 2–(–2)
Receiving: King: 1–24, Stofer: 1–14
Passing: Hopp: 1–4–24, Terlep: 1–6–14 1 INT
Punting: Zontini: 6–196, Stofer: 2–60, Hopp: 1–29
Punt Returns: Stofer: 3–15, Juzwik: 1–7
Kickoff Returns: Mutryn: 1–19, Hopp: 1–17, Thurbon: 1–15, Kulbitski: 1–13
Interception Returns: Martinelli: 1–12

September 22, 1946, Cleveland Browns vs. Buffalo Bisons
Location: Civic Stadium (Buffalo, NY)
Attendance: 30,302

	1	2	3	4	F
Cleveland Browns	21	0	0	7	28
Buffalo Bisons	0	0	0	0	0

Scoring Summary

CLE Yonakor 52-Yard Pass from Graham (Groza Kick)
CLE Motley 33-Yard Pass from Graham (Groza Kick)
CLE Smith 12-Yard Lateral from Lewis (Groza Kick)
CLE Adams 34-Yard Fumble Return (Groza Kick)

	Cleveland	Buffalo
First Downs	9	14
Total Yards	329	164
Yards Rushing	189	115
Passes Attempted	21	24
Passes Completed	8	8
Yards Passing	190	49
Interceptions	3	1
Punting Average	42.2	31.8
Penalty Yardage	11 for 95	15

Position	Cleveland	Buffalo
LE	Speedie	Klutka
LT	Daniell	Stanley
LG	Ulinski	Lahar
C	Groza	Wukits
RG	Willis	Pirro
RT	Rymkus	Pucci
RE	Yonakor	Vandeweghe
QB	Lewis	Terlep
LHB	Colella	Mutryn
RHB	Greenwood	Stofer
FB	Motley	Kulbitski

Substitutes

Cleveland
Ends: Young, Coppage, Rokisky, Harrington, Lavelli
Tackles: Blandin, Adams
Guards: Houston, Cheroke
Centers: Scarry, Gatski, Maceau
Backs: Graham, Saban, G. Fekete, Smith, Lund, Steuber, Jones, Evans

Buffalo
Ends: King, Horne, Nelson, Batorski
Guards: Perko, Jones, Klug
Centers: Prewitt, Martinelli
Backs: Dekdebrun, Stuart, Zontini, Hopp, Dudish, Fekete, Sandig, Tomasetti

Individual Statistics

Buffalo
Rushing: Kulbitski: 8–26, Hopp: 5–20, Mutryn: 5–18, Stofer: 4–13, Sandig: 4–12, Dudish: 8–10, Tomasetti: 5–10, Terlep: 3–7, Dekdebrun: 1–0, Zontini: 1–0, Fekete: 1–(–1)
Receiving: King: 3–33, Vandeweghe: 2–24, Sandig: 1–1, Kulbitski: 1–0, Hopp: 1–(–9)
Passing: Terlep: 7–20–34
Punting: Zontini: 4–128, Sandig: 1–47, Hopp: 2–27 1 Block
Punt Returns: Stofer: 2–38, Mutryn: 1–9, Sandig: 1–6
Kickoff Returns: Dudish: 2–47, Stofer: 1–36, Mutryn: 1–24
Interception Returns: Kulbitski: 1–20

Cleveland
Rushing: Motley: 4–81, Smith: 7–29, Graham: 2–17, Lewis: 4–4, Greenwood: 2–4, Steuber: 3–3, Jones: 1–3, Ulinski: 1–2, Saban: 2–2, Lund: 1–(–6)
Receiving: Yonakor: 1–52 1 TD, Saban: 1–45, Motley: 1–33 1 TD, Lavelli: 2–20, Speedie: 1–18, Harrington: 1–13, Steuber: 1–9
Passing: Graham: 5–10–153 2 TD 1 INT, Lewis: 3–11–37
Punting: Evans: 3–127, Colella: 2–84
Punt Returns: Colella: 2–56, Evans: 1–0
Kickoff Returns: Steuber: 1–20
Interception Returns: Colella: 1–12, Lewis: 2–0

September 25, 1946, Buffalo Bisons vs. Chicago Rockets
Location: Soldier Field (Chicago, IL)
Attendance: 29,618

	1	2	3	4	F
Buffalo Bisons	7	7	14	7	35
Chicago Rockets	7	7	7	17	38

Scoring Summary

BUF	Kulbitski 47–Yard Run (Zontini Kick)
CHI	Hirsch 68–Yard Pass from Hoernschemeyer (Nemeth Kick)
CHI	Hillenbrand 51-Yard Pass from Hoernschemeyer (Nemeth Kick)
BUF	Tomasetti 30-Yard Pass from Terlep (Zontini Kick)
CHI	Hillenbrand 34-Yard Run (Nemeth Kick)
BUF	King 52-Yard Pass from Dekdebrun (Zontini Kick)
BUF	Juzwik 40-Yard Pass from Terlep (Zontini Kick)
CHI	Hillenbrand 68-Yard Punt Return (Nemeth Kick)
BUF	Juzwik 24-Yard Pass from Terlep (Zontini Kick)
CHI	Heywood 5-Yard Pass from Hoernschemeyer (Nemeth Kick)
CHI	Nemeth 13-Yard Field Goal

Position	Buffalo	Chicago
LE	Batorski	Heywood
LT	Stanley	Wilkin
LG	Perko	Vogds
C	Wukits	Coleman
RG	Pirro	Sumpter
RT	Kramer	Huneke
RE	Nelson	Lahey
QB	Terlep	Nemeth
LHB	Mutryn	Hirsch
RHB	Juzwik	Griffin
FB	Kulbitski	Lewis

Substitutes

Chicago
Ends: Quillen, Morris, Motl
Tackles: Brutz, O'Neal, Verry, Wasserbach
Guards: Dove, Pearcy, Ruetz
Backs: Hoernschemeyer, Clay, Schroeder, Hillenbrand, Mathews, Kellagher, Williams

Buffalo
Ends: King, Vandeweghe, Dugger
Tackles: Matisi, Kostiuk, Doherty, Pucci
Guards: Lahar, Jones, Klug
Centers: Prewitt
Backs: Zontini, Dekdebrun, Sandig, Tomasetti, Dudish, Stuart, Stofer

Individual Statistics

Buffalo
Rushing: Kulbitski: 12–92 1 TD, Mutryn: 8–87, Stofer: 4–21, Tomasetti: 5–17, Terlep: 3–13, Sandig: 2–4, Juzwik: 7–1
Receiving: Juzwik: 3–62 2 TD, King: 1–52 1 TD, Tomasetti: 2–47 1 TD
Passing: Terlep: 4–12–92 3 TD 2 INT, Dekdebrun: 2–2–69 1 TD
Punting: Zontini: 4–140, Stofer: 1–48
Punt Returns: Tomasetti: 1–8, Mutryn: 1–8, Juzwik: 1–7
Kickoff Returns: Kulbitski: 2–33, Dekdebrun: 1–30, Terlep: 1–23, Vandeweghe: 1–15, Doherty: 1–0

Chicago
Rushing: Hillenbrand: 4–56 TD, Hoernschemeyer: 6–29, Hirsch: 3–18, Schroeder: 3–18, Clay: 5–10, Lewis: 1–5, Kellagher: 1–1, Mathews: 2–5, Griffin: 1–(-2), Williams: 1–(-4)
Receiving: Hirsch: 5–136 1 TD, Hillenbrand: 3–57 1 TD, Heywood: 3–22 1 TD, Mathews: 1–9, Motl: 1–14, Lahey: 3–13, Griffin: 1–5, Quillen: 1–4
Passing: Hoernschemeyer: 13–21–183 3 TD, Williams: 1–3–50, Clay: 2–3–14, Lewis: 1–2–13
Punting: Lewis: 4–169, Heywood: 1–17
Punt Returns: Hillenbrand: 1–68 1 TD, Hirsch: 1–21, Clay: 1–5
Kickoff Returns: Hirsch: 3–84, Mathews: 2–47, Kellagher: 1–20
Interception Returns: Clay: 2–28

September 29, 1946, Los Angeles Dons vs. Buffalo Bisons
Location: Civic Stadium (Buffalo, NY)
Attendance: 18,163

	1	2	3	4	F
Los Angeles Dons	0	0	14	7	21
Buffalo Bisons	7	0	0	14	21

Scoring Summary

BUF Mutryn 25-Yard Run (Zontini Kick)
LA Polanski 5-Yard Run (Aguirre Kick)
LA Reinhard Recovered Blocked Punt In End Zone (Aguirre Kick)
BUF Vandeweghe 8-Yard Pass from Terlep (Zontini Kick)
BUF Tomasetti 4-Yard Run (Zontini Kick)
LA Aguirre 68-Yard Pass from O'Rourke (Aguirre Kick)

	Los Angeles	Buffalo
First Downs	14	6
Total Yards	240	168
Yards Rushing	94	139
Passes Attempted	23	8
Passes Completed	11	3
Yards Passing	146	29
Interceptions	0	3
Punting Average	35.2	40.9
Penalty Yardage	20	20

Detailed Game Summaries

Position	Los Angeles	Buffalo
LE	Aguirre	Batorski
LT	Reinhard	Stanley
LG	Frankowski	Perko
C	Nolander	Wukits
RG	P. Mitchell	Pirro
RT	Artoe	Doherty
RE	Morton	Nelson
QB	O'Rourke	Terlep
LHB	Seymour	Mutryn
RHB	Nygren	Dudish
FB	Polanski	Kulbitski

Substitutes

Los Angeles
Ends: Kerr, Gentry, Krueger
Guards: Lolotai, Radovich, Yokas
Tackles: Duggan, Audet, Mihal
Center: Rockwell
Backs: Bertelli, Clarke, Elsey, Kimbrough, Marefos, Mertes, B. Mitchell, Trigilio, Vinnola

Buffalo
Ends: King, Vandeweghe, Klutka
Tackles: Dugger, Kramer, Matisi, Pucci
Guards: Klug, Lahar
Centers: Prewitt
Backs: Tomasetti, Zontini, Dekdebrun, Hopp, Black, Juzwik, Stofer

Individual Statistics

Los Angeles
Rushing: Seymour: 4–53, Clarke: 8–35, Polanski: 10–32 1 TD, Nygren: 4–27, Mertes: 6–11, Kimbrough: 3–8, Trigilio: 1–0, Elsey: 1–(–4), O'Rourke: 3–(–8), Reinhard: 1–(–30)
Receiving: Aguirre: 2–80 1 TD, Kruger: 3–29, Clarke: 1–14, Seymour: 2–12, Polanski: 1–8, Nygren: 1–2, Kimbrough: 1–1
Passing: O'Rourke: 8–16–105 1 TD 2 INT, Bertelli: 3–7–21 1 INT
Punting: Aguirre: 2–91, Bertelli: 1–40, Reinhard: 2–35 1 Block
Punt Returns: Seymour: 2–36, Fenenbock: 1–30, Elsey: 1–21, Clarke: 1–4
Kickoff Returns: Seymour: 1–27, Fenenbock: 1–24, Mertes: 1–21

Buffalo
Rushing: Kulbitski: 8–60, Tomasetti: 6–39 1 TD, Mutryn: 4–32 1 TD, Dudish: 5–24, Juzwik: 5–16, Hopp: 2–(–4), Dekdebrun: 1–(–8), Terlep: 2–(–20)
Receiving: Dudish: 1–13, Vandeweghe: 1–8 1 TD, Hopp: 1–8
Passing: Terlep: 3–8–29 1 TD
Punting: Hopp: 6–201, Zontini: 2–85, Terlep: 1–31
Punt Returns: Dudish: 1–11
Kickoff Returns: Juzwik: 4–88, Dudish: 1–30
Interception Returns: Juzwik: 1–33, Dekdebrun: 1–0, Tomasetti: 1–0

Appendix B

October 4, 1946, New York Yankees vs. Buffalo Bisons
Location: Civic Stadium (Buffalo, NY)
Attendance: 17,101

	1	2	3	4	F
New York Yankees	0	7	0	14	21
Buffalo Bisons	0	0	0	13	13

Scoring Summary

NY Kennedy 8-Yard Run (H. Johnson Kick)
BUF Terlep 3-Yard Run (Zontini Kick Failed)
NY Wagner 40-Yard Pass From Sanders (H. Johnson Kick)
NY Sanders 75-Yard Punt Return (H. Johnson Kick)
BUF Mutryn 40-Yard Pass From Dekdebrun (Zontini Kick)

Position	New York	Buffalo
LE	Russell	Ebli
LT	F. Kinard	Stanley
LG	Piskor	Perko
C	Robertson	Prewitt
RG	Riffle	Pirro
RT	N. Johnson	Doherty
RE	Alford	Nelson
QB	Morrow	Dekdebrun
LHB	Perina	Mutryn
RHB	Burrus	Juzwik
FB	H. Johnson	Zontini

Substitutes

New York
Ends: Conger, Masterson, Stanton, Schwartz
Tackles: Bentz, Palmer, McCollum
Guards: G. Kinard, Yackanich
Centers: Sossamon
Backs: Cheatham, Sanders, Wagner, Kennedy, Hare, Sinkwich

Buffalo
Ends: Klutka, Batorski
Tackles: Matisi, Pucci
Guards: Lahar, Jones, Klug
Centers: Wukits
Backs: Stofer, Dudish, Black, Kulbitski, Terlep, Hopp, Tomasetti, Thibaut

Individual Statistics

New York
Rushing: Kennedy: 9–46 1 TD, Sanders: 9–45, H. Johnson: 2–9, Sinkwich: 4–8, Perina: 7–7, Morrow: 1–3
Receiving: Wagner: 1–40 1 TD, H. Johnson: 2–19, Cheatham: 1–9, Masterson: 1–5, Burrus: 1–2, Kennedy: 1–0

Detailed Game Summaries

Passing: Sanders: 4–7–54 1 TD, Perina: 3–6–21 1 INT
Punting: Perina: 3–115, Sanders: 2–75
Punt Returns: Sanders: 1–75 1 TD, Perina: 2–29
Kickoff Returns: Sanders: 1–58, Kennedy: 1–25
Interception Returns: Perina: 1–1

Buffalo
Rushing: Mutryn: 8–40, Kulbitski: 5–30, Juzwik: 7–27, Hopp: 4–14, Zontini: 2–12, Black: 1–10, Dudish: 2–10, Nelson: 1–1, Thibaut: 1–1, Dekdebrun: 2–0, Terlep: 2-(–10) 1 TD
Receiving: Mutryn: 2–35 1 TD, Nelson: 3–34, Juzwik: 1–14, King: 1–8, Tomasetti: 1–1,
Passing: Dekdebrun: 1–1–40 1 TD, Terlep: 2–5–9
Punting: Zontini: 6–227
Punt Returns: Black: 2–58, Juzwik: 2–21, Mutryn: 1–4
Kickoff Returns: Dekdebrun: 2–28
Interception Returns: Black: 1–18, Zontini: 1–2

October 11, 1946, Miami Seahawks vs. Buffalo Bisons
Location: Civic Stadium (Buffalo, NY)
Attendance: 5,040

	1	2	3	4	F
Miami Seahawks	14	0	0	3	17
Buffalo Bisons	7	0	7	0	14

Scoring Summary

BUF Hopp 1-Yard Run (Zontini Kick)
MIA Gafford 6-Yard Run (Erdlitz Run)
MIA Gloden 6-Yard Run (Erdlitz Kick)
BUF King 9-Yard Pass From Stofer (Zontini Kick)
MIA Erdlitz 20-Yard Field Goal

	Miami	Buffalo
First Downs	11	10
Yards Rushing	205	63
Passes Attempted	25	30
Passes Completed	12	9
Interceptions	3	3
Punting Average	44	34
Penalty Yardage	30	35

Position	Miami	Buffalo
LE	L. Davis	Ebli
LT	Olenski	Pirro
LG	Jungmichel	Perko
C	Whitlow	Prewitt
RG	Taylor	Klug
RT	Ellenson	Doherty
RE	Scott	Nelson
QB	Pugh	Terlep

Position	Miami	Buffalo
LHB	Eakin	Mutryn
RHB	Erdlitz	Juzwik
FB	Reynolds	Zontini

Substitutes

Miami
Ends: Ulrich, Horne, Blount
Tackles: B. Davis, Reese
Guards: Sivell, Cato
Centers: Williams
Backs: Gafford, Gloden, J. Nelson, Price, Fox, Vardian

Buffalo
Ends: King, Batorski, Comer
Tackles: Stanley, Pucci, Kramer
Guards: Jones, Lahar, Stuart
Centers: Wukits
Backs: Hopp, Kulbitski, Dekdebrun, Dudish, Tomasetti, Johnston, Black, Stofer, Thibaut

Individual Statistics

Miami
Rushing: Reynolds: 8–32, Gafford: 1–6 1 TD, Mitchell: 2–18, Nelson: 5–17, Fox: 5–16, Gloden: 3–11 1 TD, Eakin: 1–1, Erdlitz: 2–6, Price: 3-(–7)
Receiving: Erdlitz: 6–49, McDonald: 1–47, Davis: 2–40, Mitchell: 1–39, Scott: 1–29, Gafford: 1-(–1)
Passing: Price: 7–15–132 1 INT, Nelson: 3–7–79 1 INT, Eakin: 0–1–0, Pugh: 2–5-(–8) 1 INT
Punting: Gafford: 2–76, Eakin: 1–42, Reynolds: 1–39, Fox: 1–40
Punt Returns: Gafford: 1–5
Kickoff Returns: Erdlitz: 2–39, Gafford: 1–31
Interception Returns: Gafford: 2–6, Williams: 1–3

Buffalo
Rushing: Dudish: 6–50, Kulbitski: 3–38, Juzwik: 5–30, Tomasetti: 6–20, Zontini: 2–16, Hopp: 4–13 1 TD, Mutryn: 2–4, Terlep: 1-(–11)
Receiving: King: 3–32 1 TD, Black: 1–21, Batorski: 1–11, Juzwik: 1–9
Passing: Stofer: 4–10–43 1 TD, Terlep: 1–4–11 1 INT, Dekdebrun: 1–6–9 2 INT
Punting: Zontini: 3–103, Hopp: 1–35
Punt Returns: Kuzwik: 3–51, Dudish: 1–24 (Field Goal Return)
Kickoff Returns: Juzwik: 1–24, Hopp: 2–22
Interception Returns: Dekdebrun: 2–19, Juzwik: 1–5

Detailed Game Summaries

October 19, 1946, San Francisco 49ers vs. Buffalo Bisons
Location: Civic Stadium (Buffalo, NY)
Attendance: 6,101

	1	2	3	4	F
San Francisco 49ers	0	14	0	0	14
Buffalo Bisons	3	7	0	7	17

Scoring Summary

BUF	Zontini 47-Yard Field Goal
SF	Eshmont 3-Yard Run (Vetrano Kick)
SF	Beals 39-Yard Pass From Freitas (Vetrano Kick)
BUF	Mutryn 33-Yard Pass From Dekdebrun (Zontini Kick)
BUF	King 1-Yard Pass From Dekdebrun (Zontini Kick)

	San Francisco	Buffalo
First Downs	15	6
Total Yards	281	230
Yards Rushing	193	57
Passes Attempted	22	19
Passes Completed	10	7
Yards Passing	88	173
Interceptions	2	1
Punting Average	33.6	40.1
Penalty Yardage	5	0

Position	San Francisco	Buffalo
LE	Fisk	Klutka
LT	Mellus	Klug
LG	Bassi	Perko
C	Conlee	Prewitt
RG	Banducci	Jones
RT	Woudenberg	Doherty
RE	Titchenal	Nelson
QB	Albert	Dekdebrun
LHB	Eshmont	Johnston
RHB	Strzykalski	Tomasetti
FB	Standlee	Zontini

Substitutes

San Francisco
Ends: Beals, Balatti, Norberg
Tackles: Bryant, Grgich
Guards: Gregory, Thorton
Centers: Elston
Backs: Freitas, Hall, Casanega, Parsons, Vetrano, Roskie

Buffalo
Ends: Ebli, King, Comer
Tackles: Pucci, Matisi, Kramer, Dugger

Guards: Pirro, Lahar, Stuart
Centers: Wukits
Backs: Mutryn, Juzwik, Stofer, Hopp, Dudish, Thibaut, Terlep, Sandig

Individual Statistics

San Francisco
Rushing: Standlee: 17–98, Eshmont: 12–58 1 TD, Parsons: 7–17, Vetrano: 5–17, Strzykalski: 1–1, Hall: 1–4, Freitas: 1–0, Albert: 5-(-2)
Receiving: Beals: 1–39 1 TD, Vetrano: 2–25, Eshmont: 4–24, Strzykalski: 1–2, Parsons: 2-(-2)
Passing: Freitas: 2–3–45 1 TD, Albert: 8–18–43 1 INT, Eshmont: 0–1–0
Punting: Albert: 6–202
Punt Returns: Parsons: 3–38, Eshmont: 1–20, Vetrano: 1–13
Kickoff Returns: Eshmont: 2–55, Albert: 1–22
Interception Returns: Strzykalski: 1–24, Casanega: 1–0

Buffalo
Rushing: Zontini: 1–13, Dekdebrun: 2–12, Johnston: 6–10, Hopp: 3–7, Tomasetti: 3–6, Juzwik: 7–5, Thibaut: 2–4
Receiving: Juzwik: 2–79, King: 3–52 1 TD, Mutryn: 1–33 1 TD, Klutka: 1–9
Passing: Dekdebrun: 6–11–164 2 TD 2 INT, Terlep: 1–8–9
Punting: Johnston: 4–164, Zontini: 4–162, Hopp: 1–35
Punt Returns: Mutryn: 1–6
Kickoff Returns: Juzwik: 2–32
Interception Returns: Juzwik: 1–14

October 27, 1946, Chicago Rockets vs. Buffalo Bisons
Location: Civic Stadium (Buffalo, NY)
Attendance: 15,758

	1	2	3	4	F
Chicago Rockets	0	3	7	7	17
Buffalo Bisons	0	28	14	7	49

Scoring Summary

CHI Nemeth 18-Yard Field Goal
BUF Thibaut 2-Yard Run (Zontini Kick)
BUF Johnston 4-Yard Run (Zontini Kick)
BUF Comer 48-Yard Fumble Return (Zontini Kick)
BUF Juzwik 45-Yards On Lateral From Mutryn (4-Yards) On Interception Return (Zontini Kick)
BUF Juzwik 22-Yard Run (Zontini Kick)
CHI Hirsch 88-Yard Kickoff Return On Lateral From Lewis (Boedeker Kick)
BUF Mutryn 40-Yards On Lateral From Lahar (17-Yards) On Fumble Recovery (Zontini Kick)
CHI Williams 1-Yard Run (Nemeth Kick)
BUF Dugger 22-Yard Fumble Return (Zontini Kick)

Detailed Game Summaries 141

	Chicago	Buffalo
First Downs	12	14
Total Yards	181	267
Yards Rushing	49	217
Passes Attempted	35	9
Passes Completed	13	4
Yards Passing	132	50
Interceptions	1	3
Punting Average	42.7	22.7
Penalty Yardage	65	19

Position	Chicago	Buffalo
LE	Heywood	Ebli
LT	Wilkin	Klug
LG	Pearcy	Pirro
C	Parks	Prewitt
RG	Vogds	Perko
RT	Klenk	Doherty
RE	Lahey	Nelson
QB	Hoernschemeyer	Dekdebrun
LHB	Hirsch	Johnston
RHB	Mathews	Tomasetti
FB	Lewis	Zontini

Substitutes

Chicago
Ends: Quillen, Motl, Morris
Tackles: Huneke, Brutz, Wasserbach
Guards: Dove, O'Neal, Sumpter, Ruetz
Centers: Coleman
Backs: Hillenbrand, Schroeder, Clay, Griffin, Kellagher, Cox, Nemeth, Williams, Boedeker

Buffalo
Ends: King, Comer, Klutka
Tackles: Matisi, Kramer, Dugger, Pucci, Grigg
Guards: Lahar, Jones, Lecture
Centers: Brazinsky
Backs: Terlep, Mutryn, Juzwik, Stofer, Kulbitski, Sandig, Dudish, Hopp, Thibaut

Individual Statistics

Chicago
Rushing: Williams: 6-28, Mathews: 3-9, Lewis: 5-8, Kellagher: 3-7, Hirsch: 2-3 1 TD, Clay: 1-2, Schroeder: 1-1, Hillenbrand: 2-(-2), Hoernschemeyer: 6-(-7)
Receiving: Lahey: 3-48, Hirsch: 4-33, Heywood: 2-25, Kellagher: 1-16, Motl: 1-6, Boedeker: 1-5, Mathews: 1-(-1)
Passing: Hoernschemeyer: 7-14-81 1 INT, Williams: 4-11-29 3 INT, Nemeth: 2-10-22

Punting: Williams: 2–96, Nemeth: 2–92, Kellagher: 1–56, Lewis: 1–43, Hoernschemeyer: 1–35
Punt Returns: Boedeker: 1–26, Hillenbrand: 1–10
Kickoff Returns: Hirsch: 1–88 1 TD, Hoernschemeyer: 2–58, Hillenbrand: 2–39, Lewis: 1–19
Interception Returns: Griffin: 1–19, Hirsch: 1–5

Buffalo
Rushing: Johnston: 6–69 1 TD, Juzwik: 6–67 1 TD, Thibaut: 8–44 1 TD, Tomasetti: 8–18, Hopp: 3–13, Sandig: 1–5, Terlep: 4–4, Mutryn: 2–4, Kulbitski: 1–2, Stofer: 2–1, Dekdebrun: 1-(–10)
Receiving: Juzwik: 3–25, Mutryn: 1–25
Passing: Dekdebrun: 2–5–36, Terlep: 2–4–14 2 INT
Punting: Hopp: 1–40, Sandig: 1–26, Johnston: 1–20, Zontini: 1–15
Punt Returns: Tomasetti: 3–84, Juzwik: 1–20, Dudish: 1–15
Kickoff Returns: Tomasetti: 1–27, Kulbitski: 1–26, Dekdebrun: 1–25, Mutryn: 1–21
Interception Returns: Juzwik: 1–45 1 TD, Pruitt: 1–30, Brazinsky: 2–7

November 2, 1946, Buffalo Bisons vs. San Francisco 49ers
Location: Kezar Stadium (San Francisco, CA)
Attendance: 12,500

	1	2	3	4	F
Buffalo Bisons	0	7	0	7	14
San Francisco	0	0	7	20	27

Scoring Summary

BUF Juzwik 12-Yard Pass From Dekdebrun (Zontini Kick)
SF Eshmont 20-Yard Fumble Return (Vetrano Kick)
SF Eshmont 34-Yard Run (Vetrano Kick)
SF Casanega 18-Yard Pass From Albert (Vetrano Kick)
SF Titchenal 54-Yard Pass From Albert (PAT Kick Failed)
BUF King 3-Yard Pass From Dekdebrun (Zontini Kick)

Position	Buffalo	San Francisco
LE	Daddio	Fisk
LT	Stanley	Mellus
LG	Perko	Gregory
C	Prewitt	Elston
RG	Pirro	Banducci
RT	Klug	Woudenberg
RE	Ebli	Titchenal
QB	Dekdebrun	Albert
LHB	Johnston	Eshmont
RHB	Juzwik	Strzykalski
FB	Kulbitski	Standlee

Detailed Game Summaries 143

Substitutes

San Francisco
Ends: Beals, Balatti, Norberg
Tackles: Grgich
Guards: Thornton, Pavlich
Backs: Roskie, Durdan, Parsons, Vetrano, Casanega, Mathews, Franceschi

Buffalo
Ends: King, Klutka, Nelson
Tackles: Kramer, Matisi, Doherty, Grigg
Guards: Stuart
Backs: Hopp, Mutryn, Sandig, Stofer, Terlep, Tomasetti, Zontini

Individual Statistics

Buffalo
Rushing: Kulbitski: 6–42, Mutryn: 6–22, Johnston: 3–9, Sandig: 3–9, Zontini: 2–8, Tomasetti: 2–3, Hopp: 2–0, Juzwik: 1-(–3), Dekdebrun: 5-(–11)
Receiving: King: 3–53 1 TD, Juzwik: 2–20 1 TD, Mutryn: 1–15, Tomasetti: 1–6, Johnston: 1–2
Passing: Dekdebrun: 7–13–81 2 TD 1 INT, Terlep: 1–6–15 1 INT, Zontini: 0–1–0
Punting: Johnston: 5–160 1 Block, Zontini: 3–114
Punt Returns: Tomasetti: 2–34
Kickoff Returns: Juzwik: 3–74, Dudish: 1–49
Interception Returns: Johnston: 1–15, Prewitt: 1–3

San Francisco
Rushing: Standlee: 12–67, Parsons: 11–46, Eshmont: 4–40 1 TD, Strzykalski: 5–15, Durdan: 2–12, Vetrano: 1–8, Casanega: 2–3, Franceschi: 1–3, Albert: 2-(–17)
Receiving: Beals: 4–59, Titchenal: 1–54 1 TD, Casanega: 1–18 1 TD, Fisk: 1–19, Parsons: 1–15, Strzykalski: 1–1
Passing: Albert: 9–21–166 2 TD 2 INT
Punting: Albert: 2–95
Punt Returns: Parsons: 3–47, Vetrano: 1–17, Casanega: 1–17
Kickoff Returns: Eshmont: 2–51, Gregory: 1–0
Interception Returns: Casanega: 2–0

November 10, 1946, Buffalo Bisons vs. Brooklyn Dodgers
Location: Ebbets Field (Brooklyn, NY)
Attendance: 12,820

	1	2	3	4	F
Buffalo Bisons	10	0	7	0	17
Brooklyn Dodgers	0	7	0	7	14

Scoring Summary

BUF Johnston 2-Yard Run (Zontini Kick)
BUF Zontini 14-Yard Field Goal
BKN Van Tone 16-Yard Pass From Dobbs (Martinovich Kick)

BUF Ebli 2-Yard Pass From Dekdebrun (Zontini Kick)
BKN Tackett 40-Yard Pass From Dobbs (Martinovich Kick)

Position	Buffalo	Brooklyn
LE	Ebli	McCarthy
LT	Stanley	Ruby
LG	Perko	Bernhardt
C	Prewitt	Gibson
RG	Pirro	Buffington
RT	Doherty	Mieszkowski
RE	Nelson	Davis
QB	Dekdebrun	McDonald
LHB	Johnston	Dobbs
RHB	Dudish	Van Tone
FB	Zontini	Mayne

Substitutes

Brooklyn
Ends: Judd, Adams, Perdue, McCain
Tackles: Sergienko
Guards: Freeman, Maack, Obeck, Martinovich
Centers: Warrington
Backs: Shetley, Tackett, Armstrong, Timmons

Buffalo
Ends: Klutka, Comer, King
Tackles: Klug, Pucci, Kramer
Guards: Jones, Lahar, Stuart
Centers: Brazinsky
Backs: Terlep, Mutryn, Tomasetti, Kulbitski, Thibaut

Individual Statistics

Brooklyn
Rushing: Timmons: 6-19, Dobbs: 12-12, Armstrong: 2-5, Mayne: 6-(-1), McDonald: 1-(-3), Van Tone: 1-(-5)
Receiving: Davis: 2-71, Tackett: 3-63 1 TD, Van Tone: 2-43 1 TD, Judd: 3-34, Adams: 1-25, McDonald: 1-22, Mayne: 1-12
Passing: Dobbs: 12-25-248 2 TD 1 INT, Armstrong: 1-1-22
Punting: Dobbs: 5-270
Punt Returns: Dobbs: 1-20, Armstrong: 1-16
Kickoff Returns: Mayne: 1-24, Davis: 1-17

Buffalo
Rushing: Kulbitski: 15-134, Juzwik: 5-81, Johnston: 9-73 1 TD, Mutryn: 2-16, Tomasetti: 4-12, Terlep: 3-7, Dudish: 1-1, Zontini: 1-(-3), Dekdebrun: 3-(-5)
Receiving: Ebli: 2-15 1 TD, Juzwik: 1-10, Comer: 1-6, Tomasetti: 1-(-3)
Passing: Dekdebrun: 3-8-18 1 TD, Terlep: 2-4-10
Punting: Johnston: 5-204
Punt Returns: Juzwik: 1-5

Kickoff Returns: Juzwik: 1–43, Dudish: 1–20
Interception Returns: Prewitt: 1–42

November 18, 1946, Buffalo Bisons vs. Miami Seahawks
Location: Orange Bowl (Miami, FL)
Attendance: 5,592

	1	2	3	4	F
Buffalo Bisons	0	7	7	0	14
Miami Seahawks	0	7	14	0	21

Scoring Summary

MIA Gafford 26-Yard Pass From Pugh (Erdlitz Kick)
BUF King 10-Yard Pass From Dekdebrun (Zontini Kick)
MIA Pugh 1-Yard Run (Erdlitz Kick)
MIA Blount 22-Yard Pass From Pugh (Erdlitz Kick)
BUF Juzwik 27-Yard Run (Zontini Kick)

	Miami	Buffalo
First Downs	12	9
Total Yards	290	353
Yards Rushing	152	249
Passes Attempted	16	12
Passes Completed	9	5
Yards Passing	138	104
Interceptions	3	2
Punting Average	38	27
Penalty Yardage	10	10

Position	Buffalo	Miami
LE	Ebli	Ulrich
LT	Stanley	Ellenson
LG	Perko	Sivell
C	Prewitt	Wukits
RG	Pirro	Taylor
RT	Doherty	B. Davis
RE	Nelson	Blount
QB	Dekdebrun	Pugh
LHB	Johnston	Gafford
RHB	Juzwik	L. Davis
FB	Kulbitski	Trigilio

Substitutes

Miami
Ends: Scott, Fox, Horne
Guards: Zorich
Backs: Eakin, Erdlitz, Koslowski, Nelson, Vardian, Reece, Price, Reynolds

Buffalo
Ends: Comer
Guards: Lecture
Backs: Stofer, Dudish

Individual Statistics

Miami
Rushing: Nelson: 4–41, Koslowski: 4–35, Triglio: 9–19, Erdlitz: 3–10, Paffrath: 1–9, Eakin 2–7, Reece: 5–3, L. Davis: 1–2, Vardian: 1–0, Jones: 1–0, Pugh: 2-(–9) 1 TD
Receiving: Blount: 2–36 1 TD, Scott: 3–29, Gafford: 1–26 1 TD, Ulrich: 1–25, Koslowski: 1–17, L. Davis: 1–5
Passing: Pugh: 7–13–108 2 TD 1 INT, Holley: 2–3–30 1 INT
Punting: Eakin: 5–189
Punt Returns: Eakin: 1–13, Scott: 1–6
Kickoff Returns: Nelson: 1–43, Scott: 1–27
Interception Returns: L. Davis: 1–25, Wukits: 1–12, Whitlow: 1–5

Buffalo
Rushing: Juzwik: 4–94 1 TD, Kulbitski: 10–81, Mutryn: 6–14, Hopp: 2–13, Johnston: 2–10, Terlep: 2–9, Tomasetti: 1–5, Dudish: 2–3, Zontini: 1–2, Sandig: 1–0, Dekdebrun: 3-(–18)
Receiving: Mutryn: 1–36, Juzwik: 1–35, Sandig: 1–14, King: 2–11 1 TD
Passing: Terlep: 3–8 85 2 INT, Dekdebrun: 2–4–19 1 TD 1 INT
Punting: Zontini: 3–98, Johnston: 1–10
Punt Returns: Tomasetti: 1–12, Dudish: 1–3
Kickoff Returns: Juzwik: 3–52, Dekdebrun: 1–21
Interception Returns: Prewitt: 1–14, Juzwik: 1–11

November 24, 1946, Buffalo Bisons vs. Cleveland Browns
Location: Municipal Stadium (Cleveland, OH)
Attendance: 37,054

	1	2	3	4	F
Buffalo Bisons	10	0	0	7	17
Cleveland Browns	7	7	14	14	42

Scoring Summary

CLE   Jones 46-Yard Run (Groza Kick)
BUF   Kulbitski 1-Yard Run (Zontini Kick)
BUF   Zontini 40-Yard Field Goal
CLE   Speedie 2-Yard Pass From Graham (Groza Kick)
CLE   Motley 76-Yard Run (Groza Kick)
CLE   Jones 55-Yards On A Lateral From Lavelli On A Pass From Graham (Groza Kick)
CLE   Akins 50-Yard Run (Groza Kick)
CLE   Schwenk 1-Yard Run (Groza Kick)
BUF   King 12-Yard Pass From Terlep (Juzwik Kick)

Position	Buffalo	Cleveland
LE	Elbi	Young
LT	Stanley	Blandin
LG	Perko	Ulinski
C	Prewitt	Groza
RG	Pirro	Houston

Detailed Game Summaries

Position	Buffalo	Cleveland
RT	Kramer	Rymkus
RE	Comer	Yonakor
QB	Dekdebrun	Graham
LHB	Mutryn	Jones
RHB	Juzwik	Terrell
FB	Kulbitski	Motley

Substitutes

Cleveland
Ends: Harrington, Lavelli, Coppage, Speedie
Tackles: Daniell, Adams
Guards: Cheroke, Kapter, Willis
Centers: Scarry, Gatski, Maceau
Backs: Schwenk, Saban, Fekete, Smith, Akins, Lund, Greenwood, Colella, Evans

Buffalo
Ends: King, Schilling, Nelson
Tackles: Grigg, Matisi, Doherty
Guards: Lahar, Jones, Stuart
Centers: Brazinsky
Backs: Stofer, Terlep, Zontini, Dudish, Johnston, Sandig, Tomasetti

Individual Statistics

Buffalo
Rushing: Kulbitski: 17–60 1 TD, Mutryn: 8–40, Johnston: 6–23, Dudish: 6–8, Terlep: 4–8, Juzwik: 4–4, Sandig: 1–4, Dekdebrun: 5-(–4), Zontini: 1-(–10)
Receiving: King: 6–76 1 TD, Tomasetti: 1–21, Nelson: 1–13, Dudish: 1–12, Johnston: 1–9, Juzwik: 1-(–8)
Passing: Terlep: 9–19–83 1 TD 1 INT, Dekdebrun: 2–7–40 1 INT
Punting: Johnston: 5–225, Zontini: 1–37
Kickoff Returns: Juzwik: 2–35, Dudish: 1–25

Cleveland
Rushing: Jones: 7–105 1 TD, Motley: 2–83 1 TD, Akins: 2–47 1 TD, Lavelli: 1–14, Terrell: 4–12, Fekete: 2–11, Evans: 2–9, Lund: 2–3, Schwenk: 1–1 1 TD, Graham: 3-(-2), Colella: 3-(–9)
Receiving: Jones: 1–71 1 TD, Lavelli: 3–35, Speedie: 4–31 1 TD, Motley: 1–19, Harrington: 1–7
Passing: Graham: 9–16–156 2 TD, Schwenk: 1–1–7, Jones: 0–1–0
Punting: Colella: 3–123
Punt Returns: Colella: 1–58, Graham: 2–25, Jones: 1–7
Kickoff Returns: Akins: 1–44, Motley: 1–18, Jones: 1–1
Interception Returns: Akins: 1–7, Colella: 1–0

148 Appendix B

December 1, 1946, Buffalo Bisons vs. Los Angeles Dons
Location: Los Angeles Memorial Coliseum (Los Angeles, CA)
Attendance: 22,822

	1	2	3	4	F
Buffalo Bisons	0	7	7	0	14
Los Angeles Dons	14	14	14	20	62

Scoring Summary

LA	Kimbrough 38-Yard Pass From O'Rourke (Aguirre Kick)
LA	Kimbrough 3-Yard Run (Aguirre Kick)
LA	Clarke 71-Yard Pass From Bertelli (Aguirre Kick)
BUF	Johnston 19-Yard Pass From Terlep (Zontini Kick)
LA	Gentry 8-Yard Pass From O'Rourke (Aguirre Kick)
BUF	Mutryn 24-Yard Pass From Terlep (Zontini Kick)
LA	Kimbrough 16-Yard Run (Aguirre Kick)
LA	Gentry 15-Yard Pass From Bertelli (Aguirre Kick)
LA	Bertelli 1-Yard Run (Aguirre Kick)
LA	Frankowski 54-Yard Fumble Recovery (Aguirre Kick)
LA	Polanski 7-Yard Pass From O'Rourke (PAT Attempt Failed)

	Buffalo	Los Angeles
First Downs	12	20
Total Yards	268	625
Yards Rushing	68	288
Passes Attempted	25	19
Passes Completed	14	17
Yards Passing	200	337
Interceptions	2	1
Punting Average	42.5	58.5
Penalty Yardage	22	39

Position	Buffalo	Los Angeles
LE	Ebli	Nowaskey
LT	Stanley	Reinhard
LG	Perko	Lolotai
C	Prewitt	Nelson
RG	Pirro	Radovich
RT	Doherty	Artoe
RE	Comer	Gentry
QB	Terlep	Mitchell
LHB	Juzwik	Fenenbock
RHB	Mutryn	Elsey
FB	Kulbitski	Marefos

Substitutes

Los Angeles
Ends: Aguirre, Kerr, Morton
Tackles: Audet, Mihal, Duggan
Guards: Yokas, Frankowski

Centers: Rockwell, Nolander
Backs: Bertelli, Kimbrough, Polanski, Clarke, Vinnola, Nygren, Mertes, Sneddon, O'Rourke, Seymour

Buffalo
Ends: King, Nelson, Schilling
Tackles: Matisi, Kramer, Grigg, Pucci, Dugger
Guards: Lahar, Jones
Centers: Brazinsky
Backs: Dekdebrun, Zontini, Johnston, Sandig, Tomasetti, Stofer, Dudish, Klutka, Stuart

Individual Statistics

Los Angeles
Rushing: O'Rourke: 4–56, Mertes: 6–38, Fenenbock: 5–36, Kimbrough: 6–36 2 TD, Elsey: 4–34, Nygren: 1–18, Seymour: 4–17, Vinnola: 5–17, Sneddon: 2–6, Clarke: 1–5, Polanski: 1–5, Marefos: 1–3, Bertelli: 2-(–8) 1 TD
Receiving: Kerr: 5–99, Gentry: 6–78 2 TD, Clarke: 1–71 1 TD, Kimbrough: 1–46 1 TD, Nowaskey: 1–29, Aguirre: 2–13, Polanski: 1–7 1 TD, Mitchell: 1–0
Passing: Bertelli: 11–13–203 2 TD 1 INT, O'Rourke: 7–7–141 3 TD
Punting: Reinhard: 2–117
Punt Returns: Seymour: 2–32, Fenenbock: 1–9
Kickoff Returns: Fenenbock: 2–44, Mertes: 1–14, Artoe: 1–13
Interception Returns: Sneddon: 1–15, Vinnola: 1–4

Buffalo
Rushing: Kulbitski: 8–38, Johnston: 2–16, Juzwik: 3–10, Tomasetti: 3–9, Mutryn: 3–5, Terlep: 3–1, Sandig: 4–1, Stofer: 1–0, Dekdebrun: 2-(–11)
Receiving: King: 4–74, Juzwik: 7–69, Mutryn: 1–24 1 TD, Johnston: 1–19 1 TD
Passing: Terlep: 12–18–169 2 TD 1 INT, Dekdebrun: 1–6–26 1 INT
Punting: Zontini: 6–255
Punt Returns: Mutryn: 1–30, Dudish: 1–20
Kickoff Returns: Tomasetti: 1–58, Juzwik: 2–38, Johnston: 2–21, Zontini: 1–19, Mutryn: 1–15, Dekdebrun: 1–12, Kulbitski: 1–9
Interception Returns: Jones: 1–0

1947 BUFFALO BILLS

Preseason

August 18, 1947, Buffalo Bills vs. New York Yankees
Location: Ruppert Stadium (Newark, NJ)
Attendance: 11,004

	1	2	3	4	F
Buffalo Bills	?	?	?	?	7
New York Yankees	17	?	?	?	29

150 Appendix B

Scoring Summary (Not In Order Of Scoring)

BUF Mutryn 87-Yard Kickoff Return
NYY Alford Returned Kulbitski Fumble
NYY Alford Pass From Sinkwich
NYY Johnson 21-Yard Field Goal
NYY Young 5-Yard Run

August 22, 1947, Buffalo Bills vs. Baltimore Colts
Location: (Hershey, PA)
Attendance: 7,018

	1	2	3	4	F
Buffalo Bills	?	?	0	9	29
Baltimore Colts	?	?	?	?	20

Scoring Summary (Not In Order Of Scoring)

BUF Koch 40-Yard Run
BUF Terlep 40-Yard Interception Return
BUF Mutryn 1-Yard Run
BUF Juzwick 8-Yard Field Goal
BUF Corley 40-Yard Interception Return
BAL Davis 20-Yard Pass From Galvin
BAL Castiglia 3-Yard Run

Regular Season

August 31, 1947, New York Yankees vs. Buffalo Bills
Location: Civic Stadium (Buffalo, NY)
Attendance: 32,385

	1	2	3	4	F
New York Yankees	7	7	7	3	24
Buffalo Bills	7	7	7	7	28

Scoring Summary

NY Prokop 4-Yard Run (Johnson Kick)
BUF Ratterman 1-Yard Run (Juzwick Kick)
BUF King 39-Yard Pass From Ratterman (Juzwick Kick)
NY Sanders 17-Yard Run (Johnson Kick)
NY Young 50-Yard Pass From Sanders (Johnson Kick)
BUF Koch 1-Yard Run (Juzwick Kick)
NY Johnson 20-Yard Field Goal
BUF Mutryn 4-Yard Pass From Ratternam (Juzwick Kick)

	Buffalo	New York
First Downs	11	17
Yards Rushing	138	170
Passes—Attempts	13	20
Passes—Completions	9	14
Passes—Yards	121	229

Detailed Game Summaries

	Buffalo	New York
Passes—Interceptions	1	0
Punting Average	38	23
Fumbles Recovered	2	1
Penalty Yards	20	30

Position	New York	Buffalo
LE	Russell	Gibson
LT	Palmer	Duggan
LG	Bentz	Lahar
C	Sossamon	Corley
RG	Barwegan	Pirro
RT	N. Johnson	Doherty
RE	Alford	Coppage
QB	Cheatham	Mutryn
LHB	Sinkwich	Rykovich
RHB	Wagner	Koch
FB	Young	Kulbitski

Substitutes

New York
Ends: Davis, Stanton
Tackles: Kinard, Elliott, Schleich
Guards: Yackanich, Riffle
Centers: Baldwin
Backs: H. Johnson, Prokop, Sanders, Sweiger, Burrus, Kennedy

Buffalo
Ends: Comer, King, Mazza, Baldwin, Morton
Tackles: Armstrong, Kerns, Carpenter
Guards: Hirsch, Maskas, Groves, Scott
Centers: Prewitt, Haynes
Backs: Ratterman, Juzwik, Blount, Terlep, Reisz, Tomasetti, Wizbicki

Individual Statistics

New York
Rushing: Young: 13–81, Sinkwich: 10–31, Sanders: 5–29 1 TD, Prokop: 5–29 1 TD
Receiving: Young: 2–57 1 TD, Prokop: 1–43, Wagner: 3–30, Russell: 1–28, Cheatham: 1–20, Davis: 3–19, Burrus: 1–18, Alford: 2–14
Passing: Sanders: 10–12–185 1 TD 1 INT, Sinkwich: 4–8–44
Punting: Sinkwich: 2–46 1 Block
Punt Returns: Kennedy: 1–12
Kickoff Returns: Sanders: 2–55, Prokop: 1–27, Young: 1–19

Buffalo
Rushing: Tomasetti: 7–49, Mutryn: 6–41, Koch: 7–18 1 TD, Rykovich: 7–14, Juzwik: 4–8, Blount: 2–5, Kulbitski: 1–2, Ratterman: 1–1 1 TD
Receiving: Coppage: 2–47, King: 1–39 1 TD, Rykovich: 1–23, Gibson: 1–14, Mutryn: 1–4 1 TD, Juzwik: 2-(-2), Kulbitski: 1-(-4)

Passing: Ratterman: 9–13–121 2 TD
Punting: Reisz: 5–190
Kickoff Returns: Rykovich: 2–50, Tomasetti: 2–32, Mutryn: 1–28
Interception Returns: Kulbitski: 1–14

September 5, 1947, Buffalo Bills vs. Cleveland Browns
Location: Municipal Stadium (Cleveland, OH)
Attendance: 61,442

	1	2	3	4	F
Buffalo Bills	0	0	14	0	14
Cleveland Browns	13	14	0	3	30

Scoring Summary

CLE	E. Jones 2-Yard Run (Groza Kick Failed)
CLE	Motley 3-Yard Run (Groza Kick)
CLE	Motley 48-Yard Interception Return (Groza Kick)
CLE	Lavelli 51-Yard Pass From Graham (Groza Kick)
BUF	Tomasetti 2-Yard Run (Juzwick Kick)
BUF	Coppage 3-Yard Pass From Ratterman (Juzwick Kick)
CLE	Groza 25-Yard Field Goal

	Buffalo	Cleveland
First Downs	13	11
Yards Rushing	208	193
Passes—Attempts	16	24
Passes—Completions	3	12
Passes—Yards	24	129
Passes—Interceptions	1	4
Punting Average	41	44
Fumbles Recovered	1	1
Penalty Yards	30	79

Position	Buffalo	Cleveland
LE	Gibson	Speedie
LT	Duggan	Blandin
LG	Lahar	Ulinski
C	Corley	Scarry
RG	Pirro	Willis
RT	Doherty	Simonetti
RE	Coppage	Lavelli
QB	Ratterman	Graham
LHB	Rykovich	E. Jones
RHB	Koch	Colella
FB	Tomasetti	Motley

Substitutes

Buffalo
Ends: King, Comer, Kuffel, Morton, Baldwin, Mazza
Tackles: Carpenter, Kerns, Armstrong
Guards: Maskas

Detailed Game Summaries

Centers: Prewitt
Backs: Terlep, Reisz, Blount, Wizbicki, Evans, Juzwik, Mutryn

Cleveland
Ends: Young, Gillom, Shurnas, Yonakor
Tackles: Piskor, Groza, Adams
Guards: Houston, Gaudio, Humble
Centers: Maceau
Backs: Greenwood, Saban, Adamle, Boedeker, Cowan, Dellerba, Allen, Dewar, Lund

Individual Statistics

Buffalo
Rushing: Mutryn: 12–114, Tomasetti: 14–36 1 TD, Rykovich: 5–19, Koch: 6–16, Juzwik: 3–15, Evans: 4–15, Ratterman: 2-(–7)
Receiving: Juzwik: 1–17, Tomasetti: 1–4, Coppage: 1–3 1 TD
Passing: Ratterman: 3–16–24 1 TD 4 INT
Punting: Reisz: 6–246
Punt Returns: Rykovich: 1–15, Juzwik: 2–11, Evans: 2–0
Kickoff Returns: Mutryn: 4–81, Rykovich: 2–35
Interception Returns: Hirsch: 1–21

Cleveland
Rushing: Jones: 1 TD, Motley: 1 TD
Receiving: Lavelli: 1 TD
Passing: Graham: 12–25 1 TD
Interception Returns: Motley: 1 TD

September 14, 1947, Chicago Rockets vs. Buffalo Bills
Location: Civic Stadium (Buffalo, NY)
Attendance: 33,648

	1	2	3	4	F
Chicago Rockets	0	0	6	14	20
Buffalo Bills	0	7	7	14	28

Scoring Summary

BUF Kulbitski 1-Yard Run (Juzwick Kick)
BUF King 5-Yard Pass From Ratterman (Juzwick Kick)
CHI Vananti to Scalissi To Schroeder 15-Yard Pass and Lateral (PAT failed on bad snap)
BUF Mutryn 13-Yard Run (Juzwick Kick)
BUF Evans 31-Yard Pass From Terlep (Juzwick Kick)
CHI Ramsey 41-Yard Pass From Vacanti (Rokisky Kick)
CHI Morris 6-Yard Pass From Vacanti (Roskisky Kick)

	Chicago	Buffalo
First Downs	16	11
Yards Rushing	155	163
Passes—Attempts	25	18

	Chicago	Buffalo
Passes—Completions	13	6
Passes—Yards	175	102
Passes—Interceptions	0	2
Punting Average	40	37
Fumbles Recovered	2	1
Penalty Yards	38	35

Position	Chicago	Buffalo
LE	Morris	Gibson
LT	Kuzman	Armstrong
LG	Hecht	Lahar
C	Coleman	Prewitt
RG	O'Neal	Pirro
RT	Pucci	Doherty
RE	Mulready	Coppage
QB	Dekdebrun	Mutryn
LHB	Bass	Rykovich
RHB	Ramsey	Koch
FB	Daley	Kulbitski

Substitutes
Chicago
Ends: Dove, Harrington, Rokisky, Quillen, Lahey, Berry
Tackles: Grigg, Bauman
Guards: Pearcy, Vogds, Wasserbach
Centers: Negus, Lamana
Backs: Hirsch, Kellagher, Clay, Vacanti, Scalissi, Lewis, Bertelli, Schroeder

Buffalo
Ends: Corley, Comer, King, Mazza, Baldwin
Tackles: Duggan, Kerns, Carpenter, Kozel
Guards: Maskas, Groves, Hirsch, Scott
Centers: Corley, Haynes
Backs: Ratterman, Juzwik, Blount, Terlep, Reisz, Tomasetti, Wizbicki, Evans

Individual Statistics
Chicago
Rushing: Ramsey: 8–77, Bass: 4–35, Daley: 12–25, Schroeder: 4–14, Scalissi: 3–4, Bertelli: 1–2, Lewis: 1-(-2), Dekdebrun: 3-(–3)
Receiving: Ramsey: 2–71 1 TD, Lahy: 2–21, Mulready: 1–17, Quillen: 1–15, Schroeder: 0–15 (Lateral) 1 TD, Morris: 2–13 1 TD, Dove: 1–12, Scalissi: 1–8, Bass: 3–3
Passing: Vacanti: 9–14–159 3 TD, Bass: 1–1–14, Dekdebrun: 1–3–7, Bertelli: 2–7-(–5) 2 INT
Punting: Lewis: 4–160
Punt Returns: Bass: 2–14, Ramsey: 1–10, Scalissi: 1–7
Kickoff Returns: Scalissi: 1–46, Bass: 2–35, Ramsey: 1–31

Buffalo
Rushing: Mutryn: 10–85 1 TD, Kulbitski: 10–46 1 TD, Koch: 5–16, Wizbicki: 1–7, Tomasetti: 3–6, Terlep: 1–4, Rykovich: 1–3, Evans: 1–1, Juzwik: 1-(-2), Ratterman: 2-(–3)

Receiving: Evans: 1-31 1 TD, Baldwin: 1-28, King: 2-17 1 TD, Mutryn: 1-16, Koch: 1-10
Passing: Ratterman: 5-11-71 1 TD, Terlep: 1-2-31 1 TD
Punting: Reisz: 5-185
Punt Returns: Mutryn: 2-30, Rykovich: 1-19
Kickoff Returns: Mutryn: 1-25, Kozel: 1-11
Interception Returns: Baldwin: 1-71, Koch: 1-16

September 19, 1947, Buffalo Bills vs. Chicago Rockets
Location: Soldier's Field (Chicago, IL)
Attendance: 22,685

	1	2	3	4	F
Buffalo Bills	10	7	7	7	31
Chicago Rockets	0	14	0	0	14

Scoring Summary

BUF Baldwin 9-Yard Pass From Ratterman (Juzwik Kick)
BUF Juzwick 29-Yard Field Goal
BUF Kulbitski 2-Yard Pass From Ratterman (Juzwik Kick)
CHI Hirsch 76-Yard Pass From Vacanti (Rokisky Kick)
CHI Hirsch 2-Yard Run (Rokisky Kick)
BUF Mutryn 58-Yard Pass From Ratterman (Juzwik Kick)
BUF King 18-Yard Pass From Ratterman (Juzwik Kick)

	Buffalo	Chicago
First Downs	13	9
Yards Rushing	144	83
Passes—Attempts	33	31
Passes—Completions	18	16
Passes—Yards	294	162
Passes—Interceptions	1	0
Punting Average	40	37.3
Fumbles Recovered	1	1
Penalty Yards	45	5

Position	Buffalo	Chicago
LE	Gibson	Rokisky
LT	Armstrong	Kuzman
LG	Lahar	Pearcy
C	Corley	Negus
RG	Pirro	Agase
RT	Doherty	Grigg
RE	Coppage	Mulready
QB	Ratterman	Vacanti
LHB	Rykovich	Hirsch
RHB	Mutryn	Schroeder
FB	Tomasetti	Daley

Substitutes

Buffalo
Ends: Comer, King, Mazza, Baldwin
Tackles: Kozel, Kerns, Carpenter
Guards: Scott, Maskas, Groves, Hirsch
Centers: Prewitt, Haynes
Backs: Juzwik, Kulbitski, Koch, Terlep, Reisz, Wizbicki, Evans

Chicago
Ends: Dove, Harrington, Quillen, Lahey
Tackles: Niedziela, McCollum, Sanchez, Pucci
Guards: Vogds, O'Neal, Wasserbach, Hecht
Centers: Lamana, Coleman
Backs: Kellagher, Ramsey, Bass, Lewis, Scalissi

Individual Statistics

Buffalo
Rushing: Rykovich: 10–54, Mutryn: 8–35, Kulbitski: 5–22, Tomasetti: 7–20, Evans: 3–5, Ratterman: 1–3, Juzwik: 2–0
Receiving: Mutryn: 3–82 1 TD, Baldwin: 3–75 1 TD, King 3–50 1 TD, Tomasetti: 2–44, Coppage: 3–28, Kulbitski: 3–17 1 TD, Gibson: 1–10, Juzwik: 1-(-2)
Passing: Ratterman: 18–31–294 4 TD 1 INT, Terlep: 1–2–10
Punting: Reisz: 2–80
Punt Returns: Wizbicki: 2–32, Mutryn: 2–24
Kickoff Returns: Tomasetti: 1–24

Chicago
Rushing: Scalissi: 5–31, Hirsch: 8–20 1 TD, Ramsey: 4–20, Daley: 11–9, Bass: 2–3
Receiving: Hirsch: 4–120 1 TD, Morris: 2–20, Mulready: 1–17, Scalissi: 1–9, Bass: 1–0, Ramsey: 0–2 (Lateral), Daley: 1-(–6)
Passing: Vacanti: 10–16–162 1 TD
Punting: Lewis: 6–224
Punt Returns: Hirsch: 1–3
Kickoff Returns: Hirsch: 2–67, Scalissi: 3–54, Schroeder: 1–19
Interception Returns: Ramsey: 1–8

September 28, 1947, San Francisco 49ers vs. Buffalo Bills
Location: Civic Stadium (Buffalo, NY)
Attendance: 36,099

	1	2	3	4	F
San Francisco 49ers	0	7	14	20	41
Buffalo Bills	7	10	7	0	24

Scoring Summary

BUF Rykovich 14-Yard Run (Juzwik Kick)
SF Albert 1-Yard Run (Vetrano Kick)
BUF Baldwin 58-Yard Pass From Ratterman (Juzwik Kick)

Detailed Game Summaries

BUF Juzwik 19-Yard Field Goal
BUF Mutryn 87-Yard Kickoff Return (Juzwik Kick)
SF Beals 14-Yard Pass From Freitas (Vetrano Kick)
SF Albert 15-Yard Run (Vetrano Kick)
SF Standlee 2-Yard Run (Vetrano Kick)
SF Albert 1-Yard Run (Vetrano Kick)
SF Strzykalski 1-Yard Run (Pass Failed)

	San Francisco	Buffalo
First Downs	22	8
Yards Rushing	277	145
Passes—Attempts	26	18
Passes—Completions	10	9
Passes—Yards	131	134
Punting Average	46.5	37
Fumbles Recovered	4	1

Position	San Francisco	Buffalo
LE	Fisk	Gibson
LT	Bryant	Armstrong
LG	Gregory	Lahar
C	Schiechl	Prewitt
RG	Banducci	Pirro
RT	Woudenberg	Doherty
RE	Beals	Coppage
QB	Yonamine	Hirsch
LHB	Eshmont	Mutryn
RHB	Strzykalski	Rykovich
FB	Standlee	Kulbitski

Substitutes

San Francisco
Ends: Balatti, Susoeff, Norberg
Tackles: Grgich, Thornton
Guards: Forrest, Calvelli, Bassi, Elston
Centers: Smith
Backs: Vetrano, Freitas, Mathews, Albert, Parsons

Buffalo
Ends: Comer, King, Mazza, Baldwin
Tackles: Kozel, Kerns, Carpenter
Guards: Maskas, Scott, Haynes
Centers: Corley
Backs: Evans, Tomasetti, Koch, Juzwik, Terlep, Reisz, Wizbicki

Individual Statistics

San Francisco
Rushing: Strzykalski: 18–115 1 TD, Eshmont: 11–78, Albert: 9–35 3 TD, Standlee: 11–27 1 TD, Parsons: 6–13, Yonamine: 1–4, Masini: 1–5

Receiving: Beals: 5–84 1 TD, Eshmont: 1–20, Susoeff: 1–16, Balatti: 1–5, Strzykalski: 1–4, Mathews: 1–2
Passing: Albert: 8–22–112, Freitas: 2–3–19 1 TD, Strzykalski: 0–1–0
Punting: Albert: 5–233
Punt Returns: Yonamine: 1–21, Vetrano: 1–5, Parsons: 1–0
Kickoff Returns: Vetrano: 2–40, Mathews: 1–27, Yonamine: 1–25, Parsons: 1–24
Interception Returns: Eshmont: 1–4

Buffalo
Rushing: Mutryn: 8–102, Kulbitski: 7–27, Tomasetti: 1–14, Rykovich: 4–9 1 TD, Evans: 3–(–7)
Receiving: Baldwin: 4–81 1 TD, Kulbitski: 1–25, King: 2–23, Mutryn: 1–9, Tomasetti: 1–(–4)
Passing: Ratterman: 9–16–134 1 TD 1 INT, Terlep: 0–2–0
Punting: Reisz: 4–148
Punt Returns: Evans: 1–10, Mutryn: 2–8
Kickoff Returns: Mutryn: 2–116 1 TD, Rykovich: 2–59, Wizbicki: 1–21, Kulbitski: 1–19, Evans: 1–0

October 5, 1947, Buffalo Bills vs. Los Angeles Dons
Location: Memorial Coliseum (Los Angeles, CA)
Attendance: 36,087

	1	2	3	4	F
Buffalo Bills	20	0	7	0	27
Los Angeles Dons	7	0	14	4	25

Scoring Summary

BUF Baldwin 32-Yard Pass From Ratterman (Juzwik Kick)
LA   O'Rourke 5-Yard Run (Agajanian Kick)
BUF King 61-Yard Pass From Ratterman (Juzwik Kick)
BUF Mutryn 7-Yard Run (Kick Failed)
BUF Juzwik 22-Yard Pass From Ratterman (Juzwik Kick)
LA   Aguirre 31-Yard Pass From O'Rourke (Agajanian Kick)
LA   Aguirre 4-Yard Pass From O'Rourke (Agajanian Kick)
LA   Ratterman Stepped Out of Endzone, Safety
LA   Ratterman Stepped Out of Endzone, Safety

	Buffalo	Los Angeles
First Downs	10	16
Yards Rushing	87	120
Passes—Attempts	15	20
Passes—Completions	9	13
Passes—Yards	145	227
Passes—Interceptions	2	1
Punting Average	34	32
Fumbles Recovered	3	1
Penalty Yards	9	40

Detailed Game Summaries

Position	Buffalo	Los Angeles
LE	Baldwin	Aguirre
LT	Kozel	Audet
LG	Lahar	Lolotai
C	Prewitt	Nelson
RG	Pirro	Frankowski
RT	Doherty	Artoe
RE	King	Gentry
QB	Ratterman	O'Rourke
LHB	Mutryn	Fenenbock
RHB	Juzwik	Clarke
FB	Kulbitski	Kimbrough

Substitutes

Buffalo
Ends: Gibson, Comer, Mazza, Coppage
Tackles: Armstrong, Carpenter, Kerns
Guards: Haynes, Maskas
Centers: Corley
Backs: Reisz, Blount, Hirsch, Wizbicki, Koch, Tomasetti

Los Angeles
Ends: Titchenal, Baldwin, Nowasky, Anderson
Tackles: Mitchell, Berezney
Guards: Agajanian, Gallagher, Levy
Centers: Brown
Backs: R. Reinhard, W. Reinhard, Kelly, Landsberg, Heap, Dobbs, Piggott

Individual Statistics

Buffalo
Rushing: Mutryn: 15–63 1 TD, Juzwik: 6–56, Koch: 2–12, Tomasetti: 8–8, Ratterman: 3–(-26)
Receiving: King: 3–92 1 TD, Baldwin: 3–46 1 TD, Tomasetti: 2–25, Juzwik: 1–22 1 TD
Passing: Ratterman: 9–15–185 3 TD 1 INT
Punting: Reisz: 3–103
Kickoff Returns: Mutryn: 3–117, Juzwik: 1–20
Interception Returns: Mutryn: 1–11, Prewitt: 1–10

Los Angeles
Rushing: Clarke: 8–46, Kelly: 7–31, Fenenbock: 3–22, O'Rourke: 5–19 1 TD, Kimbrough: 6–9, Reinhard: 4–7, Piggot: 4–1, Dobbs: 1–(-6)
Receiving: Aguirre: 3–63 2 TD, Fenenbock: 2–63, Kimbrough: 3–33, Nowaskey: 2–27, Clarke: 1–24, Titchenal: 1–15, Gentry: 1–2
Passing: O'Rourke: 10–15–185 2 TD 2 INT, Dobbs: 3–4–42, Reinhard: 0–1–0
Punting: Reinhard: 1–69, Dobbs: 1–35
Punt Returns: Fenenbock: 1–12, Dobbs: 1–1
Kickoff Returns: Fenenbock: 5–123, O'Rourke: 1–24, Kelly: 1–19
Interception Returns: Heap: 1–15

October 12, 1947, Baltimore Colts vs. Buffalo Bills
Location: Civic Stadium (Buffalo, NY)
Attendance: 27,345

	1	2	3	4	F
Baltimore Colts	3	12	0	0	15
Buffalo Bills	0	7	7	6	20

Scoring Summary (Not In Order Of Scoring)

BAL	Lio 22-Yard Field Goal
BAL	Phillips Tackled Ratterman For A Safety
BAL	Schwenk 6-Yard Run (Lio Kick)
BUF	Mutryn 2-Yard Run (Juzwik Kick)
BAL	Lio 19-Yard Field Goal
BUF	Baldwin 30-Yard Pass From Ratterman (Mutryn Kick)
BUF	Mutryn 7-Yard Run (Kick Failed)

	Baltimore	Buffalo
First Downs	13	14
Yards Rushing	69	239
Passes—Attempts	24	9
Passes—Completions	15	6
Passes—Yards	197	96
Passes—Interceptions	0	0
Punting Average	29.2	34.4
Fumbles Recovered	0	1
Penalty Yards	30	38

Position	Baltimore	Buffalo
LE	Davis	Gibson
LT	Perpich	Armstrong
LG	French	Lahar
C	Phillips	Prewitt
RG	Marino	Pirro
RT	Klug	Doherty
RE	Madar	Coppage
QB	Case	Hirsch
LHB	Mobley	Mutryn
RHB	Dudish	Tomasetti
FB	Mertes	Kulbitski

Substitutes

Baltimore
Ends: Bechtol, Getchell, Meyers
Tackles: Mellus, Kasap
Guards: Grain, Yokas, Zorich, Lio
Centers: Kodba, Handley
Backs: Schwenk, Hillenbrand, Black, Terrell, Vardian, Wright, Sinkwich

Buffalo
Ends: Baldwin, King, Mazza, Comer

Detailed Game Summaries 161

Tackles: Kozel, Carpenter, Kerns, Duggan
Guards: Maskas, Scott
Centers: Corley
Backs: Ratterman, Rykovich, Wizbicki, Manders, Reisz, Koch

Individual Statistics

Baltimore
Rushing: Sinkwich: 9–36, Mertes: 6–15, Schwenk: 2–10 1 TD, Mobley: 4–7, Hillenbrand: 4–6, Dudish: 1–2, Terrell: 3-(–9)
Receiving: Davis: 8–91, Hillenbrand: 3–78, Bechtol: 2–19, Dudish: 1–11, Terrell: 1-(-2)
Passing: Schwenk: 15–24–197
Punting: Galvin: 5–174
Punt Returns: Davis: 1–33, Case: 2–18, Hillenbrand: 1–9
Kickoff Returns: Hillenbrand: 2–66, Case: 1–43, Terrell: 1–25

Buffalo
Rushing: Mutryn: 20–99 2 TD, Rykovich: 7–56, Juzwik: 4–52, Kulbitski: 5–18, Tomasetti: 5–18, Koch: 2–11, Ratterman: 2-(–15)
Receiving: Baldwin: 2–48 1 TD, King: 3–34, Tomasetti: 1–14
Passing: Ratterman: 6–9–96 1 TD
Punting: Reisz: 5–147
Punt Returns: Wizbicki: 2–8
Kickoff Returns: Wizbicki: 1–19, Koch: 1–12, Baldwin: 1–6, Rykovich: 1–5

October 17, 1947, Buffalo Bills vs. Brooklyn Dodgers
Location: Ebbets Field (Brooklyn, NY)
Attendance: 9,792

	1	2	3	4	F
Buffalo Bills	7	7	0	0	14
Brooklyn Dodgers	7	0	0	7	14

Scoring Summary

BKN Akins 19-Yard Run (Martinovich Kick)
BUF Wizbicki 91-Yard Kickoff Return (Armstrong Kick)
BUF Mutryn 14-Yard Run (Armstrong Kick)
BKN Hoernschmeyer 84-Yard Run (Martinovich Kick)

	Buffalo	Brooklyn
First Downs	13	12
Yards Rushing	202	274
Passes—Attempts	13	7
Passes—Completions	7	1
Passes—Yards	84	12
Passes—Interceptions	2	0
Punting Average	36	51
Fumbles Recovered	0	1
Penalty Yards	20	35

Position	Buffalo	Brooklyn
LE	Gibson	McCarthy
LT	Armstrong	Ruby
LG	Lahar	Warrington
C	Prewitt	Gustafson
RG	Pirro	Buffington
RT	Doherty	Williams
RE	Coppage	Judd
QB	Tomasetti	Colmer
LHB	Mutryn	McDonald
RHB	Rykovich	Akins
FB	Kulbitski	Gafford

Substitutes

Buffalo
Ends: King, Kuffel, Baldwin, Mazza, Comer
Tackles: Duggan, Kerns
Guards: Scott, Maskas, Haynes
Centers: Corley
Backs: Terlep, Ratterman, Koch, Reisz, Manders, Wizbicki, Blount, Hirsch

Brooklyn
Ends: Scruggs, Nelson, Hein, Thompson
Tackles: L. Daukas, Mieszkowski, Huneke, Wetz
Guards: Jeffers, Laurinaitis, A. Harris
Centers: Gibson, N. Daukas
Backs: Perina, E. Harris, Tevis, Hoernschemeyer, Kowalski, Tackett, Martinovich

Individual Statistics

Buffalo
Rushing: Rykovich: 13–110, Mutryn: 10–76 1 TD, Koch: 2–14, Kulbitski: 4–9, Tomasetti: 5-(–1), Ratterman: 2-(–6)
Receiving: King: 4–62, Coppage: 1–14, Gibson: 1–3, Mutryn: 1–2
Passing: Ratterman: 7–13–81
Punting: Reisz: 3–109
Punt Returns: Koch: 1–30, Wizbicki: 2–28, Rykovich: 1–9
Kickoff Returns: Wizbicki: 1–91 1 TD, Mutryn: 2–82
Interception Returns: Koch: 1–0, Terlep: 1–0

Brooklyn
Rushing: Hoernschemeyer: 19–179 1 TD, Colmer: 10–42, Akins: 2–25 1 TD, Gafford: 5–23, Perina: 6–5
Receiving: Colmer: 1–12
Passing: Hoernschemeyer: 1–7–12 2 INT
Punting: Colmer: 4–205
Kickoff Returns: Gafford: 1–24, Perina: 1–24, Harris: 1–23

Detailed Game Summaries 163

October 26, 1947, Brooklyn Dodgers vs. Buffalo Bills
Location: Civic Stadium (Buffalo, NY)
Attendance: 23,762

	1	2	3	4	F
Brooklyn Dodgers	7	0	0	0	7
Buffalo Bills	0	14	21	0	35

Scoring Summary

BKN	Colmer 41-Yard Run (Martinovich Kick)
BUF	Rykovich 5-Yard Run (Armstrong Kick)
BUF	Kulbitski 38-Yard Pass From Ratterman (Armstrong Kick)
BUF	Tomasetti 1-Yard Run (Armstrong Kick)
BUF	Kulbitski 34-Yard Lateral From King From Pass From Ratterman (Armstrong Kick)
BUF	Tomasetti 41-Yard Interception Return (Armstrong Kick)

	Brooklyn	Buffalo
First Downs	6	22
Yards Rushing	112	254
Passes—Attempts	10	27
Passes—Completions	2	12
Passes—Yards	28	171
Passes—Interceptions	0	-
Punting Average	48.3	42
Fumbles Recovered	1	2
Penalty Yards	23	30

Position	Brooklyn	Buffalo
LE	McCarthy	Gibson
LT	Ruby	Armstrong
LG	Warrington	Lahar
C	Gustafson	Prewitt
RG	Buffington	Pirro
RT	Williams	Kerns
RE	Judd	Coppage
QB	McDonald	Baldwin
LHB	D. Jones	Tomasetti
RHB	Hoernschemeyer	Rykovich
FB	Colmer	Hirsch

Substitutes

Brooklyn
Ends: Thompson, Scruggs, Hein
Tackles: Huneke, Mieszkowski, Wetz
Guards: Jeffers, Martinovich, W. Jones
Centers: Gibson
Backs: E. Harris, Gafford, Perina, Tackett

Buffalo
Ends: Mazza, Comer, King, Kuffel

Tackles: Kozel, Duggan, Doherty, Carpenter
Guards: Scott, Haynes, Maskas, Groves
Centers: Corley
Backs: Ratterman, Terlep, Riesz, Koch, Kulbitski, Mutryn, Wizbicki, Manders, Blount

Individual Statistics

Brooklyn
Rushing: Colmer: 10–62 1 TD, Hoernschemeyer: 15–41, D. Jones: 4–9, Harris: 1–3, Gafford: 1-(–3)
Receiving: McCarthy: 1–20, Judd: 1–8
Passing: Hoernschemeyer: 2–9-28 2 INT, Colmer: 0–1-0
Punting: Colmer: 4–193
Punt Returns: Hoernschemeyer: 1–19, D. Jones: 1–19
Kickoff Returns: Colmer: 1–31, Gafford: 1–25, D. Jones: 1–17
Interception Returns: Perina: 1–0

Buffalo
Rushing: Tomasetti: 9–72 1 TD, Kulbitski: 10–58, Rykovich: 9–46 1 TD, Koch: 3–28, Manders: 3–15, Mutryn: 4–14, Wizbicki: 3–13, Terlep: 1–4, Hirsch: 1–3, Blount: 1–2
Receiving: Kulbitski: 2–65 2 TD, Baldwin: 4–37, King: 2–24, Tomasetti: 1–23, Rykovich: 2–22, Coppage: 1-(–1)
Passing: Ratterman: 11–22-171 2 TD 1 INT
Punting: Reisz: 2–84
Punt Returns: Koch: 1–13, Rykovich: 1–10, Wizbicki: 1–9
Kickoff Returns: Mutryn: 1–39, Tomasetti: 1–18
Interception Returns: Tomasetti: 1–41 1 TD, Rykovich: 1–5

November 2, 1947, Cleveland Browns vs. Buffalo Bills
Location: Civic Stadium (Buffalo, NY)
Attendance: 43,167

	1	2	3	4	F
Cleveland Browns	7	7	7	7	28
Buffalo Bills	0	0	0	7	7

Scoring Summary

CLE   Jones 11-Yard Run (Groza Kick)
CLE   Lavelli 11-Yard Pass from Graham (Groza Kick)
CLE   Speedie 99-Yard Pass From Graham (Groza Kick)
BUF   Baldwin 11-Yard Pass From Ratterman (Armstrong Kick)
CLE   Yonaker 39-Yard Pass From Graham (Groza Kick)

	Cleveland	*Buffalo*
First Downs	13	13
Yards Rushing	146	85
Passes—Attempts	16	2?
Passes—Completions	13	13

Detailed Game Summaries

	Cleveland	Buffalo
Passes—Yards	256	167
Passes—Interceptions	0	3
Punting Average	55.3	45
Fumbles Recovered	1	0
Penalty Yards	35	5

Position	Cleveland	Buffalo
LE	Speedie	Kuffel
LT	Adams	Armstrong
LG	Ulinski	Lahar
C	Gatski	Prewitt
RG	Houston	Pirro
RT	Rymkus	Kerns
RE	Lavelli	Comer
QB	Lewis	Baldwin
LHB	Colella	Hirsch
RHB	Mayne	Rykovich
FB	Motley	Kulbitski

Substitutes

Cleveland
Ends: Gillom, Yonakor
Tackles: Blandin, Groza
Guards: Gaudio, Humble, Piskor
Centers: Simonetti
Backs: Graham, Jones, Allen, Boedeker, Lund, Greenwood, Saban, Cowan, Adamle, Dewar, Dellerba

Buffalo
Ends: King, Coppage
Tackles: Duggan, Carpenter, Kozel
Guards: Scott, Haynes
Centers: Corley
Backs: Terlep, Tomasetti, Wizbicki, Reisz, Ratterman, Koch, Mutryn

Individual Statistics

Cleveland
Rushing: Motley: 11–72, Jones: 12–45 1 TD, Mayne: 8–21, Greenwood: 1–8, Dellerba: 1–4, Boedeker: 1–4, Adamle: 2–3, Dewar: 1–1, Allen: 1–(–5), Colella: 1–(–8), Graham: 1–(–8)
Receiving: Speedie: 7–147–1 TD, Yonaker: 2–50 1 TD, Motley: 2–37, Lavelli: 2–22 1 TD
Passing: Graham 13–16–256 3 TD
Punting: Gillom: 3–166
Punt Returns: Lewis: 1–10
Kickoff Returns: Jones: 1–23, Colella: 1–13
Interception Returns: Colella: 1–25, Allen: 1–4, Greenwood: 1–0

Buffalo
Rushing: Mutryn: 10–41, Rykovich: 7–25, Wizbicki: 3–9, Tomasetti: 4–7, Koch: 2–3

Receiving: Baldwin: 5–63 1 TD, Coppage: 2–52, Kuffel: 2–29, Mutryn: 1–16, King: 1–11, Kulbitski: 0–3, Rykovich: 1-(–1), Tomasetti: 1-(–6)
Passing: Ratterman: 13–27–167 1 TD 2 INT, Terlep: 0–2–0 1 INT
Punting: Reisz: 2–90
Punt Returns: Mutryn: 2–42, Koch: 1–33
Kickoff Returns: Mutryn: 3–70, Wizbicki: 2–33

November 9, 1947, Los Angeles Dons vs. Buffalo Bills
Location: Civic Stadium (Buffalo, NY)
Attendance: 21,293

	1	2	3	4	F
Los Angeles Dons	0	0	0	0	0
Buffalo Bills	6	0	13	6	25

Scoring Summary

BUF Baldwin 25-Yard Pass From Ratterman (Kick Failed)
BUF Mutryn 11-Yard Run (Pass Failed)
BUF Mutryn 6-Yard Run (Kulbitski Run)
BUF Kulbitski 15-Yard Pass From Terlep (Kick Failed)

	Los Angeles	Buffalo
First Downs	8	6
Yards Rushing	138	80
Passes—Attempts	10	9
Passes—Completions	5	4
Passes—Yards	42	77
Passes—Interceptions	0	3
Punting Average	40.2	37.5
Fumbles Recovered	0	3
Penalty Yards	35	5

Position	Los Angeles	Buffalo
LE	Nowasky	Kuffel
LT	Agajanian	Kozel
LG	Lolotai	Lahar
C	Brown	Prewitt
RG	Levy	Pirro
RT	Danehe	Carpenter
RE	Gentry	King
QB	O'Rourke	Tomasetti
LHB	Piggott	Mutryn
RHB	Kelly	Rykovich
FB	R. Reinhard	Wizbicki

Substitutes

Los Angeles
Ends: Anderson, Aguirre, Titchenal, B. Baldwin
Tackles: Audet, Berezney, Mitchell, Artoe, Smith
Guards: Radovich, Frankowski, Gallagher, Lennon

Centers: Nelson
Backs: Dobbs, Kimbrough, Clay, Landsberg, Hopp, Heap, Clarke, Fenenbock
Buffalo
Ends: Mazza, Coppage, Baldwin, Gibson, Comer
Tackles: Armstrong, Duggan, Doherty, Kerns
Guards: Scott, Haynes, Groves
Centers: Corley
Backs: Ratterman, Kulbitski, Terlep, Koch, Hirsch, Reisz

Individual Statistics

Los Angeles
Rushing: Kimbrough: 8–34, Reinhard: 5–34, Kelly: 4–21, Clay: 2–21, Clarke: 3–12, Piggot: 5–7, Hopp: 2–6, Fenenbock: 1–2, Dobbs: 3–1
Receiving: Hopp: 1–39, B. Baldwin: 1–7, Gentry: 1–6, Aguirre: 1–5, Landsberg: 1–0, Fenenbock: 0-(–15)
Passing: Dobbs: 4–11–35, O'Rourke: 1–7–7 3 INT, Reinhard: 0–1–0
Punting: Reinhard: 4–172, Dobbs: 1–30
Punt Returns: Dobbs: 3–20, Clarke: 1–12, Fenenbock: 1–9
Kickoff Returns: Piggot: 2–51, Reinhard: 1–26, Fenenbock: 1–26, Hopp: 1–13
Interception Returns: Dobbs: 1–0, Reinhard: 1–0

Buffalo
Rushing: Mutryn: 5–26 2 TD, Tomasetti: 13–25, Rykovich: 5–14, Reisz: 1–9, Terlep: 2–3, Hirsch: 2–2, Ratterman: 1–1, Koch: 1–1, Kulbitski: 4-(–1), {Bad Center Pass: 1-(–6)}
Receiving: Baldwin: 1–25 1 TD, Comer: 1–19, Mutryn: 1–18, Kulbitski: 1–15 1 TD
Passing: Ratterman: 3–7–62 1 TD 2 INT, Terlep: 1–2–15 1 TD
Punting: Reisz: 7–263
Punt Returns: Wizbicki: 2–28
Kickoff Returns: Mutryn: 1–51
Interception Returns: Rykovich: 1–56, Mazza: 1–26, Prewitt: 1–10

November 23, 1947, Buffalo Bills vs. Baltimore Colts
Location: (Baltimore, MD)
Attendance: 19,593

	1	2	3	4	F
Buffalo Bills	7	6	13	7	35
Baltimore Colts	0	7	0	7	14

Scoring Summary

BUF Mutryn 3-Yard Run (Juzwik Kick)
BUF Hirsch 45-Yard Interception Return (Kick Failed)
BAL Hillenbrand 18-Yard Pass From Schwenk (Lio Kick)
BUF Comer 56-Yard Pass From Ratterman (Juzwik Kick)
BUF Rykovich 1-Yard Run (Kick Failed)
BAL Dudish 1-Yard Run (Lio Kick)
BUF Mutryn 3-Yard Run (Juzwik Kick)

	Buffalo	Baltimore
First Downs	16	11
Yards Rushing	232	97
Passes—Attempts	18	21
Passes—Completions	6	10
Passes—Yards	93	143
Passes—Interceptions	3	3
Punting Average	37	42
Fumbles Recovered	0	1
Penalty Yards	34	45

Position	Buffalo	Baltimore
LE	Baldwin	Bechtol
LT	Kozel	Mellus
LG	Lahar	French
C	Prewitt	Phillips
RG	Pirro	Lio
RT	Carpenter	Perpich
RE	Coppage	Blount
QB	Ratterman	Schwenk
LHB	Mutryn	Hillenbrand
RHB	Rykovich	Vardian
FB	Hirsch	Sinkwich

Substitutes

Buffalo
Ends: Gibson, Kuffel, Mazza, Comer, King
Tackles: Duggan, Kerns, Armstrong
Guards: Scott, Groves
Centers: Corley, Haynes
Backs: Terlep, Reisz, Wizbicki, Koch, Juzwik, Kulbitski, Tomasetti

Baltimore
Ends: Konetskyy, Madar, Davis, Meyers
Tackles: Grain, Kasap
Guards: Higgins, Zorich, Yokas, Marino
Centers: Kodba, Handley
Backs: Case, Mobley, Dudish, Mertes, Wright

Individual Statistics

Buffalo
Rushing: Mutryn: 10–79 2 TD, Rykovich: 13–59 1 TD, Koch: 5–28, Tomasetti: 6–27, Kulbitski: 3–16, Wizbicki: 2–15, Ratterman: 1–6
Receiving: Comer: 1–56 1 TD, Coppage: 2–24, Tomasetti: 1–11, Baldwin: 1–6, Kulbitski: 1-(–4)
Passing: Ratterman: 5–12–97 1 TD 2 INT, Terlep: 1–6-(–4) 1 INT
Punting: Reisz: 2–75
Punt Returns: Mutryn: 3–63, Rykovich: 2–40
Kickoff Returns: Rykovich: 1–19, Coppage: 1–15
Interception Returns: Hirsch: 2–52 1 TD, Koch: 1–8

Baltimore
Rushing: Sinkwich: 16-72, Hillenbrand: 6-14, Vardian: 5-9, Dudish: 2-6 1 TD, Schwenk: 2-4, Bechtol: 1-(-8)
Receiving: Blount: 3-76, Hillenbrand: 1-18 1 TD, Davis: 2-16, Madar: 1-10, Bechtol: 2-9, Mobley: 1-9, Mellus: 0-5
Passing: Schwenk: 10-21-143 1 TD 3 INT
Punting: Sinkwich: 4-167
Punt Returns: Hillenbrand: 1-10
Kickoff Returns: Sinkwich: 2-47, Vardian: 1-23, Dudish: 1-23, Madar: 1-14, Hillenbrand: 1-10
Interception Returns: Vardian: 2-31, Bechtol: 1-7

November 30, 1947, Buffalo Bills vs. New York Yankees
Location: Yankee Stadium (New York, NY)
Attendance: 39,012

	1	2	3	4	F
Buffalo Bills	0	6	0	7	13
New York Yankees	14	0	7	14	35

Scoring Summary

NYY	Young 1-Yard Run (H. Johnson Kick)
NYY	Sossamon 59-Yard Fumble Return (H. Johnson Kick)
BUF	Rykovich 2-Yard Run (Kick Failed)
NYY	Sanders 1-Yard Run (H. Johnson Kick)
BUF	Baldwin 59-Yard Pass From Ratterman (Juzwik Kick)
NYY	Sanders 1-Yard Run (H. Johnson Kick)
NYY	Sanders 56-Yard Run (H. Johnson Kick)

	Buffalo	New York
First Downs	10	17
Yards Rushing	87	254
Passes—Attempts	21	8
Passes—Completions	9	4
Passes—Yards	115	105
Passes—Interceptions	1	3
Punting Average	33.3	40.1
Fumbles Recovered	0	1
Penalty Yards	10	5

Position	Buffalo	New York
LE	Baldwin	Russell
LT	Kozel	Kinard
LG	Lahar	Bentz
C	Prewitt	Sossamon
RG	Pirro	Barwegan
RT	Carpenter	N. Johnson
RE	Coppage	Alford
QB	Wizbicki	Cheatham
LHB	Mutryn	Sanders
RHB	Rykovich	Sweiger
FB	Tomasetti	Burrus

Substitutes

Buffalo
Ends: King, Gibson, Mazza, Kuffel, Comer
Tackles: Armstrong, Duggan
Guards: Scott, Groves
Centers: Corley
Backs: Ratterman, Terlep, Reisz, Hirsch, Kulbitski, Koch, Juzwik

New York
Ends: Ruskusky, Davis, Stanton, Kurrasch
Tackles: Durishan, Schleich, Kinard, Elliott, Palmer
Guards: Sharkey, Yackanich, Riffle
Centers: Duke, Stewart
Backs: H. Johnson, Kennedy, Sylvester, Wagner, Raimondi, Young, Proctor, Rowe

Individual Statistics

Buffalo
Rushing: Mutryn: 12–54, Tomasetti: 7–35, Rykovich: 8–1 1 TD, Koch: 1-(–3)
Receiving: Baldwin: 1–59 1 TD, Coppage: 5–33, Tomasetti: 2–15, Kuffel: 1–8
Passing: Ratterman: 9–19–115 1 TD 2 INT, Terlep: 0–2–0 1 INT
Punting: Reisz: 6–200
Punt Returns: Terlep: 1–17, Koch: 1–8, Mutryn: 1–6, Rykovich: 1–0
Kickoff Returns: Rykovich: 3–75, Mutryn: 2–57, Coppage: 1–13
Interception Returns: Baldwin: 1–19

New York
Rushing: Sanders 23–144 3 TD, Young: 12–78 1 TD, Kennedy: 5–18, Sylvester: 3–6, Proctor: 1–3, Raimondi: 1–3, Sweiger: 1–2
Receiving: Davis: 2–67, Young: 1–26, Alford: 1–13
Passing: Sanders: 3–7–94 1 INT, Kennedy: 1–1–12
Punting: Sanders: 5–200
Punt Returns: Kennedy: 1–11
Kickoff Returns: Sanders: 2–43, Young: 1–24
Interception Returns: Kennedy: 2–66, Sanders 1–1

December 7, 1947, Buffalo Bills vs. San Francisco 49ers
Location: Kezar Stadium (San Francisco, CA)
Attendance: 19,500

	1	2	3	4	F
Buffalo Bills	0	7	0	14	21
San Francisco	0	7	0	14	21

Scoring Summary

SF   Suseoff 7-Yard Pass From Albert (Vetrano Kick)
BUF Coppage 7-Yard Pass From Ratterman (Juzwik Kick)
BUF King 11-Yard Pass From Ratterman (Juzwik Kick)

Detailed Game Summaries 171

SF Mathews 1-Yard Run (Vetrano Kick)
SF Mathews 35-Yard Interception Return (Vetrano Kick)
BUF King 11-Yard Pass From Rattterman (Juzwik Kick)

	Buffalo	San Francisco
First Downs	14	11
Yards Rushing	136	153
Passes—Attempts	30	24
Passes—Completions	17	11
Passes—Yards	176	98
Passes—Interceptions	1	4
Punting Average	35	45.4
Fumbles Recovered	2	0
Penalty Yards	55	15

Position	Buffalo	San Francisco
LE	Comer	Susoeff
LT	Kozel	Bryant
LG	Lahar	Gregory
C	Corley	Calvelli
RG	Pirro	Forrest
RT	Carpenter	Woudenberg
RE	Coppage	Horne
QB	Ratterman	Vetrano
LHB	Mutryn	Eshmont
RHB	Juzwik	Strzykalski
FB	Tomasetti	Standlee

Substitutes

Buffalo
Ends: King, Mazza, Gibson
Tackles: Duggan, Armstrong, Kerns
Guards: Groves, Scott
Backs: Wizbicki, Rykovich

San Francisco
Ends: Beals, Fisk, Balatti
Tackles: Thornton
Guards: Banducci
Centers: Conlee
Backs: Freitas, Albert, Masini, Mathews, Carr, Yonamine

Individual Statistics

Buffalo
Rushing: Kulbitski: 7–52, Mutryn: 10–39, Reisz: 1–23, Tomasetti: 3–10, Rykovich: 3–4, Hirsch: 1–2, Juzwik: 6–1, Ratterman: 2-(-2)
Receiving: Gibson: 5–127, King: 5–30 2 TD, Mutryn: 1–29, Coppage: 3–26, Mazza: 2–11, Tomasetti: 1-(-1)
Passing: Ratterman: 17–33–222 3 TD 4 INT
Punting: Reisz: 5–187

Punt Returns: Juzwik: 2–25, Mutryn: 1–14, Kulbitski: 1–13
Kickoff Returns: Mutryn: 1–25, Rykovich: 1–14
Interception Returns: Corley: 1–41

San Francisco
Rushing: Standlee: 8–41, Albert: 6–40, Strzykalski: 9–22, Eshmont: 2–13, Mathews: 2–7 1 TD, Carr: 3–5, Masini: 2–2, Beals: 1–2
Receiving: Eshmont: 3–40, Suseoff: 3–25 1 TD, Beals: 2–25, Carr: 2–1, Fisk: 1–1
Passing: Albert: 11–22–92 1 TD 1 INT, Mathews: 0–1–0, Freitas: 0–1–0
Punting: Albert: 7–320, Freitas: 1–40
Punt Returns: Mathews: 1–5
Kickoff Returns: Eshmont: 1–23, Carr: 1–20
Interception Returns: Mathews: 2–77 1 TD, Scheichl: 1–21, Strzykalski: 1–0

1948 BUFFALO BILLS

Preseason

August 12, 1948, New York Yankees vs. Buffalo Bills
Location: Ruppert Stadium (Newark, NJ)
Attendance: n/a

	1	2	3	4	F
New York Yankees	?	?	?	0	28
Buffalo Bills	?	?	?	14	28

Scoring Summary (Not In Order of Scoring)

NYY Alford 15-Yard Pass From Sanders (Kick Made)
NYY Sanders 4-Yard Run (Kick Made)
NYY Young 60-Yard Pass From Sanders (Kick Made)
NYY Kennedy 4-Yard Run (Kick Made)
BUF Vic Kulbitski Run (Steuber Kick)
BUF Vic Kulbitski Run (Steuber Kick)
BUF Rykovich 2-Yard Run (Steuber Kick)
BUF Durkota 30-Yard Run (Steuber Kick)

August 17, 1948, Brooklyn Dodgers vs. Buffalo Bills
Location: Civic Stadium (Buffalo, NY)
Attendance: 27,630

	1	2	3	4	F
Brooklyn Dodgers	0	7	0	12	19
Buffalo Bills	14	0	7	0	21

Scoring Summary

BUF Gibson Pass From Ratterman (Steuber Kick)

Detailed Game Summaries 173

BUF Gibson Pass From Ratterman (Steuber Kick)
BKN Tevis 28-Yard Pass From Hoernschemeyer (Kick Made)
BUF Mutryn Pass From Ratterman (Steuber Kick)
BKN Judd Pass From Hoernschemeyer (Kick Missed)
BKN Thompson 52-Yard Pass From Hoernschemeyer, Lateral To Akins (Kick Missed)

August 22, 1948, Buffalo Bills vs. Cleveland Browns
Location: (Akron, OH)
Attendance: n/a

	1	2	3	4	F
Buffalo Bills	0	0	7	14	21
Cleveland Browns	21	7	7	0	35

Scoring Summary (Not In Order of Scoring)

CLE Lewis Touchdown (Groza Kick)
CLE Motley Touchdown (Groza Kick)
CLE Sensenbaugher Touchdown (Groza Kick)
CLE Sensenbaugher Touchdown (Groza Kick)
CLE Speedie Touchdown (Groza Kick)
BUF Baldwin Touchdown (Steuber Kick)
BUF O'Connor Touchdown (Steuber Kick)
BUF Heywood Touchdown (Steuber Kick)

Regular Season

August 29, 1948, Buffalo Bills vs. San Francisco 49ers
Location: Kezar Stadium (San Francisco, CA)
Attendance: 33,946

	1	2	3	4	F
Buffalo Bills	0	7	7	0	14
San Francisco 49ers	7	21	0	7	35

Scoring Summary

SF Schoener Pass From Albert (Vetrano Kick)
SF Cason Run (Vetrano Kick)
BUF Mutryn Run (Armstrong Kick)
SF Strzykalski 48-Yard Run (Vetrano Kick)
SF Perry 57-Yard Run (Vetrano Kick)
BUF O'Connor 5-Yard Pass From Ratterman (Armstrong Kick)
SF Cason Pass From Albert (Vetrano Kick)

	Buffalo	San Francisco
First Downs	18	12
Yards Rushing	271	225
Passes—Attempts	36	20
Passes—Completions	17	13
Passes—Yards	196	186

	Buffalo	San Francisco
Passes—Interceptions	2	1
Punts-Average	4–41.7	3–56.5
Fumbles Recovered	5	3
Penalty Yards	60	20

Position	Buffalo	San Francisco
LE	Baldwin	Shoener
LT	Armstrong	Bryant
LG	Lahar	Clark
C	Prewitt	Williams
RG	Pirro	Grgich
RT	Kerns	Woudenberg
RE	Gibson	Beals
QB	Ratterman	Albert
LHB	Steuber	Eshmont
RHB	Mutryn	Strzykalski
FB	Kulbitski	Standlee

Substitutes

Buffalo
Ends: Comer, O'Connor, Kisiday, Mazza
Tackles: Carpenter, Kissell
Guards: Hirsch, King, Scott, Wyhonic
Centers: Statuto
Backs: Bumgardner, Rykovich, Gompers, Tomasetti, Terlep, Smith, Schneider

San Francisco
Ends: Bruce, Howell, Maloney
Tackles: Mike, Collier, Land, Puddy
Guards: Cox, Matheson
Centers: Elston
Backs: Cason, Hall, Perry, Lillywhite, Sullivan, Carr, Wallace

Individual Statistics

Buffalo
Rushing: Mutryn: 14–114 1 TD, Steuber: 3–36, Tomasetti: 2–10, Gompers: 7–26, Kulbitski: 8–28, Schneider: 2–25, Rykovich: 2–25
Receiving: Baldwin: 1–49, O'Connor: 2–12 1 TD

San Francisco
Rushing: Strzykalski: 7–76 1 TD, Carr: 1–9, Perry: 3–65 1 TD, Hall: 5-(–3), Albert: 3–25, Lillywhite: 5–24, Eshmont: 4–10, Standlee: 5–13, Cason: 2–3 1 TD, Vetrano: 1–4

September 6, 1948, Chicago Rockets vs. Buffalo Bills
Location: Civic Stadium (Buffalo, NY)
Attendance: 25,816

	1	2	3	4	F
Chicago Rockets	0	0	0	7	7
Buffalo Bills	14	14	14	0	42

Detailed Game Summaries 175

Scoring Summary

BUF	Mutryn 1-Yard Run (Armstrong Kick)
BUF	Rykovich 8-Yard Run (Armstrong Kick)
BUF	Schuette 26-Yard Interception Return (Armstrong Kick)
BUF	Rykovich 7-Yard Run (Armstrong Kick)
BUF	Tomasetti 1-Yard Run (Armstrong Kick)
BUF	Rykovich 1-Yard Run (Armstrong Kick)
CHI	Proctor 1-Yard Run (Juzwik Kick)

	Chicago	Buffalo
First Downs	17	20
Yards Rushing	32	199
Passes—Attempts	49	16
Passes—Completions	21	10
Passes—Yards	258	185
Passes—Interceptions	4	1
Punting Average	45	40.5
Fumbles Recovered	2	5
Penalty Yards	81	102

Position	Chicago	Buffalo
LE	Kuffel	Baldwin
LT	Brutz	Armstrong
LG	Pearcy	Lahar
C	Rapacz	Prewitt
RG	Coleman	Pirro
RT	N. Johnson	Carpenter
RE	King	Gibson
QB	Bertelli	Ratterman
LHB	Hirsch	Mutryn
RHB	Prokop	Gompers
FB	Proctor	Kulbitski

Substitutes

Chicago
Ends: Jensen, F. Johnson, McCarthy, Owens
Tackles: Elliot, Czarobski, Uremovich, Smith
Guards: Ruetz, Urban, Piskor
Centers: Negus, Lamana
Backs: Farris, Livingstone, Perina, Vacanti, Fenenbock, Ramsey, Kellagher, Lewis, Evans, Juzwik, Simmons

Buffalo
Ends: Mazza, Comer, O'Connor
Tackles: Kissel, Kerns
Guards: Leonetti, Kisiday, Whalen, Scott, King, Wyhonic
Centers: Callahan, Statuto
Backs: Smith, Tomasetti, Still, Schuette, Rykovich, Schneider, Terlep, Bumgardner

Individual Statistics

Chicago
Rushing: Proctor: 1 TD
Passing: Vacanti: 20-42-?-0-?

Buffalo
Rushing: Rykovich: 3 TD, Mutryn: 1 TD, Tomasetti: 1 TD
Receiving: Baldwin: 1-25, Gibson: 1-30
Passing: 10-16-185-0-1

September 12, 1948, Cleveland Browns vs. Buffalo Bills
Location: Civic Stadium (Buffalo, NY)
Attendance: 35,340

	1	2	3	4	F
Cleveland Browns	14	7	7	14	42
Buffalo Bills	0	13	0	0	13

Scoring Summary

CLE	Cowan 11-Yard Pass From Graham (Groza Kick)
CLE	Motley 18-Yard Run (Groza Kick)
BUF	Rykovich 25-Yard Run (Armstrong Kick Blocked)
CLE	Speedie 10-Yard Pass From Graham (Groza Kick)
BUF	Mutryn 12-Yard Run (Armstrong Kick)
CLE	Graham 1-Yard Run (Groza Kick)
CLE	Colella 23-Yard Run (Groza Kick)
CLE	Sensanbaugher 4-Yard Run (Groza Kick)

	Cleveland	Buffalo
First Downs	20	13
Yards Rushing	268	216
Passes—Attempts	26	12
Passes—Completions	14	3
Passes—Yards	236	20
Passes—Interceptions	0	0
Punting Average	27.7	34.6
Fumbles Recovered	0	1
Penalty Yards	70	30

Position	Cleveland	Buffalo
LE	Young	Baldwin
LT	Groza	Armstrong
LG	Humble	Lahar
C	Saban	Prewitt
RG	Willis	Pirro
RT	Grigg	Carpenter
RE	Yonakor	Gibson
QB	Lewis	Bumgardner
LHB	Colella	Mutryn
RHB	James	Rykovich
FB	Adamle	Smith

Substitutes

Cleveland
Ends: Speedie, Gillom, Kosikowski
Tackles: Rymkus, Adams, Pucci, Simonetti
Guards: Ulinski, Gaudio, Houston, Agase
Centers: Gatski
Backs: Graham, Cowan, E. Jones, Boedeker, Parseghian, D. Jones, Motley, Cline, Sensenbaugher

Buffalo
Ends: Mazza, O'Connor
Tackles: Kerns, Kissell
Guards: Scott, Kisiday, Hirsch, Leonetti
Centers: Callahan, Statuto
Backs: Terlep, Still, Ratterman, Gompers, Schneider, Tomasetti, Schuette

Individual Statistics

Buffalo
Rushing: Mutryn: 18–76 1 TD, Kulbitski: 10–39, Rykovich: 12–101 1 TD, Still: 1-(–10), Ratterman: 1-(–4), Schneider: 1–4, Gompers: 2–13, Tomasetti: 1-1
Receiving: O'Connor: 2–13, Mutryn: 1–7
Passing: Ratterman: 3-9-20-0-0, Still: 0-3-0-0-0

Cleveland
Rushing: Motley: 17–136 1 TD, Cline: 1–8, Colella: 1–23 1 TD, E. Jones: 4–26, Adamle: 3–15, Boedeker: 6–40, Graham: 1–1 1 TD, D. Jones: 2–4, Parseghian: 1–5, Cowan: 2-(–1), Sensenbaugher: 1–3 1 TD, James: 1–8
Receiving: Speedie: 10–151 1 TD, Gillom: 2–24, Cowan: 2–32 1 TD, Boedeker: 1–51
Passing: Graham: 11-21-189-2-0, Lewis: 3-5-47-0-0

September 26, 1948, San Francisco 49ers vs. Buffalo Bills
Location: Civic Stadium (Buffalo, NY)
Attendance: 31,103

	1	2	3	4	F
San Francisco 49ers	7	10	14	7	38
Buffalo Bills	7	14	0	7	28

Scoring Summary

BUF Ratterman 1-Yard Run (Kulbitski Kick)
SF   Beals 29-Yard Pass From Albert (Vetrano Kick)
BUF Steuber 47-Yard run (Kulbitski Kick)
SF   Cason 59-Yard Run (Vetrano Kick)
BUF Mutryn 30-Yard Pass From Ratterman (Kulbitski Kick)
SF   Vetrano 28-Yard Field Goal
SF   Stryzalski 1-Yard Run (Vetrano Kick)
SF   Lillywhite Lateral From Stryzalski, 4-Yard Run (Vetrano Kick)

BUF Baldwin 14-Yard Pass From Ratterman (Kulbitski Kick)
SF   Albert 20-Yard Run (Vetrano Kick)

	San Francisco	Buffalo
First Downs	18	14
Yards Rushing	268	105
Passes—Attempts	25	35
Passes—Completions	14	23
Passes—Yards	268	299
Passes—Interceptions	0	2
Punts-Average	4–29.5	5–44
Fumbles Recovered	1	0
Penalty Yards	30	55

Position	San Francisco	Buffalo
LE	Beals	Baldwin
LT	Bryant	Armstrong
LG	Clark	Lahar
C	Williams	Prewitt
RG	Cox	Wyhonic
RT	Mike	Kerns
RE	Bruce	O'Connor
QB	Albert	Ratterman
LHB	Stryzkalski	Mutryn
RHB	Carr	Steuber
FB	Standlee	Kulbitski

Substitutes

San Francisco
Ends: Susoeff, Shoener, Maloney
Tackles: Woudenberg, Collier, Puddy
Guards: Grgich, Matheson, Banducci
Centers: Elston
Backs: Hall, Cason, Vetrano, Sullivan, Lillywhite, Perry

Buffalo
Ends: Gibson, Comer, Mazza, Kisiday
Tackles: Carpenter, Kozel, Kissell
Guards: King, Scott
Centers: Callahan, Hirsch, Statuto
Backs: Still, Rykovich, Bumgardner, Gompers, Akins, Wizbicki, Schneider, Schuette, Tomasetti

Individual Statistics

San Francisco
Rushing: Perry: 6–41, Lillywhite: 1 TD, Albert: 1 TD, Cason: 1 TD, Strzykalski: 1 TD
Receiving: Beals: 2–47 1 TD, Cason: 1–38, Suseoff: 1–8
Passing: Albert: 14–25–268–1–0

Buffalo
Rushing: Steuber: 1 TD, Ratterman: 1 TD

Receiving: Baldwin: 1–14 1 TD, Mutryn: 1–30 1 TD
Passing: Ratterman: 23–35–299–2–2

October 3, 1948, Brooklyn Dodgers vs. Buffalo Bills
Location: Civic Stadium (Buffalo, NY)
Attendance: 17,694

	1	2	3	4	F
Brooklyn Dodgers	0	7	7	7	21
Buffalo Bills	3	14	7	7	31

Scoring Summary

BUF	Steuber 24-Yard Field Goal
BUF	Tomasetti 15-Yard Run (Steuber Kick)
BKN	Brown 2-Yard Run (Brown Kick)
BUF	Mutryn 43-Yard Pass From Ratterman (Steuber Kick)
BKN	Brown 7-Yard Pass From Hoernschemeyer (Brown Kick)
BUF	Mutryn 9-Yard Pass From Ratterman (Steuber Kick)
BKN	Gafford 27-Yard Pass From Hoernschemeyer (Brown Kick)
BUF	Rykovich 1-Yard Run (Steuber Kick)

	Brooklyn	Buffalo
First Downs	7	17
Yards Rushing	9	222
Passes—Attempts	29	23
Passes—Completions	15	13
Passes—Yards	144	176
Passes—Interceptions	2	3
Punting Average	31.7	45.5
Fumbles Recovered	1	1
Penalty Yards	20	40

Position	Brooklyn	Buffalo
LE	Foldberg	Baldwin
LT	Ruby	Armstrong
LG	Warrington	Lahar
C	Strohmeyer	Prewitt
RG	Wozniak	Pirro
RT	Sazio	Carpenter
RE	Edwards	Comer
QB	Brown	Ratterman
LHB	Chappuis	Mutryn
RHB	Gafford	Rykovich
FB	Colmer	Kulbitski

Substitutes

Brooklyn
Ends: Morris, Thompson, Burrus, Scruggs, Judd

Tackles: Clowes, Spencer, Williams
Guards: Harris, St. John, Buffington
Centers: Gustafson
Backs: McDonald, Forkovitch, Hoernschemeyer, C. Allen, Smith, Ramsey, Tevis

Buffalo
Ends: Mazza, O'Connor, Kisiday
Tackles: Kissell, Kerns
Guards: Scott, Wyhonic, King
Centers: Callahan, Hirsch, Statuto
Backs: Still, Bumgardner, Wizbicki, Maggioli, Gompers, Steuber, Tomasetti, Schuette

Individual Statistics

Brooklyn
Rushing: Brown: 1 TD
Receiving: Gafford: 1–27 1 TD, Brown: 1–7 1 TD
Passing: Hoernschemeyer: 2 TD

Buffalo
Rushing: Tomasetti: 1 TD
Receiving: Mutryn: 2–52 2 TD
Passing: Ratterman: 13–23–176–2–3

October 10, 1948, New York Yankees vs. Buffalo Bills
Location: Civic Stadium (Buffalo, NY)
Attendance: 18,825

	1	2	3	4	F
New York Yankees	0	0	7	7	14
Buffalo Bills	7	6	0	0	13

Scoring Summary

BUF Comer 8-Yard Pass From Ratterman (Steuber Kick)
BUF Mutryn 1-Yard Run (Steuber Kick Blocked)
NY Sanders 5-Yard Run (Johnson Kick)
NY Wagner 53-Yard Pass From Sanders (Johnson Kick)

	New York	Buffalo
First Downs	13	12
Yards Rushing	99	131
Passes—Attempts	18	20
Passes—Completions	9	7
Passes—Yards	207	186
Passes—Interceptions	1	2
Punts-Average	5–37.2	6–46.3
Fumbles Recovered	1	0
Penalty Yards	67	48

Position	New York	Buffalo
LE	Russell	Baldwin
LT	Weinmeister	Armstrong
LG	Crawford	Lahar
C	Sossamon	Prewitt
RG	Signaigo	Pirro
RT	Greene	Carpenter
RE	Alford	Comer
QB	Sweiger	Ratterman
LHB	Sanders	Mutryn
RHB	Tew	Steuber
FB	Young	Tomasetti

Substitutes

New York
Ends: Schnellbacher, Davis
Tackles: Palmer, G. Johnson, Chambers, Mitchell
Guards: Riffle
Centers: Perantoni
Backs: Iverson, Magliolo, Schwenk, Wagner, H. Johnson, Daley, Kennedy

Buffalo
Ends: Mazza, O'Connor, Kisiday
Tackles: Kissell, Kerns
Guards: King, Scott, Wyhonic
Centers: Callahan, Hirsch
Backs: Still, Bumgardner, Wizbicki, Rykovich, Gompers, Kulbitski, Schuette

Individual Statistics

New York
Rushing: Sanders: 1 TD
Receiving: Wagner: 1–54 1 TD
Passing: Sanders: 1 TD

Buffalo
Rushing: Mutryn: 1 TD
Receiving: Comer: 1–8 1 TD, Mutryn: 1–71, Kulbitski: 1–41
Passing: Ratterman: 1 TD

October 17, 1948, Buffalo Bills vs. Cleveland Browns
Location: Cleveland Stadium (Cleveland, OH)
Attendance: 28,054

	1	2	3	4	F
Buffalo Bills	7	0	0	7	14
Cleveland Browns	17	0	7	7	31

Scoring Summary

CLE   E. Jones 44-Yard Pass From Graham (Groza Kick)

BUF Baldwin 22-Yard Pass From Still (Steuber Kick)
CLE Groza 45-Yard Field Goal
CLE Motley 3-Yard Run (Groza Kick)
CLE Speedie 15-Yard Pass From Graham (Groza Kick)
BUF Tomasetti 9-Yard Pass From Ratterman (Steuber Kick)
CLE Speedie 30-Yard Pass From Lewis (Groza Kick)

	Cleveland	Buffalo
First Downs	21	14
Yards Rushing	209	82
Passes—Attempts	28	35
Passes—Completions	12	19
Passes—Yards	219	260
Passes—Interceptions	0	2
Punts-Average	3–39	5–35
Fumbles Recovered	0	2
Penalty Yards	55	35

Position	Buffalo	Cleveland
LE	Baldwin	Speedie
LT	Armstrong	Groza
LG	Scott	Ulinski
C	Statuto	Gatski
RG	Pirro	Gaudio
RT	Kerns	Rymkus
RE	Comer	Gillom
QB	Still	Graham
LHB	Mutryn	E. Jones
RHB	Steuber	Cowan
FB	Tomasetti	Motley

Substitutes

Buffalo
Ends: Mazza, O'Connor, Kisiday
Tackles: Kissell, King, Whalen, Carpenter
Guards: Hirsch, Wyhonic
Centers: Callahan
Backs: Bumgardner, Gompers, Akins, Kulbitski, Schuette, Ratterman

Cleveland
Ends: Young, Yonakor, Lavelli, Kosikowski
Tackles: Adams, Pucci, Grigg, Simonetti
Guards: Humble, Agase, Willis, Houston
Centers: Saban, Maceau
Backs: Lewis, Terlep, Colella, Boedeker, Sensenbaugher, James, Parseghian, D. Jones, Adamle, Cline

Individual Statistics

Buffalo
Rushing: Mutryn: 7–13, Gompers: 5–22, Ratterman: 1-(–1), Steuber: 3–17, Tomasetti: 6–31, Kulbitski: 1–4, Bumgardner: 2-(–3), Still: 2-(–1)

Detailed Game Summaries 183

Receiving: Baldwin: 4–73 1 TD, Mutryn: 4–128, O'Connor: 6–48, Kulbitski: 1-(–4), Comer: 1-(–3), Tomasetti: 3–18 1 TD
Passing: Ratterman: 13–24–174–1–0, Still: 4–9–84–1-2, Steuber: 1–1-(–4)–0–0, Mutryn: 1–1–6–0–0

Cleveland
Rushing: Motley: 13–99 1 TD, Cowan: 4–13, E. Jones: 6–26, Graham: 2–8; Parseghian: 3–22, Cline: 1–14, Boedeker: 6–21, Lewis: 1–7, Sensenbaugher: 2-(–1)
Receiving: Speedie: 7–142 2 TD, Gillom: 1–8, E. Jones: 2–62 1 TD, Motley: 1–1, Boedeker: 1–8
Passing: Graham: 11–27–189–2–0, Lewis: 1–1–30–1–0

October 24, 1948, Buffalo Bills vs. Los Angeles Dons
Location: Memorial Coliseum (Los Angeles, CA)
Attendance: 26,818

	1	2	3	4	F
Buffalo Bills	0	14	14	7	35
Los Angeles Dons	7	7	0	7	21

Scoring Summary

LA	Aguirre 12-Yard Pass From Dobbs (Agajanian Kick)
LA	Aguirre 25-Yard Pass From Dobbs (Agajanian Kick)
BUF	Bumgardner 91-Yard Punt Return (Steuber Kick)
BUF	Mutryn 2-Yard Run (Steuber Kick)
BUF	Steuber 1-Yard Run (Steuber Kick)
BUF	Baldwin 59-Yard Pass From Ratterman (Steuber Kick)
BUF	Mutryn 21-Yard Run (Steuber Kick)
LA	Ford 26-Yard Pass From Dobbs (Agajanian Kick)

	Buffalo	Los Angeles
First Downs	16	17
Yards Rushing	173	167
Passes—Attempts	28	41
Passes—Completions	17	21
Passes—Yards	310	219
Passes—Interceptions	0	3
Punting Average	38	56
Fumbles Recovered	0	0
Penalty Yards	64	50

Position	Buffalo	Los Angeles
LE	Baldwin	Baldwin
LT	Armstrong	R. Reinhard
LG	Lahar	Levy
C	Statuto	Nelson
RG	Pirro	Ramsey
RT	Carpenter	Audet
RE	Kisiday	Ford
QB	Ratterman	Masini
LHB	Mutryn	Dobbs

Position	Buffalo	Los Angeles
RHB	Steuber	Wedemeyer
FB	Tomasetti	Clay

Substitutes

Buffalo
Ends: Mazza, O'Connor, Balatti
Tackles: Kissell, Kerns
Guards: Wyhonic, King, Scott
Centers: Callahan, Hirsch
Backs: Still, Bumgardner, Maggioli, Gompers, Akins, Kulbitski, Schuette

Los Angeles
Ends: Aguirre, Fisk, Gentry, Danehe
Tackles: Perrotti, Smith
Guards: Rockwell, Frankowski, Lolotai
Centers: Brown, Flagerman
Backs: Heap, Mitchell, W. Reinhard, Sexton, Naumu, Graham, Agajanian, Durkota, Ottele

Individual Statistics

Buffalo
Rushing: Mutryn: 12–57 2 TD, Maggioli: 2–8, Tomasetti: 6–46, Steuber: 14–61 1 TD, Still: 1-(–5)
Receiving: Baldwin: 4–154 1 TD, Mutryn: 1–35
Passing: Ratterman: 17–28–310–1–3, Steuber: 0–1–0–0–0

Los Angeles
Rushing: Dobbs: 12–64, Wedemeyer: 3–5, Clay: 6–33, W. Reinhard: 4–21, Graham: 1–5, Durkota: 3–27, Sexton: 2–18
Receiving: Aguirre: 4–63 2 TD, Ford: 1–26 1 TD
Passing: Dobbs: 21–36–219–3–0, W. Reinhard: 0–5–0–0–0

October 31, 1948, Baltimore Colts vs. Buffalo Bills
Location: Civic Stadium (Buffalo, NY)
Attendance: 23,694

	1	2	3	4	F
Baltimore Colts	7	7	3	0	17
Buffalo Bills	7	7	7	14	35

Scoring Summary

BAL   Hillenbrand 65-Yard Pass From Tittle (Grossman Kick)
BUF   Mutryn 3-Yard Run (Steuber Kick)
BUF   Gompers 43-Yard Run (Steuber Kick)
BAL   O'Rourke 1-Yard Run (Grossman Kick)
BAL   Grossman 30-Yard Field Goal
BUF   Mutryn 1-Yard Run (Steuber Kick)
BUF   Mutryn 49-Yard Pass From Ratterman (Steuber Kick)
BUF   O'Connor 35-Yard Pass From Ratterman (Steuber Kick)

	Baltimore	Buffalo
First Downs	16	20
Yards Rushing	111	218
Passes—Attempts	31	21
Passes—Completions	18	13
Passes—Yards	269	295
Passes—Interceptions	0	1
Punts-Average	5–41.4	3–32.7
Fumbles Recovered	2	1
Penalty Yards	27	33

Position	Baltimore	Buffalo
LE	Davis	Baldwin
LT	Blandin	Armstrong
LG	Barwegan	Lahar
C	Corley	Statuto
RG	Garrett	Pirro
RT	Artoe	Kerns
RE	Smith	O'Connor
QB	Tittle	Ratterman
LHB	Hillenbrand	Mutryn
RHB	Pfohl	Tomasetti
FB	Gambino	Steuber

Substitutes

Baltimore
Ends: Williams, Nowaskey, Bechtol, North, Poole
Tackles: Mellus, Spruill, Berezney
Guards: Grain, Klug
Centers: Stewart
Backs: O'Rourke, Leicht, Fowler, Vardian, Grossman, Mertes, Dellerba

Buffalo
Ends: Mazza, Balatti, Kisiday
Tackles: Kissell, Carpenter
Guards: Wyhonic, King, Scott, Whalen
Centers: n/a
Backs: Bumgardner, Schuette, Kulbitski, Gompers, Maggioli, Schneider, Still

Individual Statistics

Baltimore
Rushing: O'Rourke: 1 TD
Receiving: Hillenbrand: 1–65 1 TD
Passing: Tittle: 1 TD 0 INT

Buffalo
Rushing: Mutryn: 2 TD, Gompers: 1 TD
Receiving: Mutryn: 1–49 1 TD, Tomasetti: 1–26, O'Connor: 1–35 1 TD
Passing: Ratterman: 2 TD

November 7, 1948, Buffalo Bills vs. Brooklyn Dodgers
Location: Ebbets Field (Brooklyn, NY)
Attendance: 7,805

	1	2	3	4	F
Buffalo Bills	13	0	6	7	26
Brooklyn Dodgers	0	7	0	14	21

Scoring Summary

BUF	Mutryn 68-Yard Run (Kick Failed)
BUF	Tomasetti 15-Yard Run (Steuber Kick)
BKN	Colmer 2-Yard Run (Tevis Kick)
BUF	Mutryn 9-Yard Run (Kick Failed)
BUF	Mazza 5-Yard Lateral From Schuette After 55-Yard Interception (Steuber Kick)
BKN	Judd 57-Yard Pass From Chappius (Tevis Kick)
BKN	Ramsey 70-Yard Punt Return (Tevis Kick)

	Buffalo	Brooklyn
First Downs	16	14
Yards Rushing	414	54
Passes—Attempts	13	53
Passes—Completions	3	26
Passes—Yards	20	211
Passes—Interceptions	1	1
Punts-Average	3–34	6–43
Fumbles Recovered	1	2
Penalty Yards	65	31

Position	Buffalo	Brooklyn
LE	Mazza	Morris
LT	Kissell	Clowes
LG	Scott	Warrington
C	Hirsch	Gustafson
RG	Wyhonic	Wozniak
RT	Carpenter	Sazio
RE	Kisiday	Edwards
QB	Ratterman	Smith
LHB	Bumgardner	Chappuis
RHB	Wizbicki	Gafford
FB	Schuette	Colmer

Substitutes

Buffalo
Ends: A. Baldwin, O'Connor, Gibson, Balatti
Tackles: Armstrong, Pirro
Guards: Lahar, King, Whalen, Kerns
Centers: J. Baldwin, Statuto
Backs: Still, Mutryn, Steuber, Gompers, Schneider, Maggioli, Tomasetti, Kulbitski

Detailed Game Summaries

Brooklyn
Ends: Foldberg, Burrus, Judd, Scruggs
Tackles: Spencer, Williams, Ruby
Guards: Harris, St. John
Centers: Strohmeyer
Backs: Hoernschemeyer, McDonald, Tevis, C. Allen, Ramsey, Marcolini

Individual Statistics

Buffalo
Rushing: Mutryn: 17–185 2 TD, Tomasetti: 15–141 1 TD
Passing: Ratterman: 3–13–20–0–1

Brooklyn
Rushing: Chappuis: 4–42, Colmer: 1 TD
Receiving: Judd: 1 TD
Passing: Chappuis: 26–51–211–1–1

November 14, 1948, Los Angeles Dons vs. Buffalo Bills
Location: Civic Stadium (Buffalo, NY)
Attendance: 23,725

	1	2	3	4	F
Los Angeles Dons	0	6	14	7	27
Buffalo Bills	6	0	7	7	20

Scoring Summary

BUF A. Baldwin 30-Yard Pass From Ratterman (Armstrong Missed Kick)
LA   Agajanian 51-Yard Field Goal
LA   Agajanian 34-Yard Field Goal
LA   Dobbs 26-Yard Run (Agajanian Kick)
BUF Mutryn 36-Yard Pass From Ratterman (Kulbitski Kick)
LA   Dobbs 6-Yard Run (Agajanian Kick)
BUF A. Baldwin 38-Yard Pass From Ratterman (Kulbitski Kick)
LA   Aguirre 3-Yard Pass From Dobbs (Agajanian Kick)

	Los Angeles	Buffalo
First Downs	14	15
Yards Rushing	133	189
Passes—Attempts	29	35
Passes—Completions	16	14
Passes—Yards	149	208
Passes—Interceptions	0	3
Punting Average	52.4	39.9
Fumbles Recovered	0	2
Penalty Yards	40	35

Position	Los Angeles	Buffalo
LE	Aguirre	A. Baldwin
LT	R. Reinhard	Armstrong
LG	Levy	Lahar

Position	Los Angeles	Buffalo
C	Nelson	Statuto
RG	Agajanian	Pirro
RT	Audet	Kerns
RE	Ford	Gibson
QB	Heap	Ratterman
LHB	Dobbs	Mutryn
RHB	Wedemeyer	Steuber
FB	Clay	Tomasetti

Substitutes

Los Angeles
Ends: B. Baldwin, Gentry
Tackles: Perrotti, Smith, Johnson
Guards: Lolotai, Frankowski, Rockwell
Centers: Brown
Backs: W. Reinhard, Ottele, Durkota, Naumu, Graham, Kimbrough, Masini

Buffalo
Ends: Mazza, O'Connor, Kisiday, Balatti
Tackles: Kissell, Carpenter
Guards: King, Scott
Centers: Hirsch
Backs: Still, Bumgardner, Wizbicki, Gompers, Maggioli, Kulbitski, Schuette

Individual Statistics

Los Angeles
Rushing: Dobbs: 6–62 2 TD
Receiving: Aguirre: 1–3 1 TD
Passing: Dobbs: ?–16–149–1–0

Buffalo
Receiving: Baldwin: 2–58 2 TD, Mutryn: 1–36 1 TD
Passing: Ratterman: 1 TD

November 25, 1948, Buffalo Bills vs. Chicago Rockets
Location: Soldier Field (Chicago, IL)
Attendance: 6,305

	1	2	3	4	F
Buffalo Bills	6	13	7	13	39
Chicago Rockets	14	7	7	7	35

Scoring Summary

CHI Rykovich 1-Yard Run (McCarthy Kick)
BUF Tomasetti 5-Yard Run (Kick Failed)
CHI Fenenbock 53-Yard Pass From Freitas (McCarthy Kick)
BUF A. Baldwin 33-Yard Pass From Ratterman (Kulbitski Kick)
CHI Kellagher 5-Yard Run (McCarthy Kick)

BUF Tomasetti 7-Yard Run (Kick Failed)
BUF Tomasetti 8-Yard Run (Kulbitski Kick)
CHI King 17-Yard Pass From Freitas (McCarthy Kick)
BUF Bumgardner 90-Yard Punt Return (Kulbitski Kick)
BUF Kulbitski 64-Yard Fumble Recovery (Kick Failed)
CHI King 25-Yard Pass From Freitas (McCarthy Kick)

	Buffalo	Chicago
First Downs	14	16
Yards Rushing	179	190
Passes—Attempts	19	25
Passes—Completions	8	13
Passes—Yards	181	263
Passes—Interceptions	3	3
Punts-Average	2–47.5	7–44.7
Fumbles Recovered	4	2
Penalty Yards	20	58

Position	Buffalo	Chicago
LE	A. Baldwin	McCarthy
LT	Armstrong	Ecker
LG	Lahar	Pearcy
C	Statuto	Negus
RG	Pirro	Ruetz
RT	Kerns	N. Johnson
RE	Gibson	Jensen
QB	Ratterman	Freitas
LHB	Mutryn	Livingstone
RHB	Bumgardner	Rykovich
FB	Tomasetti	Mello

Substitutes

Buffalo
Ends: Kisiday, Mazza, O'Connor, Balatti
Tackles: Kissell, Carpenter
Guards: King, Scott, Wyhonic
Centers: J. Baldwin, Hirsch
Backs: Wizbicki, Maggioli, Schneider, Gompers, Schuette, Kulbitski

Chicago
Ends: Kuffel, King
Tackles: Kozel, Czarobski
Guards: Urban, Piskor, Bernhardt
Centers: Lamana
Backs: Farris, Fenenbock, Perina, Kellagher, Lewis

Individual Statistics

Buffalo
Rushing: Tomasetti: 3 TD
Receiving: Baldwin: 1–33 1 TD, Bumgardner: 1–63
Passing: Ratterman: 1 TD
Interception Returns:

Chicago
Rushing: Mello: 19–136, Rykovich: 1 TD, Kellagher: 1 TD
Receiving: King: 3–51 2 TD, Fenenbock: 1–52 1 TD
Passing: Freitas: 3 TD

November 28, 1948, Buffalo Bills vs. New York Yankees
Location: Yankee Stadium (New York, NY)
Attendance: 18,376

	1	2	3	4	F
Buffalo Bills	7	14	14	0	35
New York Yankees	0	7	0	7	14

Scoring Summary

BUF	Baldwin Pass From Ratterman (Armstrong Kick)
BUF	Ratterman 1-Yard Run (Armstrong Kick)
BUF	Ratterman 1-Yard Run (Armstrong Kick)
NYY	Russell 6-Yard Pass From Sanders (H. Johnson Kick)
BUF	Mutryn 88-Yard Punt Return (Armstrong Kick)
BUF	Tomasetti (Armstrong Kick)
NYY	Russell 8-Yard Pass From Sanders (H. Johnson Kick)

	Buffalo	New York
First Downs	15	9
Yards Rushing	190	70
Passes—Attempts	25	26
Passes—Completions	13	11
Passes—Yards	206	141
Passes—Interceptions	1	2
Punts-Average	6–40.8	8–41.3
Fumbles Recovered	1	0
Penalty Yards	55	52

Position	Buffalo	New York
LE	Mazza	Russell
LT	Kissell	Weinmeister
LG	Scott	Chambers
C	Hirsch	Perantoni
RG	Wyhonic	Signaigo
RT	Carpenter	Palmer
RE	Kisiday	Alford
QB	Schneider	Cheatham
LHB	Wizbicki	Layden
RHB	Bumgardner	Sweiger
FB	Schuette	Young

Substitutes

Buffalo
Ends: O'Connor, Balatti
Tackles: Armstrong, Kerns
Guards: King, Whalen, Lahar, Pirro

Centers: J. Baldwin, Statuto
Backs: Still, Kulbitski, Gompers, Mutryn, Ratterman, Tomasetti

New York
Ends: Schnellbacher, Rokisky, Davis, Cleary
Tackles: G. Johnson, Mitchell, Greene
Guards: Shirley, Garzoni, Riffle, Sharkey
Centers: Sossamon, Nabors
Backs: Iverson, Magliolo, Wagner, Rowe, H. Johnson, Tew, Kennedy, Casey, McDonald, Sanders, Schwenk

Individual Statistics

Buffalo
Rushing: Mutryn: 9–67, Ratterman: 2 TD, Tomasetti: 1 TD
Receiving: Mutryn: 4–65, Baldwin: 1 TD
Passing: Ratterman: 12–22–200–1–?

New York
Receiving: Russell: 2–14 2 TD
Passing: Sanders: 2 TD

December 5, 1948, Buffalo Bills vs. Baltimore Colts
Location: Babe Ruth Memorial Stadium (Baltimore, MD)
Attendance: 33,090

	1	2	3	4	F
Buffalo Bills	6	2	0	7	15
Baltimore Colts	7	7	7	14	35

Scoring Summary

BUF Mutryn 1-Yard Run (Kick Failed)
BAL Hillenbrand 10-Yard Run (Grossman Kick)
BAL Tittle 1-Yard Run (Grossman Kick)
BUF Tittle Tackled In Endzone By Mazza, Safety
BAL Davis 80-Yard Pass From Tittle (Grossman Kick)
BAL Tittle 1-Yard Run (Grossman Kick)
BUF Baldwin 4-Yard Pass From Ratterman (Stefik Kick)
BAL Leicht 1-Yard Run (Grossman Kick)

	Buffalo	Baltimore
First Downs	19	12
Yards Rushing	155	140
Passes—Attempts	42	14
Passes—Completions	17	8
Passes—Yards	140	163
Punts-Average	2–38	5–46
Fumbles Recovered	1	1
Penalty Yards	16	15

Position	Buffalo	Baltimore
LE	A. Baldwin	Davis
LT	Armstrong	Blandin
LG	Lahar	Barwegan
C	Statuto	McCormick
RG	Pirro	Garrett
RT	Kerns	Artoe
RE	O'Connor	North
QB	Ratterman	Tittle
LHB	Mutryn	Hillenbrand
RHB	Gompers	Pfohl
FB	Tomasetti	Mertes

Substitutes

Buffalo
Ends: Mazza, Stefik, Kisiday, Balatti
Tackles: Kissell
Guards: King, Scott, Wyhonic
Centers: Hirsch
Backs: Still, Wizbicki, Schneider, Akins, Maggioli, Kulbitski, Schuette

Baltimore
Ends: Williams, Smith, Poole, Bechtol
Tackles: Mellus, Sidorik, Berezney, Spruill
Guards: Simmons, Klug
Centers: Stewart
Backs: O'Rourke, Vacanti, Leicht, Fowler, Sylvester, Vardian, Grossman, Dellerba

Individual Statistics

Buffalo
Rushing: Mutryn: 1 TD
Receiving: Baldwin: 1–4 1 TD
Passing: Ratterman: 1 TD

Baltimore
Rushing: Tittle: 2 TD, Leicht: 1 TD, Hillenbrand: 1 TD
Receiving: Davis: 3–109 1 TD
Passing: Tittle: 1 TD

Postseason

December 12, 1948, Buffalo Bills vs. Baltimore Colts
Location: Babe Ruth Memorial Stadium (Baltimore, MD)
Attendance: 27,325

	1	2	3	4	F
Buffalo Bills	0	7	0	21	28
Baltimore Colts	3	0	14	0	17

Scoring Summary

BAL	Grossman 16-Yard Field Goal
BUF	O'Connor 8-Yard Pass From Ratterman (Armstrong Kick)
BAL	Mertes 8-Yard Run (Grossman Kick)
BAL	Mertes 1-Yard Run (Grossman Kick)
BUF	Gompers 66-Yard Pass From Ratterman (Armstrong Kick)
BUF	Baldwin 25-Yard Pass From Ratterman (Armstrong Kick)
BUF	Hirsch 19-Yard Interception Return (Armstrong Kick)

	Buffalo	Baltimore
First Downs	11	24
Yards Rushing	162	177
Passes—Attempts	18	37
Passes—Completions	10	17
Passes—Yards	135	217
Passes—Interceptions	1	1
Punts-Average	3–40	5–42
Fumbles Recovered	2	1
Penalty Yards	25	60

Position	Buffalo	Baltimore
LE	Mazza	Davis
LT	Armstrong	Blandin
LG	Scott	Barwegan
C	Hirsch	McCormick
RG	Prewitt	Garrett
RT	Carpenter	Spruill
RE	Kisiday	Williams
QB	Maggioli	Fowler
LHB	Schneider	Hillenbrand
RHB	Akins	Leicht
FB	Schuette	Mertes

Substitutes

Buffalo
Ends: Baldwin, O'Connor, Balatti
Tackles: Kissell, Kerns
Guards: Pirro, King, Lahar, Whalen
Centers: Statuto
Backs: Still, Ratterman, Wizbicki, Mutryn, Gompers, Tomasetti, Kulbitski

Baltimore
Ends: Nowaskey, North
Tackles: Mellus, Berezney, Artoe
Guards: Simmons, Klug
Centers: Vacanti
Backs: Tittle, O'Rourke, Grossman, Pfohl, Sylvester, Dellerba, Gambino

Individual Statistics

Buffalo
Rushing: Mutryn: 11–54, Gompers: 14–52, Tomasetti: 12–56

Receiving: Gompers: 1–66 1 TD, Baldwin: 3–54 1 TD, O'Connor: 3–20 1 TD
Passing: Ratterman: 10–18–135–3–1

Baltimore
Rushing: Mertes: 15–73 2 TD, Pfohl: 16–63, Leicht: 6–31
Receiving: Davis: 5–77, Hillenbrand: 6–70, Leicht: 2–31
Passing: Tittle: 17–36–217–0–1

December 19, 1948, Buffalo Bills vs. Cleveland Browns
Location: Cleveland Stadium (Cleveland, OH)
Attendance: 22,981

	1	2	3	4	F
Buffalo Bills	0	0	7	0	7
Cleveland Browns	7	7	14	21	49

Scoring Summary

CLE	E. Jones 3-Yard Run (Groza Kick), 14:50
CLE	Young 18-Yard Fumble Return (Groza Kick), 3:25
CLE	E. Jones 9-Yard Pass From Graham (Groza Kick), 2:02
CLE	Motley 29-Yard Run (Groza Kick), 10:35
BUF	Baldwin 10-Yard Pass From Still (Armstrong Kick), 14:50
CLE	Motley 31-Yard Run (Groza Kick), 0:44
CLE	Motley 5-Yard Run (Groza Kick), 9:44
CLE	Saban 39-Yard Interception Return (Groza Kick), 11:49

	Buffalo	Cleveland
First Downs	12	15
Rushing	4	6
Passing	6	7
Penalty	2	2
Total Yards Gained	167	333
Total Plays	69	66
Avg. Gain per Play	2.42	5.05
Rushing Yards	63	215
Passing Yards	104	118
Number of Rushes	33	40
Avg. Gain per Rush	1.91	5.38
Passes Attempted	36	26
Passes Completed	11	11
Percent Pass Comp.	.306	.423
Passes Intercepted	5	1
Percent Pass Int.	.139	.038
Yards Int. Return	2	80
Avg. Yards/Comp.	9.45	10.7
Avg. Yards/Att.	2.89	4.5
Number of Punts	6	3
Avg. Yards per Punt	42.5	32.7
Punts Returned By	0	4
Avg. Yards/Punt Ret.	0	10.3
Avg. Return/Punt	0	6.8

Detailed Game Summaries 195

	Buffalo	Cleveland
Kickoff Returns	3	2
Avg. Yards/Kick Ret.	17.0	33.0
Number of Penalties	7	9
Yards Penalized	27	90
Fumbles	3	6
Ball Lost	3	3
Touchdowns	1	7
Rushing	0	6
Passing	1	1
Points After Touchdown	1	7
PAT Missed	0	0
Field Goals	0	0
Field Goals Missed	0	1

Position	Buffalo	Cleveland
LE	A. Baldwin	Speedie
LT	Armstrong	Groza
LG	Lahar	Ulinski
C	Statuto	Gatski
RG	Pirro	Gaudio
RT	Kerns	Rymkus
RE	O'Connor	Lavelli
QB	Ratterman	Graham
LHB	Mutryn	E. Jones
RHB	Bumgardner	D. Jones
FB	Tomasetti	Motley

Substitutes

Buffalo
Ends: Mazza, Kisiday, Balatti, Gibson
Tackles: Kissell, Carpenter, Whalen
Guards: King, Wyhonic, Scott
Centers: Hirsch, Prewitt, J. Baldwin
Backs: Still, Schneider, Wizbicki, Maggioli, Kulbitski, Schuette

Cleveland
Ends: Young, Yonakor, Gillom, Kosikowski
Tackles: Adams, Grigg, Pucci, Simonetti
Guards: Humble, Willis, Agase, Houston
Centers: Saban, Maceau
Backs: Lewis, Colella, James, Adamle, Terlep, Boedeker, Sensenbaugher, Cowan, Parseghian, Cline

Individual Statistics

Buffalo
Rushing: Bumgardner: 11-34, Tomasetti: 11-20, Mutryn: 8-8, Kulbitski: 2-1, Still: 1-0
Receiving: O'Connor: 3-41, Mutryn: 2-5, Bumgardner: 1-25, Kulbitski: 1-14, Baldwin: 1-10, Gibson: 1-7, Schneider: 1-4, Tomasetti: 1-(-2)

Passing: Still: 6-18-80-1-2, Ratterman: 5-18-24-0-3
Punting: Still: 6-255
Punt Returns: None
Kickoff Returns: Schneider: 2-33, Mutryn: 1-18
Interception Returns: Maggioli: 1-2

Cleveland
Rushing: Motley: 14-133, E. Jones: 8-29, D. Jones: 5-22, Cline: 1-20, Parseghian: 4-14, Sensenbagher: 2-2, Colella: 1-1, Graham: 1-0, Adamle: 2-(-1), Terlep: 2-(-5)
Receiving: E. Jones: 3-39, Speedie: 2-22, Lavelli: 2-16, D. Jones: 2-13, Gillom: 1-15, Motley: 1-13
Passing: Graham: 11-24-118-1, E. Jones: 0-2-0-0
Punting: Colella: 2-31.0, Gillom: 1-36.0
Punt Returns: Lewis: 2-10, Colella: 1-18, Terlep: 1-13
Kickoff Returns: D. Jones: 1-46, Motley: 1-20
Interception Returns: James: 2-36, Saban: 1-39, Adamle: 1-4, Colella: 1-1

1949 BUFFALO BILLS

Preseason

August 5, 1949, Jersey City Giants vs. Buffalo Bills
Location: Civic Stadium (Buffalo, NY)
Attendance: 31,809

	1	2	3	4	F
Jersey City Giants	0	0	0	0	0
Buffalo Bills	21	26	12	20	79

Scoring Summary (Not In Order Of Scoring)

BUF	Baldwin 36-Yard Pass From Still, 2:10
BUF	Baldwin 20-Yard Pass From Still
BUF	Kissiday 15-Yard Fumble Return
BUF	Furse 2-Yard Run
BUF	Sutton 47-Yard Punt Return
BUF	Sutton 61-Yard Punt Return
BUF	Cline 6-Yard Run
BUF	Colella 47-Yard Run
BUF	Stanton 19-Yard Pass from DiToma
BUF	Volz 33-Yard Run
BUF	Sutton 7-Yard Run
BUF	Sutton 15-Yard Run
BUF	Adams PAT (5)
BUF	Baldwin PAT (1)
BUF	Guess PAT (2)

Position	Buffalo	Jersey City
LE	Baldwin	Lane
LT	Adams	Schuman

Position	Buffalo	Jersey City
LG	Vasicek	Oberto
C	Statuto	Zuppa
RG	Pirro	Reiss
RT	Kerns	Sartori
RE	Gibson	Girgan
QB	Mutryn	Winklereid
LHB	Colella	Nelson
RHB	Bumgardner	Berry
FB	Tomasetti	Connolly

Substitutes

Jersey City
Ends: Weis, Smith, Gorman
Tackles: Kuzman, Thropp, Hart, Gionta, Bellina
Guards: Fusella, Murphy, Back, Paradise
Centers: Valentine, Titus
Backs: Tarizian, Garofalo, Garcillo, Certisimo, Charles, Collins

Buffalo
Ends: Kisiday, Stanton, Lanza, Logel, Oristaglio, Mazza, Lukens
Tackles: Hanula, Kirkland, Carpenter, J. Kissel, McLelland, Maskas
Guards: O'Connor, King, Stautzenberger, Wyhonic, Gibron, Scott
Centers: Schuette, Herring, Hirsch
Backs: Still, Furse, DiToma, Volz, Sutton, Guess, V. Kissell, Schroll, Wyzbicki, Conwell, Cline

August 10, 1949, Buffalo Bills vs. Baltimore Colts
Location: Wilmington Park (Wilmington, DE)
Attendance: 2,953

	1	2	3	4	F
Buffalo Bills	6	0	0	6	12
Baltimore Colts	0	14	14	0	28

Scoring Summary

BUF	Baldwin Pass From Still (Adams Missed Kick)
BAL	Gambino 5-Yard Pass From Tittle (Grossman Kick)
BAL	Stone 7-Yard Pass From Tittle (Grossman Kick)
BAL	Leicht 80-Yard Run (Grossman Kick)
BAL	Touchdown (Grossman Kick)
BUF	Baldwin Pass From Still (Kick Missed)

August 14, 1949, Buffalo Bills vs. San Francisco 49ers
Location: Kezar Stadium (San Francisco, CA)
Attendance: 28,084

	1	2	3	4	F
Buffalo Bills	7	3	0	0	10
San Francisco 49ers	7	0	7	7	21

Scoring Summary

SF	Beals 34-Yard Pass From Albert (Vetrano Kick)
BUF	Bumgardner 68-Yard Run (Adams Kick)
BUF	Adams 43-Yard Field Goal
SF	Carr 24-Yard Run (Vetrano Kick)
SF	Eshmont 44-Yard Pass From Albert (Vetrano Kick)

August 19, 1949, Bethlehem Bulldogs vs. Buffalo Bills
Location: Civic Stadium (Buffalo, NY)
Attendance: 12,697

	1	2	3	4	F
Bethlehem Bulldogs	0	0	0	0	0
Buffalo Bills	14	28	0	6	48

Scoring Summary

BUF	Mutryn Run (Adams Kick)
BUF	Cline 61-Yard Run (Adams Kick)
BUF	Mutryn 59-Yard Run (Adams Kick), 5:20
BUF	Baldwin Pass from Still (Adams Kick), 7:13
BUF	Bumgardner 33-Yard Run (Adams Kick), 12:57
BUF	Colella 60-Yard Punt Return
BUF	Sutton 5-Yard Pass from Freitas (Kissell Missed Kick)

	Buffalo	Bethlehem
First Downs	10	8
Yards Rushing	391	84
Passes—Attempts	308	10
Passes—Completions	8	33
Passes—Yards	7	5
Passes—Interceptions	83	74
Punting Average	2	1
Fumbles Recovered	43.25	38.9
Penalty Yards	11	3

Position	Bethlehem	Buffalo
LE	McConnell	Mazza
LT	Sukeena	J. Kissell
LG	Perez	Maskas
C	Svendsen	Schutte
RG	Smith	Wyhonic
RT	?	?
RE	?	?
QB	?	?
LHB	Danciewicz	Colella
RHB	Parks	Wyzbicki
FB	Dedrick	Schroll

Substitutes

Bethlehem
Kline, Haffner, Cassiane, Hochbeimer, Stanczak, Son, Forte, Nojunas, Petrella, Perlow, Krasni, Zettlemoyer, Schieichar, Dipietro, Geodts, Lellnski, Chando

Detailed Game Summaries

Buffalo
Ends: Baldwin, Logel, Gibron, Mazza, Lukens
Tackles: Kerns, Kirkland, Carpenter, McLelland
Guards: Pirro, Gibron, King, Vasicek
Centers: Schuette, Herring, Hirsch

Regular Season

August 26, 1949, Buffalo Bills vs. Chicago Hornets
Location: Soldier Field (Chicago, IL)
Attendance: 23,800

	1	2	3	4	F
Buffalo Bills	7	0	0	7	14
Chicago Hornets	0	14	0	3	17

Scoring Summary

BUF Baldwin 19-Yard Pass From Still (Adams Kick)
CHI Ramsey 63-Yard Pass From Hoernschmeyer (McCarthy Kick)
CHI Patterson 35-Yard Pass From Clement (McCarthy Kick)
BUF Mutryn 13-Yard Run (Adams Kick)
CHI McCarthy 21-Yard Field Goal

Position	Buffalo	Chicago
LE	Baldwin	King
LT	Carpenter	Paine
LG	Vasicek	St. John
C	Statuto	Rapacz
RG	Pirro	Wendell
RT	Kerns	Czarobski
RE	Gibson	Edwards
QB	Still	McDonald
LHB	Mutryn	Hoernschemeyer
RHB	Bumgardner	Sweiger
FB	Cline	Ramsey

Substitutes

Buffalo
Ends: Stanton, Orstaglio, Mazza
Tackles: Maskas, Adams, J. Kissell
Guards: Wyhonic
Centers: Schuette, Herring
Backs: Colella, Wizbicki, Schroll, Sutton, Freitas, Tomasetti

Chicago
Ends: McCarthy, Jensen, Foldberg, Kuffel
Tackles: Maddock, Johnson, Clowees, Williams
Guards: Richeson, Bailey, Pearcy
Centers: Strohmeyer, Negus
Backs: Rykovich, Mello, Clement, Livingstone, Patterson, Collins, Smith

Individual Statistics

Buffalo
Rushing: Bumgardner: 16–57, Mutryn: 9–28 1 TD, Cline: 7–28, Freitas: 3–13, Colella: 1–3, Sutton: 2–(-2)
Receiving: Baldwin: 2–28 1 TD, Bumgardner: 1–21, Mutryn: 1–7, Gibson: 1–7, Cline: 3–3
Passing: Still: 4–9–56 1 TD, Freitas: 4–9–10 2 INT
Punting: Colella: 4–137, Still: 3–84
Punt Returns: Sutton: 1–22, Bumgardner: 1–16, Mutryn: 2–13, Colella: 1–8
Kickoff Returns: Bumgardner: 2–40, Mutryn: 1–15
Interception Returns: Colella: 2–27

Chicago
Rushing: Hoernschemeyer: 17–51, Clement: 7–31, Collins: 4–15, Lewis: 1–11, Ramsey: 4–(-1)
Receiving: Ramsey: 2–76 1 TD, Edwards: 3–56, Patterson: 1–35 1 TD, McCarthy: 1–19, Foldberg: 2–12
Passing: Hoernschemeyer: 7–17–150 1 TD 1 INT, Clement: 2–4–48 1 TD 1 INT
Punting: Lewis: 5–239
Punt Returns: Ramsey: 2–22
Kickoff Returns: Ramsey: 2–32
Interception Returns: Patterson: 1–23

September 5, 1949, Cleveland Browns vs. Buffalo Bills
Location: Civic Stadium (Buffalo, NY)
Attendance: 31,839

	1	2	3	4	F
Cleveland Browns	7	0	0	21	28
Buffalo Bills	0	7	21	0	28

Scoring Summary

CLE	E. Jones 12-Yard Pass from Graham (Saban Kick)
BUF	Cline 6-Yard Run (Adams Kick)
BUF	Ratterman 1-Yard Run (Adams Kick)
BUF	Ratterman 1-Yard Run (Adams Kick)
BUF	Bumgardner 3-Yard Run (Adams Kick)
CLE	E. Jones 7-Yard Pass from Graham (Saban Kick)
CLE	E. Jones 38-Yard Pass from Graham (Saban Kick)
CLE	Speedie 2-Yard Pass from Graham (Saban Kick)

	Buffalo	Cleveland
First Downs	13	7
Rushing	7	5
Passing	6	12
Total Yards	272	410
Yards Rushing	177	80
Passes Attempted	12	40
Passes Completed	7	27

Detailed Game Summaries

	Buffalo	Cleveland
Yards Passing	95	330
Interceptions	1	5
Punting Average	33.5	38.6
Penalties	1	4
Penalty Yardage	5	30

Position	Cleveland	Buffalo
LE	Speedie	Baldwin
LT	Groza	Carpenter
LG	Ulinski	Vasicek
C	Gatski	Statuto
RG	Houston	Pirro
RT	Rymkus	Kerns
RE	Lavelli	Lukens
QB	Graham	Ratterman
LHB	E. Jones	Mutryn
RHB	D. Jones	Bumgardner
FB	Motley	Cline

Substitutes

Cleveland
Ends: Young, O'Connor, Gillom, Yonakor
Tackles: Grigg, Spencer, Willis, Palmer
Guards: Humble, Agase, Gaudio
Centers: Saban, Thompson
Backs: Lewis, Horvath, Lahr, Adamle, Boedeker, Parseghian, James, Susteric

Buffalo
Ends: Mazza, Stanton, Oristaglio, Gibson
Tackles: Adams, Maskas, J. Kissell
Guards: Stautzenberger, Gibron, Hirsch
Centers: Schuette, Herring
Backs: Still, Sutton, Colella, Schroll, Wizbicki, V. Kissell, Joe, Tomasetti, Volz

Individual Statistics

Cleveland
Rushing: Motley: 8–35, E. Jones: 4–17, W. Jones: 5–16, Parseghian: 2–10, Boedeker: 1–3, Gillom: 1–(–1)
Receiving: Speedie: 10–113 1 TD, Gillom: 4–66, E. Jones: 5–64 3 TD, Motley: 4–30, Boedeker: 1–25, W. Jones: 2–24, Lavelli: 1–8
Passing: Graham: 27–40–330 4 TD 1 INT
Punting: Gillom: 5–193
Punt Returns: Lahr: 1–11
Kickoff Returns: Boedeker: 3–82, Motley: 1–27, W. Jones: 1–26
Interception Returns: Adamle: 1–10

Buffalo
Rushing: Cline: 18–76 1 TD, Mutryn: 13–60, Bumgardner: 10–27 1 TD, Ratterman: 3–8 2 TD, Sutton: 1–3, Still: 1–3

Receiving: Baldwin: 3–61, Cline: 2–14, Carpenter: 1–14, Lukens: 1–6
Passing: Ratterman: 7–12–95 1 INT
Punting: Colella: 6–201
Punt Returns: Colella: 1–11
Kickoff Returns: Colella: 1–16
Interception Returns: Schroll: 1–4

September 11, 1949, New York Yankees vs. Buffalo Bills
Location: Civic Stadium (Buffalo, NY)
Attendance: 30,410

	1	2	3	4	F
New York Yankees	7	0	0	10	17
Buffalo Bills	14	0	0	0	14

Scoring Summary

BUF Mutryn 16-Yard Run (Adams Kick)
BUF Baldwin 23-Yard Pass From Ratterman (Adams Kick)
NY   Ruby 19-Yard Interception Return (H. Johnson Kick)
NY   Tew 9-Yard Run (H. Johnson Kick)
NY   H. Johnson 21-Yard Field Goal

Position	New York	Buffalo
LE	Russell	Baldwin
LT	Ruby	Carpenter
LG	Wozniak	Gibron
C	Sossamon	Statuto
RG	Signaigo	Pirro
RT	Weinmeister	Kerns
RE	Alford	Lukens
QB	Panciera	Ratterman
LHB	Young	Mutryn
RHB	Tew	Bumgardner
FB	Colmer	Cline

Substitutes

New York
Ends: Garza, Schnellbacher, Poole, Davis
Tackles: Mitchell, Mastrangelo, Chambers, Shirley
Guards: Brown, Sharkey
Centers: Ecklund, Perantoni
Backs: G. Johnson, Layden, Landry, H. Johnson, Kusserow, Rowe, Howard, Iverson, Proctor, Kennedy

Buffalo
Ends: Mazza, Stanton, Oristaglio
Tackles: Adams, Maskas, J. Kissell, Gibson
Guards: Stautzenberger, Hirsch, Vasicek
Centers: Schuette, Herring
Backs: Still, Sutton, Wizbicki, Joe, Colella, V. Kissell, Schroll, Tomasetti

Detailed Game Summaries

Individual Statistics

New York
Rushing: Tew 14–65 1 TD, Kusserow: 8–60, Young: 6–30, Colmer: 7–8, Howard: 3–5, Proctor: 1-(–1), Panciera: 2-(–3), Kennedy: 2-(–6)
Receiving: Garza: 2–79, Landry: 2–48, Young: 3–37, Alford: 1–10, Poole: 1–7
Passing: Panciera: 6–24–142, G. Johnson: 2–3–39, Layden: 0–1–0
Punting: Layden: 1–52, Colmer: 1–51
Punt Returns: Layden: 2–21, Mitchell: 1–15, Landry: 1–9
Kickoff Returns: Kusserow: 1–31, Tew: 1–17
Interception Returns: Landry: 1–44, Rowe: 1–38, Ruby: 1–19 1 TD

Buffalo
Rushing: Mutryn: 9–58 1 TD, Cline: 9–37, Bumgardner: 2–19, Joe 2–18, Ratterman: 3–8
Receiving: Joe: 2–52, Baldwin: 4–49 1 TD, Lukens: 4–32, Cline: 1–26, Mutryn: 2–14
Passing: Ratterman: 13–23–173 1 TD 3 INT
Punting: Colella: 6–219 1 Block
Punt Returns: Bumgardner: 1–14, Sutton: 1–9
Kickoff Returns: Mutryn: 1–30, Joe 1–12, Colella: 1–9

September 25, 1949, San Francisco 49ers vs. Buffalo Bills
Location: Civic Stadium (Buffalo, NY)
Attendance: 32,097

	1	2	3	4	F
San Francisco 49ers	3	0	14	0	17
Buffalo Bills	7	7	7	7	28

Scoring Summary

SF	Vetrano 23-Yard Field Goal
BUF	Bumgardner 39-Yard Pass From Ratterman (Adams Kick)
BUF	Baldwin 6-Yard Pass From Ratterman (Adams Kick)
BUF	Tomasetti 1-Yard Run (Adams Kick)
SF	Perry 23-Yard Pass From Albert (Vetrano Kick)
SF	Carr 35-Yard Fumble Recovery (Vetrano Kick)
BUF	Cline 2-Yard Run (Adams Kick)

Position	San Francisco	Buffalo
LE	Shoener	Baldwin
LT	Mike	Carpenter
LG	Clark	Gibron
C	Johnson	Statuto
RG	Grgich	Pirro
RT	Woudenberg	Kerns
RE	Beals	Lukens
QB	Albert	Ratterman
LHB	Eshmont	Mutryn

Position	San Francisco	Buffalo
RHB	Strzykalski	Bumgardner
FB	Standlee	Cline

Substitutes

San Francisco
Ends: Susoeff, Salata, Bruce, Carr
Tackles: Morgan, Evans, Quilter
Guards: Hobbs, Banducci, Maloney
Centers: Wismann, Sabuco
Backs: Wallace, Cathcart, Cason, Wagner, Vetrano, Garlin, Lillywhite, Perry

Buffalo
Ends: Mazza, Stanton, Oristaglio
Tackles: Adams, Maskas, J. Kissell
Guards: Stautzenberger, Hirsch, Vasicek, Gibson
Centers: Schuette, Herring
Backs: Still, Sutton, Volz, Wizbicki, Colella, V. Kissell, Schroll, Tomasetti

Individual Statistics

San Francisco
Rushing: Perry: 8–70, Beals: 1–23, Cason: 2–16, Strzykalski: 7–10, Standlee: 2–7, Cathcart: 1–3, Albert: 1–3, Carr: 3–2, Morgan: 0-(–1)
Receiving: Carr: 1–25, Perry: 2–21 1 TD, Salata: 2–19, Beals: 2–13, Cason: 1–8, Eshmont: 0–8, Shoener: 1–3
Passing: Albert: 9–22–97 1 TD
Punting: Albert: 6–300
Punt Returns: Cathcart: 1–22, Strzykalski: 2–19
Kickoff Returns: Cason: 2–45, Strzykalski: 1–21

Buffalo
Rushing: Mutryn: 16–84, Bumgardner: 16–71, Cline: 14–57 1 TD, Tomasetti: 3–7 1 TD, Ratterman: 1–2
Receiving: Baldwin: 6–106 1 TD, Bumgardner: 2–45, Mutryn: 3–37, Cline: 1–13, Lukens: 1–9, Tomasetti: 1–8, Carpenter: 1–6
Passing: Ratterman: 15–20–224 2 TD
Punting: Colella: 4–178
Punt Returns: Mutryn: 2–17, Colella: 2–13, Bumgardner: 1–5
Kickoff Returns: Mutryn: 2–34, Bumgardner: 1–24, Cline: 1–21

October 2, 1949, Baltimore Colts vs. Buffalo Bills
Location: Civic Stadium (Buffalo, NY)
Attendance: 25,692

	1	2	3	4	F
Baltimore Colts	0	14	7	14	35
Buffalo Bills	7	0	7	14	28

Detailed Game Summaries 205

Scoring Summary

BUF	Bumgardner 23-Yard Pass From Ratterman (Adams Kick)
BAL	Pfohl 12-Yard Run (Grossman Kick)
BAL	Gambino 11-Yard Pass From Tittle (Grossman Kick)
BAL	Pfohl 1-Yard Run (Grossman Kick)
BUF	Ratterman 1-Yard Run (Adams Kick)
BUF	Ratterman 1-Yard Run (Adams Kick)
BAL	North 79-Yard Pass From Tittle (Grossman Kick)
BUF	Baldwin 34-Yard Pass From Ratterman (Adams Kick)
BAL	Stone 47-Yard Pass From Tittle (Grossman Kick)

Position	Baltimore	Buffalo
LE	Williams	Baldwin
LT	Blandin	Carpenter
LG	Barwegan	Gibron
C	Tillman	Statuto
RG	Garrett	Pirro
RT	Spruill	Kerns
RE	Davis	Lukens
QB	Vacanti	Ratterman
LHB	Leicht	Mutryn
RHB	Pfohl	Bumgardner
FB	Gambino	Cline

Substitutes

Baltimore
Ends: Nowaskey, Bechtol, North, Cowan
Tackles: Mellus, Sidorik, Jenkins, Stone
Guards: French, Cooper
Centers: Prewitt, Leonard
Backs: Tittle, Page, Wedemeyer, Kelly, Kingery, Grossman, Jagade, Dellerba, Ruthstrom

Buffalo
Ends: Mazza, Stanton, Oristaglio
Tackles: Adams, Maskas, J. Kissell, Gibson
Guards: Stautzenberger, Hirsch, Vasicek, Wyhonic
Centers: Schuette, Herring
Backs: Still, Sutton, Volz, Wizbicki, Colella, V. Kissell, Schroll, Tomasetti

Individual Statistics

Baltimore
Rushing: Gambino: 12–33, Stone: 2–22, Wedemeyer: 5–19, Pfohl: 3–15 2 TD, Kingery: 3–3, Jagade: 1–1
Receiving: North: 4–119 1 TD, Stone: 3–93 1 TD, Williams: 2–26, Davis: 1–22, Gambino: 1–11 1 TD, Wedemeyer: 1–5
Passing: Tittle: 12–19–276 3 TD, Vacanti: 0–1–0
Punting: Grossman: 5–209
Punt Returns: Wedemeyer: 2–26
Kickoff Returns: Wedemeyer: 4–88
Interception Returns: Cowan: 1–12, Kingery: 1-(–8)

Buffalo
Rushing: Cline: 18–91, Mutryn: 7–54, Ratterman: 10–42 2 TD, Bumgardner: 11–27
Receiving: Baldwin: 3–57 1 TD, Mutryn: 6–53, Lukens: 4–32, Bumgardner: 1–23 1 TD, Cline: 2–0
Passing: Ratterman: 16–28–165 2 TD 2 INT
Punting: Colella: 2–82
Punt Returns: Sutton: 2–27, Colella: 1–10
Kickoff Returns: Mutryn: 3–81, Sutton: 1–30, Bumgardner: 1–12

October 9, 1949, Buffalo Bills vs. Los Angeles Dons
Location: L.A. Memorial Coliseum (Los Angeles, CA)
Attendance: 16,757

	1	2	3	4	F
Buffalo Bills	7	14	7	0	28
Los Angeles Dons	0	21	14	7	42

Scoring Summary

BUF	Cline 35-Yard Run (Adams Kick)
LA	Dobbs 2-Yard Run (Nelson Kick)
BUF	Mutryn 4-Yard Run (Adams Kick)
LA	Grimes 12-Yard Pass From Dobbs (Nelson Kick)
LA	Grimes 9-Yard Run (Nelson Kick)
BUF	Baldwin 8-Yard Pass From Ratterman (Adams Kick)
BUF	Lukens 10-Yard Pass From Ratterman (Adams Kick)
LA	Wilkins 32-Yard Pass From Dobbs (Nelson Kick)
LA	Rodgers 1-Yard Run (Nelson Kick)
LA	Wimberly 33-Yard Fumble Recovery (Nelson Kick)

Position	Buffalo	Los Angeles
LE	Baldwin	Baldwin
LT	Carpenter	Reinhard
LG	Stautzenberger	Lolotai
C	Statuto	Nelson
RG	Vasicek	Dobelstein
RT	Kerns	Kelley
RE	Lukens	Wimberly
QB	Ratterman	Hoffman
LHB	Mutryn	Dobbs
RHB	Bumgardner	Grimes
FB	Cline	Rodgers

Substitutes

Buffalo
Ends: Mazza, Stanton, Oristaglio, Gibson
Tackles: Adams, Maskas, J. Kissell, Wyhonic
Guards: Hirsch
Centers: Schuette, Herring
Backs: Still, Sutton, Colella, Volz, Schroll, V. Kissell, Tomasetti, Wizbicki

Los Angeles
Ends: Holder, Ford, Wilkins
Tackles: Henke, Tinsley, Williamson
Guards: Perrotti, Ramsey
Centers: Brown, Woodard
Backs: Dworsky, Pipkin, McWilliams, Davis, Kennedy, Crowe, Spavital, Clay, Howell, Murphy

Individual Statistics

Buffalo
Rushing: Cline: 11–89 1 TD, Sutton: 3–36, Bumgardner: 7–23, Mutryn: 8–16 1 TD, Ratterman: 3–13, Tomasetti: 3–7, Kissell: 3–5, Colella: 1–(-2)
Receiving: Baldwin: 5–108 1 TD, Lukens: 5–92 1 TD, Mutryn: 2–47, Gibson: 2–25, Sutton: 2–22, Cline: 1–16, Vasicek: 0–5, Bumgardner: 1–4
Passing: Ratterman: 17–34–305 2 TD 3 INT, Still: 1–1–14
Punting: Colella: 2–74
Punt Returns: Sutton: 1–1
Kickoff Returns: Bumgardner: 3–46, Colella: 3–42, Sutton: 1–13

Los Angeles
Rushing: Rodgers: 11–65 1 TD, Grimes: 9–54 1 TD, Dobbs: 6–48 1 TD, Howell: 5–14, Spavital: 2–6
Receiving: Wilkins: 6–124 1 TD, Ford: 6–72, Rodgers: 1–44, Grimes: 2–25 1 TD, Henke: 1–15, Hoffman: 1–8, Howell: 1–(-5)
Passing: Dobbs: 18–27–283 2 TD
Punting: Dobbs: 4–159
Kickoff Returns: Grimes: 3–85, Spavital: 1–32
Interception Returns: Brown: 2–13, McWilliams: 0–9, Baldwin: 1–0

October 16, 1949, Buffalo Bills vs. San Francisco 49ers
Location: Kezar Stadium (San Francisco, CA)
Attendance: 35,476

	1	2	3	4	F
Buffalo Bills	7	0	0	0	7
San Francisco 49ers	14	23	7	7	51

Scoring Summary

SF Perry 14-Yard Run (Vetrano Kick)
SF Perry 1-Yard Run (Vetrano Kick)
BUF Sutton 21-Yard Pass From Ratterman (Adams Kick)
SF Beals 33-Yard Pass From Albert (Vetrano Kick)
SF Salata 20-Yard Pass From Albert (Vetrano Kick)
SF Wizbicki Tackled in End Zone By Evans (Safety)
SF Perry 14-Yard Run (Vetrano Kick)
SF Salata 17-Yard Pass From Albert (Vetrano Kick)
SF Wallace 1-Yard Run (Vetrano Kick)

Position	Buffalo	San Francisco
LE	Baldwin	Susoeff
LT	Carpenter	Bryant
LG	Gibron	Clark
C	Statuto	Johnson
RG	Pirro	Grgich
RT	Kerns	Mike
RE	Lukens	Bruce
QB	Ratterman	Cason
LHB	Sutton	Carr
RHB	Wizbicki	Wagner
FB	Tomasetti	Standlee

Substitutes

Buffalo
Ends: Mazza, Stanton, Oristaglio, Gibson
Tackles: Adams, Maskas, J. Kissell
Guards: Vasicek, Wyhonic, Stautzenberger, Hirsch
Centers: Schuette, Herring
Backs: Colella, Volz, V. Kissell

San Francisco
Ends: Salata, Shoener, Beals, Maloney
Tackles: Evans, Morgan, Woudenberg, Quilter
Guards: Hobbs, Banducci
Centers: Wismann, Sabuco
Backs: Albert, Wallace, Vetrano, Eshmont, Strzykalski, Garlin, Perry, Lillywhite

Individual Statistics

Buffalo
Rushing: Tomasetti: 6–20, Kissell: 6–14, Baldwin: 1–0, Sutton: 1-(-2), Ratterman: 1-(-5), Wizbicki: 3-(-6), Colella: 5-(-10)
Receiving: Baldwin: 6–52, Kissell: 3–37, Sutton: 2–25 1 TD, Tomasetti: 4–18, Oristaglio: 1–14, Lukens: 2–9, Colella: 2–6, Volz: 1–6
Passing: Ratterman: 21–36–167 1 TD
Punting: Colella: 6–163, Still: 2–98
Punt Returns: Tomasetti: 1–8
Kickoff Returns: Colella: 2–40, Sutton: 2–39, Volz: 2–28, Wizbicki: 1–22, Tomasetti: 1–19

San Francisco
Rushing: Perry: 13–88 3 TD, Eshmont: 6–47, Standlee: 5–46, Strike: 5–29, Vetrano: 1–27, Lillywhite: 7–22, Garlin: 6–21, Wagner: 2–12, Cason: 1–5, Carr: 1–4, Albert: 1–2, Wallace: 1–1 1 TD
Receiving: Salata: 3–53 2 TD, Beals: 1–33 1 TD, Strike: 1–23, Perry: 1–14, Garlin: 1–10, Cathcart: 1–4, Cason: 1–3
Passing: Albert: 9–20–140 3 TD, Wallace: 0–3–0
Punting: Albert: 2–99, Standlee: 1–37
Punt Returns: Cason: 2–48, Cathcart: 2–20, Maloney: 1–5
Kickoff Returns: Cason: 1–26, Perry: 1–15

Detailed Game Summaries

October 23, 1949, Los Angeles Dons vs. Buffalo Bills
Location: Civic Stadium (Buffalo, NY)
Attendance: 21,310

	1	2	3	4	F
Los Angeles Dons	0	0	7	7	14
Buffalo Bills	14	3	0	0	17

Scoring Summary

BUF	Tomasetti 1-Yard Run (Adams Kick)
BUF	A. Baldwin 17-Yard Pass From Ratterman (Adams Kick)
BUF	Adams 11-Yard Field Goal
LA	Crowe 56-Yard Fumble Recovery (Nelson Kick)
LA	Rodgers 1-Yard Run (Nelson Kick)

Position	Los Angeles	Buffalo
LE	Ford	Baldwin
LT	Tinsley	Gibron
LG	Ramsey	Stautzenberger
C	Nelson	Statuto
RG	Perrotti	Pirro
RT	Reinhard	Kerns
RE	B. Baldwin	Gibson
QB	Hoffman	Ratterman
LHB	Dobbs	Mutryn
RHB	Grimes	Tomasetti
FB	Rodgers	Cline

Substitutes

Los Angeles
Ends: Wimberly, Holder, Wilkins
Tackles: Kelley, Williamson, Henke
Guards: Dobelstein, Brown
Centers: Woodward
Backs: Dworsky, Pipkin, Taliaferro, McWilliams, Kennedy, Howell, Crowe, Davis, Clay, Spavital

Buffalo
Ends: Mazza, Stanton, Oristaglio, Lukens
Tackles: Adams, Maskas, J. Kissell
Guards: King, Hirsch, Vasicek
Centers: Schuette, Herring
Backs: Still, Sutton, Livingstone, Colella, Bumgardner, Wizbicki, Schroll, V. Kissell, Volz

Individual Statistics

Los Angeles
Rushing: Grimes: 11–74, Rodgers: 7–16 1 TD, Taliaferro: 3–13, Spavital: 1–4, Dobbs: 2–3
Receiving: Wilkins: 3–39, Ford: 2–34, Davis: 1–5

Passing: Dobbs: 4-11-48 1 INT, Grimes: 1-1-27, Taliaferro: 1-5-3
Punting: Dobbs: 3-114, Taliaferro: 1-23
Punt Returns: Crowe: 1-11
Kickoff Returns: Grimes: 1-32, Taliaferro: 1-24

Buffalo
Rushing: Tomasetti: 19-118 1 TD, Mutryn: 13-107, Cline: 20-81, Ratterman: 7-18, Baldwin: 1-1, V. Kissell: 1-0
Receiving: Mutryn: 5-54, Baldwin: 5-44 1 TD, Cline: 4-40
Passing: Ratterman: 14-19 138 1 TD
Punting: Still: 2-73, Colella: 1-31
Punt Returns: Mutryn: 1-11
Kickoff Returns: V. Kissell: 1-1
Interception Returns: Wizbicki: 1-1

November 6, 1949, Buffalo Bills vs. New York Yankees
Location: Yankee Stadium (New York, NY)
Attendance: 16,758

	1	2	3	4	F
Buffalo Bills	7	0	0	10	17
New York Yankees	14	0	0	0	14

Scoring Summary

NYY   Young 57-Yard Run (H. Johnson Kick)
NYY   Alford 28-Yard Pass From Panciera (H. Johnson Kick)
BUF   Baldwin 16-Yard Pass From Ratterman (Adams Kick)
BUF   Bumgardner 45-Yard Pass From Ratterman (Adams Kick)
BUF   Adams 13-Yard Field Goal

Position	Buffalo	New York
LE	Baldwin	Russell
LT	Gibron	Ruby
LG	Stautzenberger	Wozniak
C	Statuto	Ecklund
RG	Pirro	Signaigo
RT	Kerns	Weinmeister
RE	Lukens	Alford
QB	Ratterman	Panciera
LHB	Mutryn	Young
RHB	Tomasetti	Kusserow
FB	Cline	Kennedy

Substitutes

Buffalo
Ends: Mazza, Oristaglio, Gibson
Tackles: Adams, Maskas, J. Kissell
Guards: Hirsch, Vasicek
Centers: Schuette, Herring
Backs: Livingstone, Wizbicki, Bumgardner, Colella, Volz, Schroll, V. Kissell

New York
Ends: Garza, Schnellbacher, Poole, Davis
Tackles: Mitchell, Chambers
Guards: Mastrangelo, Sharkey
Centers: Perantoni, H. Johnson
Backs: Iverson, Landry, Layden, Doss, Rowe, Howard, Prokop

Individual Statistics

New York
Rushing: Young: 7–86 1 TD, Kennedy: 14–82, Howard: 14–44, Layden: 1–8, Panciera: 3–5, Landry: 5–4, Prokop: 2-(–3)
Receiving: Alford: 1–28 1 TD, Landry: 1–18, Kennedy: 2–7, Prokop: 1–7, Layden: 1–0
Passing: Panciera: 6–14–60 1 TD 1 INT
Punting: Landry: 5–180
Punt Returns: Layden: 4–52, Landry: 1–26, Young: 1–7
Kickoff Returns: Young: 2–55, Layden: 1–28, Kennedy: 1–17

November 13, 1949, Buffalo Bills vs. Cleveland Browns
Location: Cleveland Stadium (Cleveland, OH)
Attendance: 22,511

	1	2	3	4	F
Buffalo Bills	0	7	0	0	7
Cleveland Browns	7	0	0	0	7

Scoring Summary

CLE Graham 1-Yard Run (Groza Kick)
BUF Mutryn 4-Yard Run (Adams Kick)

Position	Buffalo	Cleveland
LE	Baldwin	Speedie
LT	Stautzenberger	Groza
LG	Gibron	Ulinski
C	Statuto	Gatski
RG	Pirro	Houston
RT	Kerns	Rymkus
RE	Lukens	Lavelli
QB	Ratterman	Graham
LHB	Mutryn	Boedeker
RHB	Tomasetti	D. Jones
FB	Cline	Motley

Substitutes

Buffalo
Ends: Mazza, Oristaglio
Tackles: Adams, J. Kissell
Guards: King, Vasicek
Centers: Schuette

Backs: Still, V. Kissell, Sutton, Livingstone, Wizbicki, Colella, Bumgardner, Schroll

Cleveland
Ends: O'Connor, Gillom, Yonakor
Tackles: Palmer, Grigg
Guards: Humble, Willis, Agase, Gaudio
Centers: Saban
Backs: Lewis, Lahr, Horvath, Adamle, Susteric

Individual Statistics

Buffalo
Rushing: Mutryn: 17–87 1 TD, Bumgardner: 11–36, Tomasetti: 6–19, Cline: 11–16
Receiving: Baldwin: 5–65, Mutryn: 1–17
Passing: Ratterman: 6–20–82 2 INT
Punting: Colella: 6–181
Punt Returns: Mutryn: 1–20, Livingstone: 1–0
Kickoff Returns: Mutryn: 1–26, Livingstone: 1–15

Cleveland
Rushing: Motley: 15–50, Boedeker: 4–28, Horvath: 5–15, D. Jones: 5–14, Graham: 2–7 1 TD
Receiving: Gillom: 6–65, Boedeker: 1–61, Speedie: 3–45, D. Jones: 1–5
Passing: Graham: 11–26–176
Punting: Gillom: 5–176
Punt Returns: Lewis: 1–0
Kickoff Returns: Boedeker: 1–18, Sustersic: 1–17
Interception Returns: Adamle: 1–4, Lahr: 1–2

November 20, 1949, Chicago Hornets vs. Buffalo Bills
Location: Civic Stadium (Buffalo, NY)
Attendance: 18,494

	1	2	3	4	F
Chicago Hornets	0	0	0	0	0
Buffalo Bills	0	7	0	3	10

Scoring Summary

BUF Livingstone 79-Yard Run (Adams Kick)
BUF Adams 17-Yard Field Goal

	Buffalo	Chicago
First Downs	7	7
Total Yards	163	110
Yards Rushing	143	55
Passes Attempted	4	17
Passes Completed	1	5
Yards Passing	20	55
Interceptions	2	1
Punting Average	41.7	43.3

Detailed Game Summaries 213

	Buffalo	Chicago
Penalties	9	3
Penalty Yardage	47	22

Position	Chicago	Buffalo
LE	Foldberg	Baldwin
LT	Paine	Gibron
LG	St. John	Stautzenberger
C	Negus	Statuto
RG	Wendell	Pirro
RT	Czarobski	Kerns
RE	Edwards	Lukens
QB	Brown	Ratterman
LHB	Hoernschemeyer	Mutryn
RHB	Sweiger	Bumgardner
FB	Collins	Cline

Substitutes

Chicago
Ends: Cleary, McCarthy, Jensen, Heck
Tackles: Clowes, Hazelwood, Johnson
Guards: Richeson, Bailey, Pearcy
Centers: Rapacz, Strohmeyer
Backs: McDonald, Clement, Chappuis, Patterson, Donaldson, Ramsey, Buksar

Buffalo
Ends: Mazza, Stanton, Oristaglio, Gibson
Tackles: Adams, Maskas, J. Kissell
Guards: King, Hirsch, Vasicek
Centers: Schuette, Herring
Backs: Still, Sutton, Livingstone, Schroll, Colella, Wizbicki, V. Kissell, Tomasetti, Volz

Individual Statistics

Chicago
Rushing: Clement: 10–35, Collins: 6–11, Hoernschemeyer: 12–9
Receiving: Edwards: 3–24, Patterson: 1–21, Foldberg: 1–10
Passing: Clement: 3–5–40 1 INT, Hoernschemeyer: 2–12–15 1 INT
Punting: Collins: 6–251, Hoernschemeyer: 2–106
Punt Returns: Ramsey: 3–9
Kickoff Returns: Hoernschemeyer: 3–96, Collins: 1–22
Interception Returns: Patterson: 1–55

Buffalo
Rushing: Mutryn: 15–85, Bumgardner: 11–40, Cline: 6–19, Tomasetti: 3–6, Livingstone: 1–0 1 TD, Ratterman: 4-(–7)
Receiving: Baldwin: 1–20
Passing: Passing: 1–4–20 1 INT
Punting: Still: 7–292
Punt Returns: Livingstone: 5–106, Bumgardner: 1–0
Interception Returns: Gibson: 1–9, Livingstone: 1–6

November 27, 1949, Buffalo Bills vs. Baltimore Colts
Location: Babe Ruth Memorial Stadium (Baltimore, MD)
Attendance: 16,323

	1	2	3	4	F
Buffalo Bills	7	10	14	7	38
Baltimore Colts	0	7	0	7	14

Scoring Summary

BUF	Bumgardner 30-Yard Pass From Ratterman (Adams Kick)
BUF	Adams 20-Yard Field Goal
BAL	North 80-Yard Pass From Tittle (Grossman Kick)
BUF	Lukens 14-Yard Pass From Ratterman (Adams Kick)
BUF	Tomasetti 9-Yard Pass From Ratterman (Adams Kick)
BUF	Mutryn 3-Yard Run (Adams Kick)
BUF	Volz 1-Yard Run (Adams Kick)
BAL	Stone 52-Yard Pass From Tittle (Grossman Kick)

Position	Buffalo	Baltimore
LE	Baldwin	Williams
LT	Gibron	Blandin
LG	Stautzenberger	Barwegan
C	Statuto	Prewitt
RG	Pirro	Cooper
RT	Kerns	Spruill
RE	Lukens	North
QB	Ratterman	Vacanti
LHB	Mutryn	Wedemeyer
RHB	Bumgardner	Kelly
FB	Cline	Gambino

Substitutes

Buffalo
Ends: Gibson, Mazza, Stanton, Oristaglio
Tackles: J. Kissell, Adams, Maskas
Guards: King, Vasicek
Centers: Schuette, Herring, Hirsch
Backs: Still, Livingstone, Sutton, Wizbicki, Volz, Colella, V. Kissell, Schroll, Tomasetti

Baltimore
Ends: Davis, Bechtol, Nowaskey, Leonard
Tackles: Mellus, Jenkins, Sidorik
Guards: French, Garrett
Centers: Tillman
Backs: Tittle, Stone, Leicht, Cowan, Pfohl, Kingery, Ruthstrom, Dellerba, Grossman

Individual Statistics

Buffalo
Rushing: Bumgardner: 9–74, Mutryn: 13–70 1 TD, Tomasetti: 6–42,

Detailed Game Summaries 215

	Sutton: 2–28, Volz: 4–7 1 TD, Cline: 1–7, Still: 1–3, Wizbicki: 2-(–4)
Receiving:	Mutryn: 5–59, Lukens: 5–57 1 TD, Baldwin: 7–55, Bumgardner: 1–30 1 TD, Tomasetti: 3–17 1 TD, Sutton: 1–16
Passing:	Ratterman: 21–30–218 3 TD 1 INT, Still: 1–2–16 1 INT
Punting:	Still: 2–67
Punt Returns:	Livingstone: 3–42, Sutton: 1–3
Kickoff Returns:	Livingstone: 1–20, Bumgardner: 1–18, Volz: 1–15
Interception Returns:	Colella: 1–22, Kissell: 1–14

Baltimore

Rushing:	Stone: 6–22, Wedemeyer: 6–17, Gambino: 5–4, Tittle: 2–3, Kelly: 1–0, Cowan: 1–0, Vacanti: 1–0
Receiving:	North: 2–88 1 TD, Stone: 5–84 1 TD, Davis: 3–30, Cowan: 1–26, Gambino: 1–7
Passing:	Tittle: 12–25–235 2 TD 1 INT, Wedemeyer: 0–1–0 1 INT
Punting:	Grossman: 6–269
Punt Returns:	Wedemeyer: 1–20
Kickoff Returns:	Wedemeyer: 4–67, Kelly: 2–31
Interception Returns:	Ruthstrom: 1–15, Bechtol: 1–6

Postseason

December 4, 1949, Buffalo Bills vs. Cleveland Browns
Location: Cleveland Stadium (Cleveland, OH)
Attendance: 17,270

	1	2	3	4	F
Buffalo Bills	0	14	7	0	21
Cleveland Browns	10	0	14	7	31

Scoring Summary

CLE	Lavelli 51-Yard Pass From Graham (Groza Kick)
CLE	Groza 31-Yard Field Goal
BUF	Tomasetti 4-Yard Pass From Ratterman (Adams Kick)
BUF	Mutryn 8-Yard Pass From Ratterman (Adams Kick)
CLE	E. Jones 2-Yard Run (Groza Kick)
BUF	Mutryn 30-Yard Pass From Ratterman (Adams Kick)
CLE	D. Jones 49-Yard Pass From Graham (Groza Kick)
CLE	Lahr 52-Yard Interception Return (Groza Kick)

	Buffalo	Cleveland
First Downs	19	15
Total Yards	453	398
Yards Rushing	25–80	20–72
Passes Attempted	42	43
Passes Completed	21	22
Yards Passing	293	326
Interceptions	2	2
Punting Average	40.2	41.5
Penalties	2	5
Penalty Yardage	20	58

Position	Buffalo	Cleveland
LE	Baldwin	Speedie
LT	Gibron	Groza
LG	Stautzenberger	Ulinski
C	Statuto	Gatski
RG	Pirro	Houston
RT	Kerns	Rymkus
RE	Lukens	Gillom
QB	Ratterman	Graham
LHB	Mutryn	E. Jones
RHB	Bumgardner	D. Jones
FB	Cline	Motley

Substitutes

Buffalo
Ends: Mazza, Oristaglio, Gibson
Tackles: Adams, J. Kissell
Guards: King, Vasicek
Centers: Herring
Backs: Still, Livingstone, Wizbicki, Tomasetti, Volz, Schroll, V. Kissell

Cleveland
Ends: Young, O'Connor, Yonakor, Lavelli
Tackles: Palmer, Grigg, Spencer
Guards: Agase, Willis, Humble, Gaudio
Centers: Saban, Thompson
Backs: Lewis, Lahr, James, Adamle, Sustersic

Individual Statistics

Buffalo
Rushing: Bumgardner: 10–37, Mutryn: 8–24, Cline: 3–10, Tomasetti: 4–9
Receiving: Mutryn: 6–81 2 TD, Bumgardner: 4–80, Baldwin: 2–54, Tomasetti: 3–37 1 TD, Lukens: 4–32, Cline: 2–9
Passing: Ratterman: 21–39–293 3 TD 2 INT, Still: 0–3–0
Punting: Still: 5–201
Punt Returns: Livingstone: 2–19
Kickoff Returns: Mutryn: 2–59, Livingstone: 2–33
Interception Returns: Livingstone: 2–14

Cleveland
Rushing: Motley: 8–38, D. Jones: 5–21, E. Jones: 6–10 1 TD, Graham: 1–3
Receiving: Speedie: 7–113, Lavelli: 5–96 1 TD, E. Jones: 6–73, D. Jones: 1–49 1 TD, Motley: 3–(–5)
Passing: Graham: 22–43–326 2 TD 2 INT
Punting: Gillom: 4–166
Punt Returns: Lewis: 2–19
Kickoff Returns: D. Jones: 2–40, Motley: 2–36
Interception Returns: Lahr: 1–52 1 TD, Saban: 1–36

Appendix C
All-Time Record versus Each Opponent

Note: Regular Season and Postseason results only.

Baltimore Colts

Record: 5-2-0
October 12, 1947	Baltimore Colts 15 @ Buffalo Bills 20
November 23, 1947	Buffalo Bills 33 @ Baltimore Colts 14
October 31, 1948	Baltimore Colts 17 @ Buffalo Bills 35
December 5, 1948	Buffalo Bills 15 @ Baltimore Colts 35
December 12, 1948	Buffalo Bills 28 @ Baltimore Colts 17
October 2, 1949	Baltimore Colts 35 @ Buffalo Bills 28
November 27, 1949	Buffalo Bills 38 @ Baltimore Colts 14

Brooklyn Dodgers

Record: 4-1-1
September 8, 1946	Brooklyn Dodgers 27 @ Buffalo Bisons 14
November 10, 1946	Buffalo Bisons 17 @ Brooklyn Dodgers 14
October 17, 1947	Buffalo Bills 14 @ Brooklyn Dodgers 14
October 26, 1947	Brooklyn Dodgers 7 @ Buffalo Bills 35
October 3, 1948	Brooklyn Dodgers 21 @ Buffalo Bills 31
November 7, 1948	Buffalo Bills 26 @ Brooklyn Dodgers 21

Chicago Rockets/Hornets

Record: 6-2-0
September 25, 1946	Buffalo Bisons 35 @ Chicago Rockets 38
October 27, 1946	Chicago Rockets 17 @ Buffalo Bisons 49
September 14, 1947	Chicago Rockets 20 @ Buffalo Bills 28
September 19, 1947	Buffalo Bills 31 @ Chicago Rockets 14
September 6, 1948	Chicago Rockets 7 @ Buffalo Bills 42
November 25, 1948	Buffalo Bills 39 @ Chicago Rockets 35

August 26, 1949   Buffalo Bills 14 @ Chicago Hornets 17
November 20, 1949   Chicago Hornets 0 @ Buffalo Bills 10

Cleveland Browns

Record: 0–8–2

September 22, 1946	Cleveland Browns 28 @ Buffalo Bisons 0
November 24, 1946	Buffalo Bisons 17 @ Cleveland Browns 42
September 5, 1947	Buffalo Bills 14 @ Cleveland Browns 30
November 2, 1947	Cleveland Browns 28 @ Buffalo Bills 7
September 12, 1948	Cleveland Browns 42 @ Buffalo Bills 13
October 17, 1948	Buffalo Bills 14 @ Cleveland Browns 31
December 19, 1948	Buffalo Bills 7 @ Cleveland Browns 49
September 5, 1949	Cleveland Browns 28 @ Buffalo Bills 28
November 13, 1949	Buffalo Bills 7 @ Cleveland Browns 7
December 4, 1949	Buffalo Bills 21 @ Cleveland Browns 31

Los Angeles Dons

Record: 4–3–1

September 28, 1946	Los Angeles Dons 21 @ Buffalo Bisons 21
December 1, 1946	Buffalo Bisons 14 @ Los Angeles Dons 62
October 5, 1947	Buffalo Bills 27 @ Los Angeles Dons 25
November 9, 1947	Los Angeles Dons 0 @ Buffalo Bills 25
October 24, 1948	Buffalo Bills 35 @ Los Angeles Dons 21
November 14, 1948	Los Angeles Dons 27 @ Buffalo Bills 20
October 9, 1949	Buffalo Bills 28 @ Los Angeles Dons 42
October 23, 1949	Los Angeles Dons 14 @ Buffalo Bills 17

Miami Seahawks

Record: 0–2

October 11, 1946	Miami Seahawks 17 @ Buffalo Bisons 14
November 18, 1946	Buffalo Bisons 14 @ Miami Seahawks 21

New York Yankees/Brooklyn–New York Yankees

Record: 3–5–0

September 14, 1946	Buffalo Bisons 10 @ New York Yankees 21
October 4, 1946	New York Yankees 21 @ Buffalo Bisons 13
August 31, 1947	New York Yankees 24 @ Buffalo Bills 28
November 30, 1947	Buffalo Bills 13 @ New York Yankees 35
October 10, 1948	New York Yankees 14 @ Buffalo Bills 13
November 28, 1948	Buffalo Bills 35 @ New York Yankees 14

All-Time Record versus Each Opponent 219

September 11, 1949   Brooklyn/NY Yankees 17 @ Buffalo Bills 14
November 6, 1949   Buffalo Bills 17 @ Brooklyn/NY Yankees 14

San Francisco 49ers

Record: 2-5-1
    October 19, 1946   San Francisco 49ers 17 @ Buffalo Bisons 17
    November 2, 1946   Buffalo Bisons 14 @ San Francisco 49ers 27
    September 28, 1947   San Francisco 49ers 41 @ Buffalo Bills 24
    December 7, 1947   Buffalo Bills 21 @ San Francisco 49ers 21
    August 29, 1948   Buffalo Bills 14 @ San Francisco 49ers 35
    September 26, 1948   San Francisco 49ers 38 @ Buffalo Bills 38
    September 25, 1949   San Francisco 49ers 17 @ Buffalo Bills 28
    October 16, 1949   Buffalo Bills 7 @ San Francisco 49ers 51

Appendix D
All-Time Roster

Note: The Games Started statistic can be misleading. It depends on whether the team started on offense or defense as to who was listed as the starter. Take, for instance, George Ratterman. If the defense started the game, Ratterman was on the sidelines and he came in when the offense took the field. This is not reflected in the accounts of the game or in the statistics. All individual statistics were taken from the official All-America Football Conference score sheets and the All-America Football Conference record books. Preseason statistics are not included.

Biographies are based on personal interviews with players and members of their families, as well as other resources. See the "Sources" section of this book for a complete listing of all sources used to generate player biographies.

Adams, Chester Frank (Chet) (aka Adamczyk)

Position: T; Height: 6'3"; Weight: 233; High School: South (Cleveland, OH); College: Ohio; Born: 10/24/1915, Cleveland, OH; Deceased: 10/28/1990, Cleveland, OH; 1949 Buffalo Bills (Regular Season): 13 Games Played, 1 Game Started, Extra Points: 32/32, Field Goals: 4/11; 1949 Buffalo Bills (Postseason): 1 Game Played, 0 Games Started; TOTAL (Regular Season): 13 Games Played, 1 Game Started, Extra Points: 32/32, Field Goals: 4/11; TOTAL (Postseason): 1 Game Played, 0 Games Started

Chet Adams was drafted in the twelfth round of the 1939 draft by the Cleveland Rams. He played four years for the Rams before joining the Green Bay Packers. After returning from military service, Adams joined the Cleveland Browns for three seasons. In 1949, Adams played for Buffalo before finishing his career with the 1950 New York Yankees.

Non-Buffalo Statistics

1939 Cleveland Rams: 9 Games Played, 5 Games Started
1940 Cleveland Rams: 11 Games Played, 11 Games Started, Receiving: 3–28
1941 Cleveland Rams: 11 Games Played, 11 Games Started
1942 Cleveland Rams: 11 Games Played, 11 Games Started
1943 Green Bay Packers: 10 Games Played, 6 Games Started
1946 Cleveland Browns: 14 Games Played, 0 Games Started
1947 Cleveland Browns: 13 Games Played, 7 Games Started
1948 Cleveland Browns: 14 Games Played, 0 Games Started
1950 New York Yankees: 12 Games Played, 1 Game Started

Aina, James (Jim)

Position: G; Height: 5'9½"; Weight: 220; College: Alfred; Born: 10/7/1920, Albion, NY; 1948 Buffalo Bills: on the training camp roster, but did not make the regular season roster; TOTAL: on the training camp roster, but did not make the regular season roster.

Akins, Albert George (Al)

Position: B; Height: 6'1"; Weight: 199; High School: John R. Rogers (Spokane, WA); College: Washington, Washington State; Born: 6/13/1921, Spokane, WA; Deceased: 8/29/1995, Reno, NV; 1948 Buffalo Bills (Regular Season): 5 Games Played, 1 Game Started, Receiving: 1-11; 1948 Buffalo Bills (Postseason): 1 Game Played, 1 Game Started; 1949 Buffalo Bills (Regular Season): on the preseason roster, but did not make the regular season roster. TOTAL (Regular Season): 5 Games Played, 1 Game Started, Receiving: 1-11; TOTAL (Postseason): 1 Game Played, 1 Game Started

Al Akins was drafted by the Cleveland Rams in 1944 (sixth round). He did not follow the Rams to Los Angeles, but instead signed with the Cleveland Browns. After one season with the Browns, Akins went to the Brooklyn Dodgers where he played in only three games. Akins was shipped to the Buffalo Bills for the remainder of the 1948 season and was on their preseason roster, but failed to make the regular season cut in 1949.

Non-Buffalo Statistics

1946 Cleveland Browns: 4 Games Played, 0 Games Started, Rushing: 5-42 1 TD
1947 Brooklyn Dodgers: 13 Games Played, 3 Games Started, Rushing: 15-79 1 TD, Receiving: 6-101 1 TD
1948 Brooklyn Dodgers: 3 Games Played, 1 Game Started, Rushing: 4-(-9), Receiving: 2-1

Andrejco, Joseph (Joe)

Position: B; Height: 6'0"; Weight: 190; College: Fordham; Born: 1920; 1947 Buffalo Bills: on the training camp roster, but did not make the regular season roster; TOTAL: on the training camp roster, but did not make the regular season roster.

Armstrong, Graham Leo

Position: T; Height: 6'4"; Weight: 240; High School: Cathedral Latin (Cleveland, OH); College: John Carroll; Born: 5/30/1918, Cleveland, OH; Deceased: 6/25/1960, Cuyahoga County, OH; 1947 Buffalo Bills (Regular Season): 13 Games Played, 7 Games Started, Extra Points: 8/10, Field

Goals: 0/1; 1948 Buffalo Bills (Regular Season): 16 Games Played, 14 Games Started, Receiving: 1–0, Kick Returns: 1–9, Extra Points: 15/17, Field Goals: 0/1; 1948 Buffalo Bills (Postseason): 2 Games Played, 2 Games Started; TOTAL (Regular Season): 29 Games Played, 21 Games Started, Receiving: 1–0, Kick Returns: 1–9, Extra Points: 23/27, Field Goals: 0/2; TOTAL (Postseason): 2 Games Played, 2 Games Started

Graham Armstrong earned two letters as a tackle in high school. He earned another two letters in college, but it was as a quarterback. In 1941, he played seven games for the Cleveland Rams; then entered the Navy. During his time in the Navy, Armstrong played left tackle for the Camp Peary (Virginia) team. After his military obligations, Armstrong returned to the Cleveland Rams, but only played one game. In 1947, he joined the Buffalo Bills and played two seasons for them.

During the off-season, Armstrong was a police officer.

Non-Buffalo Statistics

1941 Cleveland Rams: 7 Games Played, 0 Games Started
1945 Cleveland Rams: 1 Game Played, 0 Games Started

Balatti, Edward T. (Ed)

Position: E; Height: 6'1"; Weight: 205; High School: Oakland Technical (CA); College: (None); Born: 4/8/1924, Los Banos, CA; Deceased: 8/27/1990, Novato, CA; 1948 Buffalo Bills (Regular Season): 9 Games Played, 0 Games Started; 1948 Buffalo Bills (Postseason): 2 Games Played, 0 Games Started; TOTAL (Regular Season): 9 Games Played, 0 Games Started; TOTAL (Postseason): 2 Games Played, 0 Games Started

Non-Buffalo Statistics

1946 San Francisco 49ers: 14 Games Played, 0 Games Started, Receiving: 4–15
1947 San Francisco 49ers: 14 Games Played, 3 Games Started, Receiving: 8–98 1 TD
1948 San Francisco 49ers: 1 Game Played, 0 Games Started
1948 New York Yankees: 2 Games Played, 0 Games Started

Baldwin, Alton (Al) (Legs)

Position: E-B; Height: 6'2"; Weight: 201; High School: Hot Springs (AR); College: Arkansas; Born: 3/21/1923, Hot Springs, AR; Deceased: 5/23/1994, Hot Springs, AR; 1947 Buffalo Bills (Regular Season): 13 Games Played, 5 Games Started, Receiving: 25–468 7 TD, Interceptions: 2–90, Kick Returns: 1–6; 1948 Buffalo Bills (Regular Season): 16 Games Played, 14 Games Started, Receiving: 50–852 7 TD, Extra Points: 0/1; 1948 Buffalo Bills (Postseason): 2 Games Played, 1 Game Started, Receiving: 4–64 1 TD; 1949 Buffalo Bills (Regular Season): 13 Games Played, 13 Games Started, Rushing: 2–1, Receiving: 51–665 7 TD; 1949 Buffalo Bills (Postseason): 1 Game Played, 1 Game Started, Receiving: 2–54; TOTAL (Regular Season): 42 Games Played, 32 Games Started, Rushing: 2–1, Receiving: 126–1985 21 TD, Interceptions: 2–90, Kick Returns: 1–6, Extra Points: 0/1; TOTAL (Postseason): 3 Games Played, 2 Games Started, Receiving: 6–118 1 TD

Alton Baldwin was an All-State fullback in high school. While at Arkansas, Baldwin earned All-Southwest honors (1943) and All-Conference second team honors (1945) as a halfback. He switched to end and repeated All-Southwest honors (1946) and All-Conference honors (1946), and added All-America second team honors (1946).

Baldwin was drafted by the Buffalo Bills (first round) and the Boston Yanks (fourth round) in 1947. He signed with the Buffalo Bills and played three seasons for the team, before he joined the Green Bay Packers for one year.

Non-Buffalo Statistics

1950 Green Bay Packers: 12 Games Played, Receiving: 28–555 3 TD

Baldwin, John David (Jack)

Position: C; Height: 6'3"; Weight: 223; High School: Gladewater (TX); College: Centenary; Born: 7/31/1921, Clyde, TX; Deceased: 9/13/1989, Kerrville, TX; 1948 Buffalo Bills (Regular Season): 3 Games Played, 0 Games Started; 1948 Buffalo Bills (Postseason): 1 Game Played, 0 Games Started; TOTAL (Regular Season): 3 Games Played, 0 Games Started; TOTAL (Postseason): 1 Game Played, 0 Games Started

Non-Buffalo Statistics

1946 New York Yankees: 7 Games Played, 3 Games Started
1947 New York Yankees: 2 Games Played, 0 Games Started
1947 San Francisco 49ers: 3 Games Played, 0 Games Started

Batorski, John Michael Jr. (Bat)

Position: E; Height: 6'2"; Weight: 238; High School: Lackawanna (NY); College: Colgate; Born: 9/27/1920, Lackawanna, NY; Deceased: 11/16/1982, Old Field, NY; 1946 Buffalo Bisons (Regular Season): 7 Games Played, 2 Games Started, Receiving: 2–27; TOTAL (Regular Season): 7 Games Played, 2 Games Started, Receiving: 2–27

John Batorski captained the Lackawanna High School football team in 1939 and continued his successes while at Colgate. Batorski was named All-Conference, All-Upstate and All-American, while competing in football, baseball, basketball and track. Batorski was the only four-letter man (in one year) in the 40 years of Colgate athletics.

During World War II, Batorski served in the medical corps and spent 22 months overseas. Batorski was drafted in the 18th round of the 1944 NFL draft by the Washington Redskins, but did not join the team as he was overseas. Upon his return, he tried out for the Buffalo Bisons and made the squad in the first week of training camp.

Black, John Thomas (Blondy)

Position: B; Height: 5'11"; Weight: 195; High School: Philadelphia (MS); College: Mississippi State; Born: 8/20/1920, Philadelphia, MS; Deceased: 5/4/2000, Madison, MS; 1946 Buffalo Bisons (Regular Season): 3 Games Played, 0 Games Started, Rushing: 1–10, Receiving: 1–21, Interceptions: 1–18, Punt Returns: 2–58; 1947: Buffalo Bills (Regular Season): on the training camp roster, but did not make the regular season roster. TOTAL (Regular Season): 3 Games Played, 0 Games Started, Rushing: 1–10, Receiving: 1–21, Interceptions: 1–18, Punt Returns: 2–58

John Black was drafted by the Brooklyn Dodgers in 1943 (second round). After his military obligations, Black signed with the Buffalo Bills and played one season. He was in Buffalo's training camp in 1947, but failed to make the regular season roster. At that point, he signed on with the Baltimore Colts and played five games his final professional season.

Non-Buffalo Statistics

1947 Baltimore Colts: 5 Games Played, 0 Games Started, Rushing: 5–39, Receiving: 1–7

Blount, Lloyd Lamar (Lamar) (Pappy)

Position: B; Height: 6'1"; Weight: 190; High School: Philadelphia (MS); College: Duke, Mississippi State; Born: 4/11/1920, Decatur, MS; Deceased: 8/6/2007, Decatur, MS; 1947 Buffalo Bills (Regular Season): 5 Games Played, 0 Games Started, Rushing: 3–7, Receiving: 8–148; TOTAL (Regular Season): 5 Games Played, 0 Games Started, Rushing: 3–7, Receiving: 8–148

Lamar Blount was born April 11, 1920, to Annie Amanda Breazeale and Pleas Clayton Blount. As the youngest of twelve children, Blount always strived to be the best.

His football career started at Philadelphia High School and continued when he transferred to East Central Junior College in his junior year. There, he received a scholarship to play at Mississippi State University (MSU). While at MSU, Blount joined the team with his high school teammates "Blondy" Black, John Grace and Billy Murphy. In 1941, during his sophomore year, the MSU Bulldogs won the SEC championship.

In March of 1942, Blount enlisted in the Marine Corps and was assigned to the Marine Reserve. While awaiting orders, Blount married Naomi Gibb Foster on December 23, 1942. In July of 1943, Blount was ordered to the Marine V–12 unit at Duke University. While at Duke, Blount played for the Blue Devils and was named All-Southern Conference. In November of 1943, Blount was sent to Camp Lejeune for basic training, followed by Officer Candidate School. He earned the rank of 2nd Lieutenant in July of 1944.

On April 11, 1945, Blount was shipped out to Okinawa before being transferred to Beijing. He served in China until March of 1946 and was discharged in April of 1946.

When he returned from the war, Blount signed to play professional football with the Miami Seahawks for the 1946 season. He was drafted in the second round by the New York Giants in 1944, but he was still in the military and football was on hold. In 1947, he played part of the season with the Buffalo Bills and finished the year with the

Baltimore Colts. He retired from football after the 1947 season, after having played only two years of professional football.

After football, Blount and his wife Naomi ran a dairy farm in Decatur, Mississippi. They were also involved in beef and timber and they operated this business until their retirement.

His wife, Naomi passed away in 2006.

Non-Buffalo Statistics

1946 Miami Seahawks: 12 Games Played, 6 Games Started, Receiving: 13-218 1 TD
1947 Baltimore Colts: 5 Games Played, 3 Games Started, Rushing: 1-(-2)

Brazinsky, Samuel Joseph (Sam)

Position: C; Height: 6'1"; Weight: 215; High School: Kulpmont (PA); College: Villanova; Born: 1/9/1921, Kulpmont, PA; Deceased: 5/12/2003, Manville, NJ; 1946 Buffalo Bisons (Regular Season): 4 Games Played, 0 Games Started, Interceptions: 2-7 1947 Buffalo Bills (Regular Season): on the training camp roster, but did not make the regular season roster. TOTAL (Regular Season): 4 Games Played, 0 Games Started, Interceptions: 2-7

Sam Brazinsky captained his high school team to the state championship in 1938 and he was selected All-State two separate years. He went on to Villanova from 1939 through 1943 and was selected All-East.

Brazinsky served in the Marine Air Force during World War II. While in the service, he played for the Cherry Point Marines football team and was selected to the All-Service team of the South that played in the first Pro Bowl game against the NFL Pro Bowl team. In 1945, he was the starting center for the El Toro Flying Marines of California.

Brazinsky played for the Buffalo Bisons in 1946 and tried out for the Buffalo Bills in 1947. He was hampered by injury, however, and in the last scrimmage of training camp in 1946 he fractured his leg. He played in 4 games of the 1946 season, but failed to make the training camp cut in 1947.

Bumgardner, Rex Keith

Position: B; Height: 5'11"; Weight: 193; High School: Victory (Clarksburg, WV); College: West Virginia; Born: 9/6/1923, Clarksburg, WV; Deceased: 6/1/1998, Clarksburg, WV; 1948 Buffalo Bills (Regular Season): 14 Games Played, 4 Games Started, Rushing: 14-82, Receiving: 1-63, Interceptions: 2-7, Punt Returns: 16-336 2 TD, Kick Returns: 9-141; 1948 Buffalo Bills (Postseason): 1 Game Played, 1 Game Started, Rushing: 11-34, Receiving: 1-25; 1949 Buffalo Bills (Regular Season): 12 Games Played, 9 Games Started, Rushing: 101-391 1 TD, Receiving: 7-168 4 TD, Punt Returns: 4-35, Kick Returns: 9-163; 1949 Buffalo Bills (Postseason): 1 Game Played, 1 Game Started, Rushing: 10-37, Receiving: 4-80; TOTAL (Regular Season): 26 Games Played, 13 Games Started, Rushing: 115-473 1 TD, Receiving: 8-231 4 TD, Interceptions: 2-7, Punt Returns: 20-371 2 TD, Kick Returns: 18-304; TOTAL (Postseason): 2 Games Played, 2 Games Started, Rushing: 21-71, Receiving: 5-105

While at West Virginia, Rex Bumgardner played halfback for two years and was their leading ground gainer in 1947. While in the Army Air Force, he played under Coach Wise on the Luke Field service team. He joined the Buffalo Bills in 1948 and played two seasons for the team. After being sold to the Cleveland Browns in 1950, Bumgardner played three years before he retired from football.

Non-Buffalo Statistics

1950 Cleveland Browns: 10 Games Played, 0 Games Started, Rushing: 67-231 2 TD 1 Fumble, Receiving: 9-112 1 TD
1951 Cleveland Browns: 10 Games Played, 0 Games Started, Rushing: 45-126 1 TD 1 Fumble, Receiving: 5-61 1 TD, Kick Returns: 3-75
1952 Cleveland Browns: 11 Games, Rushing: 9-38, Interceptions: 2-33, Punt Returns: 4-24, Kick Returns: 5-89

Callahan, Robert Francis (Bob)

Position: C; Height: 6'0"; Weight: 205; High School: Beaumont (St, Louis, MO); College: Missouri, Michigan; Born: 9/26/1923, St. Louis, MO; 1948 Buffalo Bills (Regular Season): 6 Games Played, 0 Games Started; TOTAL (Regular Season): 6 Games Played, 0 Games Started

Bob Callahan played both football and basketball at Beaumont High School, captaining both teams. He earned All-State and runner-up MVP honors in 1940. After serving two years in the Marine Corps, Callahan was drafted by the Chicago Cardinals in 1947 (31st round). He decided to play for the Brooklyn Dodgers in 1947, but did not make the field for the Dodgers and left the team. Later that year, he played for the Patterson Panthers and in 1948, Callahan joined the Buffalo Bills for the first half of the season.

Carlson, Raymond (Ray)

Position: B; Height: 6'1"; Weight: 185; College: Marquette; Born: 1921; 1947 Buffalo Bills: on the training camp roster, but did not make the regular season roster. TOTAL: on the training camp roster, but did not make the regular season roster.

Carpenter, Jack Chrisman

Position: T; Height: 6'0"; Weight: 240; High School: Northeast (Kansas City, MO); College: Missouri, Michigan; Born: 7/29/1923, Kansas City, MO; Deceased: 10/16/2005 Honolulu, HI; 1947 Buffalo Bills (Regular Season): 13 Games Played, 4 Games Started; 1948 Buffalo Bills (Regular Season): 14 Games Played, 8 Games Started; 1948 Buffalo Bills (Postseason): 2 Games Played, 1 Game Started; 1949 Buffalo Bills (Regular Season): 7 Games Played, 7 Games Started; TOTAL (Regular Season): 34 Games Played, 19 Games Started; TOTAL (Postseason): 2 Games Played, 1 Game Started

Jack Carpenter was an All-City tackle for Northeast (Kansas City) High School. At Michigan, he was captain of the football team in 1946 and 1947, earning All-Big Nine honors in his senior year. He was drafted by the Cleveland Browns (third round) and the Chicago Cardinals (15th round) in 1947, but rebuffed both teams to sign with the Buffalo Bills. After three seasons in Buffalo, Carpenter finished his career with the San Francisco 49ers.

Non-Buffalo Statistics

1949 San Francisco 49ers: 3 Games Played, 0 Games Started

Check, Bernard (Bernie)

Position: E; Height: 6'3"; Weight: 200; College: Niagara; Born: 2/21/1923, Wilkes-Barre, PA; 1948 Buffalo Bills: on the training camp roster, but did not make the regular season roster; TOTAL: on the training camp roster, but did not make the regular season roster.

Cline, Oliver Monroe (Ollie)

Position: G-B; Height: 6'0"; Weight: 200; High School: Fredericktown (OH); College: Ohio State; Born: 12/31/1925, Mt. Vernon, OH; Deceased: 5/12/2001, Springfield, OH; 1949 Buffalo Bills (Regular Season): 13 Games Played, 11 Games Started, Receiving: 15–110, Kick Returns: 1–21; 1949 Buffalo Bills (Postseason): 1 Game Played, 1 Game Started, Rushing: 3–10, Receiving: 2–9; TOTAL (Regular Season): 13 Games Played, 11 Games Started, Receiving: 15–110, Kick Returns: 1–21; TOTAL (Postseason): 1 Game Played, 1 Game Started, Rushing: 3–10, Receiving: 2–9.

Ollie Cline was a fullback at Ohio State while they were running the T-formation and shifted to guard when they changed to the single wing. He was drafted by the Chicago Bears (14th round), as well as the Cleveland Browns (third round) in 1948. He signed with the Cleveland Browns, but only played one season for the team. He went to Buffalo for the 1949 season, before playing three years with the Detroit Lions.

Non-Buffalo Statistics

1948 Cleveland Browns: 11 Games Played, 0 Games Started, Rushing: 29–129, Kick Returns: 3–55
1950 Detroit Lions: 10 Games Played, 0 Games Started, Rushing: 69–227 2 TD 7 Fumbles, Receiving: 7–18, Kick Returns: 1–20

1951 Detroit Lions: 12 Games Played, 0 Games Started, Rushing: 3–15, Kick Returns: 3–48
1952 Detroit Lions: 8 Games Played, 0 Games Started, Rushing: 13–36 1 TD, Receiving: 2–45
1953 Detroit Lions: 12 Games Played, 0 Games Started, Rushing: 42–169 1 Fumble, Receiving: 10–126 1 TD, Kick Returns: 1–0

Colella, Thomas Anthony (Tom)

Position: B; Height: 6'0"; Weight: 187; High School: Albion (NY); College: Canisius; Born: 7/3/1918, Albion, NY; Deceased: 5/15/1992, Hamburg, NY; 1949 Buffalo Bills (Regular Season): 12 Games Played, 0 Games Started, Rushing: 7-(–9), Receiving: 2–6, Interceptions: 3–49, Punting: 44–1554, Punt Returns: 5–42, Kick Returns: 7–107; TOTAL (Regular Season): 12 Games Played, 0 Games Started, Rushing: 7-(–9), Receiving: 2–6, Interceptions: 3–49, Punting: 44–1554, Punt Returns: 5–42, Kick Returns: 7–107

Tom Colella had the distinction of being one of the only athletes to play his high school, college and professional careers in his hometown. As a three-sport athlete at Albion High School, Colella set the tone for his college career. While at Canisius, Colella earned Little All-American honors (twice). Because of his spectacular college career, Colella was inducted into the inaugural class of the Golden Griffin Sports Hall of Fame.

Drafted by the Detroit Lions in 1942, Colella started his professional football career. After playing the 1942 and 1943 seasons for Detroit, he was traded to the Cleveland Rams, where he spent the next two years. Colella joined the Cleveland Browns in 1946 and won championships all three years he was with the team. In 1949, Colella came home and played for the Buffalo Bills.

Colella was inducted into the Greater Buffalo Sports Hall of Fame in 2002.

Non-Buffalo Statistics

1942 Detroit Lions: 9 Games Played, 2 Games Started, Interceptions: 1–10, Punt Returns: 2–14, Kick Returns: 4–74
1943 Detroit Lions: 8 Games Played, 0 Games Started, Receiving: 1-(–1), Punt Returns: 2–11
1944 Cleveland Rams: 10 Games Played, 8 Games Started, Receiving: 2–64 1 TD, Interceptions: 4–53, Punt Returns: 4–65, Kick Returns: 10–241, Field Goals: 1/1
1945 Cleveland Rams: 10 Games Played, 1 Game Started, Receiving 7–64 2 TD, Punt Returns: 1–10, Kick Returns: 3–79
1946 Cleveland Browns: 14 Games Played, 2 Games Started, Rushing: 30–118 2 TD, Receiving: 1–12 1 TD, Interceptions: 10–110, Punting: 47–1895, Punt Returns: 8–172, Kick Returns: 1–29
1947 Cleveland Browns: 14 Games Played, 7 Games Started, Rushing: 11–77 1 TD, Receiving: 4–63 1 TD, Interceptions: 6–30 1 TD, Punting: 1–36, Punt Returns: 5–113 1 TD, Kick Returns: 1–13
1948 Cleveland Browns: 13 Games Played, 2 Games Started, Rushing: 14–60 1 TD, Receiving: 1–7, Interceptions: 2–34, Punting: 49–1716, Punt Returns: 5–60

Comer, Martin Franklin Sr. (Marty)

Position: E; Height: 6'0"; Weight: 200; High School: Horace Mann School (Gary, IN); College: Tulane; Born: 10/28/1917, Indianapolis, IN; Deceased: 3/15/1998, New Orleans, LA; 1946 Buffalo Bisons (Regular Season): 7 Games Played, 2 Games Started, Receiving: 1–6, Fumble Returns: 1–50 1 TD; 1947 Buffalo Bills (Regular Season): 13 Games Played, 2 Games Started, Receiving: 2–75 1 TD; 1948 Buffalo Bills (Regular Season): 7 Games Played, 3 Games Started, Receiving: 5–66 1 TD; TOTAL (Regular Season): 27 Games Played, 7 Games Started, Receiving: 8–147 2 TD, Fumble Returns: 1–50 1 TD

Marty Comer played under Red Dawson while at Tulane and in 1940, Comer played in the Sugar Bowl. He was named to the All-Star team of the Southeastern Conference in 1941 and 1942, where he set a school record for catching four consecutive passes for touchdowns.

After college, Comer went into the Navy where he was a Chief Petty Officer during World War II. After the war, Comer played professional football for the Buffalo Bisons/Bills, as well as for the Miami Seahawks. He was drafted in the fifth round by the Brooklyn Dodgers in 1943.

After retiring as a player, Comer coached at S.J. Peters High School. He continued his coaching career at various high schools, namely Warren Easton, Alcee Frontier and John McDonogh. He also worked for a short time as a sports writer.

Marty Comer was married to Elaine Bevinetto (who passed away in 2003) and had three children: Martin F. Comer, Jr.; Marlane N. Comer Dows and Gina M. Comer. He had four siblings: Malcolm Peek, Homer Peek, Robert Comer and Mary Francis Peek Boots.

Comer died of emphysema and pneumonia at the age of 80.

Conwell, Edward (Ed)

Position: B; Height: 5'7"; Weight: 170; High School: Palmyra (NJ); College: New York University; Born: 11/16/1924, Riverton, NJ; 1949 Buffalo Bills: On the preseason roster, but did not make the regular season roster; TOTAL: On the preseason roster, but did not make the regular season roster.

In high school, Ed Conwell was All-State in track, basketball and football. He attended NYU, but there was no football team there at the time. He did, however, set many intercollegiate sprint records while on the track team. He was also a member of the 1948 U.S. Olympic track team. His 4x100m relay team won the gold medal, but Conwell did not participate due to illness. He was replaced by Barney Ewell for that race. Conwell continued to compete in track and field events for several years after the 1948 Olympics.

To satisfy his football fix, Conwell played considerable semi-pro football and when he signed on with the Buffalo Bills in 1949, he was the first African-American player on the team.

Coppage, Alton Minor (Al) (Cop)

Position: E; Height: 6'1"; Weight: 195; High School: Hollis (OK); College: Oklahoma; Born: 2/8/1916, Hollis, OK; Deceased: 1/9/1992, Hollis, OK; 1947 Buffalo Bills (Regular Season): 14 Games Played, 11 Games Started, Receiving: 20–226 2 TD, Kick Returns: 2–28; TOTAL (Regular Season): 14 Games Played, 11 Games Started, Receiving: 20–226 2 TD, Kick Returns: 2–28

Al Coppage was a former Oklahoma sprint star that was drafted by the Chicago Cardinals in 1940 (13th round). He played for the Cardinals from 1940 through 1942, at which time he entered the Air Force. When he returned from military service, he signed on with the Cleveland Browns. After playing under Paul Brown for one year, Coppage played for the Buffalo Bills.

During the off-season, Coppage supplemented his income by owning a lumber business.

Non-Buffalo Statistics

1940 Chicago Cardinals: 11 Games Played, 7 Games Started, Receiving: 15–163 1 TD
1941 Chicago Cardinals: 9 Games Played, 2 Games Started, Receiving: 8–117
1942 Chicago Cardinals: 11 Games Played, 5 Games Started, Receiving: 20–196, Kick Returns: 1–11
1946 Cleveland Browns: 14 Games Played, 1 Game Started, Receiving: 2–34

Corley, Elbert Ellis (Bert) (Mule)

Position: E-C; Height: 6'2"; Weight: 225; High School: Okolona (MS); College: Mississippi; Born: 9/9/1920, Okolona, MS; Deceased: 9/22/1988, Tupelo, MS; 1947 Buffalo Bills (Regular Season): 14 Games Played, 4 Games Started, Interceptions: 1–41; TOTAL (Regular Season): 14 Games Played, 4 Games Started, Interceptions: 1–41

In high school, Bert Corley won five letters in football and was captain of his team for two years. In college, he won four letters as center for Mississippi and played in the 1946 North-South game.

Corley was drafted by both Buffalo (sixth round) and the New York Giants (14th round) in 1944. After graduation from Mississippi, Corley decided to play for Buffalo and spent one season with the Bills before he retired from football.

Non-Buffalo Statistics

1948 Baltimore Colts: 9 Games Played, 8 Games Started

Corriere, Louis (Lou)

Position: B; Height: 5'10"; Weight: 175; High School: Lockport; College: Buffalo; Born: 2/27/1923, Lockport, NY; 1948 Buffalo Bills: On the regular season roster, but did not play; TOTAL: On the regular season roster, but did not play.

Lou Corriere played both football and baseball in high school, winning All-Conference honors. While at the University of Buffalo, Corriere played three years under Jim Peele and was named All-Western New York for two years. Corriere spent three years in the field artillery before joining the Buffalo Bills in 1948.

Craig, Bernard (Bernie)

Position: G-E; College: Denver; 1947 Buffalo Bills: On the training camp roster, but did not make the regular season roster; TOTAL: On the training camp roster, but did not make the regular season roster.

Bernie Craig was drafted by the New York Yanks in 1949 (ninth round), but records do not show him playing a professional game in either the NFL or AAFC.

Daddio, Louis William (Bill)

Position: E; Height: 5'11"; Weight: 215; High School: Meadville (PA); College: Pittsburgh; Born: 4/26/1916, Meadville, PA; Deceased: 7/5/1989, Mount Lebanon, PA; 1946 Buffalo Bisons (Preseason): 1 Game Played, 0 Games Started, Extra Points: 2/3, Field Goals: 1; 1946 Buffalo Bisons (Regular Season): 3 Games Played, 1 Games Started, Extra Points: 3/3; TOTAL (Regular Season): 3 Games Played, 1 Games Started, Extra Points: 3/3

As an All-America selection while at the University of Pittsburgh, Bill Daddio was considered one of the best ends in school history. He was best known for his seventy-one yard touchdown run against Washington in the Rose Bowl (a Rose Bowl record at the time). He was drafted by the Chicago Cardinals in 1939 (fifth round). After graduation, Daddio went on to play two seasons with the Chicago Cardinals and made All-Pro second team in 1942.

He spent 26 months overseas as a gunnery officer during World War II and earned the Bronze Star. He played for the service champion Fleet City Blue Jackets in 1945. Upon his return, Daddio signed on with the Bills as a player-coach, but was only with the Buffalo for one year.

Non-Buffalo Statistics
1941 Chicago Cardinals: 11 Games Played, 3 Games Started, Receiving: 5–39, Extra Points: 8/9, Field Goals: 4/8
1942 Chicago Cardinals: 11 Games Played, 10 Games Started, Receiving: 11–108 1 TD, Interceptions: 1–4, Extra Points: 8/8, Field Goals: 5/10

Davis, Kenneth (Kenny)

Position: B; Height: 6'0"; Weight: 200; College: Cornell; 1946 Buffalo Bisons: On the regular season roster, but did not play; TOTAL: On the regular season roster, but did not play.

Kenneth Davis had two 100-yard games for Cornell during his college career. Before he finished college, Davis served four years in the Marines during World War II. After his return, Davis signed on with the Buffalo Bisons, but did not play. After the Bisons, Davis went back to school and finished his Bachelor's degree in 1950 and received two Master's degrees in 1954 and 1956.

Dekdebrun, Allen Edward (Al) (Dek)

Position: B; Height: 5'10½"; Weight: 180; High School: Burgard (Buffalo, NY); Wyoming Sem. (Kingston, PA); College: Cornell; Born: 5/11/1921, Buffalo, NY; Deceased: 3/29/2005, Cape Coral, FL; 1946 Buffalo Bisons (Preseason): 1 Game Played, 0 Games Started; 1946 Buffalo Bisons (Regular Season): 13 Games Played, 7 Games Started, Rushing: 22-(–55), Passing: 28-66-517 8 TD 8 INT, Interceptions: 3–19, Kick Returns: 6–116; TOTAL (Regular Season): 13 Games Played, 7 Games Started, Rushing: 22-(–55), Passing: 28-66-517 8 TD 8 INT, Interceptions: 3–19, Kick Returns: 6–116

Al Dekdebrun won three letters at Burgard Vocational High School, as well as receiving All-High honors in 1939. He went to Cornell and was All-America Mention in both 1944 and 1945. In 1945, he was captain of the team and led the nation in passing. He was voted the most valuable player in the East-West game in 1946. In the spring of 1946, he was declared ineligible from further Ivy League competition when it was discovered that he played two minutes with Columbia in 1943. He graduated from Cornell and played for the Buffalo Bisons in 1946 and the Buffalo Bills for part of the 1947 season. The remainder of the 1947 season, Dekdebrun played with the Chicago Rockets. After splitting time between the New York Yankees and the Boston Yanks in 1948, Dekdebrun spent four years in the Canadian Football League playing for the Toronto Argonauts and helped lead them to a Grey Cup victory.

Non-Buffalo Statistics

1947 Chicago Rockets: 12 Games Played, 5 Games Started, Rushing: 20–71, Passing: 45–75 556 5 TD 7 INT
1948 New York Yankees: 4 Games Played, 0 Games Started, Rushing: 7–24, Passing: 10–20 149 0 TD 2 INT, Interceptions: 1–16, Punt Returns: 1–12, Kick Returns: 1–15
1948 Boston Yanks: 2 Games Played, 0 Games Started, Rushing: 2–14, Passing: 1–3 0 TD 1 INT

DiGangi, John S. (Little John)

Position: T; Height: 6'2"; Weight: 260; High School: Boys (Brooklyn, NY); College: Holy Cross; Born: 6/24/1922, New York City, NY; 1948 Buffalo Bills: On the regular season roster, but did not play; TOTAL: On the regular season roster, but did not play.

John DiGangi was captain of his high school football team and played for three years. He was on the championship team of 1939 and earned All-Scholastic honors in 1940. At Holy Cross, DiGangi earned four letters in football and made All-New England in 1942. Before joining the Buffalo Bills in 1948, DiGangi served over three years in the Army and was stationed in the South Pacific.

DiToma, Anthony (Tony)

Position: B; Height: 6'2"; Weight: 215; College: Wake Forest, Temple; Born: 1925, Philadelphia, PA; 1949 Buffalo Bills: On the preseason roster, but did not make the regular season roster.

DiToma started as fullback while at Temple, but left to join the Army. After the war, he enrolled at Wake Forest and became a quarterback when Coach Peahead Walker changed from the single wing to the T-formation.

Doherty, George Edward

Position: T; Height: 6'1"; Weight: 218; High School: Canton (MS); College: Louisiana Tech; Born: 9/5/1920, Camden, MS; Deceased: 12/31/1987, Natchitoches, LA; 1946 Buffalo Bisons (Regular Season): 11 Games Played, 8 Games Started, Kick Returns: 1–0; 1947 Buffalo Bills (Regular Season): 12 Games Played, 8 Games Started; TOTAL (Regular Season): 23 Games Played, 16 Games Started, Kick Returns: 1–0

George Doherty earned three letters as tackle on his high school football team. In college, he also earned three letters, as well as an All-Conference selection in 1942. He turned pro after graduating from Louisiana Tech in 1943. The Brooklyn Tigers drafted him in 1944 (twelfth round) and he played 10 games for them. In 1945, Doherty went to the Boston Yanks, before joining Buffalo in 1946. Doherty played most of the season for Buffalo in 1947, but finished with the New York Yankees.

Non-Buffalo Statistics

1944 Brooklyn Tigers: 10 Games Played, 7 Games Started
1945 Boston Yanks: 9 Games Played, 7 Games Started
1947 New York Yankees: 1 Game Played, 0 Games Started

Dudish, Andrew Charles (Andy)

Position: B; Height: 6'0"; Weight: 185; High School: Hanover (PA); College: Georgia; Born: 10/13/1921, Wilkes-Barre, PA; Deceased: 1/19/2001, Lawrenceville, GA; 1946 Buffalo Bisons (Preseason): 1 Game Played, 0 Games Started; 1946 Buffalo Bisons (Regular Season): 12 Games Played, 2 Games Started, Rushing: 30–106, Receiving: 2–33, Punt Returns: 5–73, Kick Returns: 7–196; TOTAL (Regular Season): 12 Games Played, 2 Games Started, Rushing: 30–106, Receiving: 2–33, Punt Returns: 5–73, Kick Returns: 7–196

Andy Dudish served as an Infantry First Lieutenant during World War II and while in the service, he played for the 1943 Ft. Benning football team. At Georgia,

Dudish was rated second in the Southern Conference in pass interceptions and played in the Rose Bowl against UCLA. After returning from the war, Dudish signed with Buffalo and played the 1946 season. In 1947, Dudish played for the Baltimore Colts and finished his career playing for the 1948 Detroit Lions.

Non-Buffalo Statistics

1947 Baltimore Colts: 14 Games Played, 4 Games Started, Rushing: 28–30 1 TD, Receiving: 7–130 1 TD, Punt Returns: 5–121, Kick Returns: 8–184
1948 Detroit Lions: 4 Games Played, 0 Games Started, Rushing: 1–5, Punt Returns: 2–10, Kick Returns: 2–38

Duggan, Gilford Earl (Gil) (Cactus Face)

Position: T; Height: 6'3"; Weight: 229; High School: Benton (AR); College: Oklahoma; Born: 12/26/1914, Benton, AR; Deceased: 10/18/1974, Harrah, OK; 1947 Buffalo Bills (Regular Season): 10 Games Played, 2 Games Started; TOTAL (Regular Season): 10 Games Played, 2 Games Started

Gil Duggan was drafted by the New York Giants in the 1939 NFL draft (15th round). He only played one year for the Giants before joining the Chicago Cardinals for the 1942 through 1945 seasons. In 1946, Duggan jumped to the AAFC to play for the Los Angeles Dons. After only one year with the Dons, Duggan signed with the Buffalo Bills and finished his career after the 1947 season. Duggan was an Oklahoma State Trooper in the off-season.

Non-Buffalo Statistics

1940 New York Giants: 10 Games Played, 0 Games Started
1942 Chicago Cardinals: 11 Games Played, 11 Games Started, Interceptions: 1–0
1943 Chicago Cardinals: 10 Games Played, 10 Games Started
1944 Chicago-Pittsburgh Carpets: 10 Games Played, 8 Games Started
1945 Chicago Cardinals: 8 Games Played, 5 Games Started
1946 Los Angeles Dons: 11 Games Played, 0 Games Started

Dugger, John Richard (Jack)

Position: E-T; Height: 6'4"; Weight: 230; High School: McKinley (Canton, OH); College: Ohio State; Born: 1/13/1923, Pittsburgh, PA; Deceased: 2/23/1988, Charlotte, NC; 1946 Buffalo Bisons (Regular Season): 6 Games Played, 0 Games Started, Receiving: 1–15, Fumble Returns: 1–15 1 TD; TOTAL (Regular Season): 6 Games Played, 0 Games Started, Receiving: 1–15, Fumble Returns: 1–15 1 TD

While at McKinley High School, Jack Dugger earned All-State Honorable Mention in football, and was an All-Ohio and All-Tournament center in basketball. At Ohio State, Dugger was an All-America Selection and captained the team in 1943 and 1944 and was rated All-Big Ten and All-America in 1944. He also earned All-America second team in basketball in 1944. Dugger was first in the AAU in shot and discus between 1943 and 1945, was third in discus in the NCAA between 1944 and 1945, and was Big Ten Champion in discus between 1944 and 1945. After graduating in 1945, Dugger went on to coach at Lancaster High School in Ohio.

Dugger was drafted by the Pittsburgh Steelers in 1945 (second round), but elected to start his professional career with the Buffalo Bisons. After only one season with Buffalo, Dugger played two years for the Detroit Lions and one for the Chicago Bears.

Non-Buffalo Statistics

1947 Detroit Lions: 12 Games Played, 3 Games Started, Interceptions: 1–6
1948 Detroit Lions: 12 Games Played, 7 Games Started
1949 Chicago Bears: 6 Games Played, 2 Games Started, Receiving: 1–11, Kick Returns: 1–8

Durkota, Jeffrey (Jeff)

Position: B; Height: 6'0"; Weight: 205; High School: Edensburg-Cambria (PA); College: Penn State; Born: 12/20/1923, Pittsburgh, PA; 1948 Buffalo Bills: On regular season roster, but did not play; TOTAL: On regular season roster, but did not play.

In high school, Jeff Durkota played two years of football, basketball and track. While at Penn State, he played both end and right halfback. Durkota earned All-State honors in 1947, All-Eastern second team in 1947 and was voted outstanding back in 1948.

Durkota was drafted by the Philadelphia Eagles in 1947 (16th round) and the Cleveland Browns in 1948 (first round). However, after graduating from Penn State, he joined the Buffalo Bills, where coach Red Dawson switched him to fullback. He was not with the Buffalo Bills for long before he was sent to the Los Angeles Dons, where he played the majority of the season.

During World War II, Durkota served in the Ski Troops and won the Combat Infantry Badge and Bronze Star. He also captured a German General in Italy in 1945.

Non-Buffalo Statistics

1948 Los Angeles Dons: 12 Games Played, 4 Games Started, Rushing: 14–66, Receiving: 2–12, Interceptions: 1–18, Kick Returns: 9–198

Ebli, Raymond Henry (Ray) (Lil' Abner)

Position: E; Height: 6'3"; Weight: 210; High School: St. Ambrose (Ironwood, MI); College: Notre Dame; Born: 10/6/1919, Ironwood, MI; Deceased: 1/19/2005, Green Bay, WI; 1946 Buffalo Bisons (Regular Season): 9 Games Played, 8 Games Started, Receiving: 2–15 1 TD; TOTAL (Regular Season): 9 Games Played, 8 Games Started, Receiving: 2–15 1 TD

Ray Ebli went to Notre Dame on a basketball scholarship, never having played high school football. While at Notre Dame, he tried out for football and made the varsity squad. As a result, he never played basketball for Notre Dame and lost his basketball scholarship. Fortunately for Ebli, Notre Dame gave him a football scholarship.

While at Notre Dame, Ebli played three years of football under Frank Leahy, including the 1942 College All-Star Game. After graduation, he played for the Chicago Cardinals. Playing only one season of football, he entered the Navy and spent three years in the military.

Upon returning from the service, he re-joined the Cardinals. Bill Daddio, who played on the Cardinals with Ebli in 1942, had moved on to be an end coach for the Buffalo Bisons in 1946. Daddio recruited Ebli to play for Buffalo and he followed Daddio to the Bisons.

Ebli was not happy with his contract in Buffalo and asked for his release. Buffalo claimed that nobody was interested in Ebli and subsequently released him. As soon as he was released, he received a call from Jim Crowley of the Chicago Rockets and was immediately offered a contract. While with the Rockets, Ebli twisted his ankle. Soon after the injury, he was traded to the Cleveland Browns. The issue that arose in the trade is that Chicago never informed Cleveland of Ebli's ankle injury. After two weeks of evaluation, the Browns negated the trade and sent Ebli back to Chicago. The ankle never healed and he retired from football.

He took a job with the Fruehauf Corporation and was stationed in Milwaukee. He stayed with them in both Milwaukee and Green Bay for 39 years before retiring.

Ebli was inducted into the Upper Peninsula (Michigan) Sports Hall of Fame in 1978.

Non-Buffalo Statistics

1942 Chicago Cardinals: 6 Games Played, 0 Games Started, Receiving: 6–83
1947 Chicago Rockets: 5 Games Played, 2 Games Started, Receiving: 4–38 1 TD

Erdman, Verne

Position: T; 1947 Buffalo Bills: On the training camp roster, but did not make the regular season roster; TOTAL: On the training camp roster, but did not make the regular season roster.

Evans, Frederick Owens (Fred) (Dippy)

Position: B; Height: 5'11"; Weight: 185; High School: James Whitcomb Riley (South Bend, IN); College: Notre Dame; Born: 5/23/1921, Grand Rapids, MI; Deceased: 6/21/2007, Cleveland, OH; 1947 Buffalo Bills (Regular Season): 4 Games Played, 0 Games Started, Rushing: 8–27, Receiving: 1–7; TOTAL (Regular Season): 4 Games Played, 0 Games Started, Rushing: 8–27, Receiving: 1–7

Evans started his football career as an all-state running back for James Whitcomb Riley High School and went on to play for Notre Dame. While in college, Evans earned his nickname "Dippy." In the middle of a water fight with teammates,

Evans slipped on a puddle of water and hurt his knee. He hid his injury from Coach Frank Leahy and received a shot of Novocain to numb the pain, which made him "dippy."

After college, Evans served in the Army Air Corps from February 1943 through January 1946. He played football while in the service and won the national championship in 1944 on the service team.

In the 1943 NFL draft, the Chicago Bears selected Evans in the second round, but it was not until 1948 before he played for the team. Instead, Evans played for the Cleveland Browns after he left the service in 1946. He was signed by Paul Brown on May 12, 1945, and was the fourth player inked by the team. He played for the Browns in 1946, the Bills and Chicago Rockets in 1947, and the Chicago Bears in 1948. At that point, his recurring knee injury from his Notre Dame days prevented Evans from continuing his career as a football player.

Throughout his football career, he is best known for scoring the first points in Cleveland Browns history. It was a preseason game with the Brooklyn Dodgers and Evans caught a Cliff Lewis seven-yard pass for a touchdown. Evans also scored the final points in the game, when he intercepted a Glenn Dobbs pass and returned it 83 yards for a touchdown. He was also remembered as the first player to return two fumbles for touchdowns in a single game.

After retiring from football, he started a dry cleaning business in Cleveland. Evans died of bone cancer at the age of 86.

Non-Buffalo Statistics

1946 Cleveland Browns: 6 Games Played, 0 Games Started, Rushing: 8–27, Receiving: 1–7, Interceptions: 1–21, Punting: 8–296, Punt Returns: 1–0
1947 Chicago Rockets: 9 Games Played, 6 Games Started, Rushing: 20–110 1 TD, Passing: 2–0, Receiving: 4–53, Punting: 2–73
1947 Buffalo Bills and Chicago Rockets: Punt Returns: 5–30, Kick Returns: 9–159
1948 Chicago Bears: 3 Games Played, 0 Games Started, Rushing: 10–15, Receiving: 1-(-2), 2 Fumble Return TD, Punt Returns: 1–15

Fedora, Walter Jack (Walt)

Position: B; Height: 6'0"; Weight: 188; College: George Washington; High School: Stephen Decatur (Decatur, IL); Born: 9/15/1918, Decatur, IL; Deceased: 9/1968; 1946 Buffalo Bisons: On preseason and regular season roster, but did not play; TOTAL: On preseason and regular season roster, but did not play

Walt Fedora was an All-State end while at Decatur High School, but was converted to halfback when he attended George Washington University. There, Fedora was All-Southern Conference and was named All-American Honorable Mention from 1939 through 1941.

Fedora was drafted by the Brooklyn Dodgers in 1942 (22nd round) and played for them that year. At that point, Fedora entered the Navy and served in an amphibious unit in Okinawa during the occupation of Japan. He separated from the Navy as a Lieutenant Junior Grade in 1946 and joined the Buffalo Bisons.

Non-Buffalo Statistics

1942 Brooklyn Dodgers: 8 Games Played, 0 Games Started, Rushing: 16–34, Kick Returns: 4–75

Fekete, John Michael

Position: B; Height: 5'11"; Weight: 220; High School: Findley (OH); College: Ohio University; Born: 10/28/1919, Morgantown, WV; Deceased: 7/26/1988, Cleveland, OH; 1946 Buffalo Bisons (Regular Season): 2 Games Played, 0 Games Started, Rushing: 1-(–1); TOTAL (Regular Season): 2 Games Played, 0 Games Started, Rushing: 1-(–1)

John Fekete was drafted by the Brooklyn Dodgers in 1943 (14th round). However, he started his professional career with the Cleveland Browns. He attended training camp with this brother Gene, but went to Buffalo before the start the season. Fekete saw action in two games for Buffalo in his only professional season.

Freitas, Jesse

Position: B; Height: 5'10"; Weight: 170; High School: Red Bluff (CA); College: Santa Clara; Born: 2/7/1921, Red Bluff, CA; 1949 Buffalo Bills (Regular Season): 1 Game Played, 0 Games Started, Rushing: 3–13, Passing: 4–9–10 0 TD 2 INT; TOTAL (Regular Season): 1 Game Played, 0 Games Started, Rushing: 3–13, Passing: 4–9–10 0 TD 2 INT

Jesse Freitas entered Santa Clara in 1940. In April of 1942, he joined the Army field artillery.

Freitas was drafted by the Pittsburgh Steelers in 1944 (seventh round), but he joined the San Francisco 49ers instead as 49ers coach Buck Shaw was also Freitas' coach in college. He played two seasons for San Francisco before joining the Chicago Rockets. After only one season with the Rockets, Freitas was traded to Buffalo for a draft choice. He played one game for the Bills before he was cut from the team.

After football, Freitas went back to college to get his teaching credentials. He started coaching at Catholic High School and stayed there until 1974, when he retired.

Jesse Freitas has a son, Jesse Lee Freitas, who played two years for the San Diego Chargers.

Non-Buffalo Statistics

1946 San Francisco 49ers: 10 Games Played, 0 Games Started, Rushing: 6-(-21), Passing: 22–44 234 3 TD 7 INT, Interceptions: 2–40, Punt Returns: 1–10
1947 San Francisco 49ers: 10 Games Played, 0 Games Started, Rushing: 6-(–9), Passing: 13–33 215 4 TD 2 INT, Interceptions: 1–11, Punting: 8–336
1948 Chicago Rockets: 10 Games Played, 9 Games Started, Rushing: 24–25, Passing: 84–167 1425 14 TD 16 INT

Furse, Robert (Bob)(Tex)

Position: B; Height: 5'10"; Weight: 188; High School: Eastland (TX); College: Yale; Born: 7/31/1923, Eastland, TX; 1949 Buffalo Bills: On the preseason roster, but did not make the regular season roster; TOTAL: On the preseason roster, but did not make the regular season roster.

Tex Furse earned five letters as a halfback at Eastland High School. He also earned two letters as a guard in basketball and three letters on the track team and served as captain of all three teams. At Yale, Furse earned four letters as a quarterback and was named All-Ivy League second team and All-East honorable mention in 1948.

Fusci, Dominick

Position: G; Height: 6'2"; Weight: 230; College: South Carolina; Born: 5/15/1924, New York City, NY; 1948 Buffalo Bills: On the training camp roster, but did not make the regular season roster; TOTAL: On the training camp roster, but did not make the regular season roster.

Gibron, Abraham (Abe)

Position: T-G; Height: 5'11"; Weight: 243; High School: Isaac C. Elston (Michigan City, IN); College: Valparaiso, Purdue; Born: 9/22/1925, Michigan City, IN; Deceased: 9/23/1997, Belleair, FL; 1949 Buffalo Bills (Regular Season): 11 Games Played, 11 Games Started, Receiving: 3–0; 1949 Buffalo Bills (Postseason): 1 Game Played, 1 Game Started; TOTAL (Regular Season): 11 Games Played, 11 Games Started, Receiving: 3–0; TOTAL (Postseason): 1 Game Played, 1 Game Started

Abe Gibron played three years as a guard on his high school football team and spent two years on the golf team. After beginning at Valparaiso, Gibron lettered two years while at Purdue. He was selected All-Midwest Conference second team both years at Purdue and was an All-America Honorable Mention. Gibron was drafted by the New York Giants in 1949 (sixth round), as well as by the Buffalo Bills (first round) in the secret draft held by the AAFC in 1949. He signed with the Bills and became an immediate starter.

After the Bills folded, Gibron became one of Paul Brown's messenger guards, who brought plays from Brown to quarterback Otto Graham. Gibron was selected to the Pro Bowl four times (1952 through 1955) and was named All-NFL by the United Press in 1955. In the middle of the 1956 season, Gibron was traded to the Philadelphia Eagles and played for them for the 1956 and 1957 seasons. He played his final two seasons for the Chicago Bears.

In 1960, Gibron became an assistant coach for the Washington Redskins and stayed there until 1965. That same year, he joined the Chicago Bears as an assistant coach. He was promoted to head coach in 1972 and stayed through the 1974 season, amassing an 11–30–1 record. In 1975, Gibron became the head coach of the Chicago Wind of the World Football League. From 1976 through 1984, Gibron was an assistant coach of the Tampa Bay Buccaneers under John McKay.

Non-Buffalo Statistics

1950 Cleveland Browns: 12 Games Played
1951 Cleveland Browns: 12 Games Played, Kick Returns: 1–0
1952 Cleveland Browns: 12 Games Played, Kick Returns: 1–0
1953 Cleveland Browns: 10 Games Played, Rushing: 0-(–7)
1954 Cleveland Browns: 12 Games Played
1955 Cleveland Browns: 12 Games Played
1956 Cleveland Browns: 7 Games Played
1956 Philadelphia Eagles: 2 Games Played
1957 Philadelphia Eagles: 12 Games Played
1958 Chicago Bears: 12 Games Played, Kick Returns: 1–12
1959 Chicago Bears: 12 Games Played

Gibson, Paul Edward (Spider)

Position: E-T; Height: 6'2"; Weight: 195; High School: Mineral Springs (NC); College: North Carolina State; Born: 10/28/1917, Winston Salem, NC; Deceased: 8/11/1999, Charleston, SC; 1947 Buffalo Bills (Regular Season): 13 Games Played, 8 Games Started, Receiving: 8–154; 1948 Buffalo Bills (Regular Season): 8 Games Played, 5 Games Started, Receiving: 11–216; 1948 Buffalo Bills (Postseason): 1 Game Played, 0 Games Started, Receiving: 1–7; 1949 Buffalo Bills (Regular Season): 10 Games Played, 1 Game Started, Receiving: 3–32, Interceptions: 1–9; 1949 Buffalo Bills (Postseason): 1 Game Played, 0 Games Started; TOTAL (Regular Season): 31 Games Played, 14 Games Started, Receiving: 22–402, Interceptions: 1–9; TOTAL (Postseason): 2 Games Played, 0 Games Started, Receiving: 1–7

As a high school athlete, Paul Gibson earned letters in football, basketball and baseball. He was captain of his North Carolina State football team for two years, earning All-Conference honors both years. Gibson was drafted in the ninth round of the 1947 AAFC draft by the Buffalo Bills and played for them from 1947 through the end of the franchise in 1949. During the off-season, Gibson played baseball in the Florida State League.

Giles, Donald Mackay (Don)

Position: HB; Height: 6'0"; Weight: 188; High School: Milton (MA); College: Boston; Born: 7/21/1920, Milton, MA; 1948 Buffalo Bills: On the regular season roster, but did not play; TOTAL: On the regular season roster, but did not play.

Don Giles was an all-around athlete. He earned four letters in football while at Milton High School, and also participated in basketball and baseball. While at Boston University, Giles was named the captain of the squad in his senior year, as well as named All-Eastern and All-New England.

During World War II, Giles spent three years in the Coast Guard. After returning from the war, Giles signed with the Buffalo Bills, but did not play.

Gompers, William George (Bill) (Bushel Foot)

Position: B; Height: 6'1"; Weight: 185; High School: Central Catholic (Wheeling, WV); College: Notre Dame; Born: 3/20/1928, Wheeling, WV; 1948 Buffalo Bills (Regular Season): 15 Games Played, 3 Games Started, Rushing 14–48 219 1 TD, Interceptions: 2–74, Punt Returns: 1–10, Kick Returns: 4–62; 1948 Buffalo Bills (Postseason): 1 Game Played, 0 Games Started, Rushing: 14–52, Receiving: 1–66 1 TD; TOTAL (Regular Season): 15 Games Played, 3 Games Started, Rushing 14–48 219 1 TD, Interceptions: 2–74, Punt Returns: 1–10, Kick Returns: 4–62; TOTAL (Postseason): 1 Game Played, 0 Games Started, Rushing: 14–52, Receiving: 1–66 1 TD

Bill Gompers was on an accelerated graduation program while in high school. He left in the middle of his senior year to start at Notre Dame, playing football under both Hugh Devore and Frank Leahy.

Gompers was drafted by the Buffalo Bills in 1948 (3rd round) and also received interest from the Pittsburgh Steelers. Gompers called on two of his friends—John Mastragelo and Joe Gasparella—on the Steelers' roster to find out more about the team. Gasparella mentioned what practices were like under coach John Michelosen and how they compared to Frank Leahy. That was enough to convince Gompers to join his former Notre Dame coach Clem Crowe in Buffalo.

After the 1948 season, Buffalo wanted Gompers to return. However, his father had other ideas: Gompers' father was a lawyer and he wanted Bill to join the family practice. Gompers gave up football and entered Notre Dame Law School. He tried, but was unable to get his degree. At the time, his wife was pregnant with their first child, so Gompers left school to find work and joined a meat packing company outside of Wheeling, West Virginia and stayed there for three years. At that point, the plant closed and relocated about 80 miles away. Gompers did not follow the company, but instead joined MSA in Pittsburgh. He then took a sales job with the same company in Michigan and stayed there for 11 years before transferring back to Pittsburgh.

Grabinski, Taddeus (Ted) (Grebo)

Position: C; Height: 6'2"; Weight: 210; High School: Ambridge (Ambridge, PA); College: Duquesne; Born: 2/6/1916; 1946 Buffalo Bisons (Preseason): 1 Game Played, 0 Games Started; 1946 Buffalo Bisons (Regular Season): 1 Game Played, 0 Games Started; TOTAL (Regular Season): 1 Game Played, 0 Games Started

Ted Grabinski was the captain of his Duquesne football team in 1938 and earned several All-America Honorable Mentions while there. He served almost five years (four years and eleven months) in the Army, where he won five Bronze Stars and played for two years on service football teams. He was married in Kapellen, Belgium in 1945.

Non-Buffalo Statistics
1939 Pittsburgh Pirates: 10 Games Played, 2 Games Started
1940 Pittsburgh Steelers: 11 Games Played, 9 Games Started

Grigg, Forrest Porter Jr. (Chubby)

Position: T; Height: 6'2"; Weight: 330; High School: Longview (TX); College: Tulsa; Born: 1/10/1926, El Dorado, AR; Deceased: 10/10/1983, Ore City, TX; 1946 Buffalo Bisons (Preseason): 1 Game Played, 0 Games Started; 1946 Buffalo Bills (Regular Season): 6 Games Played, 0 Games Started; 1947 Buffalo Bills (Regular Season): On the training camp roster, but did not make the regular season roster; TOTAL (Regular Season): 6 Games Played, 0 Games Started

At Longview High School, Forrest Grigg was named All-State. At Tulsa, he earned All-Missouri Valley Conference and All-America Honorable Mention in 1945. He was also voted Best Blocking and Tackling for Tulsa in 1945. His ability helped take Tulsa to the Orange Bowl and the Oil Bowl Game in 1945.

The 6'2", 330-pound Grigg joined Buffalo in 1946. His 53-inch waist and 31-inch thighs made him the largest player on the team. He stayed with Buffalo throughout the 1946 season, but had difficulty removing the weight that Coach Dawson demanded. He was sent to the Chicago Rockets before the 1947 season and played one year for them. He then went to Cleveland and played four years under Paul Brown. His final professional season was in 1952 with the Dallas Texans.

Non-Buffalo Statistics

1947 Chicago Rockets: 13 Games Played, 7 Games Started
1948 Cleveland Browns: 14 Games Played, 0 Games Started
1949 Cleveland Browns: 12 Games Played, 0 Games Started, Receiving: 0-2
1950 Cleveland Browns: 11 Games Played, Extra Points: 9/9, Field Goals: 1/2
1951 Cleveland Browns: 11 Games Played
1952 Dallas Texans: 10 Games Played, Extra Points: 9/12, Field Goals: 0/3

Groves, George Noah

Position: G; Height: 5'11"; Weight: 195; High School: Rossville (IL); College: Marquette; Born: 6/10/1921, Hammond, IN; 1947 Buffalo Bills (Regular Season): 8 Games Played, 0 Games Started; TOTAL (Regular Season): 8 Games Played, 0 Games Started

George Groves started at Marquette in the fall of 1940 and played three seasons at guard under Tom Stidham. After serving four years in the Air Force, Groves left in his junior year to join Stidham with the Cleveland Browns. He was originally drafted by the Chicago Bears in 1945 (32nd round), but decided to stick with his Marquette coach. When Stidham left the Browns to join the Buffalo Bills, Groves again followed. During the 1947 preseason, Groves was injured, receiving a knee to the side of his head. This ruptured his eardrum and hampered his play. He was traded to Baltimore in the offseason and finished his playing career after only two games with the squad.

After leaving football, Groves worked for an electrical contractor for a few years before buying the business. He ran the business for 25 years before retiring.

Non-Buffalo Statistics

1948 Baltimore Colts: 2 Games Played, 0 Games Started

Guess, Frank

Position: B; Height: 6'1"; Weight: 190; College: Texas University; Born: 2/1/1924, Wharton, TX; 1949 Buffalo Bills: On the preseason roster, but did not make the regular season roster; TOTAL: On the preseason roster, but did not make the regular season roster.

Hanula, Bernard (Bernie)

Position: T; Height: 6'0"; Weight: 225; College: Wake Forest; 1949 Buffalo Bills: On the preseason roster, but did not make the regular season roster; TOTAL: On the preseason roster, but did not make the regular season roster.

Haynes, Joseph H. (Joe)

Position: G-C; Height: 6'3"; Weight: 225; College: Oklahoma, Tulsa; Born: 3/26/1921, Barnsdall, OK; Deceased: 3/9/1994 Tupelo, MS; 1947 Buffalo Bills (Regular Season): 8 Games Played, 0 Games Started; 1948 Buffalo Bills: On training camp roster, but did not make regular season roster; TOTAL (Regular Season): 8 Games Played, 0 Games Started

Joe Haynes was drafted by the Philadelphia Eagles in 1947 (23rd round). He did not play for the Eagles, but instead signed with the Buffalo Bills. He played eight games in the 1948 season, but failed to make the 1949 roster.

Heintz, Thomas

Position: T; Height: 6'2"; Weight: 250; College: Tulane; Born: 5/22/1923, Hartford, WI; 1948 Buffalo Bills: On the training camp roster, but did not make the regular season roster; TOTAL: On the training camp roster, but did not make the regular season roster.

Herring, Harold Moreland (Hal)

Position: C; Height: 6'1"; Weight: 211; High School: Lanett (AL), West Point HS (Cullman, AL); College: Auburn; Born: 2/24/1924, Lanett, AL; 1949 Buffalo Bills (Regular Season): 12 Games Played, 0 Games Started, Interceptions: 1-1; 1949 Buffalo Bills (Postseason): 1 Game Played, 0 Games Started; TOTAL (Regular Season): 12 Games Played, 0 Games Started, Interceptions: 1-1; TOTAL (Postseason): 1 Game Played, 0 Games Started

Hal Herring started at Auburn in the fall of 1942 and earned All-SEC honors while there. He entered the combat infantry and was stationed in France and Germany. Upon his return, he earned his Bachelors Degree in Education, and later earned a Masters Degree from Auburn and a PhD from Georgia.

Herring was drafted by the Chicago Cardinals in 1949 (9th round), but instead chose to play for the Buffalo Bills. After one year with the Bills, Herring played three seasons with the Cleveland Browns. In 1953, he was offered a coaching job at Auburn and accepted the position. He coached for a while, and then became a professor.

Non-Buffalo Statistics

1950 Cleveland Browns: 12 Games Played, Interceptions: 2–12
1951 Cleveland Browns: 10 Games Played, Interceptions: 1–28
1952 Cleveland Browns: 12 Games Played

Heywood, William

Position: B; Height: 5'11"; Weight: 185; College: Notre Dame; 1948 Buffalo Bills: On the regular season roster, but did not play; TOTAL: On the regular season roster, but did not play.

Hirsch, Edward Norman (Buckets)

Position: G-C-B; Height: 5'10"; Weight: 207; High School: Williamsville (NY); College: Northwestern; Born: 3/26/1921, Clarence, NY; Deceased: 1/28/2000, Irving, NY; 1947 Buffalo Bills (Regular Season): 10 Games Played, 5 Games Started, Rushing: 4–7, Interceptions: 3–73 1 TD; 1948 Buffalo Bills (Regular Season): 14 Games Played, 2 Games Started; 1948 Buffalo Bills (Postseason): 2 Games Played, 1 Game Started; 1949 Buffalo Bills (Regular Season): 8 Games Played, 0 Games Started; TOTAL (Regular Season): 32 Games Played, 7 Games Started, Rushing: 4–7, Interceptions: 3–73 1 TD; TOTAL (Postseason): 2 Games Played, 1 Game Started

Ed Hirsch played three years of high school football before attending Northwestern. While in college, Hirsch was MVP in 1942 and 1946, as well as earning All-Conference Honors in 1946. During World War II, Hirsh served as a paratrooper. He played one year of service football for the First Army Aces (1945) before returning to Northwestern. In 1947, Hirsch played on the College All-Star Team prior to joining the Buffalo Bills in 1948. He played two seasons for the Bills, before going on to play for the Hamilton Tiger Cats of the Canadian Football League in 1952.

Hodges, Robert Joseph (Bob)

Position: T; Height: 6'2"; Weight: 230; High School: Peoria Woodruff; College: Bradley Tech; Born: 12/31/1922, Peoria, IL; 1948 Buffalo Bills: On the regular season roster, but did not play; TOTAL: On the regular season roster, but did not play.

Bob Hodges played center for his high school football team. At Bradley Tech, he played tackle and earned three letters. During World War II, Hodges served three years in the Air Force and was stationed in the South Pacific.

Hopp, Harry (Hippity)

Position: B; Height: 6'0"; Weight: 215; High School: Hastings (NE); College: Nebraska; Born: 12/13/1918, Hastings, NE; Deceased: 12/22/1964, Hastings, NE; 1946 Buffalo Bisons (Preseason): 1 Game Played, 1 Game Started; 1946 Buffalo Bisons (Regular Season): 9 Games Played, 2 Games Started, Rushing: 45–129 1 TD, Passing: 11–22–190 0 TD 0 INT, Punting: 15–461 2 Blocked; TOTAL (Regular Season): 9 Games Played, 2 Games Started, Rushing: 45–129 1 TD, Passing: 11–22–190 0 TD 0 INT, Punting: 15–461 2 Blocked

Harry Hopp was an All-American, All-Big Six and All-State selection while at Nebraska. He was also an All-State selection in basketball and track. During World War II, Hopp served in the Navy. He was All-Service with the Bainbridge Naval Training Station team and played in the famous 1945 Fleet City Blue Jacket team. His brother Johnny played baseball for the Cardinals.

Hopp was drafted by the Detroit Lions in 1941 (third round). He stayed with the Lions for three years before entering the service. When he returned, Hopp played for the Buffalo Bisons and Miami Seahawks in 1946. In 1947, Hopp finished his professional career with the Los Angeles Dons.

Non-Buffalo Statistics

1941 Detroit Lions: 10 Games Played, 6 Games Started, Passing: 0–3 1 INT, Receiving: 2–7, Interceptions: 1–3
1942 Detroit Lions: 10 Games Played, 5 Games Started, Passing: 20–68 258 13 INT, Interceptions: 1–0, Punt Returns: 9–98, Kick Returns: 5–108
1943 Detroit Lions: 10 Games Played, 9 Games Started, Passing: 5–8 60, Receiving: 17–229 3 TD, Interceptions: 2–40 1 TD, Punt Returns: 1-(–7), Kick Returns: 5–57
1946 (Buffalo Bisons and Miami Seahawks): Kick Returns: 6–113
1946 Miami Seahawks: 3 Games Played, 2 Games Started, Rushing: 16–89 2 TD
1947 Los Angeles Dons: 9 Games Played, 0 Games Started, Rushing: 10–52, Passing: 11–22–190 0 TD 0 INT, Receiving: 5–58

Horne, Richard Courtland (Dick)

Position: E; Height: 6'2"; Weight: 215; High School: Woodrow Wilson (Long Beach, CA); College: Compton Junior College, Oregon; Born: 9/4/1918, Denver, CO; Deceased: 11/1964; 1946 Buffalo Bisons (Regular Season): 1 Game Played, 0 Games Started; TOTAL (Regular Season): 1 Game Played, 0 Games Started

Dick Horne played football at Woodrow Wilson High School. He attended the University of Oregon and played from 1939 through 1940. In 1941, Horne joined the New York Giants, where he played one season before entering the military. After leaving the service, Horne signed with the Miami Seahawks in 1946. He played ten games for Miami before being traded to the Buffalo Bisons for the remainder of the season. In 1947, Horne played for the San Francisco 49ers in his final season of professional football.

Non-Buffalo Statistics

1941 New York Giants: 2 Games Played, 0 Games Started
1946 Miami Seahawks: 10 Games Played, 3 Games Started, Receiving: 5–48
1947 San Francisco 49ers: 10 Games Played, 2 Games Started, Receiving: 3–69

Janiak, Leonard Joseph (Len)

Position: B; Height: 6'1"; Weight: 203; High School: South (Cleveland, OH); College: Ohio University; Born: 10/29/1915, Cleveland, OH; Deceased: 5/22/1980, Cleveland, OH; 1947 Buffalo Bills: On the training camp roster, but did not make the regular season roster; TOTAL: On the training camp roster, but did not make the regular season roster.

Len Janiak was drafted by the Brooklyn Dodgers in 1939 (sixth round). He only played one year for the Dodgers before joining the Cleveland Rams for two years. He tried out for the Buffalo Bills in 1947, but failed to make the squad.

Non-Buffalo Statistics

1939 Brooklyn Dodgers: 10 Games Played, 1 Game Started, Rushing: 18–56, Receiving: 2–6
1940 Cleveland Rams: 11 Games Played, 3 Games Started, Rushing: 19–44, Receiving: 1–3, Punting: 1–30
1941 Cleveland Rams: 10 Games Played, 4 Games Started, Rushing: 14–20, Receiving: 2–5, Interceptions: 1–19, Kickoff Returns: 2–27
1942 Cleveland Rams: 9 Games Played, 3 Games Started, Rushing: 34–108, Passing: 1-1-11 0 TD 0 INT, Receiving: 6–51

Joe, Lawrence E. (Larry) (AKA Lorenzo Guisseppe)

Position: B; Height: 5'9"; Weight: 190; High School: Derry (PA); College: Penn State; Born: 7/6/1923, New Derry, PA; Deceased: 4/1985; 1949 Buffalo Bills (Regular Season): 2 Games Played, 0 Games Started, Rushing: 2–18, Receiving: 2–52, Kick Returns: 1–12; TOTAL (Regular Season): 2 Games Played, 0 Games Started, Rushing: 2–18, Receiving: 2–52, Kick Returns: 1–12

Larry Joe was a four-letter back for Derry High School. He was also a four-letter sprinter for the track team. While at Penn State, Joe played halfback for three seasons, earning All-America Honorable Mention honors. He only participated in two games for the Buffalo Bills.

Johnson, Richard

Position: G; Height: 5'9"; Weight: 240; College: Baylor; Born: 12/4/1924, Atlanta, TX; 1948 Buffalo Bills: On the training camp roster, but did not make the regular season roster; TOTAL: On the training camp roster, but did not make the regular season roster.

Johnston, Luther Preston (Pres)

Position: B; Height: 6'0"; Weight: 205; High School: Newcastle (TX); College: Southern Methodist; Born: 10/12/1921; Deceased: 1/15/1979, Lubbock, TX; 1946 Buffalo Bisons (Regular Season): 8 Games Played, 5 Games Started, Rushing: 15–53, Receiving: 2–19 1 TD, Interceptions: 1–15, Punting: 21–783 1 Blocked, Kick Returns: 2–21; TOTAL (Regular Season): 8 Games Played, 5 Games Started, Rushing: 15–53, Receiving: 2–19 1 TD, Interceptions: 1–15, Punting: 21–783 1 Blocked, Kick Returns: 2–21

Pres Johnston was drafted by the Green Bay Packers in 1942 (seventh round). He did not play for the Packers, but instead signed on with the Miami Seahawks in 1946. After only three games, Johnston was traded to Buffalo. He finished his professional career after the 1946 season.

Non-Buffalo Statistics

1946 Miami Seahawks: 3 Games Played, 2 Games Started, Rushing: 30–165 2 TD, Passing: 1–1 9 0 TD 0 INT, Receiving: 4–35, Punting: 7–329, Extra Points: 1–1

Jones, Elmer John Jr. (Buck)

Position: G; Height: 6'0"; Weight: 233; High School: Riverside High School (Buffalo, NY); College: Franklin & Marshall, Wake Forest; Born: 8/4/1920, Buffalo, NY; Deceased: 2/21/1996, New Smyrna Beach, FL; 1946 Buffalo Bisons (Preseason): 1 Game Played, 1 Game Started; 1946 Buffalo Bisons (Regular Season): 11 Games Played, 1 Game Started, Interceptions: 2–7; TOTAL (Regular Season): 11 Games Played, 1 Game Started, Interceptions: 2–7

Elmer Jones was an All-High football player at Riverside High School. He also rowed with the West Side Club and took second place in the North American Rowing Meet in Boston in 1939.

While at Wake Forest, he was an All-Southern Selection as a sophomore in 1942 and earned the honor again in 1943. In 1943, Jones earned All-East honors and was named to the "Ten Best Athletes in the Past Ten Years" at Wake Forest.

During World War II, Jones served in the Marines. He played under "Ducky" Pond at the Georgia Pre–Flight School in 1944 and was on the Marine All-Stars in 1945.

Jones was drafted by the New York Giants in 1946 (second round), but elected to join the Buffalo Bisons that year. After a single season with Buffalo, Jones played two years for the Detroit Lions before retiring from football.

Non-Buffalo Statistics

1947 Detroit Lions: 10 Games Played, 2 Games Started
1948 Detroit Lions: 9 Games Played, 0 Games Started

Juzwik, Stephen Robert (Steve)

Position: B; Height: 5'8½"; Weight: 190; High School: DePaul Academy (Chicago, IL); College: Notre Dame; Born: 6/18/1918, Gary, IN; Deceased: 6/6/1964, Chicago, IL; 1946 Buffalo Bisons (Preseason): 1 Game Played, 1 Game Started, Rushing: 1 TD; 1946 Buffalo Bisons (Regular Season): 12 Games Played, 9 Games Started, Rushing: 71–455 7 TD, Receiving: 23–357 3 TD, Interceptions: 5–108 1 TD, Punt Returns: 11–135, Kick Returns: 21–452; 1947 Buffalo Bills (Regular Season): 9 Games Played, 2 Games Started, Rushing: 26–130, Receiving: 5–35 1 TD, Punt Returns: 4–36, Kick Returns: 1–20, Extra Points: 28/32, Field Goals: 2/3; TOTAL (Regular Season): 21 Games Played, 11 Games Started, Rushing: 97–585 7 TD, Receiving: 28–392 4 TD, Interceptions: 5–108 1 TD, Punt Returns: 15–171, Kick Returns: 22–472, Extra Points: 28/32, Field Goals: 2/3

Steve Juzwik was an All-American while at Notre Dame (1940). He led the Fighting Irish with 407 yards rushing, 205 yards passing and 89 yards receiving in his final year.

During World War II, Juzwik served in the Navy. While in the military, Juzwik played the undefeated Fleet City Blue Jackets team, as well as playing under Paul Brown at Great Lakes.

In 1942, the Washington Redskins drafted Juzwik in the 21st round. When he returned from the war, he signed on with the Buffalo Bisons and played for two seasons. Juzwik has the distinction of being the only Buffalo Bison named to the All-Conference team in 1946, being named second team halfback behind New York's Spec Sanders. Injuries cut his professional career short, as he only played a partial season for the Chicago Rockets in 1948.

Non-Buffalo Statistics

1942 Washington Redskins: 2 Games Played, 1 Game Started, Rushing: 15–75 2 TD, Punt Returns: 3–33, Kick Returns: 1–22, Extra Points: 3/3
1948 Chicago Rockets: 4 Games Played, 1 Game Started, Rushing: 13–19, Receiving: 1–5, Extra Points: 5/5

Kasap, Michael E. (Mike)

Position: T; Height: 6'2"; Weight: 255; High School: LaSalle-Peru Township (IL); College: Illinois, Purdue; Born: 11/20/1922, Oglesby, IL; Deceased: 10/20/1994, La Salle, IL; 1947 Buffalo Bills (Regular Season): 0 Games Played, 0 Games Started; TOTAL (Regular Season): 0 Games Played, 0 Games Started

Mike Kasap was the starting tackle for his high school football team. He entered

Illinois and played two seasons before joining the Marines. While in the Marine Corps, he attended the V–12 program at Purdue and helped the team to the 1943 championship. After leaving the service, he returned to Illinois to finish his schooling and graduated in 1946.

In 1945, Kasap was drafted by the Detroit Lions (twelfth round). Instead of playing for Detroit, Kasap signed on with the Buffalo Bills in 1947. He was not in Buffalo for long before being traded to the Baltimore Colts to finish his one-year professional career.

Non-Buffalo Statistics

1947 Baltimore Colts: 12 Games Played, 3 Games Started

Kerns, John Emery (Moose)

Position: T; Height: 6'3"; Weight: 243; High School: Geneva (OH); College: Ohio University, Duke, North Carolina; Born: 6/17/1923, Ashtabula, OH; Deceased: 6/1988, Leesburg, FL; 1947 Buffalo Bills (Regular Season): 13 Games Played, 2 Games Started; 1948 Buffalo Bills (Regular Season): 16 Games Played, 8 Games Started, Punt Returns: 2–0, Kick Returns: 1–3; 1948 Buffalo Bills (Postseason): 2 Games Played, 1 Game Started; 1949 Buffalo Bills (Regular Season): 13 Games Played, 12 Games Started; 1949 Buffalo Bills (Postseason): 1 Game Played, 1 Game Started; TOTAL (Regular Season): 42 Games Played, 22 Games Started, Punt Returns: 2–0, Kick Returns 1–3; TOTAL (Postseason): 3 Games Played, 2 Games Started

John Kerns played three years of high school football and lettered each year. He was All- League in 1939 and 1940. He started playing football at Ohio University, but transferred to Duke and the University of North Carolina when he went into the Marine V–12 program. While in the service, Kerns was voted All-Southern tackle in 1944. After his military obligations, Kerns went back to Ohio State to finish his schooling. There, he played in the East-West Shrine game in 1947 and earned three letters in football.

Kerns was drafted by the Philadelphia Eagles in 1946 (15th round), but elected to play for the Buffalo Bills. Kerns stayed with the Bills for their final three years of the franchise. After the AAFC folded, Kerns went to play in the Canadian Football League.

King, Edward Joseph (Ed)

Position: G; Height: 6'0"; Weight: 217; High School: Boston College (MA); College: Boston College; Born: 5/10/1925, Chelsea, MA; Deceased: 9/18/2006, Burlington, MA; 1948 Buffalo Bills (Regular Season): 15 Games Played, 0 Games Started; 1948 Buffalo Bills (Postseason): 2 Games Played, 0 Games Started; 1949 Buffalo Bills (Regular Season): 5 Games Played, 0 Games Started; 1949 Buffalo Bills (Postseason): 1 Game Played, 0 Games Started; TOTAL (Regular Season): 20 Games Played, 0 Games Started; TOTAL (Postseason): 3 Games Played, 0 Games Started

After football, King joined the accounting firm of Lybrand, Ross Bros. & Montgomery and worked there from 1953 to 1956. From 1975 to 1977, King was president of the New England Council.

In 1978, King beat then-Governor Michael Dukakis in the state's Democratic primary and went on to become Governor of the Commonwealth of Massachusetts. Dukakis beat King four years later and King switched political parties.

King then joined Hill & Knowlton, a public relations firm. In 1996, he was appointed to the Massachusetts Turnpike Authority and was in charge of their real estate holdings.

Former Governor King suffered a fall near his home in Miami in September of 2006. After the fall, King underwent brain surgery to relieve pressure from blood pooling near his brain. He died a few weeks later.

Non-Buffalo Statistics

1950 Baltimore Colts: 12 Games Played

King, Henry Lafayette (Fay) (Dolly)

Position: E; Height: 6'2½"; Weight: 200; High School: Lanier (Macon, GA); College: Georgia; Born: 3/7/1922, Dothan, AL; Deceased: 6/5/1983, Lincolnton, GA; 1946 Buffalo Bisons (Preseason): 1 Game Played, 0 Games Started; 1946 Buffalo Bisons (Regular Season): 12 Games Played, 0 Games Started, Receiving: 30–466 6 TD; 1947 Buffalo Bills (Regular Season): 13 Games Played, 2 Games Started, Receiving: 26–382 6 TD; TOTAL (Regular Season): 25 Games Played, 2 Games Started, Receiving: 56–848 12 TD

Dolly King was an all-around athlete in high school and college. In high school, King was named All-GIAA in 1940 and 1941, set records for the 120-yard high hurdles and the 220-yard low hurdles in 1941, was All-State in football for two years, and was captain of the team for one year. At Georgia, King was All-Sophomore, helped his team to the Rose Bowl in 1942 and was a star athlete in basketball, track and baseball.

King served in the Marine Corps during World War II. There, he played three years with service teams: two years with the Cherry Point Marines and one year with Dick Handley's championship El Toro team.

In 1946, King was drafted by the Los Angeles Rams (seventh round). He chose to play with the Buffalo Bisons and was the starting end for the team for two years. His final two professional years were with the Chicago Rockets/Hornets.

Non-Buffalo Statistics

1948 Chicago Rockets: 14 Games Played, 8 Games Started, Receiving: 50–647 7 TD, Kick Returns: 1–11
1949 Chicago Hornets: 8 Games Played, 3 Games Started, Receiving: 9–88 1 TD, Kick Returns: 1–13

Kirkland, Joseph (Joe)

Position: T; Height: 6'4"; Weight: 265; College: Virginia; Born: 12/18/1923, Roanoke, VA; 1948 Buffalo Bills: On the regular season roster, but did not play; TOTAL: On the regular season roster, but did not play.

Joe Kirkland was drafted by the Boston Yanks in 1946 (13th round). He chose to sign with the Buffalo Bills in 1948, but did not play.

Kisiday, George John

Position: E-G; Height: 6'1"; Weight: 220; High School: Ambridge (PA); College: Duquesne, Columbia; Born: 4/16/1923, Ambridge, PA; Deceased: 11/9/1970, Ambridge, PA; 1948 Buffalo Bills (Regular Season): 14 Games Played, 4 Games Started, Receiving: 1–20; 1948 Buffalo Bills (Postseason): 2 Games Played, 1 Game Started; TOTAL (Regular Season): 14 Games Played, 4 Games Started, Receiving: 1–20; TOTAL (Postseason): 2 Games Played, 1 Game Started

George Kisiday earned two letters as end in high school and earned another two letters as end at Duquesne before heading to Columbia. There, he switched from end to tackle. After serving in the South Pacific, where he played on the Clark Field team under Andy Tomasic, Kisiday returned and signed with the Buffalo Bills. He played one year for the Bills before retiring from football. He was drafted by the New York Giants in 1948 (22nd round).

Kissell, John Jay

Position: T; Height: 6'3"; Weight: 245; High School: Nashua (NH), La Salle Military Academy (Oakdale, NY); College: Boston College; Born: 5/14/1923, Nashua, NH; Deceased: 4/9/1992, Nashua, NH; 1948 Buffalo Bills (Regular Season): 15 Games Played, 0 Games Started; 1948 Buffalo Bills (Postseason): 2 Games Played, 0 Games Started; 1949 Buffalo Bills (Regular Season): 13 Games Played, 0 Games Started; 1949 Buffalo Bills (Postseason): 1 Game Played, 0 Games Started; TOTAL (Regular Season): 28 Games Played, 0 Games Started; TOTAL (Postseason): 3 Games Played, 0 Games Started

Brother of Bills back Vito Kissell, John Kissell was an all-around athlete in both high school and college. At Nashua High School, he lettered in football, basketball and track. He was an All-State tackle for two years. When he attended Boston College, Kissell was named All-Lithuanian for two years, All-New England for one year, and was named to the All-Opponents team.

Kissell was in the Army for three years during World War II. He played for the Camp Hood team and served some time in Europe.

He was drafted by the Los Angeles Rams in 1947 (14th round), but elected to play with the Buffalo Bills. Kissell joined the Bills in 1948 and played the final two seasons of the franchise's history. The Cleveland Browns picked him up in 1950, where he played under Paul Brown for six seasons. In 1953, he played for the Ottawa Roughriders of the Canadian Football League.

Non-Buffalo Statistics

1950 Cleveland Browns: 12 Games Played, 1 Safety
1951 Cleveland Browns: 12 Games Played
1952 Cleveland Browns: 12 Games Played
1953 Ottawa Roughriders (CFL)
1954 Cleveland Browns: 12 Games Played
1955 Cleveland Browns: 12 Games Played
1956 Cleveland Browns: 12 Games Played

Kissell, Vito Joseph

Position: B; Height: 5'10"; Weight: 205; High School: Nashua (NH); College: Holy Cross; Born: 6/13/1927, Nashua, NH; Deceased: 3/19/1997, Morris Plains, NJ; 1949 Buffalo Bills (Regular Season): 13 Games Played, 0 Games Started, Rushing: 10–19, Receiving: 3–37, Interceptions: 1–14, Kick Returns: 1–1; 1949 Buffalo Bills (Postseason): 1 Game Played, 0 Games Started; TOTAL (Regular Season): 13 Games Played, 0 Games Started, Rushing: 10–19, Receiving: 3–37, Interceptions: 1–14, Kick Returns: 1–1; TOTAL (Postseason): 1 Game Played, 0 Games Started

Brother of Bills tackle John Kissell, Vito Kissell was also an all-around athlete in high school. Earning 19 varsity letters—four as a halfback in football, four as a guard in basketball, two as a first baseman in baseball and nine in track—Kissell was a stellar athlete. In college, he played on several All-Star teams in his last two years. He was drafted by the Pittsburgh Steelers (17th round) and the Buffalo Bills (third round) in 1949. Kissell chose to follow his brother and play for the Buffalo Bills. After the Bills folded in 1949, he went on to play a season with the Baltimore Colts.

Non-Buffalo Statistics

1950 Baltimore Colts: 11 Games Played, Rushing: 2–6, Kick Returns: 2–19, Interceptions: 2–7, Extra Points: 11/11, Field Goals: 0/1

Kittrell, M.L. (Kit)

Position: B; Height: 5'9"; Weight: 190; College: Baylor; Born: 11/18/1920; 1947 Buffalo Bills: On the training camp roster, but did not make the regular season roster; TOTAL: On the training camp roster, but did not make the regular season roster.

Kit Kittrell was drafted by the New York Giants in 1944 (21st round). He signed to play with the Buffalo Bills before training camp in 1947, but failed to make the team.

Klenk, Quentin Earl (Quent)

Position: T; Height: 6'2"; Weight: 225; High School: Long Beach Polytechnic (CA); College: USC; Born: 2/3/1919, Long Beach, CA; Deceased: 1/4/1979, San Mateo, CA; 1946 Buffalo Bisons (Preseason): 1 Game Played, 1 Game Started; 1946 Buffalo Bisons (Regular Season): 2 Games Played, 2 Games Started; TOTAL (Regular Season): 2 Games Played, 2 Games Started

In college, Quent Klenk went to the Rose Bowl twice while with USC. He started his professional football career with the Los Angeles Bulldogs. He played with them for three years before he entered the Navy in 1944. While in the Navy, Klenk played two seasons for the championship Fleet City Blue Jackets.

In 1945, Klenk was drafted by the Philadelphia Eagles (18th round). He decided to play for the Buffalo Bisons and played in 2 games for Buffalo. He went to the Chicago Rockets in 1948, where he played eight games for them.

Non-Buffalo Statistics

1947 Chicago Rockets: 8 Games Played, 1 Game Started

Klug, Alfred W. (Al)

Position: T-G; Height: 6'1"; Weight: 220; High School: Bay View (Milwaukee, WI); College: Marquette; Born: 6/1/1920, Milwaukee, WI; 1946 Buffalo Bisons (Regular Season): 11 Games Played, 5 Games Started; TOTAL (Regular Season): 11 Games Played, 5 Games Started

Al Klug was a three-letter man while in high school: football, basketball and track. While at Marquette, Klug was an All-America Honorable Mention from 1940 through 1942. He also played in the East-West Game of 1943. He was drafted by the Chicago Cardinals in 1943 (sixth round).

Klug served in the armed forces during the latter half of World War II. He went overseas in the winter of 1945 and was discharged in August of 1946. After his discharge, Klug signed on with the Buffalo Bisons. He played one year for Buffalo before going to the Baltimore Colts for two seasons.

Non-Buffalo Statistics

1947 Baltimore Colts: 11 Games Played, 6 Games Started
1948 Baltimore Colts: 13 Games Played, 0 Games Started

Klutka, Nicholas (Nick)

Position: E-B; Height: 6'0"; Weight: 190; High School: New Brighton (PA); College: Florida; Born: 1/21/1921, New Brighton, PA; Deceased: 4/2/2003, Van Wert, OH; 1946 Buffalo Bisons (Preseason): 1 Game Played, 1 Game Started; 1946 Buffalo Bisons (Regular Season): 10 Games Played,

4 Games Started, Receiving: 1–9; TOTAL (Regular Season): 10 Games Played, 4 Games Started, Receiving: 1–9

Nick Klutka was a three-letter man while at Florida. He then went on to serve two years in the Air Force during World War II and played service football for the Second Air Force.

Klutka was drafted by the Boston Yanks in 1946 (13th round), but elected to play for the Buffalo Bisons. He saw action in ten games for Buffalo before retiring from football.

Koch, George Theodore

Position: B; Height: 6'0"; Weight: 200; High School: Temple (TX); College: St. Mary's (TX), Baylor; Born: 7/2/1919, Temple, TX; Deceased: 9/5/1966, Temple, TX; 1947 Buffalo Bills (Regular Season): 14 Games Played, 3 Games Started; TOTAL (Regular Season): 14 Games Played, 3 Games Started

George Koch attended Baylor from 1938 through 1939, attaining All-Conference honors in his sophomore year. He then transferred to St. Mary's and gained more ground than the rest of the team combined. In his first season there, he scored 42 points, despite having five touchdowns called back due to penalty.

Koch did not serve in the military. He did, however, work at the shipyards in Houston. The Cleveland Rams drafted Koch in 1941, but in his final game, he ran into a teammate and fractured his neck in three places. In 1942, Koch signed with the Cleveland Rams, but he did not report for training camp. He did arrive to start the 1945 season, but suffered a back injury early in the season and saw little action. He played one game for the Los Angeles Rams in 1946 and a full season for the 1947 Buffalo Bills before retiring from his playing career.

After football, Koch went back to his 3900-acre family ranch near Groesbeck, Texas and coached high school football.

Non-Buffalo Statistics

1945 Cleveland Rams: 5 Games Played, 1 Game Started, Rushing: 12–101, Kick Returns: 1–7
1946 Los Angeles Rams: 1 Game Played

Kodba, Joseph Stephen (Joe) (Jolting Joe)

Position: C-LB; Height: 5'11"; Weight: 190; High School: Michael Washington (South Bend, IN); College: Butler, Purdue; Born: 2/27/1922, Yugoslavia; Deceased: 9/7/2005, Swartz Creek, MI; 1947 Buffalo Bills (Regular Season): 0 Games Played, 0 Games Started; TOTAL (Regular Season): 0 Games Played, 0 Games Started

Joe Kodba started the 1947 season with the Buffalo Bills, but was sent to the Baltimore Colts soon after the season started. He played only one year for the Colts.

Non-Buffalo Statistics

1947 Baltimore Colts: 13 Games Played, 3 Games Started, Interceptions: 1–2

Konetsky, Floyd W.

Position: E; Height: 6'0"; Weight: 197; High School: German Twp. (McClellandtown, PA); College: Florida; Born: 5/26/1920, Marianna, PA; 1947 Buffalo Bills (Regular Season): 0 Games Played, 0 Games Started; TOTAL (Regular Season): 0 Games Played, 0 Games Started

Floyd Konetsky played football for three years at German Township High School. He also participated in shotput and discus. While at the University of Florida, Konetsky played three years at guard and was captain of the team his senior year, while earning All-American Honorable Mention honors.

Konetsky was drafted by the Cleveland Rams in 1943 (29th round) and played for the Rams from 1944 through 1945. While with Cleveland, coach Buff Donelli (1944) transferred him from guard to end. In 1946, Konetsky was traded to the Pittsburgh Steelers, but he was released before the beginning of the season. He joined the Buffalo Bills prior to the 1947 campaign, but was sent to the Baltimore Colts to finish the year.

Floyd Konetsky's brother Ted captained the University of Pittsburgh team and his other brother Francis starred for the University of Florida team. During the off-season, Floyd worked for Thompson Products.

Non-Buffalo Statistics

1944 Cleveland Rams: 8 Games Played, 6 Games Started
1945 Cleveland Rams: 10 Games Played, 4 Games Started
1947 Baltimore Colts: 6 Games Played, 1 Game Started, Interceptions: 1–15

Kormonicki, Milton (Milt)

Position: C; Height: 6'1"; Weight: 205; College: Villanova; Born: 4/15/1927, Philadelphia, PA; 1949 Buffalo Bills: On the preseason roster, but did not make the regular season roster; TOTAL: On the preseason roster, but did not make the regular season roster.

Kosikowski, Frank Leon

Position: E; Height: 6'1"; Weight: 200; High School: Cudahy (WI); College: Marquette, Notre Dame; Born: 7/23/1926, Cudahy, WI; Deceased: 11/17/1991, Milwaukee, WI; 1948 Buffalo Bills (Regular Season): 1 Game Played, 0 Games Started; TOTAL (Regular Season): 1 Game Played, 0 Games Started

Frank Kosikowski played end for his high school team, where he was voted MVP and elected captain. He was a champion boxer for three years and broke the 220-yard dash record. While at Notre Dame and Marquette, he played two seasons at end.

During World War II, Kosikowski spent 21 months in the Navy. He played for the undefeated Fleet City Blue Jackets before leaving the service.

Kosikowski was drafted by the Buffalo Bills in 1947 (16th round) and played one game for Buffalo in 1948. He was sent to the Cleveland Browns, where he finished the 1948 season under Paul Brown.

Non-Buffalo Statistics

1948 Cleveland Browns: 12 Games Played, 0 Games Started

Kostiuk, Michael (Mike)

Position: T; Height: 6'1"; Weight: 220; High School: Hamtramck High School (MI); College: Detroit Tech; Born: 8/1/1919, Krydor, Canada; Deceased: Deceased; 1946 Buffalo Bisons (Preseason): 1 Game Played, 0 Games Started; 1946 Buffalo Bisons (Regular Season): 2 Games Played, 0 Games Started; TOTAL (Regular Season): 2 Games Played, 0 Games Started

While at Hamtramck High School, Mike Kostiuk was All-City in 1935 and 1936, and was captain of his team in 1936. At Detroit Tech, he was named Little All-American his senior year. In 1941, Kostiuk played one game for the Cleveland Rams, as well as spending time with the minor-league Jersey City Giants.

During World War II, Kostiuk served two-and-a-half years in the Infantry. While in the service, he made the Mid-Atlantic All-Service Team. After his military obligations, Kostiuk signed with the Detroit Lions and played six games for them. In 1946, Kostiuk played two games for the Buffalo Bisons before retiring from football.

Non-Buffalo Statistics

1941 Cleveland Rams: 1 Game Played, 0 Games Started
1945 Detroit Lions: 6 Games Played, 3 Games Started

Kozel, Chester Richard (Chet)

Position: T; Height: 6'2"; Weight: 211; High School: Kenosha (WI); College: Mississippi; Born: 10/15/1919, Kenosha, WI; Deceased: 6/27/1982, Kenosha, WI; 1947 Buffalo Bills (Regular Season): 10 Games Played, 2 Games Started, Kick Returns: 1–11; 1948 Buffalo Bills (Regular Season): 1 Game Played, 1 Game Started; TOTAL (Regular Season): 11 Games Played, 3 Games Started, Kick Returns: 1–11

Chet Kozel played tackle for three years while at Kenosha Senior High School. He was captain of the team and earned All-Big Eight honors. While at Ole Miss, Kozel earned All-American Honorable Mention honors (1941).

During World War II, Kozel served five-and-a-half years in the Marine Corps and was stationed in the South Pacific.

Kozel played for the Buffalo Bills in 1947 and one game in 1948, at which point he was sent to the Chicago Rockets to finish the season.

Non-Buffalo Statistics
1948 Chicago Rockets: 5 Games Played, 1 Game Started

Kramer, John Francis (Jack)

Position: T; Height: 6'0"; Weight: 220; High School: Solomon Juneau (Milwaukee, WI); College: Niagara, Marquette; Born: 7/29/1919, Milwaukee, WI; Deceased: 12/15/1978, Milwaukee, WI; 1946 Buffalo Bisons (Regular Season): 10 Games Played, 2 Games Started; TOTAL (Regular Season): 10 Games Played, 2 Games Started

John Kramer began his college career at Niagara University, before shifting to Marquette. During the war, Kramer served as a Naval pilot. He was awarded the Air Medal for his service.

Kramer founded Janco Supply, Incorporated. He was there for 49 years and had three sons who ran the business.

In 1945, the Chicago Cardinals drafted Kramer in the 20th round. He chose to sign with the Buffalo Bisons and played ten games for them.

Kuffel, Raymond Francis (Ray)

Position: E; Height: 6'3"; Weight: 210; High School: Messmer (Milwaukee, WI); College: Notre Dame, Marquette; Born: 12/9/1921, Milwaukee, WI; Deceased: 12/22/1974, Brookfield, WI; 1947 Buffalo Bills (Regular Season): 7 Games Played, 2 Games Started, Receiving: 3-37; TOTAL (Regular Season): 7 Games Played, 2 Games Started, Receiving: 3-37

Ray Kuffel was an All-Conference end for Messmer High School. While in college, Kuffel was All-Catholic in 1942 and 1946 and was captain of his team in 1946. He was drafted by the Chicago Cardinals in 1944 (20th round) and by the Buffalo Bills in 1947 (third round). After graduating from Marquette in 1947, Kuffel signed with the Bills and played seven games for silver and blue. From 1948 through 1949, Kuffel played for the Chicago Rockets/Hornets.

Non-Buffalo Statistics
1948 Chicago Rockets: 14 Games Played, 7 Games Started, Receiving: 19-365 3 TD, Kick Returns: 1-16
1949 Chicago Hornets: 2 Games Played, 0 Games Started

Kulbitski, Victor John (Vic)

Position: B; Height: 5'11"; Weight: 205; High School: Central (Red Wing, MN); College: Notre Dame, Minnesota; Born: 6/15/1921, Virginia, MN; Deceased: 5/23/1998, West St. Paul, MN; 1946 Buffalo Bisons (preseason): 1 Game Played, 1 Game Started; 1946 Buffalo Bisons (Regular Season): 13 Games Played, 7 Games Started, Rushing: 97-605 2 TD,

Receiving: 1–0, Interceptions: 1–20, Kick Returns: 5–81; 1947 Buffalo Bills (Regular Season): 13 Games Played, 7 Games Started, Rushing: 56–249 1 TD, Receiving: 9–117 4 TD, Punt Returns: 1–13, Kick Returns: 1–19, Interceptions: 1–14, Extra Points: 1/1; 1948 Buffalo Bills (Regular Season): 16 Games Played, 5 Games Started, Rushing: 40–152, Receiving: 3–37, Kick Returns: 1–18, Extra Points: 8/10; 1948 Buffalo Bills (Postseason): 2 Games Played, 0 Games Started, Rushing: 2–1, Receiving: 1–14; TOTAL (Regular Season): 42 Games Played, 19 Games Started, Rushing: 193–1006 3 TD, Receiving: 13–154 4 TD, Interceptions: 2–34, Punt Returns: 1–13, Kick Returns: 7–118, Extra Points: 9/11; TOTAL (Postseason): 2 Games Played, 0 Games Started, Rushing: 2–1, Receiving: 1–14

Vic Kulbitski was an All-State guard and fullback while in high school. While in college, he played on two national championship teams. As the only Bison—other than John Perko—to play under Red Dawson before joining Buffalo, Kulbitski played on Minnesota's national championship team in 1942. In 1943, while serving in the Marine Corps, Kulbitski played on the 1943 Notre Dame undefeated team. That same year, Kulbitski earned All-America Honorable Mention honors.

Kulbitski was drafted by the Philadelphia Eagles in 1944 (seventh round). After returning from the war, he signed with the Buffalo Bisons and stayed with the team for three years.

Lahar, Harold Wade (Hal)

Position: G; Height: 6'0"; Weight: 225; High School: Central (Oklahoma City, OK); College: Oklahoma; Born: 7/14/1919, Durant, OK; Deceased: 10/20/2003, Dallas, TX; 1946 Buffalo Bisons (Preseason): 1 Game Played, 0 Games Started; 1946 Buffalo Bisons (Regular Season): 12 Games Played, 3 Games Started; 1947 Buffalo Bills (Regular Season): 14 Games Played, 14 Games Started; 1948 Buffalo Bills (Regular Season): 15 Games Played, 13 Games Started; 1948 Buffalo Bills (Postseason): 2 Games Played, 1 Game Started; TOTAL (Regular Season): 41 Games Played, 30 Games Started; TOTAL (Postseason): 2 Games Played, 1 Game Started

Hal Lahar was All-State during high school. At Oklahoma, he continued with All-State honors and was named All-Conference. Lahar was also a member of the Big Six Championship Basketball team in 1938. He graduated from Oklahoma in 1941. At that point, he was drafted by the Chicago Bears (ninth round in 1941) and played one season for the team.

In 1945, Lahar joined the Navy where served 13 months in the military. After his discharge, he joined the Buffalo Bisons, playing three seasons for the team.

After retiring from his playing career, Lahar went into coaching. From 1969 through 1973, Lahar was an assistant coach at Arkansas and West Virginia. Also during that time, he was head coach at Colgate (two stints) and Houston. He went on to become Athletic Director at Colgate from 1974 through 1984 and was the Associate Commissioner of the Southwest Athletic Conference.

Non-Buffalo Statistics

1941 Chicago Bears: 8 Games Played, 0 Games Started, Extra Points: 1/3, Field Goals: 1/1

Lanza, Nicholas, Jr. (Nick)

Position: E; Height: 6'1"; Weight: 190; College: Rice Institute; 1949 Buffalo Bills: On the preseason roster, but did not make the regular season roster.; TOTAL: On the preseason roster, but did not make the regular season roster.

Larkin, James E. (Jim)

Position: G; Height: 6'1"; Weight: 230; High School: Oil City (PA); College: Lock Haven; Born: 1921; 1946 Buffalo Bisons (Preseason): 1 Game Played, 0 Games Started; 1946 Buffalo Bisons (Regular Season): 1 Game Played, 0 Games Started; 1947 Buffalo Bills: On the training camp roster, but did not make the regular season roster; TOTAL (Regular Season): 1 Game Played, 0 Games Started

Lecture, James Wayne Jr. (Jim)

Position: G; Height: 5'10"; Weight: 220; High School: St. George (Evanston, IL); College: Washington-St. Louis, Northwestern; Born: 10/29/1924, Chicago, IL; Deceased: 12/19/1999, Cambridge, WI; 1946 Buffalo Bisons (Regular Season): 2 Games Played, 0 Games Started; TOTAL (Regular Season): 2 Games Played, 0 Games Started

Jim Lecture was drafted by the Philadelphia Eagles in 1946 (eighth round). He chose to play for the Buffalo Bisons, but was only on the field for two games.

Leonetti, Robert Phillip (Bob)

Position: G; Height: 6'0"; Weight: 185; High School: Lafayette (Buffalo, NY); College: Wake Forest; Born: 1/1/1923, Mount Carmel, PA; Deceased: 8/16/1973, Des Moines, IA; 1948 Buffalo Bills (Regular Season): 1 Game Played, 0 Games Started; TOTAL (Regular Season): 1 Game Played, 0 Games Started

Bob Leonetti was an All-America Honorable Mention selection at Wake Forest and played in the 1948 College All-Star Game. He served three years in the Army during World War II and was stationed in Europe.

He was drafted by both the San Francisco 49ers (ninth round) and the Philadelphia Eagles (ninth round) in 1947. He chose to play for the Buffalo Bills, but saw action in only one game. He was sent to the Chicago Rockets where he finished his playing career.

Non-Buffalo Statistics

1948 Brooklyn Dodgers: 9 Games Played, 0 Games Started

Livingstone, Robert Edward (Bob)

Position: B; Height: 6'0"; Weight: 173; High School: Hammond (IN); College: Notre Dame; Born: 5/11/1922, Hammond, IN; 1949 Buffalo Bills (Regular Season): 6 Games Played, 0 Games Started, Rushing: 1-0; 1949 Buffalo Bills (Postseason): 1 Game Played, 0 Games Started, Punt Returns: 2-19, Kick Returns: 2-33, Interceptions: 2-14; TOTAL (Regular Season): 6 Games Played, 0 Games Started, Rushing: 1-0; TOTAL (Postseason): 1 Game Played, 0 Games Started, Punt Returns: 2-19, Kick Returns: 2-33, Interceptions: 2-14

Bob Livingstone was drafted by the Chicago Bears in 1945 (22nd round) and the Chicago Rockets in 1947 (14th round). He played for the Rockets in 1948 and part of the 1949 season. He was sent to Buffalo where he finished the 1949 season. The Baltimore Colts drafted him in the second round of the dispersal draft and he played for the team for one year.

Non-Buffalo Statistics

1948 Chicago Rockets: 13 Games Played, 5 Games Started, Rushing: 55-174, Receiving: 15-240 2 TD, Punt Returns: 3-24, Kick Returns: 9-211
1949 Chicago Hornets: 6 Games Played, 0 Games Started, Receiving: 3-80
1949 Buffalo Bills & Chicago Hornets: Interceptions: 1-6, Punt Returns: 17-292 1 TD, Kick Returns: 6-85
1950 Baltimore Colts: 11 Games Played, Rushing: 1-(-3), Punt Returns: 3-33, Kick Returns: 1-11, Interceptions: 3-61, 1 Fumble

Logel, Robert James (Bob)

Position: E; Height: 6'3"; Weight: 210; High School: East Aurora (NY); College: Sampson CC NC; Born: 7/29/1928, East Aurora, NY; Deceased: 7/4/2001, Holland, NY; 1949 Buffalo Bills: Played on the preseason roster, but did not make the regular season roster; TOTAL: Played on the preseason roster, but did not make the regular season roster.

Bob Logel was on the roster of three teams in 1949: the Buffalo Bills, the Chicago Hornets and the Bethlehem Bulldogs. He was a fullback in high school, but did not play on the collegiate level.

Lukens, James Willie Jr. (Jim)

Position: E; Height: 6'4"; Weight: 205; High School: Swarthmore (PA); College: Washington & Lee; Born: 9/6/1924, Chester, PA; Deceased: 10/21/2002 Wernerville, VA; 1949 Buffalo Bills (Regular Season): 12 Games Played, 11 Games Started, Receiving: 24-249 2 TD; 1949 Buffalo Bills (Postseason): 1 Game Played, 1 Game Started, Receiving: 4-32; TOTAL (Regular Season): 12 Games Played, 11 Games Started, Receiving: 24-249 2 TD; TOTAL (Postseason): 1 Game Played, 1 Game Started, Receiving: 4-32

Jim Lukens was a three-sport athlete at Washington & Lee (football, basketball and track). He received All-State as well as All-American Honorable Mention honors, and was one of the nation's leading receivers in 1948 with 38 catches for 547 yards. He won the Forest Fletcher award as the track team MVP and was inducted into the Washington & Lee Hall of Fame in 1999.

Lukens was drafted by the Boston Yanks in 1948 (21st round), but chose to play for the Buffalo Bills. He finished his football career after the 1949 season.

Maggioli, Achille Fred (Chick)

Position: B; Height: 5'11"; Weight: 178; High School: Mishawaka (IN); College: Indiana, Notre Dame, Illinois; Born: 5/17/1922, Mishawaka, IN; 1948 Buffalo Bills (Regular Season): 9 Games Played, 1 Game Started, Passing: 1–1, Rushing: 11–27, Receiving: 2–23, Interceptions: 1–7, Punting: 2–95, Punt Returns: 1–0, Kick Returns: 2–38; 1948 Buffalo Bills (Postseason): 2 Games Played, 1 Game Started, Interceptions: 1–2; TOTAL (Regular Season): 9 Games Played, 1 Game Started, Passing: 1–1, Rushing: 11–27, Receiving: 2–23, Interceptions: 1–7, Punting: 2–95, Punt Returns: 1–0, Kick Returns: 2–38; TOTAL (Postseason): 2 Games Played, 1 Game Started, Interceptions: 1–2

Chick Maggioli was at Indiana for only one year before joining the Marine V–12 program at Notre Dame. Maggioli served in Okinawa, where he earned a Purple Heart when he was blown off of a bridge. He then was sent to China for almost a year before returning stateside.

Maggioli was drafted by the Washington Redskins in 1946 (eleventh round). He also received interest from the Los Angeles Rams, but decided to follow his former Notre Dame coach Clem Crowe to Buffalo.

Maggioli was injured during the 1948 season and required offseason surgery. He had heard rumors of the Bills relocating so he did not re-sign with Buffalo, but signed with the Detroit Lions instead. After one season with the lions, Coach Bo McMillan tried to scare Maggioli into signing a contract at a lower salary. Maggioli refused and McMillian put Chick on a 48-hour waiver. As soon as Maggioli was waived, Clem Crowe—now coach of the Baltimore Colts—called and immediately offered Chick a contract. McMillan also called to offer a contract after the 48-hour waiver elapsed, but Maggioli was already headed to Baltimore.

After one season with the Colts, Maggioli was offered a job with a trucking company and accepted. The Green Bay Packers were interested in signing Chick, but he refused and stayed in the business world. After being in the trucking business for a few years, Maggioli moved to Indiana and opened a restaurant.

Non-Buffalo Statistics
1949 Detroit Lions: 12 Games Played, 0 Games Started, Receiving: 1–9, Interceptions: 3–46, 1 Fumble Return TD
1950 Baltimore Colts: 8 Games Played, Interceptions: 8–165

Manders, Clarence Edward (Pug)

Position: B; Height: 6'0"; Weight: 202; High School: Milbank (SD); College: Drake; Born: 5/5/1913, Milbank, SD; Deceased: 1/20/1985, Des

Moines, IA; 1947 Buffalo Bills (Regular Season): 5 Games Played, 0 Games Started, Rushing: 3–15; TOTAL (Regular Season): 5 Games Played, 0 Games Started, Rushing: 3–15

Pug Manders was the younger brother of Jack Manders, who played eight years for the Chicago Bears and was inducted into the South Dakota Sports Hall of Fame. Drafted by the Brooklyn Dodgers in 1939 (second round), Manders immediately signed on with the Dodgers after graduating from Drake. He played six years for Brooklyn before playing a year with the Boston Yanks. Manders then joined the AAFC New York Yankees for a season and finished his career after a season with the Buffalo Bills.

Non-Buffalo Statistics

Played for 1939 Brooklyn Dodgers: 11 Games Played, 9 Games Started, Rushing: 114–482 2 TD, Receiving: 3–22
Played for 1940 Brooklyn Dodgers: 11 Games Played, 11 Games Started, Rushing: 80–311 5 TD, Passing: 1–1 0 0 TD 0 INT, Receiving: 1–38 1 TD
Played for 1941 Brooklyn Dodgers: 11 Games Played, 11 Games Started, Rushing: 111–486 5 TD, Receiving: 6–67
Played for 1942 Brooklyn Dodgers: 11 Games Played, 11 Games Started, Rushing: 93–316 6 TD, Passing 0–1 0, Receiving: 4–53
Played for 1943 Brooklyn Dodgers: 10 Games Played, 9 Games Started, Rushing: 89–266 3 TD, Passing: 4–5 31 1 TD 0 INT, Receiving: 5–68 1 TD
Played for 1944 Brooklyn Tigers: 10 Games Played, 9 Games Started, Rushing: 127–430 5 TD, Passing: 9–34 96 0 TD 4 INT, Receiving: 6–78
Played for 1945 Boston Yanks: 10 Games Played, 10 Games Started, Rushing: 76–238 6 TD, Passing: 5–9 42 0 TD 1 INT
Played for 1946 New York Yankees: 13 Games Played, 4 Games Started, Rushing: 49–168 3 TD, Passing: 2–3 14 0 TD 0 INT, Receiving: 3–49

Martinelli, Pasquale Joseph (Patsy) (Pat)

Position: C; Height: 6'0"; Weight: 227; High School: Dunmore (PA); College: Scranton; Born: 7/27/1919, Rockville, MD; Deceased: 9/7/1992, Rockville, MD; 1946 Buffalo Bisons (Preseason): 1 Game Played, 0 Games Started; 1946 Buffalo Bisons (Regular Season): 3 Games Played, 0 Games Started, Interceptions: 1–12; TOTAL (Regular Season): 3 Games Played, 0 Games Started, Interceptions: 1–12

Pat Martinelli served three years in the Army during World War II, 18 months of which was spent in Europe as a Corporal in an anti–aircraft unit. Martinelli was selected All-ETO while in the service. Upon his return, Martinelli signed with the Buffalo Bills, but only played three regular season games. Martinelli also spent time playing for the Philadelphia Eagles and the Wilmington Clippers.

Maskas, John J.

Position: T-G; Height: 5'11"; Weight: 212; High School: Monessen (PA); College: North Carolina, Virginia Tech; Born: 8/15/1920, Chios, Greece;

Deceased: 2/9/1983, Manahawkin, NJ; 1947 Buffalo Bills (Regular Season): 9 Games Played, 0 Games Started; 1949 Buffalo Bills (Regular Season): 11 Games Played, 0 Games Started; TOTAL (Regular Season): 20 Games Played, 0 Games Started

John Maskas was one of the few foreign-born football players of his time. Drafted in 1947 by Buffalo (tenth round) and the Boston Yanks (14th round), Maskas chose the Buffalo Bills. He played two seasons for Buffalo before retiring from football. Maskas was also a star heavyweight boxer and wrestler while at Virginia Tech.

Matisi, John Bernard

Position: T; Height: 6'2"; Weight: 226; High School: Union Endicott (NY); College: Duquesne; Born: 11/2/1920, New York, NY; Deceased: 4/29/1997, Youngstown, OH; 1946 Buffalo Bisons (Preseason): 1 Game Played, 0 Games Started; 1946 Buffalo Bisons (Regular Season): 10 Games Played, 0 Games Started; TOTAL (Regular Season): 10 Games Played, 0 Games Started

John Matisi was an All-State football and basketball player in high school. While in college, he was captain of the football team and made All-East in 1942. His athletic prowess was a family trait, as his brother Tony was an All-American tackle at Pittsburgh and his brother Joe was a heavyweight boxer.

He was drafted by the Brooklyn Dodgers in 1943 (seventh round) and played four games for the team before entering the military. Matisi served three years in the Army during World War II. After the war, Matisi resumed his professional football career by joining the Buffalo Bisons in 1946. He played ten games for the franchise.

Non-Buffalo Statistics

1943 Brooklyn Dodgers: 4 Games, Interceptions: 1–13

Mazza, Vincent L. (Vince)

Position: E-G; Height: 6'1"; Weight: 216; High School: Trott Vocational (Niagara Falls, NY); College: (None); Born: 3/25/1925, Niagara Falls, NY; Deceased: 12/5/1993, Winona, Canada; 1947 Buffalo Bills (Regular Season): 13 Games Played, 0 Games Started, Receiving: 2–11, Interceptions: 1–26; 1948 Buffalo Bills (Regular Season): 14 Games Played, 2 Games Started, Interceptions: 1–5 1 TD; 1948 Buffalo Bills (Postseason): 2 Games Played, 1 Game Started; 1949 Buffalo Bills (Regular Season): 13 Games Played, 1 Game Started; 1949 Buffalo Bills (Postseason): 1 Game Played, 0 Games Started; TOTAL (Regular Season): 40 Games Played, 3 Games Started, Receiving: 2–11, Interceptions: 2–31 1 TD; TOTAL (Postseason): 3 Games Played, 1 Game Started

Non-Buffalo Statistics

1945 Detroit Lions: 5 Games Played, 1 Game Started
1946 Detroit Lions: 1 Game Played, 0 Games Started

McLellan, William (Will)

Position: T; Height: 5'11½"; Weight: 235; High School: Greenfield (MA); College: Brown; Born: 10/4/1925, Greenfield, MA; 1949 Buffalo Bills: Played on the preseason roster, but did not make the regular season roster; TOTAL: Played on the preseason roster, but did not make the regular season roster.

Will McLellan was an All-State tackle in high school, earning three letters. He also earned three letters while at Brown, as well as All-New England and All-East Honors from 1946 through 1948. He was chosen to play in the Blue-Grey game in 1948.

Morton, John Joseph (Jack)

Position: E; Height: 6'0"; Weight: 200; High School: East St. Louis (IL), Maryland Heights HS (MO); College: Missouri, Purdue; Born: 7/22/1922, East St. Louis, IL; Deceased: 12/17/1983, Manteno, IL; 1947 Buffalo Bills (Regular Season): 2 Games Played, 0 Games Started; 1948 Buffalo Bills (Regular Season): 1 Game Played, 0 Games Started; TOTAL (Regular Season): 3 Games Played, 0 Games Started

Jack Morton earned three letters and All-Conference honors as an end in high school. While at Missouri, Morton made All-American Honorable Mention, as well as All-Big Six. He played professionally for the Chicago Bears, Los Angeles Dons and the Buffalo Bills.

Non-Buffalo Statistics

1945 Chicago Bears: 8 Games Played, 1 Game Started, Receiving: 1–18
1946 Los Angeles Dons: 12 Games Played, 1 Game Started, Receiving: 4–44 1 TD, Interceptions: 1–11

Mutryn, Chester A. (Chet)

Position: B; Height: 5'9"; Weight: 179; High School: Cathedral Latin (Cleveland, OH); College: Xavier (OH); Born: 3/12/1921, Cleveland, OH; Deceased: 3/24/1995, Cleveland, OH; 1946 Buffalo Bisons (Regular Season): 13 Games Played, 8 Games Started, Rushing: 57–289 1 TD, Receiving: 7–168 3 TD, Fumble Returns: 2–67 1 TD, Kick Returns: 4–79; 1947 Buffalo Bills (Regular Season): 14 Games Played, 12 Games Started, Rushing: 140–868 9 TD, Receiving: 10–176 2 TD, Interceptions: 1–11, Punt Returns: 13–187, Kick Returns: 21–691 1 TD, Extra Points: 1/2; 1948 Buffalo Bills (Regular Season): 16 Games Played, 14 Games Started, Rushing: 147–823 10 TD, Passing: 2–6 21, Receiving: 39–794 5 TD, Punt Returns: 10–171 1 TD, Kick Returns: 19–500; 1948 Buffalo Bills (Postseason): 2 Games Played, 1 Game Started, Rushing: 19–62, Receiving: 2–5, Kick Returns: 1–18; 1949 Buffalo Bills (Regular Season): 12 Games Played, 12 Games Started, Rushing: 131–696 5 TD, Receiving: 29–333, Punt Returns: 7–77, Kick Returns: 10–224; 1949 Buffalo Bills (Postseason): 1 Game Played, 1 Game Started, Rushing: 8–24, Receiving: 6–81 2 TD, Kick

Returns: 2–59; TOTAL (Regular Season): 55 Games Played, 46 Games Started, Rushing: 475–2676 25 TD, Passing: 2–6 21, Receiving: 85–1471 10 TD, Interceptions: 1–11, Fumble Returns: 2–67 1 TD, Punt Returns: 30–435 1 TD, Kick Returns: 54–1494 1 TD, Extra Points: 1/2; TOTAL (Postseason): 3 Games Played, 2 Games Started, Rushing: 27–86, Receiving: 8–86 2 TD, Kick Returns: 3–77

At Cathedral Latin High School (Cleveland, OH), Chet Mutryn earned All-Scholastic honors. Moving on to Xavier, Mutryn was a two-time Little All-American selection and was the leading scorer for his team each year. In 1942, he set records for the most touchdowns (12) and most points (96) in a season. He received Xavier's highest award: The Legion of Honor Medal, which is given for accomplishments in both athletics and academics.

He was drafted by the "Steagles" in 1943 (20th round), but was serving in the Navy at the time. Upon his return from two years of military duty he joined the Cleveland Browns, but was sent to Buffalo before the inaugural season of the franchise. He went on to become a three-time first team All-Conference player while in the AAFC. When the AAFC folded, Mutryn played a season for the Baltimore Colts before retiring from his playing career.

After retiring from his playing career, Mutryn went to work for the City of Cleveland doing real estate assessments.

In Dr. David Shapiro's book, *The 135 Greatest Pro Running Backs: How They Stack Up Against Each Other*, Mutryn was rated number one of the pre–1950 group, putting him ahead of backs Steve Van Buren, Bronco Nagurski, Spec Sanders and Beattie Feathers.

Mutryn was honored Outstanding Athlete by the Polish Everybody's Daily and the Quarterback Club of Buffalo and is a member of the Cathedral Latin School, Greater Cleveland, and Xavier Athletic Halls of Fame. He also received the Good Joe of 1988 award, as well as the Cleveland Society Heritage Award, which is given to members who foster the cultural heritage of Poland and promote the principles of American citizenship.

Non-Buffalo Statistics

1950 Baltimore Colts: 12 Games Played, Rushing: 108–355 2 TD, Passing 1–1 4 0 TD 0 INT, Receiving: 36–379 2 TD 5 Fumbles

Nelson, Herbert Russell (Herb)

Position: E; Height: 6'4"; Weight: 218; High School: William Hall (West Hartford, CT); College: Pennsylvania; Born: 4/25/1921, Hartford, CT; Deceased: 7/18/2004, Westwood, MA; 1946 Buffalo Bisons (Regular Season): 12 Games Played, 8 Games Started, Rushing: 1–1, Receiving: 4–47; TOTAL (Regular Season): 12 Games Played, 8 Games Started, Rushing: 1–1, Receiving: 4–47

Non-Buffalo Statistics

1947 Brooklyn Dodgers: 14 Games Played, 4 Games Started, Receiving: 2–17
1948 Brooklyn Dodgers: 4 Games Played, 1 Game Started

O'Connor, William Joseph (Bill)(Bucky)

Position: G; College: Notre Dame; Deceased: 9/13/1990, Oklahoma City, OK; 1949 Buffalo Bills: On the preseason roster, but did not make the regular season roster; TOTAL: On the preseason roster, but did not make the regular season roster.

Not to be confused with Bill "Zeke" O'Connor, who was the other Bill O'Connor at Notre Dame at the time, "Bucky" O'Connor was drafted by the Los Angeles Rams in 1948 (18th round). He was at Notre Dame in 1942 and 1946 and served in the Army between those years.

O'Connor, William Francis Jr. (Bill) (Zeke)

Position: E; Height: 6'4"; Weight: 220; High School: Mount St. Michael's (Bronx, NY); College: Notre Dame; Born: 5/2/1926, New York, NY; 1948 Buffalo Bills (Regular Season): 15 Games Played, 4 Games Started, Kick Returns: 1–0; 1948 Buffalo Bills (Postseason): 2 Games Played, 1 Game Started, Receiving: 6–61 1 TD; TOTAL (Regular Season): 15 Games Played, 4 Games Started, Kick Returns: 1–0; TOTAL (Postseason): 2 Games Played, 1 Game Started, Receiving: 6–61 1 TD

Zeke O'Connor was voted Most Valuable End in high school in both 1942 and 1943. In 1944, he entered the V–12 program at Notre Dame. During the two years he spent in the Navy, O'Connor played for the famed Great Lakes team under Paul Brown.

In 1948, O'Connor was drafted by the Buffalo Bills (4th round) and also received interest from the Green Bay Packers. He chose to play with Buffalo due to his numerous Notre Dame connections already on the team, including George Ratterman and Clem Crowe. He was traded to the Cleveland Browns after the 1948 season and stayed there until he was cut before the 1950 campaign. At that point, O'Connor played for the Jersey City Giants before re–entering the NFL as a member of the New York Yanks in 1951. He played the 1952 and 1953 seasons for the Toronto Argonauts, at which point he retired from football to concentrate on his business career.

While with the Yanks, O'Connor earned his Master's Degree from Columbia. Also at that time, Zeke joined Sears in Canada and stayed there for 31 years, retiring as Vice-President of Public Relations. During that time, he met Sir Edmund Hillary, who is best known as the first person to climb Mt. Everest. After reaching the summit, Hillary was enamored with the Nepalese people and devoted his life to helping the Sherpas of the region. Zeke decided to help Hillary and formed the Canadian chapter of the Sir Edmund Hillary Foundation. The Foundation concentrated on building schools and hospitals for the Sherpa people, as well as helping with education and reforestation projects in the region. O'Connor was president of the organization for over 30 years, at which point he turned it over to his daughter Karen in 2008.

Non-Buffalo Statistics

1949 Cleveland Browns: 9 Games Played, 1 Game Started
1950 Jersey City Giants
1951 New York Yankees: 12 Games Played, Receiving: 14–192
1952 Toronto Argonauts
1953 Toronto Argonauts

Oristaglio, Robert Peter (Bob)

Position: E; Height: 6'2"; Weight: 214; High School: Southeast Catholic (Philadelphia, PA); College: Pennsylvania; Born: 4/6/1924, Philadelphia, PA; Deceased: 2/14/1995, York, PA; 1949 Buffalo Bills (Regular Season): 13 Games Played, 0 Games Started, Receiving: 1–14; 1949 Buffalo Bills (Postseason): 1 Game Played, 0 Games Started; TOTAL (Regular Season): 13 Games Played, 0 Games Started, Receiving: 1–14; TOTAL (Postseason): 1 Game Played, 0 Games Started

Bob Oristaglio played fullback for three years in high school as well as played first base for the baseball team. At Penn, he earned All-East honors in 1947. Oristaglio played for the Buffalo Bills in 1949 before jumping from the Baltimore Colts to the Cleveland Browns and finally to the Philadelphia Eagles. His last season of professional football was 1952.

Non-Buffalo Statistics

1950 Baltimore Colts: 12 Games Played, 3 Games Started, Receiving: 14–134, Kick Returns: 3–32
1951 Cleveland Browns: 12 Games Played, Receiving: 1–20 1 TD
1952 Philadelphia Eagles: 4 Games Played

Paffrath, Robert William (Bob)

Position: B; Height: 5'8"; Weight: 190; High School: College: Minnesota; Born: 7/3/1918, Mankato, MN; Deceased: 5/21/2005, Beaverton, OR; 1947 Buffalo Bills: On the training camp roster, but did not make the regular season roster; TOTAL: On the training camp roster, but did not make the regular season roster.

Bob Paffrath was drafted by the Green Bay Packers in 1941 (third round). He joined the Brooklyn Dodgers in 1946, but finished the season with the Miami Seahawks.

Non-Buffalo Statistics

1946 Brooklyn Dodgers: 5 Games Played, 0 Games Started, Rushing: 8–19 1 TD, Passing: 0–1–0 0 TD 0 INT, Receiving: 2–(–3)
1946 Miami Seahawks: 7 Games Played, 2 Games Started, Rushing: 23–81 1 TD, Receiving: 2-(–3), Punts: 1–50, Punt Returns: 1–1, Kick Returns: 4–76

Pasqua, Joseph (Joe)

Position: T; Height: 6'2"; Weight: 235; College: Southern Methodist; Born: 7/31/1917, Dallas, TX; 1948 Buffalo Bills: On the training camp roster, but did not make the regular season roster; TOTAL: On the training camp roster, but did not make the regular season roster.

Perko, John Frank (Perk)

Position: G; Height: 6'1"; Weight: 225; High School: Ely (MN); College: Minnesota, Notre Dame; Born: 4/8/1918, Ely, MN; Deceased: 6/7/1994, Hibbing, MN; 1946 Buffalo Bisons (Preseason): 1 Game Played, 1 Game Started; 1946 Buffalo Bisons (Regular Season): 14 Games Played, 11 Games Started; TOTAL (Regular Season): 14 Games Played, 11 Games Started

John Perko began his college football career at Minnesota. He played first string along side Vic Kulbitski, the only other Buffalo Bison to play under Red Dawson before joining the team.

In 1943, Perko transferred to Notre Dame as a Marine Corps trainee and helped the Fighting Irish to the 1943 championship. He was discharged as a First Lieutenant on September 11, 1946 after serving 15 months in the South Pacific and Japan. He joined the Bisons training camp two days after going through the separation center at Great Lakes.

Pezelski, Joseph C. (Joe)

Position: B; Height: 5'10"; Weight: 182; High School: Kulpmont (PA); College: Villanova; Born: 1920; 1946 Buffalo Bisons (Preseason): 1 Game Played, 0 Games Started; TOTAL (Preseason): 1 Game Played, 0 Games Started

Joe Pezelski was All-State for two years while in high school and was also the leading scorer for his team one year. Accolades continued while he attended Villanova, as Pezelski earned All-America Honorable Mention honors twice.

Pezelski served 31 months in the Marine Corps with 15 of those months spent overseas.

Pfuhl, Richard (Dick)

Position: B; Height: 6'3"; Weight: 230; College: St. Louis; Born: 4/5/1919; 1947 Buffalo Bills (Regular Season): 0 Games Played, 0 Games Started; TOTAL (Regular Season): 0 Games Played, 0 Games Started

Dick Pfuhl was a First Lieutenant in the Marine Corps and fought the Pacific for 37 months. His tour included stops in Guam and Okinawa, where he was wounded in the leg.

Pfuhl returned to school, but left in 1945 to play for the Cleveland Rams. He signed a contract on November 9, 1945, but reported overweight and with a groin injury (suffered in his last collegiate game). He recovered enough to make the Buffalo Bills squad in 1947, but did not see action.

Pirro, Rocco Albert (Rocky)

Position: T-G; Height: 6'0"; Weight: 235; High School: Solvay (NY); College: Catholic University; Born: 6/30/1916, Syracuse, NY; Deceased:

1/26/1995, Solvay, NY; 1946 Buffalo Bisons (Preseason): 1 Game Played, 0 Games Started; 1946 Buffalo Bisons (Regular Season): 13 Games Played, 12 Games Started; 1947 Buffalo Bills (Regular Season): 14 Games Played, 14 Games Started; 1948 Buffalo Bills (Regular Season): 14 Games Played, 13 Games Started; 1948 Buffalo Bills (Postseason): 2 Games Played, 1 Game Started; 1949 Buffalo Bills (Regular Season): 12 Games Played, 12 Games Started; 1949 Buffalo Bills (Postseason): 1 Game Played, 1 Game Started; TOTAL (Regular Season): 53 Games Played, 51 Games Started; TOTAL (Postseason): 3 Games Played, 2 Games Started

Rocco Pirro started out as a tackle with Solvay High School, but switched to fullback by the time he reached Dutch Bergman's Catholic University team. He was drafted by the Pittsburgh Steelers in 1940 (twelfth round) and was a blocking back with the Steelers for two years.

In 1942, Pirro entered the Navy and served four years during World War II. During his time in the Navy, Pirro played center for the famous Fleet City Blue Jacket squad of 1945.

In 1946, he joined the Buffalo Bisons and played all four years of the franchise's existence. Pirro went on to be a line coach for the Baltimore Colts in 1950, before going on to coach the Montreal Alouettes of the Canadian Football League. He finished by coaching at Syracuse University for twenty-three years.

He was elected to the Catholic University and Syracuse University Halls of Fame. He also spent a year as a New York State Assemblyman and then became the executive director of the Solvay-Geddes Youth Center.

Non-Buffalo Statistics

1940 Pittsburgh Steelers: 9 Games Played, 0 Games Started
1941 Pittsburgh Steelers: 11 Games Played, 1 Game Started Rushing: 1–1, Receiving: 2–31, Interceptions: 1–2

Piskor, Roman John (Ray)

Position: T; Height: 6'0"; Weight: 245; High School: North Tonawanda (NY); College: Niagara; Born: 8/9/1919, North Tonawanda, NY; Deceased: 8/1981, North Tonawanda, NY; 1947 Buffalo Bills: On the training camp roster, but did not make the regular season roster; TOTAL: On the training camp roster, but did not make the regular season roster.

A North Tonawanda High School and Niagara University product, Ray Piskor played three years of professional football. All three years were in the All-America Football Conference. In 1946, Piskor played twelve games for the New York Yankees. He then signed with Buffalo, but failed to make the training camp cut and landed with the Cleveland Browns. He finished his career with the Chicago Rockets.

Non-Buffalo Statistics

1946 New York Yankees: 12 Games Played, 7 Games Started
1947 Cleveland Browns: 10 Games Played, 1 Game Started
1948 Chicago Rockets: 12 Games Played, 2 Games Started

Pizza, Frank

Position: T; Height: 6'2"; Weight: 268; College: Toledo; Born: 9/26/1925, Toledo, OH; 1948 Buffalo Bills: On the training camp roster, but did not make the regular season roster; TOTAL: On the training camp roster, but did not make the regular season roster.

Prewitt, Felton Winters (Felto) (Pluto)

Position: G-C; Height: 5'11"; Weight: 207; High School: Corsicana (TX); College: Tulsa; Born: 5/17/1924, Corsicana, TX; Deceased: 3/15/1998, Reno, NV; 1946 Buffalo Bisons (Preseason): 1 Game Played, 0 Games Started; 1946 Buffalo Bisons (Regular Season): 14 Games Played, 9 Games Started, Interceptions: 4–89; 1947 Buffalo Bills (Regular Season): 14 Games Played, 10 Games Started, Interceptions: 2–20; 1948 Buffalo Bills (Regular Season): 8 Games Played, 7 Games Started; 1948 Buffalo Bills (Postseason): 2 Games Played, 1 Game Started; TOTAL (Regular Season): 36 Games Played, 26 Games Started, Interceptions: 6–109; TOTAL (Postseason): 2 Games Played, 1 Game Started

Felto Prewitt was an All-America First Team Selection in 1944 while at Tulsa. He also earned All-Missouri Valley honors for three years, as well as played in three Bowl games: Sugar Bowl in 1944, Orange Bowl in 1945 and the Oil Bowl in 1946. He was drafted by the Philadelphia Eagles in 1946 (sixth round), but elected to play for the Buffalo Bisons. He played three years for Buffalo before ending his career in Baltimore.

Non-Buffalo Statistics

1949 Baltimore Colts: 12 Games Played, 7 Games Started

Pucci, Benito Modesto (Ben)

Position: T; Height: 6'4"; Weight: 261; High School: Southwest (St. Louis, MO); College: (None); Born: 1/26/1925, St. Louis, MO; 1946 Buffalo Bisons (Preseason): 1 Game Played, 0 Games Started; 1946 Buffalo Bisons (Regular Season): 11 Games Played, 1 Game Started; 1947 Buffalo Bills (Regular Season): 0 Games Played, 0 Games Started. Went to Chicago Rockets; TOTAL (Regular Season): 11 Games Played, 1 Game Started

Ben Pucci was the only player on the Buffalo Bisons' roster with no college experience. He did, however, have ample high school experience. He played varsity all four years at Southwest High School, being named All-District and All-City. Ben grew up on Elizabeth Street, in what is called The Hill in St. Louis. This same street housed baseball legends Yogi Berra and Joe Garagiola, who grew up there at the same time as Pucci (Jack Buck also lived on Elizabeth Street, but at a later time). Ben was on the same soccer team as both Berra and Garagiola.

Pucci's professional football career started in 1940 while in Hollywood. He tried out for the Hollywood Rangers and made the team, being named an All-Star of the American Association. In 1945, Pucci was offered a contract to play with the Cleveland Rams, but turned it down (the Rams went on to win the NFL Championship that year). He returned to St. Louis and was offered a scholarship to attend Tulane. In 1946, Jim Breuil offered Pucci $200/game for ten games to play with the Buffalo Bisons. The initial offer of ten games grew to 14 games and Pucci went on to sign a two-year contract. In 1947, Ben dislocated his jaw in training camp and his weight dropped to 235 pounds. Pucci and Forrest Grigg were sold to the Chicago Rockets. In 1948, Cleveland Browns coach Paul Brown traded three players to get Pucci. The following year, Ben went to Baltimore to play with the Colts. He was asked to take a pay cut and decided to leave. He went to Chicago to try out for the Cardinals, but did not make the team. He went to the Pittsburgh Steelers training camp, but when realizing that the coach ran two-a-day sessions, he decided to leave. He was offered a contract to play with Detroit, but declined.

In 1950, Pucci married Shirley, his wife of what would be 50 years. They had three children: two sons and one daughter. In 1953, Pucci started his first of two years with the St. Louis Knights of the Central State League. After retiring from football, Ben worked various jobs. He owned a cafeteria with his father. They sold the business and Pucci went to work in the breweries in St. Louis. He left the beer business and went into trucking, working his way up to vice-president when he retired in 1969, working under former Bison teammate Jack Dugger at one point. After retirement, he started his own trucking company, which he ran with his two sons. During this time, he also worked as a sports commentator for KMOX and the St. Louis Cardinals. Ben was inducted into The Hill's Hall of Fame Place in 2006, joining baseball greats Joe Garagiola and Yogi Berra, broadcaster Jack Buck, wrestling ring announcer Mickey Garagiola, Re Calcaterra (who helped develop the sport of synchronized swimming) and four World Cup players: Frank Borghi, Charlie Colombo, Gino Parlani and Frank Wallace. Hall of Fame Place is located on the 5400 block of Elizabeth Street.

Non-Buffalo Statistics

1947 Chicago Rockets: 13 Games Played, 3 Games Started
1948 Cleveland Browns: 12 Games Played, 0 Games Started

Ratterman, George William (The Kid) (Snake)

Position: B; Height: 6'1"; Weight: 185; High School: St. Xavier (Cincinnati, OH); College: Notre Dame; Born: 11/12/1926, Cincinnati, OH; Deceased: 11/3/2007, Centennial, CO; 1947 Buffalo Bills (Regular Season): 13 Games Played, 5 Games Started, Passing: 124–244 1840 22 TD 20 INT, Rushing: 17-(–49) 1 TD, Extra Points: 0/1; 1948 Buffalo Bills (Regular Season): 16 Games Played, 13 Games Started, Passing: 168–335 2577 16 TD 22 INT, Rushing: 12-(–18) 3 TD; 1948 Buffalo Bills (Postseason): 2 Games Played, 1 Game Started, Passing: 15–36–159 3 TD 4 INT; 1949 Buffalo Bills (Regular Season): 12 Games Played, 12 Games Started, Passing: 146–252 1777 14 TD 13 INT, Rushing: 36–85 4 TD; 1949 Buffalo Bills (Postseason): 1 Game Played, 1 Game Started, Passing: 2–39–293 3 TD 2 INT; TOTAL (Regular Season): 41 Games Played, 30 Games Started, Passing: 438–831 6194 52 TD 55 INT, Rushing: 65–18 8 TD, Extra Points: 0/1; TOTAL (Postseason): 3 Games Played, 2 Games Started, Passing: 17–75–452 6 TD 6 INT

Born November 12, 1926, to Leander F. and Claribel (Cahill) Ratterman, George

William Ratterman was the youngest of three children. His sister Claribel married Ray Katzenberger of Indianapolis. His brother Fred was an excellent athlete at both Withrow High School (Cincinnati, OH) and at the University of Michigan. After graduation, Fred played one game for the 1934 Cincinnati Reds of the National Football League, but his career came to a quick end after receiving a serious knee injury. George's other brother, Pat, was a Jesuit priest who became the Dean of Students and later the Vice-President of Student Affairs at Xavier University.

Since George's siblings were at least ten years older than him, he spent most of his childhood as essentially an only child. His father was a lawyer and an accountant, so they had money to travel. They took family vacations to Alaska and Cuba, as well as send him to summer camp near Traverse City, Michigan. He was a gifted student, finishing second in his class in high school. He also spent his time playing the piano. Later, while he was in Buffalo, he played piano with the Buffalo Symphony Orchestra on the same night that President Harry Truman was in town. More people went to see the Ratterman and the Symphony than to see the president.

George started playing organized football in grade school while at St. Mary's in Cincinnati. He continued into high school, where he was a classmate of Charlie Wolf, who later became the head coach of the Cincinnati Royals of the NBA. The St. Xavier High School team changed their name to the Bombers, in part due to their passing attack. Ratterman was part of that attack, playing both quarterback and tailback on the team. George had a choice to make regarding his collegiate education: He could either attend the University of Michigan or Notre Dame. He used an interesting method to make the decision. According to his book, *Confessions of a Gypsy Quarterback: Inside the Wacky World of Pro Football*, Ratterman explained,

> To choose between the two, I drove to Ann Arbor for the Notre Dame-Michigan game. At the end of sixty minutes of black-and-blue football, I carefully focused my field glasses and surveyed the backsides of three vital participants. [Angelo] Bertelli's satin pants still looked bright gold, while the two Michigan quarterbacks' britches matched the dull green stadium turf. As a quarterback myself, I had seen the advantages of a Notre Dame education.

Once at Notre Dame, the 6'0" 149-pound Ratterman saw little action until his junior year. His size was an issue. According to Ratterman, when commenting on George's diminutive frame, the Notre Dame equipment manager quipped, "Well, all right, but I'll have to give you a single-digit jersey number. You aren't wide enough to carry two digits on your back." As a freshman, George broke his collarbone during an intersquad scrimmage. In his sophomore season, Ratterman threw just four passes, with two of them being intercepted. In his junior year, Ratterman helped his team to the national championship. George was suspended for a semester in his senior year at Notre Dame. This suspension lasted through part of the football season. The Buffalo Bills offered him a two-year contract and he became a professional football player at 19 years of age. After the 1948 season, however, Bills owner Jim Breuil did not offer Ratterman a contract and he went back to Notre Dame. He also signed a contract to play with the New York Yankees of the National Football League in 1950. In that contract, Ratterman demanded that if the team were to move, he was released from his obligations. There was a rumor that the team was moving to Texas. When the team moved in 1952, Ratterman went to the Cleveland Browns, where he finished his professional football career.

After retiring from football, Ratterman worked as the sheriff of Campbell County, Kentucky. The focus of his energy was on ridding the county of organized crime. During his campaign, George was drugged with chloral hydrate and photographed with a stripper named April Flowers in an attempt to get him to drop out of the race. The blackmail attempt failed, as the plot was uncovered and made public. His political career also included failed campaigns for county judge and the United States Congress.

From 1960 through 1973, Ratterman worked in broadcasting. The first five years were with ABC and the remainder was with NBC.

In 1967, George moved his family to Denver, Colorado, where he worked in the financial services field. He eventually worked a short time as executive director of the International Association of Financial Planners. While playing football, Ratterman had earned his law degree. He passed the bar exam in Kentucky and Ohio, but never set up a law practice. He later earned his CLU, CFP and LLM degrees. With that, he worked as general counsel for the American Football League's Player's Association, while another Buffalo quarterback — Jack Kemp — was the union president. From 1976 through 2001, Ratterman wrote and taught real estate classes. He was active in the Catholic Church and in the schools of his children. According to his son Matt, "His only job in retirement was first-base coach on the family co-ed softball team. *Sports Illustrated* ran a story on him and the family softball team in its 'Catching Up With ...' segment around 2004. Dad still wanted to win at that time of his life and did not tolerate his adult kids screwing around on the field. We won several championships."

On December 27, 1947, George married Anne Hengelbrok. In their over 60 years of marriage, they had ten children: Beth, Mark, Sally, Mollie, Matt, Julie, Tim, Dave, Ned and Amy. At the time of his passing in 2007, he had 23 grandchildren and nine great-grandchildren, with two more great-grandchildren on the way.

Non-Buffalo Statistics

1950 New York Yanks: 12 Games Played, 12 Games Started, Rushing: 11–0 3 TD 4 Fumbles, Passing: 140–294 2251 22 TD 24 INT
1951 Montreal Alouettes
1951 New York Yanks: 6 Games Played, 1 Game Started, Rushing: 3–9 1 Fumble, Passing: 31–67 340 2 TD 6 INT
1952 Cleveland Browns: 6 Games Played, Rushing: 1–2, Passing: 2–6 20 1 TD 2 INT
1953 Cleveland Browns: 9 Games Played, 1 Game Started, Rushing: 2–6, Passing: 23–41 301 4 TD 0 INT
1954 Cleveland Browns: 6 Games Played, Rushing: 8-(–13) 1 TD 1 Fumble, Passing: 32–53 465 3 TD 3 INT
1955 Cleveland Browns: 10 Games Played, Rushing: 6–8 1 TD 2 Fumble, Passing: 32–47 504 6 TD 3 INT
1956 Cleveland Browns: 4 Games Played, 4 Games Started, Rushing: 10–19 1 TD 1 Fumble, Passing: 39–57 398 1 TD 3 INT

Reisz, Albert Harry (Albie)

Position: B; Height: 5'10"; Weight: 174; High School: Lorain (Lorain, OH); College: Southeastern Louisiana; Born: 11/29/1917, Lorain, OH; Deceased: 5/1/1985, New Orleans, LA; 1947 Buffalo Bills (Regular Season): 13 Games Played, 0 Games Started, Rushing: 2–32, Punting: 57–2111; TOTAL (Regular Season): 13 Games Played, 0 Games Started, Rushing: 2–32, Punting: 57–2111

Albie Reisz was one of the first two-sport star athletes in Southeastern Louisiana University history. He earned Little All-America honors three years, was All-League halfback in 1941 and 1942, and was the Associated Press' Little All-American in 1942. He was inducted into Southeastern Louisiana's Hall of Fame in 1942.

After college, Reisz played three years for the Cleveland Rams. In 1947, he played 13 games for the Buffalo Bills before retiring from football.

Non-Buffalo Statistics

1944 Cleveland Rams: 10 Games Played, 2 Games Started, Rushing: 69–134 2 TD, Passing: 49–113 777 8 TD 10 INT, Interceptions: 3–72, Punting: 24–959, Punt Returns: 5–68, Kick Returns: 12–285
1945 Cleveland Rams: 10 Games Played, 0 Games Started, Rushing: 12-(-2) 3 Fumbles, Passing: 8–21 146 2 TD 3 INT, Receiving: 1–11, Interceptions: 2–55, Punting: 7–258, Punt Returns: 8–78
1946 Los Angeles Rams: 2 Games Played, 1 Game Started

Ruthstrom, Ralph David

Position: B; Height: 6'5"; Weight: 212; High School: Milby (Houston, TX); College: Sam Houston State, Southern Methodist; Born: 7/12/1921, Schenectady, NY; Deceased: 3/29/1962, Houston, TX; 1948 Buffalo Bills: On the regular season roster, but did not play; TOTAL: On the regular season roster, but did not play.

Non-Buffalo Statistics

1945 Cleveland Browns: 6 Games Played, 1 Game Started, Rushing: 10–74
1946 Los Angeles Rams: 6 Games Played, 4 Games Started, Rushing: 2-(-4), Receiving: 1–9
1947 Washington Redskins: 2 Games Played, 1 Game Started, Rushing: 2–5
1949 Baltimore Colts: 4 Games Played, 0 Games Started

Rykovich, Julius Alphonsus (Julie) (Big Train)

Position: B; Height: 6'2"; Weight: 204; High School: Lew Wallace (Gary, IN); College: Notre Dame, Illinois; Born: 4/6/1923, Gary, IN; Deceased: 12/22/1974, Merrillville, IN; 1947 Buffalo Bills (Regular Season): 12 Games Played, 10 Games Started, Receiving: 4–44, Interceptions: 2–61, Punt Returns: 7–93, Kick Returns: 12–257; 1948 Buffalo Bills: Receiving: 2-(–6), Interceptions: 3–65, Punt Returns: 1–23, Kick Returns: 7–129; 1948 Buffalo Bills (Regular Season): 6 Games Played, 2 Games Started; TOTAL (Regular Season): 18 Games Played, 12 Games Started, Receiving: 6–38, Interceptions: 5–126, Punt Returns: 8–116, Kick Returns: 19–386

In high school, Julie Rykovich played end and left halfback. He captained the team to the Indiana State Championship in 1941. He became an All-Conference halfback while at Illinois.

In 1943, he was transferred to Notre Dame as a Marine Corps trainee and played on the undefeated 1943 squad. While in the Marine Corps, Rykovich played under Cliff Battles on the Marine All-Star team. After he was discharged from the Marine Corps in 1946, he returned to Illinois and helped them to a Rose Bowl victory the following year.

In 1946, Rykovich was drafted in the second round by the Chicago Bears, but he opted to play for the Buffalo Bills. During the 1948 season, he was traded to the Chicago Rockets. In 1949, he started his first of three years with the Chicago Bears before playing two years for the Washington Redskins.

Non-Buffalo Statistics

1948 Chicago Rockets: 6 Games Played, 4 Games Started, Rushing: 53–176 1 TD, Passing: 1–1 12 0 TD 0 INT, Receiving: 3–78
1949 Chicago Bears: 11 Games Played, 3 Games Started, Rushing: 88–340 6 TD, Receiving: 16–210 2 TD
1950 Chicago Bears: 12 Games Played, Rushing: 122–394 7 TD, Receiving: 21–344
1951 Chicago Bears: 12 Games Played, Rushing: 83–399 4 TD, Passing: 0–3, Receiving: 6–133
1952 Washington Redskins: 11 Games Played, Rushing: 94–361 1 TD, Receiving: 16–283 1 TD
1953 Washington Redskins: 12 Games Played, Rushing: 73–251, Receiving: 7–73 1 TD

Sandig, Curtis Walter (Curt) (Two Tone)

Position: B; Height: 5'10"; Weight: 180; High School: Mart (TX); College: Baylor, St. Mary's (San Antonio, TX); Born: 7/12/1918, Mart, TX; Deceased: 2/13/2006, San Antonio, TX; 1946 Buffalo Bisons (Preseason): 1 Game Played, 0 Games Started; 1946 Buffalo Bisons (Regular Season): 9 Games Played, 1 Game Started, Rushing: 22–52 1 TD, Receiving: 2–15, Punting: 4–155 0 Blocked, Punt Returns: 2–20, Kick Returns: 2–43; TOTAL (Regular Season): 9 Games Played, 1 Game Started, Rushing: 22–52 1 TD, Receiving: 2–15, Punting: 4–155 0 Blocked, Punt Returns: 2–20, Kick Returns: 2–43

Curt Sandig started his football career at Mart High School, where he played all four years. Sandig transferred from Baylor to St. Mary's in 1938. In his first year with the team, Sandig racked up 770 yards rushing and scored 121 points to put him third in the country. He was a Little All-America selection for four years at St. Mary of Texas. Also, played basketball and baseball while in college.

In 1942, the Chicago bears drafted Sandig, but his rights were traded away to the Pittsburgh Steelers. He played all eleven games for the Steelers, earning $150 per game.

After only one year with the Steelers, Sandig left to serve in the Navy. There, he helped the City Blue Jackets to an undefeated season in 1945. He left the Navy after three years and signed on with the Buffalo Bisons to play for $1250 a year plus a $1500 signing bonus. His tenure with Buffalo was a short one, as injuries prevented him from continuing after the 1946 season.

After football, Sanding moved to San Antonio, where he worked at Butter Krust Bakery. He enjoyed hunting and fishing in his leisure time.

Curt Sandig died of congestive heart failure at the age of 87. He had one daughter, Carol Ann.

Non-Buffalo Statistics

1942 Pittsburgh Steelers: 11 Games Played, 8 Games Started, Rushing: 50–116 3 TD, Passing: 2–4 10, Receiving: 6–103, Interceptions: 5–94, Punting: 37–1437, Punt Returns: 6–142 1 TD, Kick Returns: 7–168

Schilling, Ralph Franklin

Position: E; Height: 6'3"; Weight: 218; College: Oklahoma City; Born: 7/5/1921, Morris, OK; Deceased: 5/9/1994, McAllen, TX; 1946 Buffalo Bisons (Regular Season): 2 Games Played, 0 Games Started; TOTAL (Regular Season): 2 Games Played, 0 Games Started

Non-Buffalo Statistics

1946 Washington Redskins: 5 Games Played, 0 Games Started, Receiving: 1–14

Schneider, Donald Paul (Don)

Position: B; Height: 5'9"; Weight: 170; High School: J.P. McCaskey (Lancaster, PA); College: Pennsylvania; Born: 4/3/1923, Crafton, PA; Deceased: 7/13/2009, West Chester, PA; 1948 Buffalo Bills (Regular Season): 12 Games Played, 1 Game Started, Rushing: 15–70, Receiving: 1–14, Punt Returns: 1–4, Kick Returns: 4–77; 1948 Buffalo Bills (Postseason): 2 Games Played, 1 Game Started, Receiving: 1–4, Kick Returns: 2–33; TOTAL (Regular Season): 12 Games Played, 1 Game Started, Rushing: 15–70, Receiving: 1–14, Punt Returns: 1–4, Kick Returns: 4–77; TOTAL (Postseason): 2 Games Played, 1 Game Started, Receiving: 1–4, Kick Returns: 2–33

Born April 3, 1923, to Paul and Margaret Schneider, Don Schneider loved football. He dedicated his life to teaching and coaching after he retired from the Buffalo Bills. But first came World War II. During the war, Schneider was in Denver for pilot training. The military realized that Don was not suited for this position and made him a tail gunner. He fell ill, however, before being shipped overseas. A severe case of pneumonia kept Don state-side for several months and he was discharged after serving two years in the military.

Once returning from military service, Don got his Bachelor of Arts in Education from the University of Pennsylvania. While at Penn, Don played first string and was drafted by both the Chicago Bears (fifth round in 1946) and the Buffalo Bills (23rd round in 1947). He chose the Buffalo Bills because it was closer to home and he wanted his family and friends to be able to attend the games.

Don only played one year of professional football before receiving a head coaching offer at Sharon Hill. His love of coaching outweighed his love of playing and Don started his long coaching and teaching career, coaching football and teaching English and Physical Education. After one successful season, Schneider moved on to Springfield to be an assistant coach for one year. North Lancaster High School was his next stop, where he was head coach for five years. He continued coaching at Bethlehem High School, Lehigh University, Springfield (New Jersey) and Watchyoung Hills. He retired

All-Time Roster 277

from coaching and took a position as a middle school principal. He then became assistant principal at East High School before retiring.
Don was married June 21, 1946, and has four children: three sons and a daughter.

Schroll, Charles William (Bill) (Bonk)

Position: B; Height: 6'0"; Weight: 214; High School: Jesuit (Alexandria, LA; College: Louisiana State; Born: 1/24/1926, Alexandria, LA; 1949 Buffalo Bills (Regular Season): 12 Games Played, 0 Games Started, Interceptions: 1-4 ;1949 Buffalo Bills (Postseason): 1 Game Played, 0 Games Started; TOTAL (Regular Season): 12 Games Played, 0 Games Started, Interceptions: 1-4; TOTAL (Postseason): 1 Game Played, 0 Games Started

Bill Schroll played quarterback, fullback and tackle in high school, earning All-Stat honors in 1942. While in the service, he played on the Camp Cooke Engineers team, which won five out of six games in 1945.

He was drafted by the Los Angeles Rams in 1948 (14th round), but elected to play for the Buffalo Bills. After the Bills folded, Schroll played a year for the Baltimore Colts and a year for the Green Bay Packers.

Non-Buffalo Statistics

1950 Detroit Lions: 12 Games Played, Rushing: 1-1, Interceptions: 2-8
1951 Green Bay Packers: 12 Games Played

Schuette, Charles William (Carl) (Bull)

Position: C-B; Height: 6'1"; Weight: 206; High School: Sheboygan Central (WI); College: Marquette; Born: 4/4/1922, Sheboygan, WI; Deceased: 12/9/1975, Boston, MA; 1948 Buffalo Bills (Regular Season): 16 Games Played, 2 Games Started, Interceptions: 4-97 1 TD; 1948 Buffalo Bills (Postseason): 2 Games Played, 1 Game Started; 1949 Buffalo Bills (Regular Season): 12 Games Played, 0 Games Started; TOTAL (Regular Season): 28 Games Played, 2 Games Started, Interceptions: 4-97 1 TD; TOTAL (Postseason): 2 Games Played, 1 Game Started

Carl Schuette played fullback for three years at Sheboygan Central High School and earned All-Conference and MVP honors in 1940. He alternated between right halfback and fullback while at Marquette, and earned three letters.

After spending over three years in the Marine Corps, Schuette signed with the Buffalo Bills. He was drafted by the Detroit Lions in 1947 (22nd round), but received a better offer from the Bills. He spent two seasons in Buffalo, before playing two years for the Green Bay Packers.

Non-Buffalo Statistics

1950 Green Bay Packers: 12 Games Played, Interceptions: 1-0
1951 Green Bay Packers: 12 Games Played

Schwenk, Wilson Rutherford (Bud)

Position: B; Height: 6'2"; Weight: 200; High School: Beaumont (St. Louis); College: Washington (St. Louis); Born: 8/26/1918, St. Louis, MO; Deceased: 10/1/1980, St. Louis, MO; 1947 Buffalo Bills (Regular Season): 0 Games Played, 0 Games Started. Went to Baltimore Colts; TOTAL (Regular Season): 0 Games Played, 0 Games Started

Bud Schwenk was MVP at Beaumont High School in 1937 and 1938. He earned All-Conference honors three straight years while at Washington University, as well as MVP honors in 1940 and 1942.

Schwenk was drafted by the Chicago Cardinals in 1942 (third round) and spent one year with the team before entering military service. After three years in the armed forces, Schwenk continued his professional football career when he joined the Cleveland Browns. After one year with the Browns, Schwenk signed with the Buffalo Bills. He did not see action with Buffalo, but was instead traded to the Baltimore Colts. After the 1947 season, Schwenk joined the New York Yankees for his final season.

Non-Buffalo Statistics

1942 Chicago Cardinals: 10 Games Played, 9 Games Started, Rushing: 111–313 2 TD, Passing: 122–295–1360 6 TD 27 INT, Interceptions: 1–21, Punts: 3–114, Kick Returns: 2–24

1946 Cleveland Browns: 4 Games Played, 0 Games Started, Rushing: 6-(–1) 1 TD, Passing: 15–23–276 4 TD 0 INT

1947 Baltimore Colts: 14 Games Played, 2 Games Started, Rushing: 25–58 1 TD, Passing: 168–327–2236 13 TD 20 INT

1948 New York Yankees: 8 Games Played, 0 Games Started, Rushing: 3–6, Passing: 6–17–52 0 TD 3 INT

Scott, Vincent Joseph (Vin) (Vince) (Boomer)

Position: G; Height: 5'8"; Weight: 215; High School: LeRoy (NY); College: Notre Dame; Born: 7/10/1925, LeRoy, NY; Deceased: 7/13/1992, Hamilton, Canada; 1947 Buffalo Bills (Regular Season): 11 Games Played, 0 Games Started; 1948 Buffalo Bills (Regular Season): 16 Games Played, 3 Games Started; 1948 Buffalo Bills (Postseason): 2 Games Played, 1 Game Started; TOTAL (Regular Season): 27 Games Played, 3 Games Started; TOTAL (Postseason): 2 Games Played, 1 Game Started

Known as "Pretty Boy" to his Buffalo teammates, Vince Scott came to the Bills in 1947. A graduate of LeRoy High School, Scott earned four letters as a fullback. He made All-Western New York State in 1941 and 1942 and was captain of the team in 1943. Not only was he a good football player, but he also earned a letter as a guard on the basketball team, as well as two letters as a left fielder on the baseball team. He earned four letters in shot-put, winning the Western New York Championship in 1943. His athletic prowess continued into his collegiate career, earning two letters in shot-put. His football career spanned three coaches: Ed McKeever, Hugh Devore and Frank Leahy.

Shurnas, Marshall Kenneth (Iggie)

Position: E; Height: 6'1"; Weight: 205; High School: Central (St. Louis, MO); College: Missouri; Born: 4/1/1922, St. Louis, MO; Deceased: 8/19/2006, Columbia, MO; 1948 Buffalo Bills: On the regular season roster, but did not play; TOTAL: On the regular season roster, but did not play.

Marshall Shurnas played end for three years while at Central High School and continued as end while at Missouri. He was drafted by the Boston Yanks in 1944 (17th round). He played for the Cleveland Browns in 1947 and joined Buffalo in 1948. While with the Bills, he was on the roster, but did not play.

Non-Buffalo Statistics

1947 Cleveland Browns: 11 Games Played, 1 Game Started, Receiving: 2–30

Smith, James Robert (Bob)

Position: B; Height: 6'1"; Weight: 191; High School: Will Rogers (Tulsa, OK); College: Tulsa, Iowa; Born: 8/20/1925, Ranger, TX; Deceased: 3/1/2002, Flower Mound, TX; 1948 (Buffalo Bills and Brooklyn Dodgers): 13 Games, Rushing: 1–7, Interceptions: 4–29, Punting: 14–538, Punt Returns: 1–1; 1948 Buffalo Bills (Regular Season): 2 Games Played, 0 Games Started; TOTAL (Regular Season): 2 Games Played, 0 Games Started

Bob Smith played halfback for four years under Eddie Anderson at Iowa. His most notable accomplishment while in college was scoring three touchdowns in one quarter against Tulsa.

Smith was drafted by both the Brooklyn Dodgers (eleventh round) and the Washington Redskins (24th round) in 1947. In 1948, he split time between the Buffalo Bills and the Brooklyn Dodgers. He started the 1949 season with the Chicago Hornets, but finished with the Detroit Lions. He spent the next five seasons with the Lions before retiring from football.

Non-Buffalo Statistics

1949 Chicago Hornets: 3 Games Played, 0 Games Started, Receiving: 1–31
1949 Detroit Lions: 12 Games Played, 2 Games Started, Rushing: 33–162, Interceptions: 9–218 1 TD, Punting: 0–0 4 Fumbles, Receiving: 2–16, Punt Returns: 2–25, Kick Returns: 7–172
1950 Detroit Lions: 12 Games Played, Interceptions: 5–128 1 TD, Punting: 32–1310
1951 Detroit Lions: 12 Games Played, Interceptions: 3–70, Punting: 49–2082
1952 Detroit Lions: 12 Games Played, Rushing: 3–12, Interceptions: 9–184 1 TD, Punting: 61–2729 1 Fumble, Receiving: 1–18
1953 Detroit Lions: 12 Games Played, Interceptions: 3–119, Punting: 40–1647
1954 Detroit Lions: 2 Games Played

Stanley, C.B.

Position: T; Height: 6'4"; Weight: 225; High School: Holdenville (OK); College: Tulsa; Born: 1/25/1919; Deceased: 4/1977, Tulsa, OK; 1946 Buffalo Bisons (Preseason): 1 Game Played, 1 Game Started; 1946 Buffalo Bisons (Regular Season): 12 Games Played, 11 Games Started; TOTAL (Regular Season): 12 Games Played, 11 Games Started

C.B. Stanley played four years of varsity football at Tulsa. He was a three-time All-America Honorable Mention selection, as well as a three time All-State selection from 1943 through 1945. He helped Tulsa reach the Sugar Bowl in 1943, the Orange Bowl in 1944 and the Oil Bowl in 1945. Stanley also played in the College All-Star game against the Los Angeles Rams in 1946. He was drafted by the Chicago Bears in 1944 (sixth round).

Stanton, William McKimmon (Bill)

Position: E; Height: 6'2"; Weight: 210; High School: South Robeson (Rowland, NC); College: North Carolina State; Born: 4/21/1924, Dillon, SC; 1949 Buffalo Bills (Regular Season): 10 Games Played, 0 Games Started; TOTAL (Regular Season): 10 Games Played, 0 Games Started

Bill Stanton attended North Carolina State on a baseball scholarship. He left for the war — was part of the 84th Infantry — and when he returned he was a much larger man. As a result, the coaches pushed him towards football. He was drafted by the Philadelphia Eagles in 1948 (27th round), but chose to play for the Buffalo Bills in 1949.

After the Bills folded, Stanton went to the Canadian Football League and was part of the Ottawa Roughrider Grey Cup team, earning MVP honors. The following year, he blew out his knee and that ended his playing career.

We went into coaching, accepting a job at Illinois and then at Carlton College. After coaching, Stanton used his forestry degree to get a job as a Forestry Agent at North Carolina State. He was there for 40 years before retiring.

Statuto, Arthur Gaetano (Art)

Position: C; Height: 6'2"; Weight: 221; High School: Saugus (MA); College: Notre Dame; Born: 7/17/1925, Saugus, MA; 1948 Buffalo Bills (Regular Season): 15 Games Played, 8 Games Started, Receiving: 2–0; 1948 Buffalo Bills (Postseason): 2 Games Played, 1 Game Started; 1949 Buffalo Bills (Regular Season): 13 Games Played, 13 Games Started; 1949 Buffalo Bills (Postseason): 1 Game Played, 1 Game Started; TOTAL (Regular Season): 28 Games Played, 21 Games Started, Receiving: 2–0; TOTAL (Postseason): 3 Games Played, 2 Games Started

Art Statuto played three years at center while in high school. He went to Notre Dame in the spring of 1943. In July of that year, Statuto joined the Navy and a few months later was sent to Midshipman's School. While in the Navy, Statuto played football under former Chicago Bears standout Hamp Pool.

Statuto signed with the Buffalo Bills after graduating from Notre Dame. Later, he discovered that he was drafted by the Philadelphia Eagles (31st round in 1948), but since he had already signed with Buffalo, he stayed with the Bills.

After playing two seasons with the Bills and one season with the Los Angeles Rams, Statuto retired from football. He went into industrial sales with Boston Gear and stayed with the company for five years. After that, he went into business for himself, doing training for distribution. He retired after 31 years in the business.

Non-Buffalo Statistics

1950 Los Angeles Rams: 12 Games Played

Stautzenberger, Weldon Odell (Odell)

Position: G; Height: 6'0"; Weight: 218; High School: Thomas Jefferson (San Antonio, TX); College: Texas A&M; Born: 10/23/1924, San Antonio, TX; Deceased: 5/5/2002, Alexandria, LA; 1949 Buffalo Bills (Regular Season): 12 Games Played, 7 Games Started; 1949 Buffalo Bills (Postseason): 1 Game Played, 1 Game Started; TOTAL (Regular Season): 12 Games Played, 7 Games Started; TOTAL (Postseason): 1 Game Played, 1 Game Started

Odell Stautzenberger was born to Oscar A. Stautzenberger and his wife Myrtle (Greebon) on May 5, 1924. He had an older brother (Lee) and a younger sister (Eunice). His parents were very poor, so Odell spent his summers and holidays working on his grandparent's farm in Seguin, TX. Using the money he earned to help support his family, Odell hitchhiked everywhere and did not own a car until 1949.

Odell started playing organized footall in junior high school. He could play any position on the line, but always preferred guard. He graduated from Thomas Jefferson High School in 1942. At that point, Odell joined the Marines and served with distinction. He was a member of the Carlson's Second Marine Raider Battalion and after the Raiders were disbanded in 1944, he served as an Automatic Rifleman in the 2nd Battalion, 4th Marine Regiment. He was wounded twice and won the Bronze Star for heroic achievement during the battle of Mt. Yaetake on the island of Okinawa. He was also a member of Task Force 31 and was in the first group of Marines that landed in Japan at 5:50AM on August 30, 1945, prior to the official surrender ceremony aboard the U.S.S. Missouri. His unit was responsible for seizing the main armory and to destroy all powerful fortifications. While with the Raiders, Stautzenberger served with Hank Bauer of the New York Yankees and the Kansas City Athletics. Bauer and Stautzenberger were members of both the Raiders and the 4th Marine Regiment.

After serving in the Marine Corps, Odell received a scholarship to attend Texas A&M. Starting in September of 1946, he attended classes year-round and graduated in May of 1949. While at Texas A&M, he lettered all three years, won MVP of the 1946 season, was captain of the 1948 season, was named all-Southwest Conference in 1948, played in the 1949 East-West Shrine game and the 1949 College All-Star game. In 1947, the Boston Yanks drafted him in Round 27, but he opted to stay in school and get his degree. He married Cora Elizabeth Chapman on June 6, 1949.

After college, Odell received interest from the Chicago Bears, but signed with the Cleveland Browns because they offered more money. Cleveland promptly traded Stautzenberger to the Buffalo Bills, where he played the 1949 season. After the Bills disbanded in 1950, he had a contract to play football, but decided to retire. His wife,

Cora, was pregnant with their first child and Odell needed steady income with a benefit package. He interviewed with Proctor & Gamble, as well as the Federal Bureau of Investigation. He was offered a job with Proctor & Gamble and began working for them June 1, 1950, retiring exactly 40 years later. In that time, Odell and Cora had five children (four boys and one girl). Cora and Odell divorced in 1970.

Odell Stautzenberger died May 5, 2002, of complications from Alzheimer's disease. He was at the VA hospital in Alexandria, LA.

Stefik, Robert Mathias (Bob)

Position: E; Height: 5'11"; Weight: 180; High School: St. Mary's (Niagara Falls, NY); College: Niagara; Born: 10/8/1923, Madison, WI; Deceased: 4/9/2008, Lewiston, NY; 1948 Buffalo Bills (Regular Season): 1 Game Played, 0 Games Started, Extra Points: 0/1; TOTAL (Regular Season): 1 Game Played, 0 Games Started, Extra Points: 0/1

Bob Stefik was born in Madison, Wisconsin and moved to Niagara Falls when he was young. He attended St. Mary's High School and Niagara University, playing football for both schools. During World War II, Stefik served in the Army in Europe. Upon returning home, he signed to play with the Buffalo Bills for one year. After seeing limited playing time, Stefik retired and went into real estate, soon opening his own company, Stefik Realty.

Stefik was active in the community, serving on several local boards including the Niagara Falls Boys Club, Cerebral Palsy Association and the Niagara Falls Rotary Club, among others. He was active in golf, as well as other sports. His wife Rosemary passed away in 2002, and they had three sons and two daughters.

Steuber, Robert James (Bob)

Position: B; Height: 6'2"; Weight: 200; High School: Christian Brothers Academy (St. Louis, MO); College: Missouri, DePauw; Born: 10/25/1921, Wenonah, NJ; Deceased: 11/29/1996, St. Louis, MO; 1948 Buffalo Bills (Regular Season): 9 Games Played, 7 Games Started, Passing: 2–1 5 –4, Receiving: 2–14, Punting: 1–40, Kick Returns: 6–123, Extra Points: 20/23, Field Goals: 1/2; TOTAL (Regular Season): 9 Games Played, 7 Games Started, Passing: 2–1 5 –4, Receiving: 2–14, Punting: 1–40, Kick Returns: 6–123, Extra Points: 20/23, Field Goals: 1/2

In high school, Bob Steuber was All-Prep and All-District in 1937 and 1938. While at Missouri, Steuber earned All-Conference honors in 1941 and 1942. He was MVP in the Missouri Valley in 1941 and was All-American in 1942.

Steuber has the distinction of being the only player to knowingly play for a major professional club and then be allowed to return to the college ranks to play another season. From 1941 through 1942, Steuber played for Missouri. He was drafted by the Chicago Bears in 1943 (first round) and on September 26, 1943, was a substitute for the Chicago Bears in their game against the Green Bay Packers. The following day, Steuber was ordered by the Navy to report to DePauw University for flight training. He played the final six games for DePauw. In those six games, Steuber racked up an impressive 129 points, rushed for over 1,000 yards and helped his team outscore their

opponents 206-6. After two years in the military, Steuber returned to professional football.
He was plagued by injuries his entire professional career. After the 1948 season, he retired from football.

Non-Buffalo Statistics

1943 Chicago Bears: 1 Game Played, 0 Games Started, Rushing: 1-3
1946 Cleveland Browns: 6 Games Played, 1 Game Started, Rushing: 8-19, Receiving: 1-9, Interceptions: 1-52, Kick Returns: 2-53
1947 Los Angeles Dons: 3 Games Played, 0 Games Started, Rushing: 1-2

Still, James Edward Jr. (Jim)

Position: B; Height: 6'3"; Weight: 193; High School: Panama City (FL); College: Mississippi Gulf Coast CC; Georgia Tech; Born: 3/5/1924, Columbia, SC; Deceased: 1/3/1999, Green Cove Springs, FL; 1948 Buffalo Bills (Regular Season): 15 Games Played, 1 Game Started, Passing: 5-14 89 1 TD 3 INT, Rushing: 5-(-26), Interceptions: 1-37, Punting: 47-1825; 1948 Buffalo Bills (Postseason): 2 Games Played, 0 Games Started, Rushing: 1-0, Passing: 6-18-80 1 TD 2 INT, Punting: 6-255; 1949 Buffalo Bills (Regular Season): 11 Games Played, 1 Game Started, Passing: 6-12 86 1 TD 1 INT, Rushing: 2-6, Punting: 16-614; 1949 Buffalo Bills (Postseason): 1 Game Played, 0 Games Started, Passing: 0-3-0, Punting: 5-201; TOTAL (Regular Season): 26 Games Played, 2 Game Started, Passing: 11-26 175 2 TD 4 INT, Rushing: 7-(-20), Interceptions: 1-37, Punting: 63-2439; TOTAL (Postseason): 3 Games Played, 0 Games Started, Rushing: 1-0, Passing: 6-21-80 1 TD 2 INT, Punting: 11-456

Jim Still was drafted by the Los Angeles Dons (26th round) and the Chicago Cardinals (16th round) in 1948. He signed with Los Angeles, but was traded to Buffalo before the season began. He played two seasons with the Bills before retiring from professional football.

Stofer, Kenneth Lamont (Ken)

Position: B; Height: 5'9 1/2"; Weight: 188; High School: Olmstead Falls, OH; Dickinson Seminary (Williamsport, PA); College: Cornell; Born: 8/10/1919, Lakewood, OH; Deceased: 5/4/2006, Westlake, OH; 1946 Buffalo Bisons (Preseason): 1 Game Played, 0 Games Started, Rushing: 1 TD; 1946 Buffalo Bisons (Regular Season): 13 Games Played, 1 Game Started, Passing: 9-26-86 1 TD 1 INT, Receiving: 1-14, Punting: 3-108 0 Blocked, Punt Returns: 5-53, Kick Returns: 2-81; TOTAL (Regular Season): 13 Games Played, 1 Game Started, Passing: 9-26-86 1 TD 1 INT, Receiving: 1-14, Punting: 3-108 0 Blocked, Punt Returns: 5-53, Kick Returns: 2-81

Ken Stofer captained the football team while in high school, as well as played guard on a championship basketball team. He entered Cornell in 1939 and became All-East Honorable Mention Selection in 1941.

Stofer entered the Army Corps of Engineers in 1942 and was shipped to Japan. After 42 months in the service, he separated from the Army with the rank of Captain. During his time in the service, he played a few games of football.

After leaving the service, Stofer returned to Cornell to finish his civil engineering degree. He used his degree to form Gordon F. Stofer & Brother Company with his brother Gordon. Stofer was heavily involved in various civil engineering organizations, as well as served in many Cornell alumni groups.

Stofer only played one season of major league professional football—for the Buffalo Bisons. He had an opportunity to play with the Washington Redskins while in the service, but his commander refused to give him time off to play. After leaving the Bisons, Stofer played with the semi-pro Elmira Gliders. He was one of only two players who were paid on the team.

Later in life, Stofer served as historian for the Lakewood Country Club and Forest Country Club.

Stuart, Roy J.

Position: G-B; Height: 5'8"; Weight: 195; High School: Shawnee (OK); College: Tulsa; Born: 7/25/1920, Shawnee, OK; 1946 Buffalo Bisons (Preseason): 1 Game Played, 0 Games Started; 1946 Buffalo Bisons (Regular Season): 9 Games Played, 0 Games Started; TOTAL (Regular Season): 9 Games Played, 0 Games Started

While at Tulsa, Roy Stuart earned All-America Honorable Mention and All-Missouri Valley honors. He played in the Sun Bowl in 1942 and was inducted into the Tulsa University Hall of Fame in 1992.

After graduating from Tulsa, Stuart joined the Cleveland Rams. He only played one season before entering the Army. Within two weeks of commission from OCS, he left the Army and joined the Navy. While in the Navy, Stuart helped the Norman Navy Zoomers to an undefeated season and simultaneously played for the Detroit Lions.

In July of 1945, Stuart was offered a contract to play with the Cleveland Rams, but did not play again until joining the Buffalo Bisons in 1946. After one season with Buffalo, Stuart retired from playing football and went into coaching. He coached his old high school team before moving to Louisiana to coach high school football, making the finals two years in a row.

He left football and joined Warren Petroleum selling liquid petroleum gas. He retired from Warren in 1982, when they were sold to Gulf Oil.

Non-Buffalo Statistics

1942 Cleveland Rams: 10 Games Played, 6 Games Started, Interceptions: 1–25
1943 Detroit Lions: 6 Games Played, 0 Games Started

Sutton, Joseph Boyle (Joe)

Position: B; Height: 5'11"; Weight: 180; High School: Northeast (Philadelphia, PA); College: Temple; Born: 4/26/1924, Philadelphia, PA; 1949 Buffalo Bills (Regular Season): 11 Games Played, 1 Game Started, Rushing: 9-63, Receiving: 5-63 1 TD, Punt Returns: 6-62, Kick Returns: 4-82; TOTAL (Regular Season): 11 Games Played, 1 Game Started, Rushing: 9-63, Receiving: 5-63 1 TD, Punt Returns: 6-62, Kick Returns: 4-82

Joe Sutton was born April 26, 1924. He grew up in Philadelphia, attending Northeast High School. After getting his degree in Physical Education from Temple, Joe served for three years in the Army. He landed at Normandy ten days after D-Day and fought in the Battle of the Rhine and the Battle of the Bulge.

Upon returning from the war, Joe decided to play football. He was contacted by the Buffalo Bills in 1949 and signed a one-year contract. After the Bills were disbanded, he played three years for his hometown team, the Philadelphia Eagles. He was paid $6000 to play for Buffalo and $5000 for each of the three years with the Eagles. He received a $27 bonus for playing in the December 4, 1949 playoff game with the Cleveland Browns.

Joe met his future wife Pat Garmong in 1950, while playing baseball for the Oil City Refiners. The Refiners were the farm club for the Cincinnati Reds.

After football, Joe went into sales and spent his free time fishing and playing golf. He has three children, two daughters and a son.

Non-Buffalo Statistics

1950 Philadelphia Eagles: 9 Games Played, Rushing: 1-1, Interceptions: 8-67 2 Fumbles, Punt Returns: 9-75, Kick Returns: 1-21
1951 Philadelphia Eagles: 11 Games Played, Interceptions: 2-8
1952 Philadelphia Eagles: 10 Games Played, Interceptions: 3-54

Swan, Edward

Position: E; Height: 6'2½"; Weight: 230; College: (None); Born: 12/1/1925, Buffalo, NY; 1948 Buffalo Bills: On the training camp roster, but did not make the regular season roster; TOTAL: On the training camp roster, but did not make the regular season roster.

Terlep, George Rudolph (Duke)

Position: B; Height: 5'10"; Weight: 180; High School: Elkhart Central (IN); College: Notre Dame; Born: 4/12/1923, Elkhart, IN; 1946 Buffalo Bisons (Preseason): 1 Game Played, 0 Games Started; 1946 Buffalo Bisons (Regular Season): 13 Games Played, 5 Games Started, Rushing: 36-29 1 TD, Passing: 48-123-574 7 TD 14 INT, Punting: 1-31 0 Blocked, Kick Returns: 1-23; 1947 Buffalo Bills (Regular Season): 12 Games Played, 0 Games Started, Rushing: 4-11, Passing: 5-23-51 2 TD 3 INT, Interceptions: 1-0, Punt Returns: 1-17; 1948 Buffalo Bills (Regular Season): 3 Games Played, 0 Games Started, Passing: 0-2-0 1 INT; TOTAL (Regular Season): 28 Games Played, 5 Games Started, Rushing: 40-40 1 TD, Passing: 53-148-625 9 TD 18 INT, Interceptions: 1-0, Punting: 1-31 0 Blocked, Punt Returns: 1-17, Kick Returns: 1-23

After gaining All-Conference and All-State honors in high school, George Terlep earned a football scholarship to Notre Dame. He played a year-and-a-half for the Irish before entering the Navy V-12 program. While in the Navy, he was ordered to report to the Great Lakes Training Facility, where he played football under the legendary Paul Brown. He quarterbacked the team to a 6-3 record and beat his former Notre Dame teammates 39-6.

After leaving the service, Terlep signed with the Buffalo Bisons instead of returning to Notre Dame. He stayed with Buffalo throughout the 1946 and 1947 seasons. Partway into the 1948 season, Terlep was traded to the Cleveland Browns to be reunited with Paul Brown. After one season with Cleveland, Terlep received a call from his former Notre Dame coach Frank Leahy. Leahy mentioned that the University of South Carolina was looking for a backfield coach. Terlep wanted to get into coaching, so this was a perfect fit. Terlep retired from professional football and accepted the job at South Carolina. He stayed there for two years before accepting the same position at Vanderbilt. After Vanderbilt, he took coaching jobs at Pennsylvania and Indiana, before landing the assistant coaching position in the Canadian Football League, winning two Grey Cups.

He retired from coaching and went into the mobile home business. After 25 years, he retired as Vice-President of the company.

Non-Buffalo Statistics

1948 Cleveland Browns: 9 Games Played, 0 Games Started, Rushing: 1-4, Passing: 1-2 27 0 TD 1 INT

Thames, Richard (Dick)

Position: G; 1947 Buffalo Bills: On the training camp roster, but did not make the regular season roster; TOTAL: On the training camp roster, but did not make the regular season roster.

Thibaut, James Pierre (Jim)

Position: B; Height: 5'11"; Weight: 205; College: Tulane; Born: 8/31/1919, New Orleans, LA; Deceased: 4/5/2006, Kenner, LA; 1946 Buffalo Bisons (Regular Season): 5 Games Played, 0 Games Started, Rushing: 10-48 1 TD; TOTAL (Regular Season): 5 Games Played, 0 Games Started, Rushing: 10-48 1 TD; Jim Thibaut was a member of the service champion Fleet City Blue Jackets in 1945. He was drafted by the Brooklyn Dodgers in 1942 (twelfth round)

Thurbon, Robert William (Bob)

Position: B; Height: 5'10½"; Weight: 181; High School: Erie Academy (PA); College: Pittsburgh; Born: 2/22/1918, Erie, PA; Deceased: 9/20/2000, Charlotte, NC; 1946 Buffalo Bisons (Preseason): 1 Game Played, 0 Games

Started, Rushing: 1 TD; 1946 Buffalo Bisons (Regular Season): 2 Games Played, 0 Games Started, Rushing: 3-2, Receiving: 1-(-3), Kick Returns: 1-15; TOTAL (Regular Season): 2 Games Played, 0 Games Started, Rushing: 3-2, Receiving: 1-(-3), Kick Returns: 1-15

Bob Thurbon's college career was highlighted by making the "Play of the Year" in 1939. In a game against Carnegie Tech, Thurbon caught a touchdown pass from Edgar "Special Delivery" Jones to win the game in the last seconds of the fourth quarter. "Greasy" Neale referred to him as "the best back I have seen within the ten-yard line." He played in the North-South game in 1940, where he rushed an average of 19.2 yards per carry.

In 1943, Thurbon joined the combined Pittsburgh-Philadelphia team in the NFL and led the team in scoring with six touchdowns. He went to the combined Chicago-Pittsburgh squad for one season. Thurbon finished his professional career with the 1946 Buffalo Bisons.

Non-Buffalo Statistics

1943 Philadelphia-Pittsburgh: 10 Games Played 1 Game Started, Rushing: 71-291 5 TD, Receiving: 6-100 1 TD, Interceptions: 1-3, Punt Returns: 2-19, Kick Returns: 6-150
1944 Chicago-Pittsburgh: 10 Games Played, 7 Games Started, Rushing: 69-185 4 TD, Receiving: 7-134 1 TD, Interceptions: 2-14, Punting: 15-450, Punt Returns: 1-2, Kick Returns: 12-291

Tomasetti, Louis Vincent (Lou) (Babe)

Position: B; Height: 6'0"; Weight: 218; High School: Old Forge (PA); College: Bucknell; Born: 1/8/1916, Old Forge, PA; Deceased: 3/23/2004, Doylestown, PA; 1946 Buffalo Bisons (Preseason): 1 Game Played, 1 Game Started; 1946 Buffalo Bisons (Regular Season): 13 Games Played, 2 Games Started, Rushing: 43-139 1 TD, Receiving: 6-81 1 TD, Interceptions: 1-0, Punt Returns: 7-138, Kick Returns: 2-85; 1947 Buffalo Bills (Regular Season): 14 Games Played, 7 Games Started, Rushing: 92-326 2 TD, Receiving: 13-125, Interceptions: 1-44 1 TD, Kick Returns: 4-74; 1948 Buffalo Bills (Regular Season): 15 Games Played, 9 Games Started, Rushing: 134-716 7 TD, Receiving: 22-213 8 TD, Kick Returns: 2-14; 1948 Buffalo Bills (Postseason): 2 Games Played, 1 Game Started, Rushing: 23-76, Receiving: 1-(-2); 1949 Buffalo Bills (Regular Season): 11 Games Played, 5 Games Started, Rushing: 54-249 2 TD, Receiving: 9-56 1 TD, Punt Returns: 2-13, Kick Returns: 1-19; 1949 Buffalo Bills (Postseason): 1 Game Played, 0 Games Started, Rushing: 4-9, Receiving: 3-37 1 TD; TOTAL (Regular Season): 53 Games Played, 23 Games Started, Rushing: 323-1430 12 TD, Receiving: 50-475 10 TD, Interceptions: 2-44 1 TD, Punt Returns: 9-151, Kick Returns: 9-192; TOTAL (Postseason): 3 Games Played, 1 Game Started, Rushing: 27-85, Receiving: 4-35 1 TD

Lou Tomasetti was one of only two players to play all four years for Buffalo (the other was Rocco Pirro). He was captain of both his high school and college football teams. While at Bucknell, he was named All-State, All-Eastern and All-American Honorable Mention.

Tomasetti entered the Navy in 1943 and spent nearly a year in the South Pacific. He emerged as an Ensign in 1946.
Tomasetti was drafted in the eleventh round of the 1939 NFL draft by the Pittsburgh Pirates. He played for Pittsburgh for two years before joining the Philadelphia Eagles. He split time between the Eagles and Detroit Lions in 1941 and played a full season for the Eagles in 1942. He then joined the minor league Hollywood Bears. In 1946, Tomasetti joined the Buffalo Bisons. Both Tomasetti and Rocco Pirro played in 56 games for Buffalo, which is the most in franchise history.
Tomasetti also coached football at North Tonawanda High School.

Non-Buffalo Statistics

1939 Pittsbugh Pirates: 11 Games Played, 6 Games Started, Passing: 13-47 140 1 TD 7 INT, Receiving: 4-22, Punting: 3-111
1940 Pittsburgh Steelers: 10 Games Played, 9 Games Started, Passing: 3-6 30 1 TD 2 INT, Receiving: 6-129 1 TD
1941 Philadelphia Eagles: 6 Games Played, 3 Games Started, Receiving: 5-54 1 TD, Punt Returns: 2-30
1941 Detroit Lions: 4 Games Played, 2 Games Started, Interceptions: 1-13, Punt Returns: 1-18, Kick Returns: 1-18
1942 Philadelphia Eagles: 10 Games Played, 5 Games Started, Receiving: 4-22, Interceptions: 1-23, Punt Returns: 3-37, Kick Returns: 4-90

Vandeweghe, Alfred Bernard (Al)

Position: E; Height: 5'11"; Weight: 201; High School: Ridgefield Park (NJ), Hampton (VA); College: William & Mary; Born: 10/25/1920, Wyckoff, NJ; 1946 Buffalo Bisons (Preseason): 1 Game Played, 1 Game Started; 1946 Buffalo Bisons (Regular Season): 5 Games Played, 3 Games Started, Receiving: 6-67 1 TD, Fumble Returns: 1-97 1 TD, Kick Returns: 1-15; TOTAL (Regular Season): 5 Games Played, 3 Games Started, Receiving: 6-67 1 TD, Fumble Returns: 1-97 1 TD, Kick Returns: 1-15

Al Vandeweghe's father was the 13th of 18 children. Born in Belgium, Al's father saw five of his siblings die from the flu in a mere ten days. He was a soccer player that played on a team made up of strictly Vandeweghe's. The team traveled all of Europe to play.

Al Vandeweghe's football career started when he was at Ridgefield High School in New Jersey. There, he won All-County and All-State honors and was later inducted into their Hall of Fame. Vandeweghe transferred to Hampton High School in Virginia and continued his athletic success. For the first time in school history, the basketball team won the state championship. Vandeweghe won All-State honors.

Vandeweghe attended the College of William & Mary, where he converted from back to end. He was an All-American mention in 1942.

After college, Vandeweghe enlisted in the Navy. He was stationed at Bainbridge Naval Station for two years, playing on two undefeated football teams. This earned him Mid-Atlantic All-Service honors. After Bainbridge, Vandeweghe went to Shoemaker, CA to play a year of football on the Fleet City Blue Jacket team that went 8-0-1 in 1945.

After only playing a few games with the Buffalo Bisons, Vandeweghe was contacted by Rube McCray of the College of William & Mary. He was offered a job coaching ends and accepted. In 1947, the team went 9-2 and played in the Dixie Bowl.

In 1950, Vandeweghe left William & Mary to be an Education Advisor at the Army Education Center in Ft. Eustis, VA. He stayed there until he retired as the Chief of Army Education.

Vasicek, Victor Frederick (Vic)

Position: G; Height: 5'11"; Weight: 223; High School: El Campo (TX); College: USC, Texas; Born: 5/5/1926, Austin, TX; Deceased: 6/20/2003, Midland, TX; 1949 Buffalo Bills (Regular Season): 12 Games Played, 2 Games Started, Receiving: 5-0; 1949 Buffalo Bills (Postseason): 1 Game Played, 0 Games Started; TOTAL (Regular Season): 12 Games Played, 2 Games Started, Receiving: 5-0; TOTAL (Postseason): 1 Game Played, 0 Games Started

Vic Vasicek was drafted in the eighth round by the Buffalo Bills and the tenth round by the Washington Redskins in 1949. He signed with Buffalo and played the final season of the franchise's history. In 1950, he was drafted by the Los Angeles Rams in the dispersal draft and played one season for the team.

Non-Buffalo Statistics

1950 Los Angeles Rams: 12 Games Played, Interceptions: 1-52, Kick Returns: 2-30

Vogt, Alois (Allie)

Position: B; Height: 6'0"; Weight: 185; High School: Rufus King (Milwaukee, WI); College: Marquette; Born: 6/20/1921, Germany; Deceased: 2/26/2002, Milwaukee, WI; 1946 Buffalo Bisons (Preseason): 1 Game Played, 0 Games Started; 1946 Buffalo Bisons (Regular Season): 1 Game Played, 0 Games Started; TOTAL (Regular Season): 1 Game Played, 0 Games Started

Born in Germany, Vogt came to the United States when he was four years old. Attending Marquette, he played under future Buffalo Bison's assistant coach Tom Stidham. Vogt received All-America mention in 1943. During World War II, Allie joined the Navy and played football on the Great Lakes military team under Paul Brown. In 1946, Vogt joined the Buffalo Bisons, but only played in one regular season game. After leaving the Bisons, Vogt went to play for the Toronto Argonauts, but a heel injury ended his football career.

After football, Vogt applied his civil engineering training, working in the Milwaukee area. After a while, he formed his own company, A. Vogt Construction, Inc. He and his wife Betty had one daughter and two sons.

Volz, Wilbur Edward

Position: B; Height: 6'0"; Weight: 192; High School: Edwardsville (IL); College: Missouri; Born: 1/1/1924, Edwardsville, IL; 1949 Buffalo Bisons (Regular Season): 8 Games Played, 0 Games Started, Rushing: 4–7 1 TD, Receiving: 1–6, Kick Returns: 3–43; 1949 Buffalo Bills (Postseason): 1 Game Played, 0 Games Started; TOTAL (Regular Season): 8 Games Played, 0 Games Started, Rushing: 4–7 1 TD, Receiving: 1–6, Kick Returns: 3–43; TOTAL (Postseason): 1 Game Played, 0 Games Started

Wilbur Volz started at Missouri in 1942, but entered the Air Force in February of 1943. As a gunner on a B-17, Volz was shot down over the Bay of Biscayne and fought with the French Underground for a few months. Toward the end of 1945, Volz left the service and returned to Missouri.

Volz was drafted by the Bills in 1949 (fourth round) and played one season for the team. After the season was over, Volz returned to Missouri to get his Master's Degree. He started coaching on the high school level. Two weeks before his first game, he was recalled into the service and spent one year fighting in the Korean War. When he returned, he tried out for the Green Bay Packers, but did not make the team.

Volz then went back into coaching and signed on to be the football and baseball coach in Clovis, New Mexico. He then went to the University of Denver on his way to Dartmouth, where he coached for ten years. He then became the Director of Physical Education and Intramurals and remained in that position until retirement.

Whalen, Gerald Cornelius (Jerry)

Position: G-T; Height: 6'1"; Weight: 235; High School: Canisius Prep (Buffalo, NY); College: Canisius; Born: 4/23/1928, Buffalo, NY; Deceased: 11/1973, Buffalo, NY; 1948 Buffalo Bills (Regular Season): 6 Games Played, 0 Games Started; 1948 Buffalo Bills (Postseason): 2 Games Played, 0 Games Started; TOTAL (Regular Season): 6 Games Played, 0 Games Started; TOTAL (Postseason): 2 Games Played, 0 Games Started

Jerry Whalen earned three letters as a halfback while at Canisius Prep. He attended Canisius College for only one year before he was forced to leave. At that point, he joined the Buffalo Bills. He received special approval from the AAFC Commissioner to play while he went back to school to finish his degree.

White, Eugene G. (Gene)

Position: G; Height: 6'0"; Weight: 205; College: Indiana; Born: 8/3/1919, South Bend, IN; Deceased: 4/24/1989, South Bend, IN; 1946 Buffalo Bisons (Regular Season): 1 Game Played, 0 Games Started; TOTAL (Regular Season): 1 Game Played, 0 Games Started

Gene White earned All-State and All-Conference honors while at Indiana. He was captain of the 1941 team and played in the 1946 College All-Star game.

White enlisted in the Infantry in 1942 and fought in the ETO (Europe) with the 100th Division. He earned a Bronze Star, Combat Infantry Badge and the Purple Heart.

Wizbicki, Alexander John (Alex)

Position: B; Height: 5'11"; Weight: 188; High School: Boys (Brooklyn, NY); College: Dartmouth, Holy Cross; Born: 10/6/1921, Brooklyn, NY; 1947 Buffalo Bills (Regular Season): 13 Games Played, 2 Games Started, Rushing: 9–44, Punt Returns: 9–105, Kick Returns: 5–164 1 TD; 1948 Buffalo Bills (Regular Season): 10 Games Played, 1 Game Started, Interceptions: 3–49, Punt Returns: 3–33; 1948 Buffalo Bills (Postseason): 2 Games Played, 0 Games Started; 1949 Buffalo Bills (Regular Season): 13 Games Played, 1 Game Started, Rushing: 5-(–10), Interceptions: 1–1, Kick Returns: 1–22; 1949 Buffalo Bills (Postseason): 1 Game Played, 0 Games Started; TOTAL (Regular Season): 36 Games Played, 4 Games Started, Rushing: 14–34, Interceptions: 4–50, Punt Returns: 12–138, Kick Returns: 6–186 1 TD; TOTAL (Postseason): 3 Games Played, 0 Games Started

Alex Wizbicki started at Holy Cross in 1941, but left in 1943 to serve in the Marine Corps. While in the service, Wizbicki played football for Dartmouth before being shipped overseas. While abroad, he did reconnaissance work for the 6th Marine Division, earning a Bronze Star. He spent over two years in the military before returning to Holy Cross in 1946.

Wizbicki was drafted by the Pittsburgh Steelers in 1945 (18th round), but was traded before the season. He was offered a contract with the Buffalo Bills and accepted, playing two seasons for the franchise. In 1950, the Cleveland Browns selected him in the dispersal draft, but he was traded to the Green Bay Packers. He retired from football after playing one season with Green Bay.

He went into sales and marketing, and retired in 1994.

Non-Buffalo Statistics

1950 Green Bay Packers: 11 Games Played, Interceptions: 2–38

Wukits, Albert Robert (Al) (Buckets)

Position: C; Height: 6'3"; Weight: 218; High School: Millvale (PA); College: Duquesne; Born: 12/16/1917, Millvale, PA; Deceased: 10/15/1978, Pittsburgh, PA; 1946 Buffalo Bisons (Preseason): 1 Game Played, 1 Game Started; 1946 Buffalo Bisons (Regular Season): 8 Games Played, 5 Games Started, Interceptions: 2–26; TOTAL (Regular Season): 8 Games Played, 5 Games Started, Interceptions: 2–26

Al Wukits was the captain of both the football and basketball teams while at Duquesne. After graduating from college, he immediately signed with the combined Pittsburgh-Philadelphia franchise in the NFL. He played three straight seasons for Pittsburgh before heading to Buffalo, where he signed the same day as Duquesne and Steeler teammate Ted Grabinski. Midway through the 1946 season, Wukits was sent to the Miami Seahawks.

Non-Buffalo Statistics

1943 Philadelphia-Pittsburgh: 10 Games Played, 1 Game Started, Interceptions: 1–7, 1 Fumble TD

1944 Chicago-Pittsburgh: 10 Games Played, 3 Games Started
1945 Pittsburgh Steelers: 3 Games Played, 1 Game Started, 2 Fumbles
1946 Miami Seahawks: 7 Games Played, 3 Games Started

Wyhonic, John N. (aka John Wyhowanec)

Position: T-G; Height: 6'0"; Weight: 213; College: Alabama; Born: 12/23/1919, Tiltonville, OH; Deceased: 7/17/1989, Arcadia, FL; 1948 Buffalo Bills (Regular Season): 11 Games Played, 2 Games Started; 1948 Buffalo Bills (Postseason): 1 Game Played, 0 Games Started; 1949 Buffalo Bills (Regular Season): 4 Games Played, 0 Games Started; TOTAL (Regular Season): 15 Games Played, 2 Games Started; TOTAL (Postseason): 1 Game Played, 0 Games Started

John Wyhonic was drafted by the Philadelphia Eagles in 1942 (14th round) and spent two seasons with the team. He spent part of the 1948 season with the Baltimore Colts before being shipped to Buffalo for the remainder of the season. He was an All-America Honorable Mention at Alabama.

Non-Buffalo Statistics

1946 Philadelphia Eagles: 11 Games Played, 2 Games Started
1947 Philadelphia Eagles: 12 Games Played, 2 Games Started

Yagiello, Raymond (Ray)

Position: G; Height: 6'2"; Weight: 220; High School: Kearny (NJ); College: Franklin & Marshall, Catawba College; Born: 9/23/1923, Orange, NJ; Deceased: 6/9/1999; 1947 Buffalo Bills: On the training camp roster, but did not make the regular season roster; TOTAL: On the training camp roster, but did not make the regular season roster.

Ray Yagiello was a four-letter winner while at Kearny High School (football, basketball, baseball and track). He graduated in 1941 and entered Catawba College, where he played four years of football. He was unanimous All-Conference in both 1946 and 1947, MVP of the conference in 1947, Associated Press Little All-America second team in 1946 and 1947, and was the only small college player named All-State.

Yagiello spent over three years in the Navy, serving in the South Pacific. He was drafted by the Los Angeles Rams in 1948 (22nd round). While playing football, he worked on his Masters Degree in Physical Education at North Carolina.

Non-Buffalo Statistics

1948 Los Angeles Rams: 12 Games Played, 0 Games Started
1949 Los Angeles Rams: 12 Games Played, 7 Games Started, Fumbles: 1–0

Yelich, Steve

Position: G; Height: 6'2"; Weight: 205; College: Syracuse, Canisius; Born: 7/14/1923, Lackawanna, NY; 1948 Buffalo Bills: On the training camp roster, but did not make the regular season roster; TOTAL: On the training camp roster, but did not make the regular season roster.

Zontini, Louis Rogers (Lou)

Position: B; Height: 5'9"; Weight: 199; High School: Sherman (Seth, WV); College: Notre Dame; Born: 8/30/1917, Whitesvills, WV; Deceased: 8/6/1986, Richmond Heights, OH; 1946 Buffalo Bisons (Preseason): 1 Game Played, 0 Games Started; 1946 Buffalo Bisons (Regular Season): 13 Games Played, 7 Games Started, Passing: 0–1–0 0 TD 0 INT, Interceptions: 1–2, Punting: 44–1597 0 Blocked, Kick Returns: 1–19, Extra Points: 30/31, Field Goals: 4/8; TOTAL (Regular Season): 13 Games Played, 7 Games Started, Passing: 0–1–0 0 TD 0 INT, Interceptions: 1–2, Punting: 44–1597 0 Blocked, Kick Returns: 1–19, Extra Points: 30/31, Field Goals: 4/8

Lou Zontini was All-State in football and an All-Tournament guard in basketball while at Sherman High School. He earned All-America Honorable Mention honors at Notre Dame in 1938.

While serving in the Navy, Zontini played with the undefeated Fleet City Blue Jackets. He was one of nine Bison players who played for that service championship team.

Non-Buffalo Statistics

1940 Chicago Cardinals: 8 Games Played, 0 Games Started, Rushing: 1–1, Interceptions: 1–20, Punting: 2–92, Extra Points: 10/10, Field Goals: 2/5
1941 Chicago Cardinals: 8 Games Played, 1 Game Started, Rushing: 1–(–9), Receiving: 1–22, Punting: 12–446, Extra Points: 5/7, Field Goals: 0/4
1944 Cleveland Rams: 10 Games Played, 0 Games Started, Rushing: 33–105 3 TD, Passing: 2–2 18, Receiving: 3–88 1 TD, Interceptions: 2–14, Punt Returns: 4–47, Kick Returns: 3–66, Extra Points: 14/16, Field Goals: 3/6

Chapter Notes

Prologue

1. Jeffrey Miller. *Tommy Hughitt: Mr. Everything* (The Historical Society of the Buffalo All-Americans, Bisons and Rangers).
2. Kenneth R. Crippen. "The 1918 Buffalo Semi-Professional Football League," *Coffin Corner* vol. 25, no. 1, 2003.
3. Kenneth R. Crippen. "1919 Buffalo Prospects." *Coffin Corner*, vol. 23, no. 5, 2001.
4. Jeffrey J. Miller. *Buffalo's Forgotten Champions: The Story of Buffalo's First Professional Football Team and the Lost 1921 Title* Philadelphia: Xlibris, 2004.
5. Bob Carroll and Bob Gill, eds., *Bulldogs on Sunday*. (Professional Football Researchers Association, 1921). Jeffrey Miller. *Buffalo's Forgotten Champions: The Story of Buffalo's First Professional Football Team and the Lost 1921 Title* (Philadelphia: Xlibris, 2004).
6. Jeffrey J. Miller. *Buffalo's Forgotten Champions: The Story of Buffalo's First Professional Football Team and the Lost 1921 Title.* (Philadelphia: Xlibris Corporation, 2004).
7. Bob Gill and Tod Maher. *The Outsiders: The Three American Football Leagues of 1936–1941* (Professional Football Researchers Association, 1989).
8. Tony Barnhart. "The '40s: NFL Goes to War," *Coffin Corner*, vol. 9, no. 8.
9. Ibid.
10. "Pro Football Battle is Now in Earnest," *Nebraska State Journal*, August 3, 1944.
11. "Pro Football's Future Studied," *Piqua Daily Call*, April 4, 1945.
12. "Secret Meet by Pro Grid Club Owners: Two Proposed Rival Loops in Trouble," *Council Bluffs Nonpareil*, June 2, 1945.
13. "Grid Leagues do 'Elfoldo,'" *San Mateo Times*, June 5, 1945.
14. "Red Grange to Head New Pro Grid Ring," *Nebraska State Journal*, November 28, 1944.
15. Martin Witney. "Honolulu Gridders Planning to Carry a Sideshow, Too," *Morning Herald*, December 26, 1944.
16. "Red Grange to Head New Pro Grid Ring," *Nebraska State Journal*, November 28, 1944.
17. "NFL Doubts Soundness of Rival Loops," *Mason City Globe-Gazette*, May 22, 1945.
18. "Secret Meet by Pro Grid Club Owners: Two Proposed Rival Loops in Trouble," *Council Bluffs Nonpareil*, June 2, 1945.
19. Ibid.
20. Ibid.
21. "Grid Leagues do 'Elfoldo,'" *San Mateo Times*, June 5, 1945.

Chapter 1

1. Grantland Rice. "Rice Sees Room for Two Major Football Leagues," *Syracuse Herald Journal*, January 16, 1946.
2. Bob Meyer. "Coast Cities Seek Berth in Pro Football Circuit: San Francisco, Los Angeles in Post-War Setup," *Nevada State Journal*, January 13, 1944.
3. John M. Flynn. "The Referee's Sporting Chat," *Berkshire Evening Eagle*, January 10, 1944.
4. Thomas M. Tarapacki. *The Rise and Fall of the Buffalo Bills* (Unpublished).
5. "Cordovano Seeks Buffalo Franchise," *Nebraska State Journal*, January 9, 1944.
6. Charles Chamberlain. "Big Scramble for Players by Pros Seen," *Titusville Herald*, January 13, 1944.
7. "Pro Grid Moguls Return Coast Money, Keep Buffalo's," *Berkshire Evening Eagle*, January 14, 1944.
8. Bob Meyer. "Coast Cities Seek Berth in Pro Football Circuit: San Francisco, Los Angeles in Post-War Setup," *Nevada State Journal*, January 13, 1944.
9. Charles Chamberlain. "Big Scramble for Players by Pros Seen," *Titusville Herald*, January 13, 1944.

295

10. "Buffalo to Field Pro Grid Team," *Coshocton Tribune*, January 23, 1944.
11. Hugh Fullerton, Jr. "Pro Football Expansion to be Delayed," *Evening Tribune*, April 21, 1944.
12. Thomas M. Tarapacki. *The Rise and Fall of the Buffalo Bills* (Unpublished).
13. Lee Dunbar. "What, Another Pro Loop?," *Oakland Tribune*, August 9, 1944.
14. "Wieman signs as Lion Mentor," *Stars and Stripes Mediterranean*, July 7, 1944.
15. "New Pro Grid Loop Planned," *Oakland Tribune*, September 2, 1944.
16. "All-American Pro Grid Conference, Rival to National Loop, Set for '45," *Nevada State Journal*, September 17, 1944.
17. "Tunney Named in New Pro Football Loop," *Stars and Stripes London*, September 4, 1944.
18. Ibid.
19. "Miami Granted Franchise in New Grid Loop," *Troy Record*, December 11, 1944.
20. Sgt. Merrell Whittlesey. "The Boys of Shekel U. Make Ready for a Bitter Civil War," *Stars and Stripes Mediterranean*, October 28, 1945.
21. Walter Byers. "New Grid Circuit Will Raid National League of Players," *Nevada State Journal*, September 2, 1945.
22. "Pros Squabble About Hirsch," *Nevada State Journal*, November 27, 1945.
23. Ibid.
24. "Sports Before Your Eyes," *Gettysburg Times*, November 15, 1945.
25. Joe Clifford and Denny Lynch. *The 1946–49 Buffalo Bisons/Bills: Members of the All-America Football Conference* (Archives Department — Buffalo Bills Football Team, Inc., 2006).
26. "General Sports Topics," *Olean Times Herald*, April 1, 1946.
27. "Buffalo Eleven to Make Debut Sept. 8," *Blizzard*, December 14, 1945.
28. "Two Stars Lost," *Ada Weekly News*, December 20, 1945.
29. "'Skins Lose Juzwik to Buffalo Eleven of New Pro League," *Kingsport News*, December 20, 1945.
30. Bill Murdock. "Verne Gagne: A Wrestler's Wrestler." *The Wrestling Gospel*. URL: http://www.mikemooneyham.com/pages/viewfull.cfm?ObjectID=55D14610-7990-4AB8-A688B6397F132041. Accessed October 6, 2007.
31. Sgt. Merrell Whittlesey. "The Boys of Shekel U. Make Ready for a Bitter Civil War," *Stars and Stripes Mediterranean*, October 28, 1945.
32. Ibid.

Chapter 2

1. "All-America Loop Membership Held to Eight for '46," *Middle Pacific Stars and Stripes*, January 5, 1946.
2. "New Pro Gridiron League Sets Up New Draft Deal," *Fresno Bee Republican*, January 6, 1946.
3. Ibid.
4. Letter from Ed McKeever to Fiore A. Cesare, dated November 14, 1946.
5. Letter from Albert E. Humphreys to Fiore A. Cesare dated November 22, 1946; Letter from Jack Harding to Fiore A. Cesare dated November 18, 1946; Letter from John "Ox" Dagrosa to Fiore A. Cesare dated November 15, 1946.
6. At this point, I could go into the connection between the Philadelphia Eagles and the Frankford Yellowjackets, who were members of the NFL from 1924 through 1931. The new Philadelphia franchise could technically be considered a continuation of the Frankford Yellowjacket team as the incorporation papers for the Philadelphia Eagles were just a name change and not a new corporation. The Eagles also assumed some of the debt owned by the Yellowjackets. The official NFL standpoint is that the Philadelphia Eagles are a new franchise. Since this distinction is really not relevant to the discussion, no further details will be provided and no further arguments will be made.
7. Pro Football Hall of Fame, "Bert Bell: The Commissioner," *Coffin Corner*, vol. 18, no. 3.
8. Pro Football Hall of Fame, "Dan Reeves Moves West," *Coffin Corner*, vol. 20, no. 1.
9. "National League Enlists Pacific Coast Aid in Grid War," *Syracuse Herald Journal*, January 16, 1946.
10. Ibid.
11. Ibid.
12. "Buffalo Signs Batorski, Former Colgate Gridder," *Blizzard*, January 24, 1946.
13. "Two Gridders to Join Bisons," *Syracuse Herald Journal*, March 16, 1946.
14. "New Loop Adds Gridiron Talent," *Coshocton Tribune*, April 2, 1946.
15. "Bisons Sign Two More Grid Players," *Times Record*, April 3, 1946.
16. "General Sports Topics," *Olean Times Herald*, April 9, 1946.
17. "Dugger Signs with Buffalo," *Blizzard*, April 12, 1946.
18. "General Sports Topics," *Olean Times Herald*, May 14, 1946.
19. "General Sports Topics," *Olean Times Herald*, April 25, 1946.

20. "General Sports Topics," *Olean Times Herald*, April 26, 1946.
21. "Sam Cordovano Quits as General Manager Buffalo Pro Gridders," *Olean Times Herald*, May 28, 1946.
22. Hugh Fullerton, Jr. "The Roundup," *Lowell Sun*, January 14, 1946.
23. Aldo T. "Buff" Donelli obituary *Columbia University Record*, vol. 20, no. 1, September 9, 1994.
24. Lowell "Red" Dawson Biography, University of Wisconsin-River Falls website. URL: http://www.uwrf.edu/sportsrecords/hall-of-fame–1977.php. Accessed August 27, 2007.
25. Alex Wizbicki, exclusive interview, March 8, 2008.
26. Ray Schmidt. "Welcome to L.A.," *Coffin Corner*, vol. 25, no. 6.
27. Joe Clifford and Denny Lynch. "The 1946–49 Buffalo Bisons/Bills: Members of the All-America Football Conference." (Archives Department — Buffalo Bills Football Team, Inc., 2006).
28. "Buffalo Bisons Sign Dekdebrun," *Olean Times Herald*, June 10, 1946.
29. Lawrence J. Skiddy, "Dekdebrun Votes For His Home Team," *Syracuse Herald Journal*, June 13, 1946.
30. "Buffalo Bisons Sign Dekdebrun," *Olean Times Herald*, June 10, 1946.
31. Charles E. Fish. "Sideline Sidelights," *Olean Times Herald*, June 26, 1946.
32. "Buffalo Bisons to Train at Oconomowoc, Wis.: Shift Caused by Student Load at Bonaventure," *Olean Times Herald*, July 9, 1946.
33. *Ibid.*
34. Benito Pucci, exclusive interview, September 11, 2007.

Chapter 3

1. Edward N. Feinen. "Two Big Lines Feature Bison Footballers Bid for Conference Honors," *Olean Times Herald*, August 27, 1946.
2. Arthur Statuto, exclusive interview, June 7, 2008.
3. Achille Maggioli, exclusive interview, December 26, 2007.
4. Thomas M. Tarapacki. *The Rise and Fall of the Buffalo Bills* (Unpublished).
5. George Buksar, exclusive interview, March 29, 2008.
6. *Ibid.*
7. Robert Elmer. "Clash Marked By Long Runs," *Buffalo News*. August 30, 1946.
8. *Ibid.*
9. *Ibid.*
10. Ray Ryan. "25,489 See Dodgers Win Grid Opener," *Buffalo News*, September 9, 1946.
11. Bob Braunwart and Bob Carroll. "Glenn Dobbs," *Coffin Corner*, vol. 2, no. 9.
12. Ray Ryan. "25,489 See Dodgers Win Grid Opener," *Buffalo News*, September 9, 1946.
13. *Ibid.*
14. *Ibid.*
15. Benito Pucci, exclusive interview, September 11, 2007.
16. Mike Kanaley. "Bison Pro Gridders Bow to Yankees by Score of 21 to 10," *Buffalo Courier-Express*, September 14, 1946.
17. *Ibid.*
18. "Nelson to Join Bison Gridders," *Olean Times Herald*, September 20, 1946.
19. Harold Sauerbrei. "Graham Pitches Two Scoring Passes as Browns Blast Buffalo, 28–0," *The Plain Dealer*, September 22, 1946.
20. Otto Schnellbacher, exclusive interview by Andy Piascik, April 13, 2004.
21. Harold Sauerbrei. "Graham Pitches Two Scoring Passes as Browns Blast Buffalo, 28–0," *The Plain Dealer*, September 22, 1946.
22. Andy Piascik. "Marion Motley," *Coffin Corner*, vol. 24, no. 4.
23. Otto Schnellbacher, exclusive interview by Andy Piascik, April 13, 2004.
24. Harold Sauerbrei. "Graham Pitches Two Scoring Passes as Browns Blast Buffalo, 28–0." *The Plain Dealer*, September 22, 1946.
25. Tony Wurzer. "Same Old Story — Bisons Rated 1–3 Against AAC Foe," *Buffalo Evening News*, September 25, 1946.
26. Ron Wolf, exclusive interview, September 4, 2008.
27. Edward Prell. "Chicago Rally in 4th Quarter Whips Bisons," *Buffalo News*, September 25, 1946.
28. *Ibid.*
29. Tony Wurzer. "Scoring 59 Points In Two Games, Herd Salvages Only Tie," *Buffalo Evening News*, September 30, 1946.
30. *Ibid.*
31. "Grid Bisons Add Strength for Yankees," *Olean Times Herald*, October 3, 1946.
32. Albert Vandeweghe, exclusive interview via letter, September 10, 2007.
33. "Gridiron Yanks Defeat Bisons by 21 to 13 Tally," *Times Record*, October 5, 1946.
34. "Hawks Quit Cellar on Erlitz' Boot," *Buffalo Evening News*, October 12, 1946.
35. *Ibid.*
36. "Dawson Names New Bison Backfield," *Dunkirk Evening Observer*, October 18, 1946.

37. Mike Kanaley. "Football Bisons Beat Frisco, 17 to 14," *Buffalo Courier-Express*, October 20, 1946.
38. Raymond Ebli, exclusive interview by Andy Piascik, December 21, 2004.
39. Mike Kanaley. "Football Bisons Beat Frisco, 17 to 14," *Buffalo Courier-Express*, October 20, 1946.
40. "Buffalo Bisons Seek Second Win in Sunday Tilt," *Olean Times Herald*, October 26, 1946.
41. George Ratterman. *Confessions of a Gypsy Quarterback: Inside the Wacky World of Pro Football* (New York: Coward-McCann, 1962).
42. Mike Kanaley. "Football Bisons Blast Chicago Rockets to Defeat With Record 49 to 17," *Buffalo Courier-Express*, October 28, 1946.
43. "49ers, Bisons Meet At Kezar," *Oakland Tribune*, November 1, 1946.
44. Mike Kanaley. "Bisons Bow to 49ers, 27–14," *Buffalo Courier-Express*, November 2, 1946.
45. Mike Kanaley. "Buffalo Suffers Second Loss To Trailing Eleven," *Buffalo Courier-Express*, November 18, 1946.
46. Harold Sauerbrei. "Browns' Long Runs Clinch Western Title and Playoff Role, 42–17," *The Plain Dealer*, November 24, 1946.
47. *Ibid.*
48. *Ibid.*
49. *1947 All-America Football Conference Record Manual.*
50. *Ibid.*
51. *Ibid.*
52. Thomas M. Tarapacki. *The Rise and Fall of the Buffalo Bills* (Unpublished).
53. *1947 All-America Football Conference Record Manual.*
54. *Ibid.*
55. *Ibid.*
56. Bob Carroll, Michael Gershman, David Neft, and John Thorn, *Total Football: The Official Encyclopedia of the National Football League* (New York: HarperCollins, 1997).
57. Raymond Ebli, exclusive interview by Andy Piascik, December 21, 2008.

Chapter 4

1. Game program, Cleveland Browns vs. Buffalo Bills, October 17, 1948.
2. *Ibid.*
3. Thomas M. Tarapacki. *The Rise and Fall of the Buffalo Bills* (Unpublished).
4. Arthur Statuto, exclusive interview, June 7, 2008.
5. "Frank Dunn Quits Bison Footballers," *Olean Times Herald*, February 12, 1947.
6. *1947 All-America Football Conference Record Manual.*
7. *Ibid.*
8. *Ibid.*
9. *1946 Buffalo Bisons Football Team 50th Anniversary: WNY's Pro Football Pioneers* (Buffalo Bills Football Club, Inc. 1996).
10. Joe Cronin, et al., *1947 Buffalo Bills Press Guide*, 2007.
11. Benito Pucci, exclusive interview, September 11, 2007.
12. "Yankees Thump Bills 29–7, In Newark Go," *Dunkirk Evening Observer*, August 19, 1947.
13. "Buffalo Bills Trim Baltimore," *Syracuse Herald Journal*, August 23, 1947.
14. Jim Campbell. "Dick Barwegan," *Coffin Corner*, vol. 27, no. 2.
15. William Fay, "Buffalo All-Americas Upset New York, 28–24," *Chicago Daily Tribune*, September 1, 1947.
16. Ratterman was incorrect in his description of the play. It was actually a thirty-nine-yard pass play, not thirty-two yards.
17. George Ratterman. *Confessions of a Gypsy Quarterback: Inside the Wacky World of Pro Football* (New York: Coward-McCann, 1962).
18. *Ibid.*
19. William Fay. "Buffalo All-Americas Upset New York, 28–24," *Chicago Daily Tribune*, September 1, 1947.
20. *Ibid.*
21. *Ibid.*
22. Alex Wizbicki, exclusive interview, March 8, 2008.
23. Edward Prell. "All-America Browns Rout Buffalo, 30–14," *Chicago Daily Tribune*, September 6, 1947.
24. *Ibid.*
25. John Henshan. "Ratterman, Who Beat Bears, Says Browns Are Stronger," *The Plain Dealer*, September 5, 1947.
26. Edward Prell. "All-America Browns Rout Buffalo, 30–14," *Chicago Daily Tribune*, September 6, 1947.
27. John Henshan. "Ratterman, Who Beat Bears, Says Browns Are Stronger," *The Plain Dealer*, September 5, 1947.
28. *Ibid.*
29. *Ibid.*
30. *Ibid.*
31. *Ibid.*
32. *Ibid.*
33. *Ibid.*
34. William Fay. "Bills Beat Rockets,

28–20," *Chicago Daily Tribune*, September 15, 1947.
35. *Ibid.*
36. *Ibid.*
37. *Ibid.*
38. *Ibid.*
39. *Ibid.*
40. William Fay. "Ratterman's Passes Beat Rockets, 31–14: Buffalo Hands Chicago 4th Straight Loss," *Chicago Daily Tribune*, September 20, 1947.
41. *Ibid.*
42. *Ibid.*
43. "Forty-Niners Top Buffalo by 41–24," *New York Times*, September 29, 1947.
44. *Ibid.*
45. Alex Wizbicki, exclusive interview, March 8, 2008.
46. Dick Hyland. "Ratterman Stars as Bills Edge Dons, 27 to 25," *Los Angeles Times*, October 6, 1947.
47. *Ibid.*
48. *Ibid.*
49. *Ibid.*
50. "Bills Win, 20 to 15, As Colts Protest," *New York Times*, October 13, 1947.
51. *Ibid.*
52. *Ibid.*
53. *Ibid.*
54. *Ibid.*
55. Louis Effrat. "Dodgers Tie Buffalo in 4th, 14–14, on Hoernschemeyer's 84-Yard Run," *New York Times*, October 18, 1947.
56. Alex Wizbicki, exclusive interview, March 8, 2008.
57. Louis Effrat. "Dodgers Tie Buffalo in 4th, 14–14, on Hoernschemeyer's 84-Yard Run," *New York Times*, October 18, 1947.
58. *Ibid.*
59. *Ibid.*
60. *Ibid.*
61. "Ratterman Leads Buffalo to Victory in Pro Conference Game," *New York Times*, October 27, 1947.
62. *Ibid.*
63. *Ibid.*
64. According to Conference scoring rules, George Ratterman was credited with the touchdown pass.
65. "Ratterman Leads Buffalo to Victory in Pro Conference Game," *New York Times*, October 27, 1947.
66. Harold Sauerbrei. "Graham Fires 3 Scoring Passes as Browns Hurdle Buffalo, 28–7," *The Plain Dealer*. November 2, 1947.
67. *Ibid.*
68. *Ibid.*
69. *Ibid.*
70. *Ibid.*

71. "Bills Blank Dons, 25–0 in Mudfest," *Los Angeles Times*, November 10, 1947.
72. *Ibid.*
73. *Ibid.*
74. *Ibid.*
75. "Buffalo Downs Baltimore, 34–14, Stays in Race for Division Title," *New York Times*, November 24, 1947.
76. *Ibid.*
77. *Ibid.*
78. Louis Effrat. "Yankees Smother Buffalo and Retain Eastern Division All-America Honors," *New York Times*, December 1, 1947.
79. *Ibid.*
80. "Forty-Niners Tie Buffalo, 21 to 21," *New York Times*, December 8, 1947.
81. *Ibid.*
82. *Ibid.*

Chapter 5

1. Bob Carroll, Michael Gershman, David Neft, John Thorn. *Total Football: The Official Encyclopedia of the National Football League* (New York: HarperCollins, 1997).
2. Joe Clifford and Denny Lynch. "The 1946–49 Buffalo Bisons/Bills: Members of the All-America Football Conference" (Archives Department — Buffalo Bills Football Team, Inc., 2006).
3. "Buffalo Bills and New York Yankees Play to 28–28 Tie," *Syracuse Herald Journal*, August 13, 1948.
4. "Rickey Moves For 2-a-Week Grid Schedule," *Syracuse Herald Journal*, August 18, 1948.
5. *Ibid.*
6. George Ratterman. *Confessions of a Gypsy Quarterback: Inside the Wacky World of Pro Football* (New York: Coward-McCann, 1962).
7. Bills Defeat Dodgers in Grid Battle. *Syracuse Herald Journal*. August 18, 1948.
8. George Ratterman. *Confessions of a Gypsy Quarterback: Inside the Wacky World of Pro Football* (New York: Coward-McCann, 1962).
9. Browns Batter Bills for 35–21 Victory. *Dunkirk Evening Observer*. August 23, 1948.

Chapter 6

1. William O'Connor. Exclusive Interview. May 4, 2008.
2. "Forty-Niners Stop Buffalo, 35–14," *New York Times*, August 30, 1948.
3. Robert Cromie. "Bills Swamp Rockets in East, 42 to 7," *Chicago Daily Tribune*, September 7, 1948.

4. Harold Sauerbrei. "Browns Pile Up 504 Yards in Whipping Buffalo, 42–13, for Second Straight," *The Plain Dealer*, September 12, 1948.
5. Ibid.
6. Ibid.
7. "Forty-Niners Halt Buffalo, 38 to 28," *New York Times*, September 27, 1948.
8. Joseph Hession. "Frankie Albert: "Mr. 49er," *Coffin Corner*, vol. 7, no. 5.
9. "Forty-Niners Halt Buffalo, 38 to 28," *New York Times*, September 27, 1948.
10. Ibid.
11. "Football Dodgers Bow to Bills, 31–21," *New York Times*, October 4, 1948.
12. Ibid.
13. Joseph M. Sheehan. "Yankees Score Two Last-Half Touchdowns to Top Buffalo," *New York Times*, October 11, 1948.
14. Arthur Statuto, exclusive interview. April 20, 2008, and June 7, 2008.
15. Harold Sauerbrei. "Browns Win, 31–14, For Seventh in Row," *The Plain Dealer*, October 17, 1948.
16. Ibid.
17. Dick Hyland. "Bills Batter Dons, 35 to 21; Dobbs Hurt," *Los Angeles Times*, October 25, 1948.
18. Ibid.
19. Ibid.
20. Ibid.
21. Ron Wolf, exclusive interview. September 4, 2008.
22. "Buffalo Conquers Colt Eleven, 35–17," *New York Times*, November 1, 1948.
23. Ibid.
24. Ibid.
25. Roscoe McGowen. "Chappuis Sets New Passing Record As Buffalo Halts Brooklyn, 26–21," *New York Times*, November 8, 1948.
26. Ibid.
27. Ibid.
28. Arthur Statuto, exclusive interview. June 7, 2008.
29. Dick Hyland. "Dons Upset Bills in Final Minute," *Los Angeles Times*, November 15, 1948.
30. Ibid.
31. Ibid.
32. Ibid.
33. Ibid.
34. Ibid.
35. Robert Cromie. "Bills Overcome Rockets in 4th Quarter, 39–35," *Chicago Daily Tribune*, November 26, 1948.
36. Ibid.
37. Ibid.
38. Ibid.

39. Joseph M. Sheehan. "Buffalo Topples Yankees at Stadium: Alert Bills Rout Bombers by 35–14," *New York Times*, November 29, 1948.
40. Thomas M. Tarapacki. "The Rise and Fall of the Buffalo Bills," (Unpublished).
41. Joseph M. Sheehan. "Buffalo Topples Yankees at Stadium: Alert Bills Rout Bombers by 35–14," *New York Times*, November 29, 1948.
42. Louis Effrat. "Baltimore Downs Buffalo, Forcing Play-off for All-America Eastern Title," *New York Times*, December 6, 1948.
43. Ibid.
44. Arthur Statuto, exclusive interview. June 7, 2008.
45. Joseph M. Sheehan. "Bills Conquer Baltimore, 28–17, on 3 Touchdowns in Last Period," *New York Times*, December 13, 1948.
46. Ibid.
47. William Gompers, exclusive interview. September 8, 2007.
48. Joseph M. Sheehan. "Bills Conquer Baltimore, 28–17, on 3 Touchdowns in Last Period," *New York Times*, December 13, 1948.
49. Alex Wizbicki, exclusive interview. March 8, 2008.
50. Ibid.
51. Thomas M. Tarapacki. "The Rise and Fall of the Buffalo Bills," (Unpublished).
52. William O'Connor, exclusive interview. May 4, 2008.
53. Harold Sauerbrei. "Browns Win Third Title, 49 to 7," *The Plain Dealer*, December 19, 1948.
54. Ibid.
55. Arthur Statuto, exclusive interview. April 20, 2007.
56. Arthur Statuto, exclusive interview. June 7, 2008.
57. Harold Sauerbrei. "Browns Win Third Title, 49 to 7," *The Plain Dealer*, December 19, 1948.
58. Thomas M. Tarapacki. *The Rise and Fall of the Buffalo Bills* (Unpublished).
59. AAFC attendees were Ben Lindheimer (Los Angeles Dons), Dan Topping (New York Yankees), Arthur McBride (Cleveland Browns), Anthony Morabito (San Francisco 49ers) and Jim Breuil (Buffalo Bills).

Chapter 7

1. *1949 All-America Football Conference Record Manual*.
2. Jesse Freitas, exclusive interview. June 14, 2008.
3. "Bills Wallop Jersey Giants," *Syracuse Herald Journal*, August 6, 1949.

4. Joseph Sutton, exclusive interview. September 11, 2007.
5. "Bills Cut Squad; Play Colts Tonight," *Olean Times Herald*, August 10, 1949.
6. "Colts Down Bills in Exhibition," *The Capital*, August 11, 1949.
7. "49ers Defeat Bills, 21–10," *Oakland Tribune*, August 15, 1949.
8. "Bills Batter Bulldogs, 48–0," *Dunkirk Evening Observer*, August 20, 1949.
9. "Hornets Defeat Buffalo, 17–14," *Chicago Daily Tribune*, August 27, 1949.
10. *Ibid*.
11. *Ibid*.
12. Jesse Freitas, exclusive interview. June 14, 2008.
13. Thomas M. Tarapacki. *The Rise and Fall of the Buffalo Bills* (Unpublished).
14. Harold Sauerbrei. "Graham's 3 Scoring Passes in Last Period Give Browns 18–18 Tie at Buffalo," *The Plain Dealer*, September 5, 1949.
15. *Ibid*.
16. *Ibid*.
17. Arthur Statuto, exclusive interview. June 7, 2008.
18. The Brooklyn-New York team was a combination of the Brooklyn Dodgers and the New York Yankees. Hereafter, the team will simply be referred to as the New York Yankees, to make it easier for the reader.
19. "Football Yankees Topple Buffalo on H. Johnson's Field Goal, 17–14," *New York Times*, September 12, 1949.
20. *Ibid*.
21. *Ibid*.
22. "Bills Score 28–17 Upset Over '49ers," *Los Angeles Times*, September 26, 1949.
23. *Ibid*.
24. "Albert Involved in Affray with Buffalo Rooter," *Los Angeles Times*, September 26, 1949.
25. *Ibid*.
26. "Colts Check Bills on Late Pass, 35–28," *Chicago Daily Tribune*, October 3, 1949.
27. Dick Hyland. "Dons Upset Bills, 42–28, In Thriller," *Los Angeles Times*, October 10, 1949.
28. *Ibid*.
29. *Ibid*.
30. "Red Dawson Resigns," *Los Angeles Times*, October 10, 1949.
31. Joseph Sutton, exclusive interview. September 11, 2007.
32. *Ibid*.
33. Thomas M. Tarapacki. *The Rise and Fall of the Buffalo Bills*, (Unpublished).
34. Alex Wizbicki, exclusive interview. March 8, 2008.
35. Arthur Statuto, exclusive interview. April 20, 2008.
36. "49ers Smash Bills, 51 to 7," *Chicago Daily Tribune*, October 17, 1949.
37. "Dons Lose Brutal Tilt at Buffalo," *Los Angeles Times*, October 24, 1949.
38. *Ibid*.
39. "Pro Grid Loop Merger Looms, Says Sun-Times," *Los Angeles Times*, October 24, 1949.
40. *Ibid*.
41. *Ibid*.
42. *Ibid*.
43. Joseph M. Sheehan. "Buffalo Downs Yanks on Adams' Last-Period Field Goal at Stadium," *New York Times*, November 7, 1949.
44. *Ibid*.
45. *Ibid*.
46. Harold Sauerbrei. "Buffalo Ties Browns 2nd Time This Season, 7–7; Keeps Play-off Hopes Alive," *The Plain Dealer*, November 13, 1949.
47. *Ibid*.
48. *Ibid*.
49. Robert Cromie. "10–0 Buffalo Victory Dims Chicago Hope," *Chicago Daily Tribune*, November 21, 1949.
50. *Ibid*.
51. *Ibid*.
52. "Bills Win, 38–14, As Ratterman Passes Click," *Chicago Daily Tribune*, November 28, 1949.
53. Alex Wizbicki, exclusive interview. March 8, 2008.
54. Harold Sauerbrei. "Browns Whip Bills, 31–21; Tackle 49ers," *The Plain Dealer*, December 4, 1949.
55. *Ibid*.
56. *Ibid*.
57. *Ibid*.

Chapter 8

1. Mark L. Ford. "The 75 Days of the NAFL," *Coffin Corner*, vol. 26, no. 4.
2. *Ibid*.
3. Thomas M. Tarapacki. *The Rise and Fall of the Buffalo Bills* (Unpublished).
4. *Ibid*.
5. *Ibid*.
6. Joe Marren. "The Other Buffalo Bills," *Coffin Corner*, vol. 19, no. 1.
7. Untitled article, *Buffalo Evening News*, December 28, 1949.
8. *Ibid*.
9. "Buffalo's Pro Football Drive Gets a $199,770 'Retainer,'" *Buffalo Evening News*, December 14, 1949.

10. Thomas M. Tarapacki. *The Rise and Fall of the Buffalo Bills* (Unpublished).
11. Tony Wurzer. "Drive for Bills Really Rolling, $209,770 Now In," *Buffalo Evening News*, December 14, 1949.
12. "Buffalo's Pro Football Drive Gets a $199,770 'Retainer,'" *Buffalo Evening News*, December 14, 1949.
13. *Ibid*.
14. Tony Wurzer. "Bills' Chances Brighten After N.Y. Conference," *Buffalo Evening News*, December 20, 1949.
15. *Ibid*.
16. *Ibid*.
17. *Ibid*.
18. Mark L. Ford. "The 75 Days of the NAFL," *Coffin Corner*, vol. 26, no. 4.
19. Thomas M. Tarapacki. *The Rise and Fall of the Buffalo Bills* (Unpublished).
20. Mark L. Ford. "The 75 Days of the NAFL," *Coffin Corner*, vol. 26, no. 4.
21. Tony Wurzer. "Bills' Chances Brighten After N.Y. Conference," *Buffalo Evening News*, December 20, 1949.
22. Thomas M. Tarapacki. *The Rise and Fall of the Buffalo Bills* (Unpublished).
23. *Ibid*.
24. Mark L. Ford. "The 75 Days of the NAFL," *Coffin Corner*, vol. 26, no. 4.
25. *Ibid*.
26. Joe Clifford and Denny Lynch. *The 1946–49 Buffalo Bisons/Bills: Members of the All-America Football Conference* (Archives Department — Buffalo Bills Football Team, Inc., 2006).
27. Joseph Sutton, exclusive interview. September 11, 2007.
28. Thomas M. Tarapacki. *The Rise and Fall of the Buffalo Bills* (Unpublished).
29. Blair Stautzenberger, exclusive interview. October 3, 2007.
30. Thomas M. Tarapacki. *The Rise and Fall of the Buffalo Bills* (Unpublished).
31. *Ibid*.
32. *Ibid*.
33. *Ibid*.

Epilogue

1. George Ratterman. *Confessions of a Gypsy Quarterback: Inside the Wacky World of Pro Football* (New York: Coward-McCann, 1962).
2. Samuel S. Cordovano, Co-Founded 1946 Bills. *Buffalo Evening News*. July 16, 1995.

Bibliography

"10 Teams Enter New Grid League." *Coshocton Tribune*. July 24, 1944.
1946 Buffalo Bisons Media Guide.
1946 Buffalo Bisons Football Team 50th Anniversary: WNY's Pro Football Pioneers. Buffalo Bills Football Club, Inc., 1996.
1946–49 Buffalo Bills/Bisons: Members of the All-America Football Conference; Buffalo Bills Archive Department; 2006.
1947 All-America Football Conference Record Manual.
1948 All-America Football Conference Record Manual.
1948 Buffalo Bills Media Guide.
1949 All-America Football Conference Record Manual.
1949 All-America Football Conference Record Manual (Supplement).
1949 Buffalo Bills Media Guide.
"33,090 Watch Colts Topple Bills, 35–15." *Buffalo Evening News*. December 5, 1948.
"'49ers, Bills Battle to 21–21 Grid Deadlock." *Los Angeles Times*. December 8, 1947.
"49ers, Bisons Meet at Kezar." *Oakland Tribune*. November 1, 1946.
"'49ers Blast Bills, 51–7, In Rough Mix." *Los Angeles Times*. October 17, 1949.
"49ers Defeat Bills, 21–10." *Oakland Tribune*. August 15, 1949.
"49ers Defeat Buffalo, 41–24, On Late Drive." *Chicago Daily Tribune*. September 29, 1947.
"'49'ers Explode To Top Bills." *Los Angeles Times*. September 29, 1947.
"49ers Smash Bills, 51 to 7." *Chicago Daily Tribune*. October 17, 1949.
"49ers Win 5th Straight, Beat Bills, 38–28." *Chicago Daily Tribune*. September 27, 1948.
"AAC Leaders Meet Runners-up; 49ers At Buffalo Friday." *Dunkirk Evening Observer*. October 17, 1946.
"AA Signs Two Panthers." *Nebraska State Journal*. February 20, 1946.
"Adams Kicks Yankees Out of AAC Lead." *Los Angeles Times*. November 7, 1949.
"Albert Involved in Affray with Buffalo Rooter." *Los Angeles Times*. September 26, 1949.
"Albert Leads 49ers To 35–14 Circuit Win." *Los Angeles Times*. August 30, 1948.
Aldo T. "Buff" Donelli. Obituary. *Columbia University Record* Volume: 20, Number 1. September 9, 1994.
"Alert Bills Rout Bombers by 35–14." *Buffalo Evening News*. November 28, 1948.
Alford, Bruce, Sr. Exclusive Interview by Jay Langhammer. March 26, 2008.
"All-America Grid Clubs Open Conference Today." *Post-Standard*. April 7, 1946.
"All-America Loop Membership Held to Eight for '46." *Middle Pacific Stars and Stripes*. January 5, 1946.
"All-America Loop to Sponsor Grid in Baseball Towns." *Port Arthur News*. May 8, 1946.
"All-American Football League to Cover Nation Announced." *Independent Record*. September 3, 1944.
"All-American Pro Grid Conference, Rival to National Loop, Set for '45." *Nevada State Journal*. September 17, 1944.
"Ando, Michael. T Formation Will Be Used By Majority of Area Football Teams." *Olean Times Herald*. September 17, 1946.
Barnhart, Tony. "The '40s: NFL Goes to War." *Coffin Corner*: vol. 9, no. 8.
"Ben Lindheimer Denies Reports on Pro Merger." *Chicago Daily Tribune*. October 24, 1949.
Berstein, Ralph. "New Major League Pro Grid Circuit to Open in 1945." *Daily News*. July 24, 1944.
_____. "Plan New Major Pro Grid League; May begin in '45." *Daily Register*. July 24, 1944.
"Bills, 33; Colts, 14." *Chicago Daily Tribune*. November 24, 1947.
"Bills, 35; Dodgers, 7." *Chicago Daily Tribune*. October 27, 1947.
"Bills Batter Bulldogs, 48–0." *Dunkirk Evening Observer*. August 20, 1949.

"Bills Batter Colts for 35–17 Triumph." *Los Angeles Times.* November 1, 1948.
"Bills Blank Dons, 25–0 in Mudfest." *Los Angeles Times.* November 10, 1947.
"Bills Bowl Over Colts to Stay in Title Chase." *Los Angeles Times.* November 24, 1947.
"Bills Bowls Over Rockets, 31 to 14." *Los Angeles Times.* September 20, 1947.
"Bills Conquer Baltimore, 28–17, On 3 Touchdowns in Last Period." *Buffalo Evening News.* December 12, 1948.
"Bills Cut Squad; Play Colts Tonight." *Olean Times Herald.* August 10, 1949.
"Bills Defeat Dodgers in Grid Battle." *Syracuse Herald Journal.* August 18, 1948.
"Bills' Early Attack Beats Dons, 17 to 14." *Chicago Daily Tribune.* October 24, 1949.
"Bills' Early Drive Checks Dons, 17–14." *New York Times.* October 24, 1949.
"Bills Halt 49ers in Surprise, 28–17." *New York Times.* September 26, 1949.
"Bills Knock Over Rockets." *Los Angeles Times.* November 26, 1948.
"Bills Nod Colts, 20–15, but Losers to Protest." *Los Angeles Times.* October 13, 1947.
"Bills Overcome Dons, 27 to 25." *Chicago Daily Tribune.* October 6, 1947.
"Bills Rally to Top Colts." *Los Angeles Times.* December 13, 1948.
"Bills Score 28–17 Upset Over '49ers." *Los Angeles Times.* September 26, 1949.
"Bills Spank Dodgers, 31–21." *Los Angeles Times.* October 4, 1948.
"Bills Stop Rockets in 4th Period, 39–35." *Buffalo Evening News.* November 25, 1948.
"Bills Stop Rockets in 4th Period, 39–35." *New York Times.* November 26, 1948.
"Bills Survive Surge by Rockets to Take 28–20 Game at Buffalo." *New York Times.* September 15, 1947.
"Bills Thump Dodgers, 35–7." *Los Angeles Times.* October 27, 1948.
"Bills Tie 49ers, 21–21." *Chicago Daily Tribune.* December 8, 1947.
"Bills Top Hornets, Gain Fourth Place." *New York Times.* November 21, 1949.
"Bills Upset 49ers, 28–17; First Defeat." *Chicago Daily Tribune.* September 26, 1949.
"Bills Wallop Jersey Giants." *Syracuse Herald Journal.* August 6, 1949.
"Bills Wallop Yanks, 35–14." *Los Angeles Times.* November 29, 1948.
"Bills Win, 20–15, As Colts Protest." *Buffalo Courier-Express.* October 13, 1947.
"Bills Win, 20–15, As Colts Protest." *New York Times.* October 13, 1947.
"Bills Win, 31–21; Run Dodgers' Losses to Five." *Chicago Daily Tribune.* October 4, 1948.
"Bills Win, 38–14, As Ratterman Passes Click." *Chicago Daily Tribune.* November 28, 1949.
"Bills Win Home Final, 25 to 0." *Chicago Daily Tribune.* November 10, 1947.
"Bisons Battle Los Angeles to 21–21 Tie Before 18,163." *Buffalo Courier-Express.* September 29, 1946.
"Bisons Lose to Miami Seahawks In Last Minute." *Olean Times Herald.* October 12, 1946.
"Bisons Set Scoring Record in 49–17 Win Over Chicago Rockets." *Troy Record.* October 28, 1946.
"Bisons Sign Two More Grid Players." *Times Record.* April 3, 1946.
"Bisons Tip Brooklyn." *Buffalo Evening News.* November 10, 1946.
Braunwart, Bob, and Bob Carroll. "Glenn Dobbs." *Coffin Corner,* vol. 2, no. 9.
"Brevities." *Middle Pacific Stars and Stripes.* September 13, 1945.
"Brooklyn, Held to 9 Yards on Ground, Suffers 5th Defeat in Buffalo Encounter." *Buffalo Evening News.* October 3, 1948.
"Brooklyn Ties Buffalo, 14–14, On Hunchy's Run." *Chicago Daily Tribune.* October 18, 1947.
"Browns Batter Bills for 35–21 Victory." *Dunkirk Evening Observer.* August 23, 1948.
"Browns Blast Bills, 30–14." *Los Angeles Times.* September 6, 1947.
"Browns Score 35–21 Victory Over Buffalo." *The Bradford Era.* August 23, 1948.
"Browns Trip Bills in Opener, 30 to 14." *New York Times.* September 6, 1947.
"Buffalo Aerials Top Rockets, 31–14." *New York Times.* September 20, 1947.
"Buffalo Ahead: 16,000 Fans See Seahawks Bow To Bisons At Baltimore." *Buffalo News.* August 31, 1946.
"Buffalo All-American Football Team Will Train at St. Bonas." *Olean Times Herald.* April 4, 1946.
"Buffalo Beaten by Dons, 27–20, In Final Minute." *Chicago Daily Tribune.* November 15, 1948.
"Buffalo Beats Yankees, 35–14; Gain Title Tie." *Chicago Daily Tribune.* November 29, 1948.
"Buffalo Bills and New York Yankees Play to 28–28 Tie." *Syracuse Herald Journal.* August 13, 1948.
"Buffalo Bills Come To Life — In Court — As Reese Sues Breuil." *Buffalo News.* April 29, 1953.

"Buffalo Bills Romp to 79–0 Win Over JC." *Olean Times Herald.* August 6, 1949.
"Buffalo Bills Trim Baltimore." *Syracuse Herald Journal.* August 23, 1947.
"Buffalo Bills Whip Dons, 35–21." *Chicago Daily Tribune.* October 25, 1948.
"Buffalo Bills Wreck Rockets in 42–7 Tilt." *Los Angeles Times.* September 7, 1948.
"Buffalo Bisons Seek Second Win in Sunday Tilt." *Olean Times Herald.* October 26, 1946.
"Buffalo Bisons Sign Dekdebrun." *Olean Times Herald.* June 10, 1946.
"Buffalo Bisons to Train At Oconomowoc, Wis.: Shift Caused By Student Load At Bonaventure." *Olean Times Herald.* July 9, 1946.
"Buffalo Conquers Colt Eleven, 35–17." *Buffalo Evening News.* November 1, 1948.
"Buffalo Conquers Colt Eleven, 35–17." *New York Times.* November 1, 1948.
"Buffalo Defeats Dons' Eleven, 25–0." *New York Times.* November 10, 1947.
"Buffalo Downs Baltimore, 34–14, Stays in Race for Division Title." *New York Times.* November 24, 1947.
"Buffalo Downs Rockets, 28–20." *Chicago Daily Tribune.* September 15, 1947.
"Buffalo Eleven to Make Debut Sept. 8." *Blizzard.* December 14, 1945.
Buffalo Evening News. December 28, 1949.
"Buffalo Fails to Stop Albert; 49ers Win, 35–14." *Chicago Daily Tribune.* August 30, 1948.
"Buffalo Hands Hornets 10-to-0 Defeat in Mud." *Los Angeles Times.* November 21, 1949.
"Buffalo Is Victor Over Rockets, 42–7." *New York Times.* September 7, 1948.
"Buffalo Loses to Colts, 35–15; Tied For Lead." *Chicago Daily Tribune.* December 6, 1948.
"Buffalo Pros Want Dekdebrun." *Syracuse Herald Journal.* March 2, 1946.
"Buffalo to Field Pro Grid Team." *Coshocton Tribune.* January 23, 1944.
"Buffalo Signs Batorski, Formaer Colgate Gridder." *Blizzard.* January 24, 1946.
"Buffalo Tops Dons in Passing Display." *Buffalo Evening News.* October 24, 1948.
"Buffalo Tops Dons in Passing Display." *New York Times.* October 25, 1948.
"Buffalo Upsets Yanks, 17–14, on Field Goal." *Chicago Daily Tribune.* November 7, 1949.
"Buffalo Wins, 35–17; Ties for Lead in East." *Chicago Daily Tribune.* November 1, 1948.
"Buffalo Won First Title in 1920: The All-Americans Launched Championship Tradition Here." *Buffalo Evening News.* December 26, 1964.
"Buffalo's Eleven Downs Dons, 27–25." *New York Times.* October 6, 1947.
"Buffalo's Pro Football Drive Gets a $199,770 'Retainer.'" *Buffalo Evening News.* December 14, 1949.
Buksar, George. Exclusive Interview. March 29, 2008.
Byers, Walter. "New Grid Circuit Will Raid National League of Players." *Nevada State Journal.* September 2, 1945.
Campbell, Jim. "Dick Barwegan." *Coffin Corner,* vol. 27, no. 2.
Carroll, Bob. *Coffin Corner,* vol. 6, no. 2, 1948.
_____. "How to Get from Dayton to Indianapolis By Way of Brooklyn, Boston, New York, Dallas, Hershey and Baltimore." *Coffin Corner,* vol. 17, no. 5.
_____. "Mini-Bio: Abe Gibron." *Coffin Corner,* vol. 16, no. 5.
_____. "Mini-Bio: George Ratterman." *Coffin Corner,* vol. 17, no. 4.
_____, and Bob Gill. *Bulldogs on Sunday.* Professional Football Researchers Association, 1921.
Chamberlain, Charles. "Big Scramble for Players by Pros Seen." *Titusville Herald.* January 13, 1944.
_____, Michael Gershman, David Neft, and John Thorn. *Total Football: The Official Encyclopedia of the National Football League.* New York: HarperCollins, 1997.
_____. "Grid League Hesitates to Expand Now." *Daily Times-News.* January 14, 1944.
"Chappuis Sets New Passing Record As Buffalo Halts Brooklyn, 26–21." *Buffalo Evening News.* November 8, 1948.
"Chappuis Sets Records, But Bills Win, 26 to 21." *Los Angeles Times.* November 8, 1948.
Clary, Jack. "Paul Brown." *Coffin Corner,* vol. 14, no. 1.
"Cleveland Browns, in Fast Start, Topple Bisons in Buffalo by 28–0." *Buffalo Evening News.* September 23, 1946.
"Cleveland Squad Beats Bills, 42–13." *Buffalo Evening News.* September 13, 1948.
"Cleveland Stops Buffalo, 31 to 14, For 7th in Row as Graham Stars." *Buffalo Evening News.* October 18, 1948.
"Cleveland Victor Over Bills by 49–7." *Buffalo Evening News.* December 20, 1948.
Clifford, Joe, and Denny Lynch. *The 1946–49 Buffalo Bisons/Bills: Members of the All-America Football Conference* (Archives Department—Buffalo Bills Football Team, Inc., 2006).

"Colts Check Bills on Late Pass, 35–28." *Chicago Daily Tribune.* October 3, 1949.
"Colts Down Bills in Exhibition." *The Capital.* August 11, 1949.
"Colts Protest After Buffalo Wins, 20 to 15." *Chicago Daily Tribune.* October 13, 1947.
"Colts Protest Game After Bills Register Fifth Triumph, 20–15." *Buffalo Evening News.* October 13, 1947.
"Colts Top Bills, Gain Tie for Eastern Lead." *Los Angeles Times.* December 6, 1948.
"Colts Upset Bills, 35–28." *Los Angeles Times.* October 3, 1949.
"Cordovano Resigns as Coach, Pilot of Buffalo Eleven." *Wisconsin State Journal.* May 29, 1946.
"Cordovano Seeks Buffalo Franchise." *Nebraska State Journal.* January 9, 1944.
"Cordovano Signs Pirro." *Bradford Era.* February 18, 1946.
"Coughlin, W.S. Dons Set Scoring Record As Herd Completes Season." *Buffalo Courier-Express.* December 1, 1946.
Crippen, Kenneth R. "Buffalo Semi-Professional Football League." *Coffin Corner,* vol. 25, no. 1. 1918.
Crippen, Kenneth R. "Buffalo Prospects." *Coffin Corner,* vol. 23, no. 5. 1919.
Cromie, Robert. "10–0 Buffalo Victory Dims Chicago Hope." *Chicago Daily Tribune.* November 21, 1949.
_____. "Bills Overcome Rockets in 4th Quarter, 39–35." *Chicago Daily Tribune.* November 26, 1948.
_____. "Bills Swamp Rockets in East, 42–7." *Chicago Daily Tribune.* September 7, 1948.
Cronin, Joe, et al. *1947 Buffalo Bills Press Guide.* 2007.
Curt Sandig obituary. *San Antonio Express-News.* February 19, 2006.
Daley, Art. "What Are We Doing in Buffalo?" *Coffin Corner,* vol. 10, no. 6.
Dawson, Adrienne. Exclusive Interview. September 9, 2007.
_____. Exclusive Interview. September 22, 2007.
_____. Exclusive Interview. January 26, 2008.
_____. Exclusive Interview. June 7, 2008.
"Dawson Names New Bison Backfield." *Dunkirk Evening Observer.* October 18, 1946.
"Dawson Out as Buffalo Bills' Coach, Report." *Chicago Daily Tribune.* October 10, 1949.
"Dodgers Lose to Bills, 26–21; 2 Marks Broken." *Chicago Daily Tribune.* November 8, 1948.
"Dodgers Tie Bills, 14–14." *Los Angeles Times.* October 18, 1947.

"Dons, Bisons Even at Buffalo, 21–21." *Buffalo Evening News.* September 30, 1946.
"Dons Defeat Bills in Air Battle, 42–28." *New York Times.* October 10, 1949.
"Dons Lose Brutal Tilt at Buffalo." *Los Angeles Times.* October 24, 1949.
"Dons' Strong Finish Beats Bills, 42 to 28." *Chicago Daily Tribune.* October 10, 1949.
"Dons Upset Bills at Buffalo, 27–20." *Buffalo Evening News.* November 15, 1948.
"Dons Upset Bills at Buffalo, 27–20." *New York Times.* November 15, 1948.
"Dugger Signs With Buffalo." *Blizzard.* April 12, 1946.
Dunbar, Lee. "What, Another Pro Loop?" *Oakland Tribune.* August 9, 1944.
Ebli, Raymond. Exclusive Interview by Andy Piascik. December 21, 2004.
Effrat, Louis. "40,606 See Yanks Halt Bisons, 21–10." *Buffalo Evening News.* September 14, 1946.
_____. "Baltimore Downs Buffalo, Forcing Play-Off for All-America Eastern Title." *New York Times.* December 6, 1948.
_____. "Dodgers Tie Buffalo in 4th, 14–14, on Hoernschemeyer's 84-Yard Run." *New York Times.* October 18, 1947.
_____. "Yankees Smother Buffalo and Retain Eastern Division All-America Honors." *New York Times.* December 1, 1947.
_____. "Yankees Upset by Buffalo in Pro Football Opener." *New York Times.* September 1, 1947.
Elaine Bevinetto Comer obituary. *Times-Picayune.* July 15, 2003
"Elect Grid Loop Officials Sunday: New Pro Circuit Will Not Operate Until After War." *The Stars and Stripes London.* May 24, 1944.
Elmer, Robert. "Clash Marked By Long Runs." *Buffalo News.* August 30, 1946.
Fay, William. "Bills Beat Rockets, 28–20." *Chicago Daily Tribune.* September 15, 1947.
_____. "Buffalo All-Americas Upset New York, 28–24." *Chicago Daily Tribune.* September 1, 1947.
_____. "Ratterman's Passes Beat Rockets, 31–14: Buffalo Hands Chicago 4th Straight Loss." *Chicago Daily Tribune.* September 20, 1947.
Feinen, Edward N. "Two Big Lines Feature Bison Footballers Bid for Conference Honors." *Olean Times Herald.* August 27, 1946.
Fish, Charles E. "Sideline Sidelights." *Olean Times Herald.* June 26, 1946.
_____. "Sideline Sidelights." *Olean Times Herald.* August 5, 1946.

Flynn, John M. "The Referee's Sporting Chat." *Berkshire Evening Eagle.* January 10, 1944.
———. "The Referee's Sporting Chat." *Berkshire Evening Eagle.* May 3, 1945.
"Football Dodgers Bow to Bills, 31–21." *New York Times.* October 4, 1948.
"Football Yankees Topple Buffalo on H. Johnson's Field Goal, 17–14." *New York Times.* September 12, 1949.
Ford, Mark L. "The 75 Days of the NAFL." *Coffin Corner,* vol. 26, no. 4.
"Forty-Niners Down Buffalo Bills, 38–28." *Los Angeles Times.* September 27, 1948.
"Forty-Niners Halt Buffalo, 38 to 28." *Buffalo Evening News.* September 27, 1948.
"Forty-Niners Halt Buffalo, 38 to 28." *New York Times.* September 27, 1948.
"Forty-Niners Rout Bills, 51 to 7, As Perry, Albert Pace Offensive." *New York Times.* October 17, 1949.
"Forty-Niners Stop Buffalo, 35 to 14." *Buffalo Evening News.* August 30, 1948.
"Forty-Niners Stop Buffalo, 35–14." *New York Times.* August 30, 1948.
"Forty-Niners Tie Buffalo, 21 to 21." *New York Times.* December 8, 1947.
"Forty-Niners Top Buffalo By 41–24." *New York Times.* September 29, 1947.
"Frank Dunn Quits Bison Footballers." *Olean Times Herald.* February 12, 1947.
Freitas, Jesse. Exclusive Interview. June 14, 2008.
Fullerton, Hugh, Jr. "Fullerton's Roundup." *Athens Messenger.* January 15, 1946.
———. "Pro Football Expansion to be Delayed." *Evening Tribune.* April 21, 1944.
———. "The Roundup." *Lowell Sun.* January 14, 1946.
Game Film. Baltimore Colts vs. Buffalo Bills. October 2, 1949.
Game Film. Buffalo Bills vs. Cleveland Browns. December 4, 1949.
Game Film. Buffalo Bills vs. New York Yankees. November 28, 1948.
Game Program. Buffalo Bills vs. Baltimore Colts. October 31, 1948.
Game Program. Buffalo Bills vs. Brooklyn Dodgers. August 17, 1948.
Game Program. Buffalo Bills vs. Brooklyn Dodgers. October 3, 1948.
Game Program. Buffalo Bills vs. Chicago Rockets. September 14, 1947.
Game Program. Buffalo Bills vs. Chicago Rockets. September 6, 1948.
Game Program. Buffalo Bills vs. Cleveland Browns. November 2, 1947.
Game Program. Buffalo Bills vs. Cleveland Browns. September 12, 1948.
Game Program. Buffalo Bills vs. New York Yankees. October 10, 1948.
Game Program. Buffalo Bills vs. San Francisco 49ers. September 25, 1949.
Game Program. Buffalo Bisons vs. Cleveland Browns. November 24, 1946.
Game Program. Buffalo Bisons vs. San Francisco 49ers. November 2, 1946.
Game Program. Chicago Rockets vs. Buffalo Bisons. September 25, 1946.
Game Program. Cleveland Browns vs. Buffalo Bills. September 5, 1947.
Game Program. Cleveland Browns vs. Buffalo Bills. October 17, 1948.
Game Program. Cleveland Browns vs. Buffalo Bills. November 13, 1949.
Game Program. Cleveland Browns vs. Buffalo Bisons. September 22, 1946.
Game Program. Los Angeles Dons vs. Buffalo Bills. October 5, 1947.
Game Program. Los Angeles Dons vs. Buffalo Bills. October 24, 1948.
Game Program. Los Angeles Dons vs. Buffalo Bills. October 9, 1949.
Game Program. New York Yankees vs. Buffalo Bisons. September 14, 1946.
Game Program. New York Yankees vs. Buffalo Bills. November 28, 1948.
Game Program. New York Yankees vs. Buffalo Bills. November 6, 1949.
Game Program. San Francisco 49ers vs. Buffalo Bills. December 7, 1947.
Game Program. San Francisco 49ers vs. Buffalo Bills. August 29, 1948.
Game Program. San Francisco 49ers vs. Buffalo Bills. August 14, 1949.
Game Program. San Francisco 49ers vs. Buffalo Bills. October 16, 1949.
"General Sports Topics." *Olean Times Herald.* April 1, 1946.
"General Sports Topics." *Olean Times Herald.* April 9, 1946.
"General Sports Topics." *Olean Times Herald.* April 25, 1946.
"General Sports Topics." *Olean Times Herald.* April 26, 1946.
"General Sports Topics." *Olean Times Herald.* May 14, 1946.
Gill, Bob. "PCPFL: 1940–45." *Coffin Corner,* vol. 4, no. 7.
———, and Tod Maher. The Outsiders: The Three American Football Leagues of 1936–1941. Professional Football Researchers Association, 1989.
Gompers, William. Exclusive Interview. September 8, 2007.
Grayson, Harry. "Rumor Leahy Headed for Pro Ranks." *Council Bluffs Iowa Nonpareil.* September 2, 1945.

"Grid Bisons Add Strength For Yankees." *Olean Times Herald.* October 3, 1946.
"Grid Bisons Face Rockets, Dons in Four Day Period." *Olean Times Herald.* September 24, 1946.
"Grid Bisons Get Three Players In Deal With Browns." *Olean Times Herald.* February 4, 1947.
"Grid Bisons Lost to Hapless Hawks for Second Time." *Buffalo Evening News.* November 19, 1946.
"Grid Bisons Set for Opener with Brooklyn Sunday." *Olean Times Herald.* September 7, 1946.
"Grid Leagues Do 'Elfoldo.'" *San Mateo Times.* June 5, 1945.
"Gridiron Yanks Defeat Bisons by 21 to 13 Tally." *Times Record.* October 5, 1946.
Grosshandler, Stan. "All-America Football Conference." *Coffin Corner,* vol. 2, no. 7.
———. "From One War to Another — NFL Season of '46." *Coffin Corner,* vol. 13, no. 6.
———. "Spec Sanders: A Memorable Runner on a Forgotten League." *Coffin Corner,* vol. 18, no. 5.
Groves, George. Exclusive Interview. May 4, 2008.
"Hanley Signs to Coach Pro Grid Eleven." *Evening Tribune.* March 1, 1945.
"Hawks Quit Cellar on Erdlitz' Boot." *Buffalo Evening News.* October 13, 1946.
Henshan, John. "Ratterman, Who Beat Bears, Says Browns are Stronger." *The Plain Dealer.* September 5, 1947.
Herring, Hal. Exclusive Interview via letter. June 24, 2008.
Hession, Joseph. "Frankie Albert: 'Mr. 49er.'" *Coffin Corner,* vol. 7, no. 5.
"Honolulu Eleven Seeks Loop Berth." *Gettysburg Times.* April 8, 1944.
"Honolulu Wants Pro Grid Berth." *Fresno Bee Republican.* April 8, 1944.
"Hopp, Juzwik Snatched from National Loop." *San Antonio Light.* December 20, 1945.
"Hornets Conquer Buffalo by 17–14." *New York Times.* August 27, 1949.
"Hornets Defeat Buffalo, 17–14." *Chicago Daily Tribune.* August 27, 1949.
"Hornets Win Grid Opener from Bills." *Los Angeles Times.* August 27, 1949.
Horrigan, Joe, and Bob Carroll. "'Earth, to Ratterman' and Other Hall of Fame Artifacts." *Coffin Corner,* vol. 15, no. 4.
Hyland, Dick. "Bills Batter Dons, 35 to 21; Dobbs Hurt." *Los Angeles Times.* October 25, 1948.
———. "Dons Upset Bills, 42–28, in Thriller." *Los Angeles Times.* October 10, 1949.
———. "Dons Upset Bills in Final Minute." *Los Angeles Times.* November 15, 1948.
———. "Ratterman Stars as Bills Edge Dons, 27 to 25." *Los Angeles Times.* October 6, 1947.
Kanaley, Mike. "Bison Pro Gridders Bow To Yankees By Score of 21 to 10." *Buffalo Courier-Express.* September 14. 1946.
———. "Bisons Bow to 49ers, 27–14." *Buffalo Courier-Express.* November 2, 1946.
———. "Browns Batter Bisons, 28–0, Before 30,302." *Buffalo Courier-Express.* September 22, 1946.
———. "Buffalo Suffers Second Loss to Trailing Eleven." *Buffalo Courier-Express.* November 18, 1946.
———. "Football Bisons Beat Frisco, 17–14." *Buffalo Courier-Express.* October 20, 1946.
———. "Football Bisons Blast Chicago Rockets to Defeat With Record 49–17." *Buffalo Courier-Express.* October 28, 1946.
———. "Ratterman Sets Record As Bills Win, 31 to 14." *Buffalo Courier-Express.* September 19, 1947.
King, Steve. "Dippy" Evans Passes Away. Cleveland Browns website. http://www.clevelandbrowns.com/article.php?id=6892. Accessed: August 28, 2007.
"Kittrell Signed by Buffalo." *Stars and Stripes London.* September 22, 1945.
Latterman, Mark. "Hunchy." *Coffin Corner,* vol. 15, no. 1.
Letter from John "Ox" Dagrosa to Fiore A. Cesare. Dated November 15, 1946.
Letter from Red Dawson to Bill Gompers. Dated May 19, 1949.
Letter from Albert E. Humphreys to Fiore A. Cesare. Dated November 22, 1946.
Letter from Jack Harding to Fiore A. Cesare. Dated November 18, 1946.
Letter from Ed McKeever to Fiore A. Cesare. Dated November 14, 1946.
Letter from Roland D. Payne to Fiore Cesare. Dated April 11, 1944.
Letter from Ken Stofer to Mel Bashore. Dated August 20, 1992.
Liska, Jerry. "Pro Football Marking Time Until End of the Year: Fur Will Fly After V-J Day." *Daily Globe.* May 16, 1945.
———. "Red Grange Thinks There is Room for More Pro Football." *Ada Evening News.* December 18, 1945.
———. "Room for Two Pro Leagues, Says Grange." *Council Bluffs Nonpareil.* December 18, 1945.
Lloyd Lamar Blount obituary. *The Meridian Star.* August 8, 2007.

"Loop Is Charged with Bad Faith." *Council Bluffs Nonpareil*. April 10, 1946.
Lowell "Red" Dawson Biography. University of Wisconsin-River Falls website. http://www.uwrf.edu/sportsrecords/hall-of-fame-1977.php. Accessed August 27, 2007.
Maggioli, Achille. Exclusive Interview. December 26, 2007.
Marren, Joe. *A Brief History of the AAFC*. Unpublished.
———. "NFL Called on Buffalo in 1940." *Coffin Corner*, vol. 19, no. 5.
———. "The Other Buffalo Bills." *Coffin Corner*, vol. 19, no. 1.
Martin Franklin Comer Sr. obituary. *Times-Picayune*. March 18, 1998.
Martin, Whitney. "Honolulu Gridders Planning to Carry a Sideshow, Too." *Morning Herald*. December 26, 1944.
Matthews, Anne McIlhenney. "Bills Get Gift from City." *Buffalo Courier-Express*. January 24, 1967.
McCarty, Bernie. "The Best Pro a College Ever Had." *Coffin Corner*, vol. 3, no. 9.
McGowen, Roscoe. "Chappuis Sets New Passing Record as Buffalo Halts Brooklyn, 26–21." *New York Times*. November 8, 1948.
Meyer, Bob. "Coast Cities Seek Berth in Pro Football Circuit: San Francisco, Los Angeles in Post-War Setup." *Nevada State Journal*. January 13, 1944.
"Miami Granted Franchise in New Grid Loop." *Troy Record*. December 11, 1944.
"Miami Granted Franchise in Pro Grid Loop." *San Antonio Express*. December 12, 1944.
Miller, Jeffrey J. *Buffalo's Forgotten Champions: The Story of Buffalo's First Professional Football Team and the Lost 1921 Title*. Philadelphia: Xlibris, 2004.
Miller, Jeffrey. *Tommy Hughitt: Mr. Everything*. The Historical Society of the Buffalo All-Americans, Bisons and Rangers.
Morrison, Bruce. "Wanted: One Pass Defender — Rockets." *Chicago Tribune*. September 19, 1947.
Murdock, Bill. "Verne Gagne: A Wrestler's Wrestler." *The Wrestling Gospel*. http://www.mikemooneyham.com/pages/viewfull.cfm?ObjectID=55D14610-7990-4AB8-A688B6397F132041. Accessed October 6, 2007.
"National League Enlists Pacific Coast Aid in Grid War." *Syracuse Herald Journal*. January 16, 1946.
"Nelson to Join Bison Gridders." *Olean Times Herald*. September 20, 1946.

"New Football League Plans Baltimore Meet." *Modesto Bee and News-Herald*. November 11, 1944.
"New Loop Adds Gridiron Talent." *Coshocton Tribune*. April 2, 1946.
"New Pro Grid League Sets Up New Draft Deal." *Fresno Bee Republican*. January 6, 1946.
"New Pro Grid Loop Planned." *Oakland Tribune*. September 2, 1944.
"New Yankee Owners May Block Rivals of National Grid Loop." *Dothan Eagle*. January 28, 1945.
Newland, Russ. "Newland's Streamliner." *Fresno Bee Republican*. November 4, 1944.
"NFL Doubts Soundness of Rival Loops." *Mason City Globe-Gazette*. May 22, 1945.
"No Peace in Sight on Pro Grid Front." *Daily News*. May 22, 1945.
O'Connor, William. Exclusive Interview. May 4, 2008.
Palmer, Pete, Ken Pullis, Sean Lahman, Tod Maher, Matthew Silverman, Christina Kahrl and Gary Gillette. *The ESPN Pro Football Encyclopedia*. New York: Sterling, 2007.
Pavlick, Ed. "Pro Football Records Should Include the AAFC." *Coffin Corner*, vol. 2, no. 7.
Piascik, Andy. "AAFC vs. NFL: The Attendance Battle." *Coffin Corner*, vol. 29, no. 3.
———. *The Best Show in Football: The 1946–1955 Cleveland Browns, Pro Football's Greatest Dynasty*. New York, New York: Taylor Trade Publishing, 2007.
———. "Comparing the NFL, AFL, and AAFC." *Coffin Corner*, vol. 29, no. 4.
———. "Marion Motley." *Coffin Corner*, vol. 24, no. 4.
———. "Why the AAFC Cleveland Browns were the Best Team in Football from 1946 Through 1949." *Coffin Corner*, vol. 27, no. 3.
"Players Divide $38,621 in Conference Play-Off." *Buffalo Evening News*. December 19, 1948.
Prell, Edward. "2 Football Leagues Hurt by Cash War." *Chicago Daily Tribune*. November 1, 1948.
———. "All-America Browns Rout Buffalo, 30–14." *Chicago Daily Tribune*. September 6, 1947.
———. "Bills Rally to Beat Colts in Play-Off, 28–17." *Chicago Daily Tribune*. December 13, 1948.
———. "Chicago Rally in 4th Quarter Whips Bisons." *Buffalo News*. September 26, 1946.

"Pro Dodgers Beat Buffalo by 27–14." *Buffalo Evening News.* September 9, 1946.
"Pro Football Battle Is Now in Earnest." *Nebraska State Journal.* August 3, 1944.
Pro Football Hall of Fame. "Bert Bell: The Commissioner." *Coffin Corner,* vol. 18, no. 3.
Pro Football Hall of Fame. "Dan Reeves Moves West." *Coffin Corner,* vol. 20, no. 1.
Pro Football Hall of Fame. "Marion Motley: Some Say He Was 'Greatest Football Player Ever.'" *Coffin Corner,* vol. 13, no. 2.
"Pro Football's Future Studied." *Piqua Daily Call.* April 4, 1945.
"Pro Grid Bisons Seek First Win." *Olean Times Herald.* October 11, 1946.
"Pro Grid Confab Postponed." *The Stars and Stripes* (London). May 29, 1944.
"Pro Grid Loop Merger Looms, Says Sun Times." *Los Angeles Times.* October 24, 1949.
"Pro Grid Moguls Return Coast Money, Keep Buffalo's." *Berkshire Evening Eagle.* January 14, 1944.
"Pro Grid Peace Talks on Today." *Los Angeles Times.* December 20, 1948.
Professional Football Researchers Association Research. "1948 AAFC Championship: Perfect Ending." *Coffin Corner,* vol. 18, no. 4.
Professional Football Researchers Association Research. "1949 AAFC Championship: Finishing In Style." *Coffin Corner,* vol. 18, no. 2.
"Pros Squabble About Hirsch." *Nevada State Journal.* November 27, 1945.
Pucci, Benito. Exclusive Interview. September 11, 2007.
Ratterman, George. *Confessions of a Gypsy Quarterback: Inside the Wacky World of Pro Football.* New York: Coward-McCann, 1962.
"Ratterman Leads Buffalo to Victory in Pro Conference Game." *New York Times.* October 27, 1947.
Ratterman, Matt. Exclusive Interview. January 7, 2008.
"Ratterman Sets Pace as Bills Beat Colts, 38–14." *Los Angeles Times.* November 28, 1949.
"Recalling Ed King, Who 'Loved Being Governor.'" *The Patriot Ledger.* September 19, 2006.
"Red Dawson Resigns." *Los Angeles Times.* October 10, 1949.
"Red Grange to Head New Pro Grid Ring." *Nebraska State Journal.* November 28, 1944.
"Red Grange Resigns Pro Grid Loop Job." *The Stars and Stripes* (European). June 4, 1945.
Rice, Grantland. "Rice Sees Room for Two Major Football Leagues." *Syracuse Herald Journal.* January 16, 1946.
"Rickey Moves For 2-A-Week Grid Schedule." *Syracuse Herald Journal.* August 18, 1948.
"Robert M. Stefik, Realtor, Bills Kicker One Season." *Buffalo News.* April 12, 2008.
"Roland Payne to Call Meeting." *Ogden Standard-Examiner.* November 11, 1944.
Ryan, Ray. "25,489 See Dodgers Win Grid Opener." *Buffalo News.* September 10, 1946.
"Rykovich Scores Three Times—Ratterman Passes Spark Drives Before 25,816." *Buffalo Evening News.* September 7, 1949.
"Sam Cordovano Quits as General Manager Buffalo Pro Gridders." *Olean Times Herald.* May 28, 1946.
"Sanders Sets Pace in 14–13 Triumph." *Buffalo Evening News.* October 11, 1948.
Sauerbrei, Harold. "Browns' Long Runs Clinch Western Title and Playoff Role, 42–17." *The Plain Dealer.* November 24, 1946.
_____. "Browns Pile Up 504 Yards in Whipping Buffalo, 42–13, for Second Straight." *The Plain Dealer.* September 12, 1948.
_____. "Browns Whip Bills, 31–21; Tackle 49ers." *The Plain Dealer.* December 4, 1949.
_____. "Browns Win, 31–14, For Seventh in Row." *The Plain Dealer.* October 17, 1948.
_____. "Browns Win Third Title, 49 to 7." *The Plain Dealer.* December 19, 1948.
_____. "Buffalo Ties Browns 2nd Time This Season, 7–7; Keeps Play-off Hopes Alive." *The Plain Dealer.* November 13, 1949.
_____. "Graham Fires 3 Scoring Passes as Browns Hurdle Buffalo, 28–7." *The Plain Dealer.* November 2, 1947.
_____. "Graham Pitches Two Scoring Passes as Browns Blast Buffalo, 28–0." *The Plain Dealer.* September 22, 1946.
_____. "Graham's 3 Scoring Passes in Last Period Give Browns 18–18 Tie at Buffalo." *The Plain Dealer.* September 5, 1949.
Schmidt, Ray. "Welcome to L.A." *Coffin Corner,* vol. 25, no. 6.
Schneider, Donald and Lilly. Exclusive Interview. November 26, 2007.
Schnellbacher, Otto. Exclusive Interview by Andy Piascik. April 13, 2004.
"Secret Meet by Pro Grid Club Owners: Two Proposed Rival Loops in Trouble." *Council Bluffs Nonpareil.* June 2, 1945.
Sheehan, Joseph M. "Bills Conquer Balti-

more, 28–17, On 3 Touchdowns in Last Period." *New York Times.* December 13, 1948.

———. "Buffalo Topples Yankees at Stadium: Alert Bills Rout Bombers by 35–14." *New York Times.* November 29, 1948.

———. "Buffalo Downs Yanks on Adams' Last-Period Field Goal at Stadium." *New York Times.* November 7, 1949.

———. "Yankees Score Two Last-Half Touchdowns to Top Buffalo." *New York Times.* October 11, 1948.

Sheer, Harry. "Ratterman, 31; Rockets, 14." *Chicago Tribune.* September 19, 1947.

Shoemaker, Lisle. "Coasting Along: Long-Range Plan to Place Honolulu in Fast Pro Post-War Grid Loop is Under Way." *Nevada State Journal.* August 6, 1944.

Silvers, Amy Rabideau. "Vogt Made His Mark In Football, Then Engineering." *Milwaukee Journal Sentinel.* March 2, 2002.

"Skiddy, Lawrence J. Dekdebrun Votes For His Home Town." *Syracuse Herald Journal.* June 13, 1946.

"'Skins Lose Juzwik to Buffalo Eleven of New Pro League." *Kingsport News.* December 20, 1945.

"Sports Before Your Eyes." *Gettysburg Times.* November 11, 1945.

Statuto, Arthur. Exclusive Interview. April 20, 2008.

———. Exclusive Interview. June 7, 2008.

Stautzenberger, Blair. Exclusive Interview. October 3, 2007.

Stuart, Roy. Exclusive Interview. April 4, 2008.

Sutton, Joseph. Exclusive Interview. September 11, 2007.

Tarapacki, Thomas M. *The Rise and Fall of the Buffalo Bills.* Unpublished.

Terlep, George. Exclusive Interview. September 29, 2007.

———. Exclusive Interview by Andy Piascik. May 11, 2004.

Tomasetti, Louis. Exclusive Interview. August 8, 1998.

Troup, T.J. "Frank Sinkwich and the Contending Lions of 1944." *Coffin Corner,* vol. 24, no. 1.

"Tunney Named in New Pro Football Loop." *Stars and Stripes London.* September 4, 1944.

Turkin, Hy. "Grid Yanks Rally to Down Bisons 21–10, in 4th Period." *Buffalo News.* September 15, 1946.

"Two Gridders to Join Bisons." *Syracuse Herald Journal.* March 16, 1946.

"Two Star Backs are Signed by Buffalo Club." *Bradford Era.* December 20, 1945.

"Two Stars Lost." *Ada Weekly News.* December 20, 1945.

USFL Organizational Meeting Minutes. April 2, 1944.

Vandeweghe, Albert. Exclusive Interview via letter. September 10, 2007.

Volz, Wilbur. Exclusive Interview. April 27, 2008.

Whittlesey, Sgt. Merrell. "The Boys of Shekel U. Make Ready for a Bitter Civil War." *Stars and Stripes Mediterranean.* October 28, 1945.

"Wieman Signs as Lion Mentor." *Stars and Stripes Mediterranean.* July 7, 1944.

Wizbicki, Alex. Exclusive Interview. March 8, 2008.

Wolf, Ron. Exclusive Interview. September 4, 2008.

Wurzer, Tony. "Bills' Chances Brighten After N.Y. Conference." *Buffalo News.* December 20, 1949.

———. "Bisons to Pit Ground Game Against Miami Air Power." *Buffalo Evening News.* October 12, 1946.

———. "Drive for Bills Really Rolling, $209,770 Now In." *Buffalo News.* December 14, 1949.

———. "Ratterman's Passes Gain a Record 294 Yards." *Buffalo Evening News.* September 21, 1947.

———. "Same Old Story—Bisons Rated 1–3 Against AAC Foe." *Buffalo Evening News.* September 26, 1946.

———. "Scoring 59 Points In 2 Games, Herd Salvages Only Tie." *Buffalo Evening News.* October 1, 1946.

———. "Youth, Bulk Combined with Blazing Speed—That's 1948 Grid Bills." *Buffalo Evening News.* {No Date}.

"Yankees Edge Bills, 14–13." *Chicago Daily Tribune.* October 11, 1948.

"Yankees Edge Bills, 14–13." *Los Angeles Times.* October 11, 1948.

"Yankee Grids Whip Bills in Final Minute." *Los Angeles Times.* September 12, 1949.

"Yankees Halt Bills, 17–14, On Field Goal." *Chicago Daily Tribune.* September 12, 1949.

"Yankees Nab East Grid Title, 35–13." *Los Angeles Times.* December 1, 1947.

"Yankees Thump Bills 29–7, In Newark Go." *Dunkirk Evening Observer.* August 19, 1947.

"Yankees Top Buffalo; Gain East Crown." *Chicago Daily Tribune.* December 1, 1947.

Index

Akron Pros 4–5
Albert, Frankie 34–35, 61, 72, 75, 89, 94, 96, 111
Ameche, Don 9, 11–12
American Football League (1926) 6
American Football League (1940–1941) 5–8, 112
American Professional Football Association (APFA) 4–5, 19

Baldwin, Alton 51–52, 54–56, 59, 61, 63, 67, 70, 72, 74–75, 77–79, 81, 83, 89–91, 93–95, 97, 101, 107, 111, 113, 120, 123, 125, 222–223
Baltimore Colts 27, 41, 48, 56, 60, 64, 66, 73–76, 78–82, 85, 87, 90, 95, 97–100, 102, 106–107, 112–114, 116–120, 122, 124–125, 224–225, 230, 234, 242, 249–250, 252–255, 260–261, 265, 267, 269–271, 274, 278, 292
Batorski, John 20–22, 27
Bell, Bert 19, 104–105, 111
Bennett, William 9–10, 12
Bertelli, Angelo 24–25, 33, 51–52, 66
Boston Braves 19
Boston Yanks 14, 24–25, 42–43, 223, 232–233, 251, 254, 261–263, 279
Brazinsky, Sam 22, 46, 118, 120, 225
Breuil, James F. 9–12, 23, 39, 45, 63, 67, 69, 89, 91–92, 95, 102–103, 112, 114, 118, 120, 123, 125, 272
Brooklyn Dodgers 14, 16, 22–23, 25, 28–29, 32,
36, 38–39, 56–58, 64–67, 69, 70, 72, 76–77, 79–80, 85–87, 90, 110–111, 117–118, 120, 122, 221, 226, 229, 237–238, 246, 259, 262–263, 265, 267, 279
Brooklyn Tigers 13–14, 233
Brown, Paul 13–14, 27, 30, 50–51, 82, 96, 106, 110, 114, 239, 242, 248, 251, 271, 286, 289
Buffalo All-Americans 4–5, 19
Buffalo Bills Football Club, Inc. 103–104
Buffalo Indians 6, 112
Buffalo Prospects 4
Buffalo Tigers 6, 112

Canton Bulldogs 4–5, 39
Cesare, Fiore 6–7, 19
Chicago Bears 6, 10, 14, 42–45, 84, 104, 106–109, 113, 235, 237, 239–240, 258, 260, 262, 264, 275–276, 280–283; see also Chicago Staleys
Chicago Cardinals 6, 10, 13, 21–22, 33, 42–43, 79, 85, 106–109, 227, 230–231, 234, 236, 244, 253, 257, 271, 278, 283, 287, 292–293
Chicago Hornets 42, 65, 87, 90–91, 97–100, 107–109, 125, 250, 257, 260, 279; see also Chicago Rockets
Chicago Rockets 15, 31–32, 35, 39, 43, 51–54, 64, 66, 70, 75, 78–79, 85–87, 106, 111, 117–118, 120, 122–123, 232, 236–238, 242, 248, 250, 253,
256–257, 259–260, 269, 271, 275; see also Chicago Hornets
Chicago Staleys 5; see also Chicago Bears
Cleveland Browns 29–31, 35, 38–39, 41–42, 44, 48, 50–51, 58–59, 61, 63–66, 69, 70–74, 78, 80, 82–86, 91–103, 105–111, 113–114, 116–120, 122–123, 125, 220–221, 226–228, 230, 237–238, 240, 242, 244, 251–252, 255–256, 265–267, 269, 271–274, 278–279, 281, 283, 286, 291
Cleveland Rams 6, 9–10, 15, 19, 21–23, 44, 220–222, 228, 246, 254–256, 268, 270–271, 274, 284, 293; see also Los Angeles Rams
Collins, Ted 14, 102
Conkright, William "Red" 44, 69, 120, 123
Cordovano, Sam 9–13, 15–16, 20, 22–23, 25, 44, 115
Crosby, Bing 9, 11
Crowe, Clem 27, 44, 63, 69, 85, 89, 95–97, 110, 114, 118, 120, 123, 125, 241, 261
Crowley, James 13–15, 28, 39, 43, 45

Daddio, Bill 20–22, 27–28, 44, 118, 231
Dawson, Lowell "Red" 24–25, 29–30, 35, 44, 47–48, 50–51, 63, 69, 89–91, 95–96, 115, 118, 120, 123, 125, 229, 235, 242, 258, 268

313

Index

Dayton Triangles 5
Dekdebrun, Al 25, 27, 31, 32–36, 39, 51–52, 118, 232
Detroit Heralds 3
Detroit Lions 7, 9–10, 16, 21–22, 27, 42–43, 48, 65, 85–86, 106–109, 113–114, 116, 227–228, 234–235, 245, 247–249, 256, 261, 263, 277, 279, 284, 288
Detroit Tigers 5
Dobbs, Glenn 12, 28–29, 36, 59, 74–75, 77–78, 95, 108, 111, 237
Donnelli, Aldo "Buff" 23, 255

Embry, Robert C. 66

Flaherty, Ray 29, 79
Freitas, Jesse 78–79, 89, 91, 113, 126, 238
Frontier Oil Refining Corporation 9–10, 12

Gagne, Verne 16
Gallery, Tom 13
Gehrig, Eleanor 12–13, 23
Gibron, Abe 85, 89, 103, 113, 126, 239
Globe Construction Company 9, 115
Gompers, Bill 64, 69, 75, 81, 108, 123, 241
Governali, Paul 15–16, 22, 25
Graham, Otto 30–31, 38, 50–51, 53, 58–59, 70, 72–73, 75, 91–92, 98, 101, 111, 239
Grange, Red 6, 8
Green Bay Packers 10, 17, 20, 43, 87, 102, 106–109, 113–114, 220, 223, 247, 261, 277, 282, 290–291
Grigg, Forrest "Chubby" 27, 35, 47, 63, 118, 121, 242

Halas, George 5, 39, 104–105
Hanley, Dick 13, 15, 31–32
Herring, Hal 89, 107, 113, 126, 243–244
Hester, Harvey 13, 39
Hirsch, Elroy "Crazylegs" 14–15, 32, 52–53, 66

Hopp, Harry 16, 22, 27–31, 118, 245
Ingram, Jonas 45–46, 56, 89
Isbell, Cecil 56

Jaskwhich, Chuck 44, 63, 69, 120, 123
Jersey City Giants 21, 89–90, 124, 256, 266
Juzwik, Steve 15–16, 22, 27–28, 30, 32–33, 36, 39, 44, 47, 49, 52–53, 56, 60, 63, 70, 118, 121, 248

Keeshin, John 12–14, 39
Kessing, Oliver O. 45–46, 58, 89
King, Dolly 29, 32, 34–36, 39, 44, 47–48, 53–55, 58, 61, 63, 67, 79, 111, 118, 121, 250
Klenk, Quentin 22, 27, 31, 118, 253
Klug, Al 16, 22, 27, 118, 253
Kostiuk, Michael 21–22, 118, 256
Kulbitski, Vic 20–22, 27, 31–32, 36, 38–39, 44, 47–48, 51–52, 57–59, 63, 67, 73, 118, 121, 123, 257–258

Lavelli, Dante 30, 38, 58, 83, 91–92, 100, 111
Layden, Elmer 6, 8, 13–14, 19, 23
Lillywhite, Verl 72
Lindheimer, Benjamin 45
Los Angeles Dons 19, 23–25, 32–33, 39, 41, 51–52, 54–55, 59–60, 64, 74–78, 85, 95, 97, 99–100, 108–111, 117–118, 120, 122–123, 125, 234–235, 245, 264, 283
Los Angeles Rams 20, 97, 105–107, 114, 250–251, 254, 261, 266, 274, 277, 280–281, 289, 292; see also Cleveland Rams

Maggioli, Chick 27, 69, 123, 261
Mandel, Frank 9
Maxwell, Clayton 9–10
McBride, Arthur 12

McKeever, Ed 19, 66, 278
Meagher, Jack 13, 36
Meehan, Chick 7
Miami Seahawks 28, 34, 36–41, 224–225, 229, 245–247, 267, 292
Morabito, Anthony J. 9, 11–13, 105
Motley, Marion 30–31, 58, 70, 73–74, 83, 98, 111
Murray, Charles 9–10
Mutryn, Chet 27–28, 33, 39, 44, 47–54, 56–58, 60, 63, 67, 69, 72–77, 79–82, 89, 91, 94, 96, 98–99, 101, 106–107, 111, 114, 119, 121, 124, 126, 264–265

Nesmith, Ole 6
Nevers, Ernie 13
New York Giants 6, 14, 20–22, 29, 42–43, 84–85, 89, 97, 102, 106–109, 230, 234, 239, 246–247, 251–252
New York Yankees 13–14, 29–30, 32–33, 39, 41–42, 44–45, 48–51, 60–61, 64, 67, 73–76, 78–80, 85–87, 93–94, 97–99, 108–111, 117–120, 122, 125, 220, 222–223, 232–233, 262, 266, 269, 278
New York Yanks 87, 106–109, 114, 116, 231, 266, 273

O'Connor, Bill "Zeke" 64, 69, 70, 75–76, 81–82, 124, 266
O'Neill, Albert T. 103–104
O'Rourke, Charlie 33, 54–55, 59, 75

Payne, Roland D. 7–8
Philadelphia Eagles 6, 19, 22, 65, 85, 87, 106–110, 113–114, 235, 239–240, 243, 249, 253, 258–259, 262, 267, 270, 281, 285, 287–288, 291–292
Philadelphia Quakers 4–5
Pirro, Rocco 20–22, 27, 52, 63, 67, 69, 89, 113, 119, 121, 124, 126, 268–269, 287
Pittsburgh Steelers 6, 21–23, 27, 42–43, 65, 91,

102, 106–109, 241, 252, 255, 269, 271, 275–276, 287–288, 291–292
Pucci, Ben 22, 26, 29, 33, 47, 51, 63, 119, 121, 270–271

Ratterman, George 44–45, 47–49, 51–61, 63, 67, 69, 70, 72–75, 77–81, 83, 89–95, 97–98, 100–101, 110–111, 114, 121, 124, 126, 271–273
Reeves, Dan 9, 19, 97, 105
Rickey, Branch 14, 66–67
Rochester Jeffersons 3, 5
Rodenberg, Robert 39, 56
Rooney, Art 19, 104
Ryan, Ray 12–14

San Francisco 49ers 34–36, 41, 53, 61, 66, 70–72, 75, 80, 85, 89–90, 93–97, 100, 102, 106–109, 116–118, 120, 122–125, 222–223, 227, 238, 246, 259
Sanders, Orban "Spec" 29, 33, 48, 61, 67, 73, 79, 109, 111, 248, 265
Schneider, Don 42, 69, 83, 124, 276–277

Seick, Earl 6
Shaw, Lawrence T. "Buck" 12, 238
Sorrell, Allen E. 12
Speedie, Mac 30, 38, 58, 70, 74, 83, 92, 101, 111
Stanton, Bill 89, 109, 113, 126, 280
Statuto, Art 27, 45, 73, 77, 81, 83, 89, 92, 96, 107, 124, 126, 280–281
Stautzenberger, Odell 99, 106–107, 113, 126, 281–282
Steuber, Bob 14, 67, 69, 72, 74–76, 124, 282–283
Stidham, Tom 27, 44, 118
Strader, Red 79
Stuart, Roy 119, 284
Sutton, Joe 89–90, 92, 95–97, 105, 108, 114, 126, 284–285

Terlep, George 27, 30, 32–34, 39, 47, 52–53, 59, 63, 67, 69, 73, 119, 121, 124, 285–286
Tittle, Y.A. 75, 80–81, 90, 95, 100
Tomasetti, Lou 22, 32–35, 49, 51–52, 56, 58–59, 61, 63, 69, 72, 74, 76–79, 89, 101, 109, 113, 119, 124, 126, 287–288
Topping, Dan 13–14, 18, 45, 89
Trans-America League 6–8, 16
Tunney, Gene 12–13

United States Football League (USFL) 6–8, 14, 16

Vandeweghe, Al 21, 29, 33, 39, 119, 288–289
Volz, Wilbur 86, 108, 113, 126, 290

Walsh, Christy 11–13
Ward, Arch 11–14, 28
Washington Redskins 16, 19–20, 22, 39, 84, 87, 102, 104, 106–109, 223, 239, 248, 261, 274–276, 279, 284, 289
West Buffalo 4
Wizbicki, Alex 24, 47, 52–53, 57, 60, 63, 69, 73, 82, 89, 96, 100, 108, 114, 121, 124, 126, 291

www.ingramcontent.com/pod-product-compliance
Ingram Content Group UK Ltd.
Pitfield, Milton Keynes, MK11 3LW, UK
UKHW050023050125
453157UK00016B/171